中等职业教育"十三五"规划教材

中职中专国际商务专业创新型系列教材

外贸单证实训

杨 遐 傅德明 主编

潘 柠 张立强 谢 江 副主编

科学出版社

北 京

内 容 简 介

本书涵盖了我国现阶段进出口贸易所有环节中通用的、以安全结汇或对外结算为终极目标的大部分单证,从贸易合同的签订到货物的国际运输、通关,最后到结汇、付汇,涉及贸易合同、信用证、商业发票、运输单证、保险单证、原产地证书、报检报关单证、结汇单证、议付单证等主要单证的缮制方法与审核事项。本书案例中援引了大量近年来对外贸易各环节,来自专业银行和进出口公司以及报关、国际运输公司的真实单证,具有较强的实用性。本书的内容编排以外贸业务各个环节的单证种类及其业务逻辑展开为依据,实用、有效。

本书可作为中等职业学校、中职升为高职学校的国际商务等相关专业的教材,也可供商贸专业教师及有志于从事对外贸易行业的人士学习、参考。

图书在版编目(CIP)数据

外贸单证实训/杨遐,傅德明主编. —北京:科学出版社,2016
ISBN 978-7-03-049003-2

Ⅰ. ①外… Ⅱ. ①杨…②傅… Ⅲ. ①进出口贸易-原始凭证-中等专业学校-教材 Ⅳ. ①F740.44

中国版本图书馆 CIP 数据核字(2016)第 141253 号

责任编辑:贾家琛 李 娜 / 责任校对:王万红
责任印制:吕春珉 / 封面设计:艺和天下

科学出版社 出版
北京东黄城根北街 16 号
邮政编码:100717
http://www.sciencep.com

三河市骏杰印刷有限公司印刷
科学出版社发行 各地新华书店经销
*
2016 年 8 月第 一 版 开本:787×1092 1/16
2016 年 8 月第一次印刷 印张:19 1/4
字数:456 000
定价:39.00 元
(如有印装质量问题,我社负责调换〈骏杰〉)

销售部电话 010-62136230 编辑部电话 010-62135763-2041

前　　言

外贸单证运作是国际贸易流程的重要环节，以单证处理为工作核心的单证员，是外贸企业不可或缺的基础性人才，单证操作实务更是每一位外贸从业人员必备的基本功。为了满足外贸及流通企业对单证操作人才的需要，适应职业院校商贸类专业"理实一体化"的教学要求，编者精心编写了本书。

本书主要有以下几个特点。

（1）实操性。在全书内容上，力求做到"实用"和"适用"，完全从实训出发，不作繁复的理论知识讲解，基础知识"以够用为度"，注重培养学生动手操作能力。

（2）仿真性。在编写过程中，编者深入企业，获得企业的第一手业务资料，力求以真实的业务案例作为实训背景，为学生创建亲历式、场景化的训练模式。学生将以公司单证员的角色置身每一个项目的实训中，对每一步操作形成全新的感受。

（3）过程性。根据外贸单证员岗位核心技能要求，以单证员工作过程为主线，编排典型的项目和工作任务，主要包括合同、信用证制单单项训练，综合制单、审单等实训项目；每一项目下设置若干实训任务，每一任务安排"任务导航"、"任务准备"、"任务实施"、"任务再现"等环节；每一项目后安排"知识巩固"和"技能提高"（知识巩固为二维码形式，实现了在线测试学习效果的目的），以"项目导向、任务驱动"模式引领学生递进式、全方位展开模拟训练。

（4）多样性。全书选取不同外贸公司、不同交易条件的众多业务资料，既设置了各种单据的单项训练，又设置了贯穿同笔业务前后的综合训练，使学生获得多元兼容的模拟实训体验。

（5）立体化。本书关注每一个细节，配备图片、视频、微课等直观形象的表现形式，立体化地展示全书内容，以增强学生的感性认识，激发学生学习和探究的积极性。

本书由广东省对外贸易职业技术学校杨遐、肇庆市第一中等职业学校傅德明任主编；由宁波鄞州职业高级中学潘柠、肇庆市技师学院张立强、广东省对外贸易职业技术学校谢江任副主编；宁波鄞州职业高级中学陈淑女、侯慧微、陈慕飞和宁波东钱湖旅游学校董婕参与了本书的编写。全书具体编写分工为：项目一由谢江编写，项目二由杨遐编写，项目三由陈淑女编写，项目四由董婕编写，项目五由侯慧微编写，项目六由陈慕飞编写，项目七由潘柠编写，项目八、项目十一由傅德明编写，项目九由梁英华编写，项目十由张立强编写。

在编写本书的过程中，编者得到了中国银行柳州分行、广东肇庆土产进出口有限公司、广东顺德纺织品进出口有限公司、肇庆卓瑞轻工业品有限公司和肇庆报关公司相关人士的大力支持和帮助，广州立纬进出口贸易有限公司部门经理甘晓晴女士对本书的编写提出了宝贵的意见和建议，谨在此一并表示诚挚的谢意！

在编写本书的过程中，编者参考了大量相关文献，个别地方引用了现有资料，在此特向这些文献的作者致以衷心的感谢！

由于编者的学识水平和实践经验有限，书中的不足之处在所难免，恳请广大读者批评指正，以便我们不断修订完善。

编　者

2016 年 5 月

目　录

项目一

初识单证工作

1. 了解并掌握国际商务单证的含义、作用和分类;
2. 了解单证相关工作岗位及其要求;
3. 认知贸易合同。

能力目标

1. 了解国际商务单证工作的有关内容、流程;
2. 掌握制单依据和要求;
3. 识读贸易合同。

任务一 认知单证

任务导航

小张毕业于某省贸易学校，刚刚就职于南方纺织品进出口有限公司。该公司是一家国有企业，主要经营各类轻纺产品的进出口业务，产品远销世界各地，深受客户欢迎。因为是公司的一名新成员，小张被公司安排到单证部工作，先从单证员做起。

要求：

（1）了解单证工作在国际贸易中的重要性。

（2）掌握单证工作的主要内容和流程。

（3）正确理解单证工作的要求。

任务准备

一、国际商务单证的含义

单证是国际货物贸易业务的重要组成内容。广义的国际商务单证（international trade documents）是国际贸易中使用的各种单据、文件与证书的统称。从贸易合同的签订到备货、商检、托运、投保、报关、装船、货款支付以及进口商提货，整个业务过程的每个环节都需要相应的单证的缮制、处理、交接和传递，以满足进出口双方、运输部门、保险公司、商检机构、海关、银行、政府有关机构等多方面的需要。

狭义的国际商务单证通常是指货物支付环节的结算单证，特别是信用证支付方式下的结算单证。

二、国际商务单证的种类

国际贸易单证，从不同角度可以分为不同的种类。

根据贸易双方的不同，国际贸易单证可分为出口单证、进口单证。其中，进口方涉及的单证包括进口许可证、开证申请书、进口报关单、报检单、FOB 和 CFR 术语下的保险单或预约保险单等。出口方涉及的单证种类比较多，包括出口许可证、出口报关单、包装单、出口货运单据、商业发票、CIF 项下的保险单、商检证、原产地证书等（见表 1.1）。

根据单证的性质，国际贸易单证可分为金融单据、商业单据。其中，金融单据包括汇票、本票、支票或其他类似用以取得货款的凭证；商业单据包括发票、装箱单、运输单据、保险单等其他非金融单据。

表 1.1 出口方单据

结汇单据					非结汇单据	
金融单据	商业单据		官方单据	附属单据	商业单据	官方单据
	商业发票		商检证书	受益人证明	报关单 报关委托书	配额证明 出口许可证
	装箱单	装箱单、重量单、尺码单、 磅码单、花色搭配单	原产 地证 明书	一般原产地 证书	电抄	报检单 报检委托书	
				普惠制原产 地证书	船籍证明	托运单	
					船舱证明	投保单	
汇票	运输 单据	提单/海运单/空运单/铁 路运单副本/承运货物收 据/邮包收据/联合运输 单据	海关发票/领事发票	航线证明	装货单	通关单 换证凭条
				寄单证明	场站数据	
				寄样证明	大副数据	
				装船通知		
	保险单	保险单/保险凭证		船长收据	报检单 报检委托书	
	其他		其他	其他	其他	其他

根据用途，国际贸易单证可分为金融单证、商业单证、货运单证、保险单证、官方单证和附属单证等。根据国际惯例，国际贸易单证的分类如表 1.2 所示。

表 1.2 根据国际惯例的分类方法

《托收统一规则》的 分类	金融单据		汇票、本票、支票
	商业单据	基本单据	商业发票、提单、保险单
		附属单据 进口国官方要求	领事发票/海关发票、原产地证明等
		进口方要求	装箱单、商检证书、寄单证明、寄样证明、装运通知、船龄证明等
《跟单信用证统一惯 例》的分类	运输单据		海运提单，海运单，多式联运单，航空运单，快递收据，邮政收据，公路、铁路和内陆水运单据等
	保险单据		保险单、保险凭证、投保声明、预约保险单等
	商业发票		
	其他单据		装箱单、重量单、原产地证明、普惠制单据、商检证书、受益人证明等
UN/EDIFACT 的分类	生产单证、订购单证、销售单证、银行单证、保险单证、货运代理服务单证、运输单证、出口单证、进口和转口单证九大类		
单证形式	纸面单证		
	电子单证		

注：UN/EDIFACT 指联合国欧洲经济理事会从事国际贸易程序简化工作的第四工作组制订的 EDI 国际通用标准（United Nations/Electronic Data Interchange for Administration, Commerce, and Transport）。

三、单证工作在外贸业务中的重要性

国际商务单证种类多，制证工作量大、时间性强、涉及面广，而且环环相扣，互相影响，互为条件，是外贸业务过程中重要的工作内容之一。其重要性主要体现在以下几方面：

（一）国际商务单证是履行合同的必要手段

国际贸易是跨国的商品买卖，买卖双方分处于不同国家，在绝大多数情况下，货物与货款不能进行简单的直接交换，而必须以单证作为交换的媒介，货物买卖通过单证买卖来实现。《联合国国际货物销售合同公约》对卖方基本义务的规定是，卖方必须按照合同和本公约的规定，交付货物，移交一切与货物有关的单据并转移货物所有权。卖方交单意味着交付了货物，买方付款则是以得到单据代表买到了货物，双方的交易不以货物为核心，而是以单证为核心。

单证工作种类繁多，贯穿于进出口业务的全过程。各种单证的签发、组合、流转、交换和应用，反映了合同履行的进程，也反映了买卖双方权责的发生、转移和终止。例如，CIF 条件出口货物，卖方需要根据合同或信用证向承运人发出托运单进行租船订舱，取得装货单时，即意味着托运工作已落实；在装船前需要凭装货单、报关单、商业发票、装箱单等向海关办理出口报关。货物装船后凭大副收据向船公司换取正本提单，证明卖方已完成交货义务；买方通过付款得到卖方所提交的代表物权的提单及相关单据，等于是得到货物。由此可见，国际商务单证是完成合同履行的必要手段。

参考答案

▌课堂思考 ▬▬▬▬▬▬▬▬▬▬

什么是海运提单？它的性质与作用是什么？

（二）国际商务单证是结算货款的基本工具

在国际贸易结算中，不论采取哪一种交易条件、支付方式，买卖双方之间都要发生单据的交接。单据代表着货物，交接单据等于交接货物。

从交货条件看，国际贸易多数按 FOB/CFR/CIF 或 FCA/CPT/CIP 条件成交，这类合同都是凭单交货、凭单付款的象征性交货合同，都是以单证为桥梁实现货款交割的，其性质同样是单证买卖。卖方按合同规定的时间和地点将货物装上运输工具或交付承运人后，只要向买方提供合格的包括物权证书在内的有关单证，买方就必须付款，卖方无须保证到货。

从国际贸易货款的结算方式看，在信用证支付方式下，出口方以受益人的身份向开证行提交发票、提单等有关单据，只要单单一致、单证一致，开证行就必须给予付款。然后买方通过向开证行付款赎单，得到有关单据，即是得到了货物的所有权。如果单据不符合要求，银行及买方可以拒绝付款（见图 1.1）。

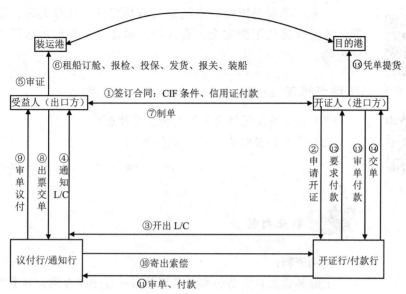

图 1.1　信用证业务流程

在 D/P 托收支付方式下，出口方交货后通过银行向进口商提示有关单据，表明已经交货，只要出口方提交了必要的和符合合同要求的单据，进口方就必须付款，从而得到单据并提取货物。如果单据不符合要求，进口方有权拒付或承兑。可见，托收也是以单据买卖代表货物买卖（见图1.2）。

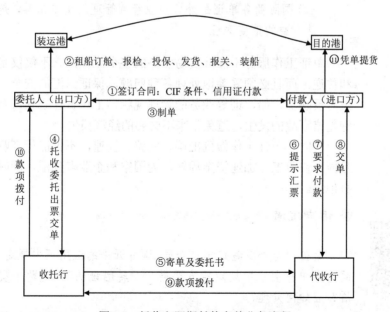

图 1.2　托收之即期付款交单业务流程

可见，单证是国际贸易结算的基础工具，只有正确、及时缮制单据，才能保证收汇的安全。有人说：单证就是外汇，这话也不是没有道理的。

（1）参考答案

（2）参考答案

课堂思考

（1）什么是象征性交货？其特点是什么？
（2）什么是信用证？其特点是什么？

职业判断

案例资料：

上海某进出口贸易公司与日商签订一份出口合同。该公司按合同规定的品质、数量、交货时间等条款履行后，持全套单据向银行交单，要求付款。开证行审单无误，准备付款时收到日商通知：发现货物数量短缺，要求停止付款。

思考：

银行应如何处理？

参考答案

（三）国际商务单证是外贸企业经营管理的重要工具，是提高经济效益的重要保证

单证工作服务于国际贸易业务的整个流程，它不仅仅是单证的缮制和传递，而且必须妥善地处理各种问题，保证结汇的安全。单证工作能及时反映货、船、证等业务的管理现状，工作责任心强可及时解决、杜绝差错事故的发生，避免带来不必要的经济损失。

同时，单证工作做到准确、完整、快速，不仅能保证收汇安全，而且能加快收汇，加速资金周转，为国家和企业多创汇，同时树立企业自身信誉。

课堂思考

参考答案

某公司与外商签订出口合同，国外开来的信用证中规定"允许转船"，同时在单据要求中规定卖方要提交"转船证明"。这两个规定是否有矛盾？应如何处理？

职业判断

案例资料：

广州某公司与美国客户签订 CIF 出口合同总值 10 万美元，远期见票后 60 天付款的信用证付款。国外开来信用证，最迟装运期是 2014 年 10 月 31 日，交单期是提单日后 15 天，信用证到期日 2014 年 11 月 20 日。该公司于 10 月 10 日完成装运并取得提单。

思考：

（1）该公司最迟应于何时交单？

参考答案

（2）假如适逢人民币汇率发生较大变动，10 月 20 日为 1 : 6.22，25日为 1 : 6.20，该公司于 10 月 20 日交单与 10 月 25 日交单，有何不同？

（四）国际商务单证是进出口企业形象的重要体现

作为商务文件的单证能起到对外宣传的作用，正确、整洁、清晰的单证能展现进出口企业优质的服务水准，为企业塑造良好的品牌，有利于业务的开展；反之，潦草、粗劣、错讹的单证则容易影响银行、客户审单，容易引起误判而拒付，甚至影响客户顺利提货。客户对企业印象不良，必然会给企业带来负面效益。

（五）国际商务单证是政策性很强的涉外工作

国际商务单证作为一种涉外商业文件，必须严格按照国家有关外贸的各项法规和制度办理。例如，出口许可证、配额证关系到国家对出口商品的管理，甚至牵涉到两国之间的贸易协定。

国际商务单证又是重要的涉外法律文件。它不仅是收汇的依据，当发生纠纷时，又常常是处理争议的依据。例如，货物在运输途中受损，被保险人向保险公司索赔，保险单就是索赔的依据，也是保险公司理赔的依据；如关系到赔偿额的计算，发票又是计算赔偿的依据；如货物受损是属于承运人的责任，提单或运输单据就是处理索赔的依据；品质检验证书是处理品质纠纷的依据。所以单证员必须认真做好单据的归档和保管工作。

四、单证工作的主要内容与要求

（一）单证工作的内容

国际贸易中，合同采用的贸易术语和结算方式不同，出口方履行合同的工作程序和内容也不同，对单据的要求也有所不同。以 CIF 条件成交、L/C 方式结算的合同为例，其业务履行程序可以简单地归纳为"证、货、船、款"四个基本环节，单证工作内容主要包括审证、制单、审单、交单、归档五个环节。

1. 信用证的登录、审核和修改

信用证一般由当地的通知行传递给出口企业，出口企业单证员在收到信用证后即应做好登记工作。登记的内容主要包括信用证的号码、信用证的主要当事人、装运期、有效期、交单期及有关货物和装运方面的说明等，以便查考和管理，有利于公司单证工作的顺利开展。同时，对信用证在出口企业各部门流转情况也应做好记录，最后送银行议付后退回出口企业，并与其他资料一起归档保存。

信用证的审核尤为重要。进口方按合同规定的内容向开证行申请开立信用证，信用证内容理应与合同条款保持一致，这是出口方履行交货义务的前提。但实践中，国外开来的信用证由于开证行疏忽、电文传递错误、贸易习惯差异，甚至故意行为等种种原因，往往会出现信用证与合同不符或相关条款卖方无法接受的情况。有时进口商还会有意利用其开证主动权，在证中加列一些限制性条款（俗称"软条款"）。

出口方为确保收汇安全和合同的顺利履行，要对来证认真审核，对信用证的全文和附件以及证实书等，从头到尾、上下前后、逐条、逐字仔细审核。

出口方审证的依据是合同，并结合《国际贸易术语解释通则（2010年）》等国际惯例和卖方实际情况，以及进出口双方国家的相关法规来审核。

课堂思考

某信用证中要求有下面这样一种单据：

Inspection certificate issued by the representative of the applicant whose signature must be in compliance with the one in the file of the issuing bank.

该单据内容的规定对出口商有什么影响？

参考答案

2. 制单

缮制单据主要根据信用证的要求，结合合同、双方往来函电以及实际交货情况等。制单工作贯穿于履行合同的全过程，每一个环节都需要有单证的缮制、处理、交换和传递，全程不能存在丝毫差错，否则就有可能给企业带来经济损失。因此，缮制单证时必须做到正确、完整、及时、简明、整洁。

（1）正确

正确是一切单证工作的前提，是安全收汇的保证。它包括两个方面的内容。

1）要求各种单据必须做到"四个一致"，即证（信用证）同合同一致、单证一致、单单一致、单货一致。证同一致是出口方履行合同的前提；单证一致、单单一致是开证行或付款行付款的条件；单货一致的侧重点在备货工作上，对制单所需资料必须核实，保证单据中的货物描述与实物一致，此为出口方树立信誉所必需的内容。

2）要求各种单据必须符合有关国际惯例和进出口国有关法令和规定。

（2）完整

完整是构成单证合法性的重要条件之一，是单证成为有价证券的基础。它包含三个方面的内容。

1）单据内容完整，即每一种单据本身的内容（包括单据本身的格式、项目、文字和签章、背书等）必须完备齐全，否则就不能构成有效文件，也就不能为银行所接受。

2）单据种类完整，即单据必须是成套齐全的而不是单一的，遗漏一种单据，就是单据不完整。单据应严格按照信用证规定一一照办，除主要单据外，一些附属证明、收据一定要及时办理，不得遗漏。

3）单据份数完整，即要求在信用证项下的交易中，进出口商需要哪些单据、一式几份都要明确，尤其是提单的份数，更应注意按要求出齐，避免多出或少出。

（3）及时

进出口单证工作的时间性很强，所谓及时，包括以下两个方面的内容。

1）及时出单：各种单据的出单日期必须符合逻辑。也就是说，每一种单据的出单日期不能超过信用证规定的有效期限或按商业习惯的合理日期。如保险单、检验证的日期应早于提单的日期，而提单的日期不应晚于信用证规定的最迟装运期限，否则，就会造成单证不符。

2）及时交单：交单议付不得超过信用证规定的交单有效期。如信用证不做规定，国际商会《跟单信用证统一惯例》规定："银行将拒绝接受迟于运输单据出单日期21天后提交的单据，但无论如何，单据也不得迟于信用证到期日提交。"

 课堂思考

中国甲公司与外商签订一份 CIF 出口合同，以 L/C 为支付方式。国外银行开来的信用证中规定："信用证有效期为 2011 年 6 月 16 日，装运期为 2011 年 5 月。"甲公司加紧备货出运，于 5 月 20 日取得大副收据，并换回正本已装船清洁提单。甲公司最迟应于何日交单？

参考答案

9

（4）简明

简明是指单证的内容应按照信用证、合同和国际惯例填写，力求简化，切勿加入不必要的内容，以免弄巧成拙。国际商会《跟单信用证统一惯例》指出"为了防止混淆和误解，银行应劝阻在信用证或其任何修改书中加注过多细节的内容"，其目的也是避免单证的复杂化，提高工作效率。简化单证，不仅可以减少工作量和提高工作效率，而且有利于提高单证的质量和减少单证的差错。

（5）整洁

单证表面要整洁、美观、大方，单证内容要简洁明了。

如果正确和完整是单证的内在质量要求，那么整洁则是单证的外观质量要求，它在一定程度上反映了一个国家的科技水平和一个企业的业务水平。单证是否整洁，不但反映出制单人的业务熟练程度和工作态度，而且直接影响出单的效果。

单证的整洁还体现在单证格式的设计及缮制力求标准化和规范化，单证内容的排列要行次整齐、主次有序、重点项目突出醒目，单证字迹清晰，语言通顺，语句流畅，用词简明扼要、恰如其分，更改处要盖校对章或简签。如单证涂改过多，应重新缮制。

3．审单

在交单前，必须汇集各项单据，以发票为中心，以信用证为主要依据，结合合同、《跟单信用证统一惯例》，逐项审核单据，保证做到单证一致、单单一致，防止错单、缺单，务必完整无误。

4．交单

交单是议付和结汇的基础，外贸企业只有按时交单才能顺利收回货款。交单时应做到单据齐全、内容正确、提交及时。

5．归档

出口方交单后，寄送国外的单据就成了涉外文件。如果发生退单、拒付、索赔、争议等事项，出口方需要有副本单据来核对、处理。所以出口方务必将一套完整的副本单据妥善归档保管，并编排做好索引，以便发生问题时及时查找、应对。

（二）单证工作的特点与要求

单证工作量大、涉及面广。一名单证员往往要负责跟进多名外贸业务员的业务单证，在每天有限的时间内同时处理多笔进度各不相同的业务单据，工作量非常大。在处理每票单据的过程中，单证员需要完成与业务员、跟单员、财务，以及客户、货运代理、报关行、银行、办证机构等各方面的沟通协调工作。

单证工作对时间要求比较高。每个业务操作环节都有时间上的严格要求。以信用证作为出口结算方式为例，单证员需要及时催证、审证，若发现信用证与合同不符，要在最短时间内要求客户改证；一定要提前租船订舱，把握好商检、截关、开船时间，确保按时送货和及时制作报关资料安排报关；货物装船后，尽快核对提单，并发装船通知给进口商；保险单的签发日期既不能早于报关单日期，也不能晚于提单签发日期；单据要在信用证规定的交单期内尽早向银行提交，如果银行审单出现不符点，还能有沟通修改的补救机会。只有把握好时间这条主线，才能分清轻重缓急，高效地完成单证工作。

因为单证工作涉及面广、工作量大，制单和交单时间都有相关严格要求，所以要求单证员有扎实的国际贸易理论知识和专业外语知识、娴熟的计算机操作能力，更需要有良好的沟通协调能力、高度的责任心和严谨细致、耐心的工作态度，能够不断地提高、完善制单技巧，具备独立处理变化多端单证的能力，以保证货物按时、按质、按量运出，又能确保及时收汇。许多单证员都有过因单证制作错误"花钱买教训"的经历，制单过程中最忌粗心大意，急于求成。要善于进行时间管理，勤于记录备案，重视协调沟通，能够在工作中不断思考、总结，养成良好的工作习惯，这些都是高素质外贸单证员的必备条件。

▌ 课堂思考 ▌

（1）CIF 交货条件、信用证支付方式的合同项下，出口方办理租船订舱、报关、投保、商检、装船、信用证，这几项工作的先后顺序有何要求？

（1）参考答案

（2）某公司按 FOBC5%广州每箱 100 美元出口某商品 1000 台，D/P at sight 支付方式。在制作发票时，发票总值应为多少？应付佣金多少？

（2）参考答案

（3）某公司按 CIF 汉堡每件 110 美元出口某商品 5000 件，合同规定按发票价值的 110%投保一切险加战争险。单证员在办理投保时查得一切险的保险费率为 0.5%，战争险的保险费为 0.8%。该公司在投保时需要支付多少保险费？保险单上保险金额应为多少？

（3）参考答案

（4）信用证中规定提单收货人留空不填，但船公司规定提单抬头必须填写，怎么处理？

（4）参考答案

小贴士

根据国际惯例，开证行如发现单证不符，必须：①在合理的时间内提出，即在开证行收到单据次日起算的 5 个工作日之内向单据的提示者提出不符点；②无延迟地以电信方式，如做不到，须以其他快捷方式将不符点通知提示者；③一次性提出，即如第一次所提不符点不成立，即使单据还存在实质性不符点，开证行也无权再次提出；④通知不符点同时，必须说明单据代为保管听候处理，或径退交单者。以上条件必须同时满足，如有一项条件开证行未做到，开证行便无权声称单据有不符点而拒付。

任务实施

1. 了解单证工作在国际贸易中的重要性

国际商务单证是履行合同的必要手段，也是结算货款的基本工具，是外贸企业经营管理的重要工具、提高经济效益的重要保证，同时也是企业形象的重要体现。国际商务单证工作是政策性很强的涉外工作，要遵守国内的、相关国家的和国际上的相关规定，有关单证也是在处理纠纷时的重要依据。

2. 掌握单证工作的主要内容和工作要求

单证工作主要包括审证、制单、审单、交单、归档 5 个环节，要求做到正确、完整、及时、简明、整洁。单证工作工作量大，涉及面广，时间性强，必须严格做到单单一致、单证一致、单同一致、单货一致，才能确保安全收回货款。

（1）参考答案

（2）参考答案

任务再现

（1）描述 D/P 30days after sight 方式下的支付流程。

（2）如果某出口业务按 CIF DUBAI、即期信用证方式付款的条件成交，履行合同的主要环节有哪些？与国外结算货款时一般需要提交哪些单据？制单的依据是什么？

任务二　　解读贸易合同

任务导航

任务导航

小张所在 ABC 服饰有限公司与外商签订了一份关于童装的合同，具体如下：

ABC Garments & Accessories Co., Ltd (1)

SALES CONTRACT (2)

(3) Contract No.: ABC091102
(4) Date 　　　: NOV. 02,2009
(5) Signed AT 　: HANGZHOU

Buyer(6): Arrabon Trading Co.

　　　　Unit 9,Central Office Park,257Jean Ave. Centurion, South Africa

Seller(7): ABC Garments & Accessories Co., Ltd

　　　　HONGXI ROAD, HANGZHOU, ZHEJIANG, CHINA

The Buyer agree to buy and the Seller agree to sell the following goods on terms and conditions as set forth below:

(8) Name of Commodity, Specification	(9) Quantity	(10) Unit Price CFR LIMASSOL	(11) Total Amount
Boy's denim long pant　No.100	1000pcs	USD9.50	USD9500.00
Boy's twill long pant　No. 101	1000pcs	USD10.00	USD10000.00
		TOTAL	USD19500.00

(12) Packing: 50pcs/Carton

(13) Shipping Marks:　　　ABC/ABC091102/LIMASSOL/NOS.1-40

(14) Shipping Quantity:　　Five Percent More or Less Allowed.

(15) Time of Shipment:　　50 days after the Seller receive the L/C.

(16) Port of Loading:　　　SHANGHAI

(17) Port of Destination:　　LIMASSOL CYPRUS

(18) Insurance:　　　　　TO be covered by Buyer

(19) Terms of Payment:　　IRREVOCABLE L/C AT SIGHT. The covering Letter of Credit must reach the Seller in 45 days after the date of this Contract and is to remain valid in above indicated Loading Port 15 days after the date of shipment, failing which the Seller reserve the right to cancel the Sales Contract and to claim from the Buyer compensation for loss resulting therefrom.

(20) Quality/Quantity Discrepancy: In case of quality discrepancy, claim should be filed by the Buyer within 30 days after the arrival of the goods at Port of destination, while for quantity discrepancy, claim should be filed by the Buyer within 15 days after the arrival of the goods at Port of destination. In all cases, Claims must be accompanied by Survey Reports of Recognized Public Surveyors agreed to by the Seller. Should the responsibility of the subject under claim be found to rest on part of the Seller, the Seller shall, within 20 days after receipt of the claim, send his reply to the Buyer together with suggestion for settlement.

(21) Inspection: The Certificate of Origin and/or the Inspection Certification of Quality/Quantity/Weight issued by the relative institute shall be taken as the basis for the shipping Quality/Quantity/Weight.

(22)Force Majeure: The Seller shall not be held responsible if they owing to Force Majeure cause or causes fail to make delivery within the time stipulated in this Sales Contract or cannot deliver the goods. However, the Seller shall inform immediately the Buyer by fax. The Seller shall deliver to the Buyer by registered letter, if it is requested by the Buyer, a certificate issued by the China Council for the Promotion of International Trade or by any competent authority, certifying to the existence of the said cause or causes. Buyer's failure to obtain the relative Import License is not to be treated as Force Majeure.

(23)Arbitration: All disputes arising in connection with the Sales Contract of the execution thereof shall be settled amicably by negotiation. In case no settlement can be reached, the case under dispute shall then be submitted for arbitration to the Foreign Trade Arbitration Commission of the China Council for the Promotion of International Trade in accordance with the Provisional Rules of Procedure of the Foreign Trade Arbitration Commission of the China Council for the Promotion of International Trade . The decision of the Commission shall be accepted as final and binding upon both parties.

The Buyer   The Seller

要求：

（1）翻译合同，找出交易条件、品名、品质、数量、包装、单价、装运期和装运港、目的港、支付方式等。

（2）掌握合同履行的相关程序。

一、国际贸易合同的重要性

任务准备

国际货物买卖合同是国际贸易中买卖双方通过一定的磋商程序，就有关货物的买卖规定各方权利义务所达成的书面协议。买卖双方要根据合同履行各自的权利和义务。发生违约行为时，合同是解决贸易纠纷，进行调节、仲裁与诉讼的法律依据。

信用证是银行应申请人（进口方）的要求向受益人（出口方）开立的有条件的付款保证书。它是一种银行信用，只要受益人提交符合信用证要求的单据，做到单单一致、单证一致，银行就必须付款。而且信用证是一种独立于合同之外的文件，银行在处理付款过程中，只按信用证的要求来审核单据，银行付款与否和合同、货物无关。

所以，在合同规定的支付方式为信用证时，进口方必须按合同规定向开证行申请信用证，开证行所开立的信用证必须与合同要求相符，这是出口方履行交货义务的前提。合同就是出口方审核信用证的依据。所以，进出口双方都必须认真理解合同的各项条款。

在合同规定的支付方式为托收时，合同更是出口方履行交货义务、缮制单据的主要依据。只要出口方单据符合合同，进口方就必须按规定时间付款。

二、国际贸易合同的形式与内容

国际贸易合同形式包括书面合同与口头合同。根据我国法律和国际贸易一般的习惯做法，交易双方通过口头或来往函电磋商达成协议后，通常要签订一份格式正式的书面合同。

书面合同的名称并无统一规定，内容繁简也不一致。常见的形式包括合同（contract）、确认书（confirmation）等，法律效力相同，只是内容繁简有所差异，确认书是合同的简化形式。

根据起草者的不同，国际贸易合同可分为销售合同（确认书）和购买合同（确认书），前者由出口方草拟提出，后者由进口方草拟提出。

无论哪种形式的合同，其内容通常都包括约首、本文、约尾三部分。

1. 约首

约首部分一般包括合同的名称、合同编号、缔约双方的名称和地址、电话和电报挂号、订约时间与地点等内容。

2. 本文

本文即合同的各项条款，具体列明各项交易条件，包括品名、品质、数量、包装、单价和总值、交货条件、运输、保险、支付、商检、不可抗力、索赔、仲裁等条款。这些条款是根据交易磋商的结果，体现了买卖双方的权利和义务。

3. 约尾

约尾部分主要是进出口双方当事人的签字、盖章等内容，有时还会注明本合同的份数，使用的文字及其效力、生效等。

三、国际贸易合同条款的内容

1. 品质规格条款

品质规格是指商品所具有的内在质量与外观形态，商品品质规格条款的主要内容是品名、规格或牌名。商品合同中规定品质规格的方法有两种：凭样品和凭文字与图样。

（1）在凭样品确定商品品质的合同中，卖方要承担货物品质必须同样品完全一致的责任。为避免发生争议，合同中应注明"品质与样品大致相同"。商品凭样品成交适用于从外观上即可确定商品品质的交易。

（2）商品凭文字与图样的买卖包括凭规格、等级或标准的买卖，凭说明书的买卖以及凭商标、牌名或产地的买卖。卖方所交货物必须与文字描述或图样相符。

2. 数量条款

数量条款的主要内容是交货数量、计量单位与计量方法。商品制定数量条款时应注意明确计量单位和度量衡制度。通常在数量条款中还会增订"溢短装条款",明确规定溢短装幅度,如"东北大米 500 公吨,溢短装 3%",同时规定溢短装的作价方法。

3. 包装条款

包装是指为了有效地保护商品的数量完整和质量要求,把货物装进适当的容器。商品包装条款的主要内容有包装方式、规格、包装材料、费用和运输标志。商品制定包装条款要明确包装的材料、造型和规格,不应使用"适合海运包装""标准出口包装"等含义不清的词句。

4. 价格条款

价格条款的主要内容有每一计量单位的价格金额、计价货币、贸易术语与商品的计价单位等。

5. 装运条款

装运条款的主要内容是装运时间、运输方式、装运地与目的地、装运方式以及装运通知。根据不同的贸易术语,装运的要求是不一样的,所以应按照贸易术语来确定装运条款。

6. 保险条款

国际货物买卖中的保险条款主要内容包括确定投保人及支付保险费,投保险别及其对应的保险条款。

7. 支付条款

国际贸易常见的支付方式包括信用证、托收、汇付。合同中需要规定具体的支付方式、时间和地点。

8. 检验条款

商品检验条款主要内容包括检验机构、检验权与复验权、检验与复验的时间与地点、检验标准与方法以及检验证书。

9. 异议与索赔条款

异议与索赔条款是合同中关于处理和索赔违约责任的规定，一般内容包括索赔的依据、索赔期限、索赔方法和索赔金额等。

10. 不可抗力条款

不可抗力条款是合同中的免责条款，指合同订立以后发生的当事人订立合同时不能预见的、不能避免的、人力不可控制的意外事故，导致合同不能履行或不能按期履行，遭受不可抗力一方可由此免除责任，而对方无权要求赔偿。

一般来说，不可抗力来自两个方面：自然条件和社会条件。商品前者如水灾、旱灾、地震、海啸、泥石流等，后者如战争、暴动、罢工、政府禁令等。商品不可抗力是一个有确切含义的法律概念，并不是所有的意外事故都可构成不可抗力，双方需要在合同中定明双方公认的不可抗力事故。

11. 仲裁条款

仲裁条款是双方当事人自愿将其争议提交第三者进行裁决的意思表示。商仲裁条款的主要内容有仲裁机构、适用的仲裁程序规则、仲裁地点及裁决效力。在国际贸易实践中，仲裁机构、仲裁地点都由双方约定产生，仲裁程序规则一般由选择的仲裁机构决定，仲裁裁决的效力一般是一次性的、终局的，对双方都有约束力，凡订有仲裁协议的双方，不得向法院提起诉讼。

课堂思考

（1）销售合同和销售确认书在合同条款上有什么不同？
（2）买卖双方对一般交易条件如何处理？

（1）参考答案

（2）参考答案

小张对公司的合同解读如表 1.3 所示。

表 1.3 合同的解读

合同原文	解读
① ABC Garments & Accessories Co., Ltd.	ABC 服饰有限公司
② SALES CONTRACT	销售合同
③ CONTRACT NO.：ABC091102	合同号码：ABC091102
④ DATE: NOV. 02, 2009	合同签订日期：2009.11.02
⑤ SIGNED AT:HANGZHOU	合同签订地点：杭州
⑥ BUYER: Arrabon Trading Co Unit 9, Central Office Park, 257 Jean Ave; Centurion, South Africa	买方：Arrabon 贸易公司 南非杉球恩市珍恩大道 257 号中央办公区第 9 单元
⑦ SELLER: ABC GARMENTS & ACCESSORIES CO., LTD HONGXIN ROAD, HANGZHOU, ZHEJIANG, CHINA	卖方：ABC 服饰有限公司 中国浙江杭州红星路
⑧ Name of Commodity, Specifications: Boy's denim long pant NO.100 Boy's twill long pant NO.101	品名和规格： 男童牛仔长裤 货号 100 男童斜纹布长裤 货号 101
⑨ Quantity: 1000PCS、1000PCS	数量：各 1000 件
⑩ Unit Price: CFR LIMASSOL USD9.50、USD10.00	单价：CIF 利马索尔 （贸易术语） 9.50 美元、10 美元
⑪ Total Amount: TOTAL USD19500.00	总值：合计 19500 美元
⑫ PACKING: 50 pcs /carton	包装：50 件/纸箱
⑬ Shipping Marks: ABC/ABC091102/LIMASSOL/NOS.1-40	运输标志（唛头）：ABC/ABC091102/利马索尔
⑭ Shipping Quantity: Five Percent More or Less Allowed	装运数量允许有 5%增减
⑮ Time of Shipment: 50 DAYS AFTER THE SELLER RECEIVE THE L/C.	装运期：卖方收到信用证后 50 天内
⑯ Port of Loading: SHANGHAI	装运港：上海
⑰ Port of Destination: LIMASSOL, CYPRUS	目的港：塞浦路斯利马索尔
⑱ Insurance: TO BE COVERED BY BUYER	保险：由买方自理
⑲ Terms of Payment: IRREVOCABLE L/C AT SIGHT. The covering Letter of Credit must reach the Seller in 45 days after the date of this Contract and is to remain valid in above indicated Loading Port 15 days after the date of shipment, failing which the Seller reserve the right to cancel this Sales Contract and to claim from the Buyer compensation for loss resulting therefrom	支付条款：不可撤销即期信用证。该信用证必须在本合同签订日后 45 天内开到卖方。信用证的有效期应为装船期后 15 天，在上述装运口岸到期。否则卖方有权取消本售货合约并保留因此而发生的一切损失的索赔权
⑳ QUALITY/QUANTITY DISCREPANCY: In case of quality discrepancy, claim should be filed by the Buyer within 30 days after the arrival of the goods at Port of destination, while for quantity discrepancy claim should be filed by the Buyers within 15 days after the arrival of the goods at port of destination. In all cases, claims must be accompanied by Survey Reports of Recognized Public Surveyors agreed to by the Seller. Should the responsibility of the subject under claim be found to rest on part of the Seller, the Seller shall, within 20 days after receipt of the claim, send his reply to the Buyer together with suggestion for settlement	品质/数量异议：品质异议须于货到目的口岸之日起 30 天内提出，数量异议须于货到目的口岸之日起 15 天内提出，但均须提供经卖方同意的公证行的检验证明。如责任属于卖方者，卖方于收到异议 20 天内答复买方并提出处理意见

续表

合同原文	解读
㉑ INSPECTION: The Certificate of Origin and/or the Inspection Certification of Quality/Quantity/Weight issued by the relative institute shall be taken as the basis for the shipping Quality/Quantity/Weight	商品检验：产地证明书或中国有关机构所签发的品质数量/重量检验证，作为品质数量/重量的交货依据
㉒ Force Majeure: The Sellers shall not be held responsible if they owing to Force Majeure cause or causes fail to make delivery within the time stipulated in this Sales Contract or cannot deliver the goods. However, the Seller shall inform immediately the Buyer by fax. The Seller shall delivery to the Buyer by registered letter, if it is requested by the Buyer, a certificate issued by the China Council for the Promotion of International Trade or by any competent authority, certifying to the existence of the said cause or causes. Buyer's failure to obtain the relative Import license is not to be treated as Force Majeure	不可抗力：因人力不可抗拒事故，使卖方不能在本售货合约规定期限内交货或不能交货，卖方不负责任，但是卖方必须立即以传真通知买方，如果买方提出要求，卖方应以挂号函向买方提供由中国国际贸易促进委员会或有关机构出具的证明，证明事故的存在。买方不能领到进口证不能被认为系属人力不可抗拒范围
㉓ ARBITRATION: All disputes arising in connection with the Sales Contract of the execution thereof shall be settled amicably by negotiation. In case no settlement can be reached, the case under dispute shall then be submitted for arbitration to the Foreign Trade Arbitration Commission of the China Council for the Promotion of International Trade in accordance with the Provisional Rules of Procedure of the Foreign Trade Arbitration Commission of the China Council for the Promotion of International Trade. The decision of the Commission shall be accepted as final and binding upon both parties	仲裁：凡因执行本合约或有关本合约所发生的一切争执，双方应以友好方式协商解决，如果协商不能解决，应提交北京中国国际贸易促进委员会对外贸易仲裁委员会根据中国国际贸易促进委员会对外贸易仲裁委员会的仲裁程序暂行规则进行仲裁。仲裁裁决是终局的，对双方都有约束力

任务再现

南京某公司出口高尔夫球帽，与日本某客户经过磋商达成协议，双方同意签订如下合同，阅读理解合同内容。

任务再现

Sales Confirmation(1)

Seller (2):
NANJING LANXING Co., LTD
ROOM 2501, JIAFAMANSTION, BEIJING WEST ROAD, NANJING

(4) Contract No.03TG28711
(5) Date: July 22, 2003

(6) Signed at: NANJING

Buyer (3):
EAST AGENT COMPANY
3-72,OHTAMACHI,NAKA-KU,YOKOHAMA, JAPAN231

(7)This Sales Contract is made by and between the Seller and Buyer, whereby the Seller agree to sell and the Buyer agree to buy the under-mentioned goods according to the terms and conditions stipulated below:

(8)NAME OF COMMODITY & SPECIFICATION	(9) UNIT PRICE	(10)QUANTITY	(11) AMOUNT & PRICE TERMS
H6-59940BS GOLF CAPS	USD 8.10	1800 DOZS	CIF AKITA USD14580.00
		TOTAL	USD14580.00

(12) 10% more or less both in amount and quantity allowed.

(13)Packing: 10 DOZS per CARTON

(14)Delivery: From NANJING to AKITA

(15) Shipping Marks: V.H

LAS PLAMS

C/NO.1-180

(16) Time of Shipment: Within 30 days after receipt of L/C, allowing transshipment and partial shipments.

(17) Terms of Payment: by 100% Confirmed, Irrevocable Letter of Credit in favor of the Seller to be available by sight draft to be opened and to reach China before JULY 30,2003, and to remain valid for negotiation in China until the 15th day after the foresaid Time of Shipment.

L/C must mention this contract number, L/C advised by BANK OF CHINA NANJING BRANCH.

TLX: 44U4K NJBC, CN. All banking charges outside China(the Mainland of China) are for account of the Drawee.

(18) Insurance: to be effected by Seller for 110% of full invoice value covering FPA up to AKITA.

(19) Arbitration: All disputes arising from the execution of or in connection with this contract shall be settled amicably by negotiation. In case of no settlement can be reached through negotiation, the case shall then be submitted to China International Economics & Trade Arbitration Commission in NANJING for arbitration in act with its rules of Procedures. The arbitral award is final and binding upon both parties for settling the dispute. The fee for arbitration shall be borne by the losing party unless otherwise awarded.

The Buyer: The Seller:

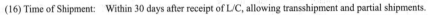

参考答案

技能强化训练

项目小结

技 能 提 高

1. 阅读理解以下合同。

Sales Contract （1）

(2)Seller:

FEI YANG IMPORT & EXPORT CO., LTD

256,TIANHE EAST ROAD,GUANGZHOU, CHINA

(3)Buyer:

BRTRADING CORPORATION

21014AST, TORONTO CANADA

(4)Contract No.G2201 2076

Date: Apr. 15,2012

Signed at: GUANGZHOU

在线测试及

参考答案

WE HEREBY AGREE TO SELL AND BUY THE COMODITIES MENTIONED IN THIS CNTRACT SUBJECT TO THE TERMS AND CONDITIONS STIPULATED AS FOLLOWS:

NAME OF COMMODOTY &SPECIFICATION (5)	QUANTITY (6)	UNIT PRICE (7)	AMOUNT (8)
Child's cap with pompon		CIF TORONTO	

Art. No. S12	1 000pcs	USD12.00	USD12 000.00
Art. No. A12	2 000pcs	USD10.00	USD20 000.00
(9)Packing:		TOTAL	USD32 000.00
Each in one plastic bag, 15pcs to a carton, totaling:200 cartons			
(10)SHIPPING MARKS: FFQ　　TORONTO　　NO.1-200			

参考答案

(11)TOTAL VALUE: SAY US DOLLARS THIRTY FIVE THOUSAND ONLY.

(12) Time of Shipment: Within 45 days of receipt of Letter of Credit and not later than the end of Aug.,2012 with partial shipments and transshipment allowed.

(13) Port of Loading: Guangzhou, China.

(14) Port of Destination: Toronto, Canada.

(15) Terms of Payment: by 100% irrevocable sight Letter of Credit opened by the Buyer to reach the Seller not later than July,25th,2012 and to be available for negotiation in China until the 15th day after the date of shipment.

In case of late arrival of L/C, the Seller shall not be liable for any delay in shipment and shall have the right to rescind the contract and /or claim for damages.

(16)Insurance: to be effected by the Seller for 110% of the CIF invoice value covering All Risks and WAR Risk only as per China Insurance Clauses.

(17) General Terms:

1. Reasonable tolerance in quality, weight, measurements, designs and colors, is allowed, for which no claims will be entertained.

2. The buyer are to assume full responsibilities for any consequences arising from the late establishment of L/C.

Confirmed by the Buyer:	The Seller:
BRTRADING CORPORATION	FEIYANG IMPORT AND EXPORT CO., LTD.
JOHN	

2. 根据下列买卖双方磋商的结果，填制一份合同。

致：加拿大 ABC 进口贸易公司

敬启者：

　　我们很高兴地通知贵公司，我们已收到并接受贵公司 4 月 25 日的还盘，现确认与贵公司达成如下交易：

　　4000 套茶碟，规格：4′和 6′，纸箱包装，每箱装 8 套，4′货共计 260 箱，6′货共计 240 箱。价格为 CIF 温哥华每套 8.90 美元，含佣金 5%。货物将于 2003 年 7 月底前由中国大连装船运出，不允许转船。保险由我公司根据中国保险条款（1981.1.1）按发票 110%投保一切险。唛头由我方制定。装运前 60 天贵公司须将不可撤销即期信用证开到我方，有效期为装运后 21 天内，以便按期备货装运。信用证以我方为受益人，包括 95%的发票金额。

　　现将我方签好的合同 03DO9084 号寄给贵公司，请签字并退一份供我方存档。

广东东方工艺品贸易公司

李广

2003 年 5 月 5 日

参考答案

项目二

开证、审证和改证实训

知识目标

1. 理解信用证的含义和特点；
2. 掌握信用证业务流程；
3. 熟悉信用证的基本内容和主要条款；
4. 掌握信用证审核要点和修改程序。

能力目标

1. 能根据进口合同向银行申请开证；
2. 能分析信用证的主要条款；
3. 能对照合同内容进行审证、改证。

任务一　申请开立信用证

任务导航

2015 年 3 月,南方纺织品进出口有限公司(以下简称"南方公司")根据公司生产需要,与印度 JAMES EXPORT 公司签订了一笔棉纱(100% cotton yarn)进口合同,合同约定 CIF FOSHAN 交易条件,即期信用证方式付款,金额为 USD43 700.00。

合同签订后,作为进口方,南方公司必须按照合同规定及时向中方银行申请开立信用证。小张是南方公司的单证员,她首先必须对该笔合同十分熟悉,对合同主要条款做到心中有数,以便顺利完成进口单证处理工作。

要求:

请以单证员小张的身份,根据合同内容,向中信银行广州分行申请开立一份以印度 JAMES EXPORT 公司为受益人的即期信用证。

棉纱

中信银行

购货合同

任务准备

一、申请开立信用证的程序

申请开证是整个进口信用证处理业务的第一个环节。当进出口双方在贸易合同中确定以信用证方式结算时,进口方(开证申请人)必须在合同规定的时间向所在地银行申请开立信用证,具体办理手续如图 2.1 所示。

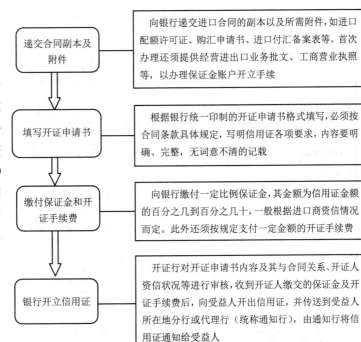

图 2.1　申请开证流程

图中流程内容如下:

- **递交合同副本及附件** —— 向银行递交进口合同的副本以及所需附件,如进口配额许可证、购汇申请书、进口付汇备案表等。首次办理还须提供经营进出口业务批文、工商营业执照等,以办理保证金账户开立手续

- **填写开证申请书** —— 根据银行统一印制的开证申请书格式填写,必须按合同条款具体规定,写明信用证各项要求,内容要明确、完整,无词意不清的记载

- **缴付保证金和开证手续费** —— 向银行缴付一定比例保证金,其金额为信用证金额的百分之几到百分之几十,一般根据进口商资信情况而定。此外还须按规定支付一定金额的开证手续费

- **银行开立信用证** —— 开证行对开证申请书内容及其与合同关系、开证人资信状况等进行审核,收到开证人缴交的保证金及开证手续费后,向受益人开出信用证,并传送到受益人所在地分行或代理行(统称通知行),由通知行将信用证通知给受益人

申请开证一般要交多少保证金？

如果在银行有授信关系，信用证保证金比例一般为 20%～50%，剩余部分占用企业授信额度；如果没有授信就需要全额保证金或全额担保了。

实际业务中，银行推出了减免保证金开证业务。银行应外贸公司要求，为外贸公司减收或免收保证金开出信用证，这种贸易融资方式适用于具有进出口经营权的银行已授信的外贸公司，其所进口的商品必须符合国家政策和相关规定。

二、填写信用证申请书

一般情况下，开证申请书（irrevocable documentary credit application）都由开证银行事先印就，申请人直接填制。各家银行出立的申请书格式不尽相同，但主要内容基本一致（见图 2.2）。开证申请书通常为一式两联，申请人除填写正面内容外，还须签具背面的开证申请人承诺书，这是申请人对开证行的声明，用以明确双方责任。开证申请书正面内容及填制方法见表 2.1。

IRREVOCABLE DOCUMENTARY CREDIT APPLICATION

TO:　　　　　　　　　　　　　　　　　　　　DATE:

Beneficiary(full name and address)	L/C No.
	Ex-Card No. / Contract No.
	Date and place of expiry of the credit
Partial Shipments ( )allowed ( )not allowed / Transshipment ( )allowed ( )not allowed	( ) Issue by airmail ( ) With brief advice by teletransmission ( ) Issue by express delivery
Loading on board/dispatch/taking in charge at/from / not later than / for transport to	( ) Issue by teletransmission (which shall be the operative instruction) / Amount(both in figures and words)
Description of goods: / Packing:	Credit available with ( )by sight payment ( )by acceptance ( )by negotiation ( )by deferred payment at / against the documents detailed herein ( )and beneficiary's draft for 100% of the invoice value at / on ( ) FOB ( ) CFR ( ) CIF ( ) or other terms

图 2.2　信用证开证申请书

```
Document required:(marked with × )
1.(  ) Signed Commercial Invoice in _____copies indicate L/C No. and Contract No._____.
2.(  ) Full set of clean on board ocean Bills of Lading made out _____and (  ) blank endorsed, marked "freight"
  (  ) to collect/ (  ) prepaid.
3.(  ) Air Waybills showing "freight (  ) to collect / (  ) prepaid (  )  indicating freight amount" and consigned to
_____
4.(  ) We normal issued by _____ consigned to _____.
5.(  ) Insurance Policy / Certificate in _____ copies for _____% of the invoice value showing claims paypable in China in
currency of the draft,blank endorsed, covering (  ) Ocean Marine Transportation / (  ) Air Transportation / (  ) Over Land
Transporation (  ) All risks, War Risks.
6.(  ) Packing List / Weight Memo in _____ copies indicating quantity / gross and net weights of each package and packing
conditions as called for by the L/C.
7.(  ) Certificate of Quantity / Weight in copies issued by an independent surveyor at the loading port, indicating the actual
surveyed quantity / weight of shipped goods as well as the packing condition.
8.(  ) Certificate of Quality in 1 copies issued by (  ) manufacturer / (  ) public recognized surveyor / (  ).
9.(  ) Beneficiary's Certified copy of cable / fax dispatched to the accountees within _____ days after shipment advising
(  ) name of vessel / (  ) flight No. / (  ) wagon No. , date, quantity, weight and value of shipment.
10. (  ) Beneficiary's certificate Certifying that extra copies of the documents have been dispatched according to the contract
terms.
11.(  ) Shipping Co's certificate attesting that the carrying vessel is chartered or booked by accountee or their shipping agent.
12.(  ) Other documents, if any.
  Additional Instructions:
1.(  ) All banking charges outside the opening bank are for beneficiary's account.
2.(  ) Documents must be presented within _____ days atrer the date of issuance of the transport documents but within the
3.(  ) Third party as shipper is not acceptable. Short Form / Blank Back B/L is not acceptable.
4.(  ) Both quantity and amout _____ % more or less are allowed.
5.(  ) Prepaid freight drawn in excess of L/C amount is acceptable against presentation of original charges voucher issued by
shipping Co. / Air Line / or it's agent.
6.(  ) All documents to be for warded in one cover, unless otherwise stated above.
7.(  ) Other terms, if any.
```

图 2.2 信用证开证申请书（续）

表 2.1 信用证申请书内容及填制方法一览表

序号	项目名称	填制方法
1	TO（致）	申请书上事先都会印就开证银行的名称、地址，银行的 SWIFT CODE、TELEX NO 等也可同时显示
2	DATE（申请开证日期）	在申请书右上角填写实际申请日期，必须符合日期格式且在合同日期之后
3	L/C NO.（信用证号码）	此栏由银行随机生成
4	Beneficiary（受益人）	填写受益人的全称及详细地址
5	Contract NO.（合同号码）	填写合同号码
6	Date and place of expiry（信用证有效期及地点）	有效期为日期格式（YYYYMMDD），且须在申请开证日期之后。信用证的到期地点可以规定在出口地（议付行所在地，通常也是受益人所在地）、进口地（开证行所在地）或第三国（付款行所在地）
7	开证方式	Issue by airmail（以航空信开）；With brief advice by teletransmission（以简电开）；Issue by express delivery（以快递信开）；Issue by teletransmission（which shall be the operative instrument）（以全电开）。如今大多银行以"SWIFT"方式开证
8	Amount（信用证金额）	填写币种和合同金额，分别用数字和文字两种形式
9	装运条件	Partial shipments（是否允许分批装运）；Transshipment（是否允许转运）；Loading on board/dispatch/taking in charge at/from（装运港名称）；not later than（最迟装运期）；For transportation to（目的港）

续表

序号	项目名称	填制方法
10	Description of goods（货物描述）	包括商品编号、商品名称、商品描述（必须与合同上商品描述完全一致）、商品数量（与合同一致，注意单位的单复数）、商品单价、包装、唛头等
11	价格条款	根据合同内容选择填写贸易术语
12	Credit available with（付款方式）	① 填写此信用证可由____银行即期付款、承兑、议付、延期付款，即押汇银行（出口地银行）名称。如果信用证为自由议付信用证，银行可用"ANY BANK IN…（地名/国名）"表示。如果该信用证为自由议付信用证，而且对议付地点也无限制时，可用"ANY BANK"表示 ② Sight payment 勾选此项，表示开具即期付款信用证；negotiation 勾选此项，表示开具议付信用证；deferred payment at 勾选此项，表示开具延期付款信用证 ③ against the documents detailed herein and beneficiary's draft(s) for____% of invoice value at____sight drawn on____。此栏为汇票信息，解释如下： 　a. 受益人按发票金额×%，填制成限制为×天、付款人为××的汇票。如是"即期付款信用证"，此栏可选可不选；如是"承兑信用证"或"议付信用证"，必须选择此栏；如是"延期付款信用证"，则不需要选择连同此单据 　b. "at____sight"为付款期限。如果是即期，需要在"at____sight"之间填"***"或"----"，不能留空 　c. 远期有几种情况：at ×× days after date（出票后××天），at ××days after sight（见票后××天）或 at ×× days after date of B/L（提单日后××天）等 　d. "drawn on"为指定付款人，汇票付款人应为开证行或指定的付款行
13	Documents required: (marked with ×) [信用证需要提交的单据（用"×"标明）]	已印就单据条款十几条，最后一条是 OTHER DOCUMENTS, IF ANY（其他单据），对上述没有印就的单据可填写在该处；在所要的单据前打"×"。一般要求提示的单据有海运提单（或空运单、收货单）、发票、箱单、重量证明、保险单、数量证明、质量证明、产地证、装船通知、商检证明以及其他申请人要求的证明等；在该单据条款后填上具体要求，如一式几份，应包括什么内容等。如信用证申请书印制好的要求不完整，可在该条款后面填写清楚
14	Additional instructions（附加条款）	是对以上各条款未述之情况的补充和说明，也包括对银行的要求等
15	Name，Signature of Authorised Person，Tel. No., Fax, Account No.（开证申请人信息）	申请书最下面一栏填写有关开证申请人的开户银行（填银行名称）、账户号码、执行人、联系电话、申请人（法人代表）签字等内容

▌ 课堂思考 ▌

参考答案

（1）信用证付款方式下，汇票的付款人可以填为开证申请人，如 drawn on ABC CO. 吗？

（2）在 CIF 价格条件下，开证申请书应表明要求卖方提交"Freight Prepaid（运费预付）"的提单，这种说法对吗？

三、申请开证时应注意的问题

申请人申请开立信用证时应注意以下问题。

（1）申请开证前，要落实进口批准手续及外汇来源。

（2）开证时间。开证申请人必须在合同规定的时间，向所在地银行申请开证，合同中如果没有规定开证日期，一般掌握在合同规定的装运期前一个月到一个半月。总之，开证时间应在卖方收到信用证后能在合同规定的装运期内出运为原则。

 职业判断

案例资料：

2月26日，深圳富通机械工业有限公司与瑞士旁尔公司签订了一份金额为320万美元的食品机械进口合同，见票后30天远期信用证付款，最迟装运期为8月30日。合同签订后，富通公司单证员小刘准备向中信银行深圳分行申请开立信用证。

思考：

小刘应在什么时间向银行申请开证？

参考答案

任务实施

（1）南方公司单证员小张填制的信用证申请书如图2.3所示。

IRREVOCABLE DOCUMENTARY CREDIT APPLICATION	
TO: CHINA CITIC BANK（GUANZGHOU BRANCH），GUANGZHOU	**DATE:** 150410
Beneficiary(full name and address) JAMES EXPORTS. 506 SHARDA CHAMBERS，19 NEW MARINE LINES MUMBAI-400030，INDIA	L/C No. Ex-Card No. Contract No. 001/M/2015-13
	Date and place of expiry of the credit 150516　INDIA
Partial Shipments （　）allowed （×）not allowed	Transshipment （×）allowed （　）not allowed	（　）Issue by airmail　（　）With brief advice by teletransmission （　）Issue by express delivery （×）Issue by SWIFT
Loading on board/dispatch/taking in charge at/from ANY PORT IN INDIA not later than　150501 for transport to　FOSHAN，CHINA	Amount(both in figures and words) USD43700.00 SAY US DOLLARS FORTY THREE THOUSAND SEVEN HUNDRED ONLY.

图2.3　南方公司信用证申请书

Description of goods: 100% COTTON YARN NE 16/1 GREY OPEN END WEAVING UNWAXED 100PCT CARDED YARN ON CHEESE BRAND:KIKANI SALE CONTRACT NO.001/M/2015-13 PROFORM INVOICE NO. 001/M/2015-13 QUANTITY:19000KGS UNIT PRICE:USD2.30 PER KG COUNTRY OF ORIGIN AND SUPPLY: INDIA Packing：NET WEIGHT 2.25KGS/CHEESE，24CHEESE/PP BAG，NEUTRAL PACKING	Credit available with （ ）by sight payment（ ）by acceptance（×）by negotiation （ ） by deferred payment at against the documents detailed herein （×） and beneficiary's draft for 100% of the invoice value at SIGHT on US
	（ ） FOB （ ） CFR （×） CIF （ ） or other terms

Document required:(marked with ×)

1. （×）Signed Commercial Invoice in 3 ORIGINALS AND 3 COPIES indicate L/C No. and Contract No..

2. （×）Full set of clean on board ocean Bills of Lading made out TO ORDER and （×）blank endorsed, marked "freight" （ ）to collect/ （×）prepaid , notifying the applicant.

3. （ ）Air Waybills showing "freight （ ） to collect / （ ） prepaid （ ） indicating freight amount" and consigned to_____ .

4. （ ）We normal issued by _____ consigned to _____ .

5. （×）Insurance Policy / Certificate in 1 ORIGINAL AND 2 COPIES for 110% of the invoice value showing claims payable in China in currency of the draft, blank endorsed, covering （×）Ocean Marine Transportation / （ ） Air Transportation / （ ） Over Land Transportation （ ） All risks, War Risks. INSTITUTE CARGO CLAUSES （A），INSTITUTE WAR CLAUSES （CARGO） AND INSTITUTE STRIKES CLAUSES （CARGO）.

6. （×）Packing List / Weight Memo in3 ORIGINALS AND 3 COPIES indicating quantity / gross and net weights of each package and packing conditions as called for by the L/C.

7. （ ） Certificate of Quantity / Weight in copies issued by an independent surveyor at the loading port, indicating the actual surveyed quantity / weight of shipped goods as well as the packing condition.

8. （ ） Certificate of Quality in 1 copies issued by （ ） manufacturer / （ ） public recognized surveyor / （ ）.

9. （ ） Beneficiary's Certified copy of cable / fax dispatched to the accountee within _____ days after shipment advising （ ） name of vessel / （ ） flight No. / （ ） wagon No. , date, quantity, weight and value of shipment.

10. （×）Beneficiary's certificate Certifying that extra copies of the documents have been dispatched according to the contract terms.

11. （ ） Shipping Co's certificate attesting that the carrying vessel is chartered or booked by accountee or their shipping agent.

12. （×）Other documents, if any.

（×）ASIA PACIFIC TRADE AGREEMENT (APTA) CERTIFICATE ISSUSED BY INDIAN AUTHORITY IN 1 ORIGINAL AND 2 COPIES INDICATING L/C NO. AND CONTRACT NO.

Additional Instructions:

1. （×）All banking charges outside the opening bank are for beneficiary's account.

2. （×）Documents must be presented within 15 days after the date of issuance of the transport documents but within the validity of the credit.

3. （ ） Third party as shipper is not acceptable. Short Form / Blank Back B/L is not acceptable.

4. （×）Both quantity and amount 5 % more or less are allowed.

图 2.3 南方公司信用证申请书（续）

5. （ ） Prepaid freight drawn in excess of L/C amount is acceptable against presentation of original charges voucher issued by shipping Co. / Air Line / or it's agent.

6. （ ） All documents to be for warded in one cover, unless otherwise stated above.

7. （ ） Other terms, if any.

Account No.   with＿＿＿＿＿＿＿＿＿＿＿＿＿＿＿＿＿ (name of bank)

＿＿ NANFANG TEXTILES IMP. AND EXP. CO. LTD ＿＿

（Applicant: name, signature of authorized person）

图 2.3 　南方公司信用证申请书（续）

（2）中信银行广州分行开立的信用证如图 2.4 所示。

Issue of a Documentary Credit

27/ Sequence of Total: 1/1

40 A/ Form of　Doc. Credit: IRREVOCABLE

20/ Doc. Credit Number: 51000LC1500460

31 C/ Date of Issue: 150410

31 D/ Date and Place of Expiry: 150516 INDIA

40E/ Applicable Rules: UCP LATEST VERSION

50/ Applicant: NANFANG TEXTILES IMP. AND EXP.CO.,LTD.

             ADDRESS SEE FIELD 47A

59/ Beneficiary: JAMES EXPORTS.

             ADDRESS SEE FIELD 47A

32B/ Currency Code，Amount: USD43700.00

39/ Percentage Credit Amount Tolerance: 05/05

41D/ Available with/By: ANY　BANK BY NEGOTIATION

42 C/ Drafts at…: AT SIGHT FOR 100PCT OF INVOICE VALUE

42A/ Drawee: CIBKCNBJ510

             CHINA CITIC BANK(GUANZGHOU BRANCH),GUANGZHOU

43P/ Partial Shipments: NOT ALLOWED

43 T/ Transshipment: ALLOWED

44E/ Port of　Loading/Airport of Departure: ANY PORT IN INDIA

44F/ Port of Discharge/Airport of Destination: FOSHAN，CHINA

44 C/ Latest Date of Shipment: 150501

45A/ Description of Goods and/or Services:

图 2.4 　银行信用证

100% COTTON YARN

NE 16/1 GREY OPEN END WEAVING UNWAXED 100PCT CARDED YARN

ON CHEESE

SALE CONTRACT NO.001/M/2015-13

PROFORM INVOICE NO. 001/M/2015-13

QUANTITY: 19000KGS

BRAND: KIKANI

PACKING: NET WEIGHT 2.25KGS/CHEESE, 24CHEESE/PP BAG, NEUTRAL PACKING

UNIT PRICE: USD2.30 PER KG

COUNTRY OF ORIGIN AND SUPPLY: INDIA

CIF FOSHAN，CHINA

46A/ Documents Required:

1. SIGENDE COMMERCIAL INVOICE IN 3 ORIGINALS AND 3 COPIES INDICATING L/C NO. AND CONTRACT NO.

2. FULL SET(3 ORIGINALS AND 3 NON NEGOTIABLE COPIES)OF CLEAN ON BOARD BILLS OF LADING MADE OUT TO ORDER AND BLANK ENDORSED, MARKED FREIGHT PREPAID, NOTIFYING APPLICANT WITH FULL NAME, ADDRESS TELEPHONE NUMBERS AND FAX NUMBER.

3. FULL SET(1 ORIGINAL AND 2 COPIES) OF INSURANCE POLICY/CERTIFICATE FOR AT LEAST 110PCT OF THE INVOICE VALUE SHOWING CLAIMS PAYABLE IN CHINA IN CURRENCY OF THE CREDIT，BLANK ENDORSED，COVERING INSTITUTE CARGO CLAUSES(A)，INSTITUTE WAR CLAUSES(CARGO)AND INSTITUTE STRIKES CLAUSES(CARGO).

4. PACKING LIST/WEIGHT MEMO IN 3 ORIGINALS AND 3 COPIES ISSUED BY BENEFICIARY INDICATING L/C NO. AND CONTRACT NO.

5. ASIA PACIFIC TRADE AGREEMENT (APTA) CERTIFICATE ISSUSED BY INDIAN AUTHORITY IN 1 ORIGINAL AND 2 COPIES INDICATING L/C NO. AND CONTRACT NO.

6. BENEFICIARY'S CERTIFICATE CERTIFYING THAT EXTRA COPIES OF ALL DOCUMENTS REQUIRED IN THIS CREDIT HAVE BEEN SENT VIA DHL. COURIER SERVICE TO THE APPLICANT WITHIN 10 DAYS AFTER SHIPMENT.

47 / Additional Conditions:

1. T/T REIMBURSEMENTS ARE NOT ALLOWED.

2. DRAFTS DRAWN HEREUNDER MUST BEAR OUR NAME，THE CREDIT NO. AND DATE.

3. IF DOCUMENTS ARE PRESENTED WITH DISCREPANCYIES, A DISCREPANCY FEE OF USD80.00 OR EQUIVALENT WILL BE DEDUCTED FROM THE PROCEEDS.

4. ALL DOCUMENTS SHOULD BE ISSUED IN ENGLISH AND INDICATE THIS CREDIT NUMBER.

5. IF THIS L/C IS NEGOTIATED BY A BANK OTHER THAN THE ADVISING BANK，THE NEGOTIATING BANK IS TO CERTIFY ON COVERING SCHEDULE THAT THE ADVISING BANK CHARGES ARE PAID.

图 2.4　银行信用证（续）

6. BOTH QUANTITY AND AMOUNT 5 PCT MORE OR LESS ARE ALLWED.

7. DOCUMENTS MUST NOT BE DATED PRIOR TO THE ISSUANCE DATE OF THIS CREDIT.

8. APPLICANT'S ADDRESS:

  ROOM 211，128 DONGXIAO SOUTH ROAD

  GUANGZHOU，CHINA

  TEL: +86-22-93115583   FAX: 93115161

9. BENEFICIARY'S ADDRESS:

  506 SHARDA CHAMBERS，19 NEW MARINE LINES MUMBAI-400030，INDIA

  TEL: +91-22-29617500   FAX: 22005082

  71B/ Charges: ALL BANK CHARGES AND INSTEREST, IF ANY, OUTSIDE ISSUING BANK AND PEIMBURSEMENT CHARGE ARE FOR ACCOUNT OF THE BENEFICIARY.

图 2.4　银行信用证（续）

 任务再现

木制花架
和花盆

2015 年 10 月，广州海达国际公司与加拿大 HAROLD 公司签订一笔园艺产品（木制花架和花盆）进口合同（见图 2.5），即期信用证付款，CFR MONTREAL 成交，合同金额为 244 000 美元。

试为广州海达国际公司向中国银行广东省分行申请开证，填写信用证申请书，申请开证时间为 2015 年 10 月 28 日。

我国四大商业银行

销 售 合 同
SALES　CONTRACT

NO.:2015G02350

DATE: SEP. 10,2015

The Seller:

HAROLD CO., LTD.

FOERETA 6 S-23237 MONTREAL,CANADA

The Buyer:

GUANGZHOU HAIDA INTERNATIONAL CORP.

NO.336 TIANHE SOUTH STREET, TIANHE

DISTRICT, GUANGZHOU, CHINA

This Contract is made by and between the Seller and the Buyer, whereby the Seller agree to sell and the buyer agree to buy the under-mentioned goods according to the terms and conditions stipulated below:

图 2.5　销售合同

（1）货号\品名及规格 Name of commodity and specifications	（2）数量 Quantity	（3）单价 Unit Price	（4）金额 Amount	（5）包装 Packing
WOODEN GARDEN PRODUCTS				
WOODEN FLOWER STANDS	3 500PCS	USD 20.00/PC	USD70 000.00	20PCS/CTN
WOODEN FLOWER POTS	6 000PCS	USD 29.00/PC	USD174 000.00	40PCS/CTN
TOTAL	9 500PCS	CFR MONTREAL,CANADA	USD244 000.00	325 CTNS

（6）Loading in charge: MONTREAL, CANADA

（7）For Transport to: GUANGZHOU, CHINA

（8）Transshipment: ALLOWED

（9）Partial Shipments: NOT ALLOWED

（10）The Latest Date Of Shipment: NOV. 30, 2015

（11）Insurance: BE EFFECTED BY THE BUYER

参考答案

（12）Payment: BY IRREVOCABLE L/C, IN FAVOR OF THE SELLER. TO BE AVAILABLE BY SIGHT DRAFT, REACHING THE SELLER BEFORE OCT. 30, 2015, REMAIN VALID FOR NEGOTIATION IN CANADA UNTIL THE 15TH DAYS AFTER THE FORESAID TIME OF SHIPMENT. ALL COMMISSION AND CHARGES OUTSIDE CHINA ARE FOR ACCOUNT OF THE SELLER.

The Seller:

HAROLD CO. LTD

JUSTIN

The Buyer:

GUANGZHOU HAIDA INTERNATIONAL CORP.

杨立胜

图 2.5 销售合同（续）

任务二 分析信用证

任务导航

胶管接头

2015 年 8 月 9 日，广迪机械进出口有限公司（以下简称"广迪公司"）与阿联酋 WLL MARKETING ENGINEERING MATERIALS LTD. 公司经反复磋商，达成一笔胶管接头（HYDRAULIC HOSE FITTINGS）出口交易，双方贸易合同约定 CIF DUBAI 价格条件，即期信用证付款，成交金额为 58 605 美元。

2015 年 8 月 17 日，阿联酋 WLL MARKETING ENGINEERING MATERIALS LTD 公司按照合同规定，开出了以广迪公司为受益人的信用证，编号为 DER260635，如图 2.6 所示。

Issue of a Documentary Credit

APPLICATION HEADER 0 700 1915 150817 HBZUAEADAXXX 2572 542494 150817

2315 N   *HABIB BANK AG ZURICH

*DUBAI

Sequence of Total	*27 : 1 / 2
Form of Doc. Credit	*40 A : IRREVOCABLE
Doc. Credit Number	*20 : DER260635
Date of Issue	31 C : 150817
Date and Place of Expiry	*31 D : DATE151030 PLACE CHINA
Applicant	*50 : WLL MARKETING ENGINEERING MATERIALS LTD
	PO BOX6747, SHARJAH，U.A.E.
	PHONE 065337338 FAX 065335883
Beneficiary	*59: GUANGDI MACHINERY IMPORT AND EXPORT CO., LTD.
	726 DONGFENG ROAD EAST，
	GUANGZHOU, CHINA
Currency Code, Amount	*32 B: CURRENCY USD AMOUNT 58600.00
Available with/By	*41 A: ANY BANK BY NEGOTIATION
Drafts at…	42 C: AT SIGHT
Drawee	42 A: HBZUAEADA×××
	* HABIB BANK AG ZURICH
	* DUBAI
Partial Shipments	43 P: NOT ALLOWED
Transshipment	43 T: ALLOWED
Loading In Charge	44 A: CHINA
For Transport To…	44 B: DUBAI，UNITED ARAB EMIRATES
Latest Date of Shipment	44 C: 151015
Description of Goods	45A:

HYDRAULIC HOSE FITTINGS

S91-001	3000SETS	USD9.10/SET	USD27 300.00
F91-002	460SETS	USD8.30/SET	USD3 818.00
H 91-003	22SETS	USD8.50/SET	USD187.00
991-006	3000SETS	USD9.10/SET	USD27 300.00

TRADE TERM: CIF DUBAI

AS PER SALES CONFIRMATION NO.HF60809 DATED AUGUST 09, 2015

Documents Required   46 A:

1. 5 SIGNED COMMERCIAL INVOICE IN THE NAME OF BENEFICIARY CERTIFING MERCHANDISE TO BE CHINA ORIGIN.

2. 4 PACKING LIST/WEIGHT LIST.

3. CERTIFICATE OF ORIGIN ISSUED BY CCPIT IN 1 ORIGINAL AND 2 COPIES.

图 2.6   对方开来的信用证

4. FULL SET OF CLEAN SHIPPED ON BOARD OCEAN BILL OF LADING DRAMN OR ENDORSED TO THE ORDER OF HABIB BANK AG ZURICH, SHOWING BENEFICIARY AS SHIPPER，MARKED NOTIFY APPLICANT, BEARING OUR CREDIT NO., SHOWING FREIGHT PREPAID.

5. 2 MARINE INSURANCE POLICY/CERTIFICATE, ENDORSED IN BLANK, FOR FULL INVOICE VALUE PLUS 10 PERCENT, COVERING INSTITUTE CARGO CLAUSES（A）,SHOWING CLAIMS IF ANY PAYABLE IN UNITED ARAB EMIRATES.

6. ALL SHIPMENT UNDER THIS CREDIT MUST BE ADVISED BY BENEFICIARY WITHIN 5 WORKING DAYS. FROM SHIPMENT DATE DIRECTLY BY FAX OR POST OR COURIER TO APPLICANT. A COPY OF EACH OF ABOVE ADVICES TO ACCOMPANY THE ORIGINAL SET OF DOCUMENTS.

7. BENEFICIARY'S CERTIFICATION，CERTIFING THAT ONE SET OF NON NEGOTIABLE DOCUMENT MUST BE SENT TO THE APPLICANT ON FAX.NO.9716 5331819 IMMEDIATELY AFTER SHIPMENT.

Additional Conditions   47A:

1. THIRD PARTY DOCUMENTS ARE NOT ACCEPTABLE.

2. DOCUMENTS ISSUED OR DATED PRIOR TO THIS CREDIT ISSUANCE DATE NOT ACCEPTABLE.

3. ALL DOCUMENTS TO BE MADE IN ENGLISH.

4. IF SHIPMENT IN CONTAINER, BILL OF LADING TO SHOW CONTAINER NUMBER AND SEAL NUMBER.

Details Of Charges   71B: ALL BANK CHARGES RECORDING FEE AND COMMISSION OUTSIDE UNITED ARAB EMIRATES INCLUDING REIMBURSEMENT CHARGES ARE FOR BENEFICIARY'S ACCOUNT.

Presentation Period   48:

DOCUMENTS TO BE PRESENTED WITHIN 21 DAYS AFTER THE DATE OF ISSUANCE OF THE SHIPPING DOCUMENTS，BUT WITHIN THE VALIDITY OF THE CREDIT.

Confirmation   *49: WITHOUT

Instructions   78:

1. THE NEGOTIATING BANK MUST FORWORD THE DRAFTS AND ALL DOCUMENTS BY REGISTERED AIRMAIL DIRECT TO US IN ONE LOT.

2. IF THIS LC IS NEGOTIATED BY A BANK OTHER THAN THE ADVISING BANK, THE NEGOTIATING BANK IS TO CERTIFY ON COVERING SCHEDULE THAT THE ADVISING BANK CHARGES ARE PAID.

3. THIS DOCUMENTARY CREDIT ISSUED IS SUBECT TO UCP600.

Instr. to Pay/Accept. /Neg.   78:

UPON RECEIPT OF ORIGINAL SHIPPING DOCUMENTS COMPLYING WITH CREDIT TERMS, WE SHALL EFFECT PAYMENT AS PER INSTRUCTION OF NEGOTIATING BANK/ COLLECTING BANK.

Advise Through   57A: BKCHCNBJ400
                 *BANK OF CHINA GUANGDONG BRANCH
                 *GUANGZHOU

Trailer: MAC: 1F858B75
            CHK: 2C08BC31E9C6

图 2.6 对方开来的信用证（续）

补充交易资料如下：

发票号：A12-234-8256   发票日期：OCT.09,2015
提单号：HUPDXB06A0306   提单日期：OCT.13,2015

船名航次：WAN HAN 303 V.W049　　　　装运港：HUANGPU，CHINA

集装箱号：1×20'FCL CY/CY

　　　WHLU5165067　　　SEAL NO.WH04341085

保单号：6697256　　　　　　　　原产地证号：120387253

HS CODE: 8302.4100　　　　　　　唛头：N/M

原材料情况：完全中国产，不含任何进口成分

货物装箱情况：

S91-001	3000SETS	20 SETS/CTN	150 CTNS
F91-002	460SETS	20 SETS/CTN	23CTNS
H 91-003	22SETS	22 SETS/CTN	1CTNS
991-006	3000SETS	20 SETS/CTN	150CTNS
	6482SETS		324CTNS

净重：1KG/SET　　毛重：1.3KG/SET　　尺码：（56×38×31）CM/CTN

出口口岸：黄埔关区（5200）　　　生产厂家：广东顺德立欧金属制品厂

经营单位编码：4401967226　　　　贸易方式：一般贸易

运费：1200美元　　　　　　　　保险费：500美元

报检单位登记号：4401004899　　　报关报检员：陈丽

要求：

以广迪公司单证员的身份，阅读理解该信用证，找出以下内容：

（1）信用证号、开证日期；

（2）信用证有效期及到期地点；

（3）开证人、受益人名称和地址；

（4）信用证金额；

（5）汇票期限和汇票付款人；

（6）装运港、目的港、装运期限、分批装运和转运的要求；

（7）商品名称、数量及贸易术语；

（8）合同号及日期；

（9）要求的单据；

（10）交单期限。

知识准备

一、收到信用证通知书

实际业务中，通知行收到国外开证行开立的信用证后，会通知出口

信用证通知书

人（受益人），并将信用证正本或复印件（一般是复印件，如无必要，正本建议留在银行保存）交给出口人。一般来说，从国外客户开证，到出口方收到信用证快则一周，慢则 10 天左右。

跟随信用证一起交给出口人的通常还有一页通知行出具的信用证通知书，主要列明了此份信用证的基本情况，如信用证编号、开证行、金额、有效期等，同时由通知行盖章。

参考答案

■ 课堂思考 ━━━━━━━

（1）信用证和买卖合同有什么关系？
（2）信用证支付方式有哪些特点？

小 贴 士

信用证业务流程

信用证种类和信用证条款的规定不同，其业务流程有所差异，但就其基本环节而言，则大致相同，具体如图 2.7 所示。

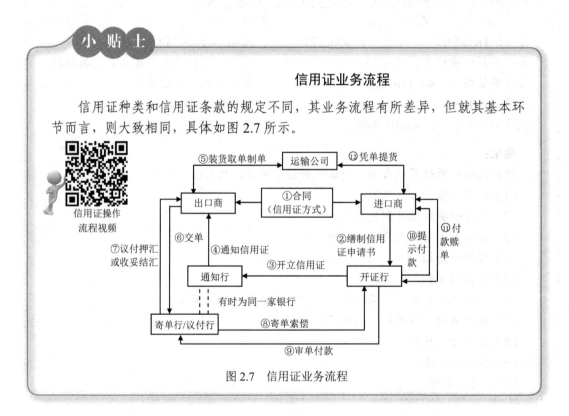

图 2.7　信用证业务流程

二、信用证的基本内容

目前国际信用证大多采用"SWIFT"报文格式开出，虽然各银行使用的格式并不尽相同，文字语句也有一些差别，但基本内容大致相同，如表 2.2 所示。

表2.2 信用证的主要项目内容

序号	主要内容		SWIFT 项目代号
1	对信用证本身的说明	①信用证的类型，如说明可否撤销、转让，是否经另一家银行保兑，偿付方式等；②信用证号码和开证日期；③有效期及到期地点；④信用证的金额：币别代号、金额、加减百分率	40A、20、31C、31D、41A、42P、49、32B、39A
2	信用证的当事人	必须记载的当事人，如申请人、开证行、受益人、通知行；可能记载的当事人，如保兑行、指定议付行、付款行、偿付行等	50、59A、51A、52A、53A、57A
3	对汇票的要求	汇票条款：出票人、付款人、付款期限、汇票金额	42A、42C
4	对运输的要求	包括运输方式、装运地和目的地、最迟装运日期、可否分批装运或转运	43P、43T、44A、44B、44C、44D
5	货物条款	包括货物名称、规格、数量、包装、单价以及合约号码等	45A
6	对单据的要求	说明要求提交的单据种类、份数、内容要求等，基本单据包括商业发票、运输单据和保险单；其他单据有检验证书、原产地证书、装箱单或重量单等	46A
7	其他规定	对交单期的说明；银行费用的说明；对议付行寄单方式、议付背书和索偿方法的指示等	47A、48、71B、72、78
8	银行责任文句	通常说明应根据《跟单信用证统一惯例》开立以及开证行保证付款的承诺，电开信用证可以省略	47A、78

SWIFT 银行结算系统

SWIFT 全称为"环球同业银行金融电讯协会"，是国际银行同业间的国际合作组织，成立于 1973 年，目前全球大多数国家大多数银行已使用 SWIFT 系统。SWIFT 的使用，为银行的结算提供了安全、可靠、快捷、标准化、自动化的通信业务，从而大大提高了银行的结算速度。由于 SWIFT 的格式具有标准化，目前大多银行信用证主要通过 SWIFT 电文开立。

三、阅读信用证

卖方收到信用证后应仔细阅读，快速理解和分析信用证，做到对信用证内容和具体要求了然于胸。

单证员可根据 SWIFT 代号看信用证，一目了然。通过"代号看证法"，能快速熟悉信用证基本框架结构，一拿到信用证就可轻车熟路地找出其基本信息了。例如，40A 条款看信用证类型、31D 条款看有效期、50 条款看开证人（客户）名址、59 条款看受益人、45A 条款看货物描述、32B 条款看金额、44C 条款或 44D 条款看交货期、46A 条款看单据要求、

47A 条款看特别要求、48 条款看交单期限等，一份信用证的核心内容基本如此。对信用证中的重要部分，如日期、金额、单证项目等涂画出来，这样方便下一步备货制单时一目了然。在实际工作中，常常还自行填制一份信用证分析单，这样使信用证各条款的内容更加清晰明了，便于下一步备货、制单，提高工作效率，减少差错。

小贴士

SWIFT 开立信用证常用项目如表 2.3 所示。

表 2.3　SWIFT 开立信用证常用项目

代号	英文	中文含义
20	DOCUMENTARY CREDIT NUMBER	信用证号码
27	SEQUENCE OF TOTAL	电文页次
31C	DATE OF ISSUE	开证日期
31D	DATE AND PLACE OF EXPIRY	信用证有效期和到期地点
32B	CURRENCY CODE, AMOUNT	信用证结算的货币和金额
39A	PERCENTAGE CREDIT AMOUNT TOLERANCE	信用证金额上下浮动允许的最大范围
40A	FORM OF DOCUMENTARY CREDIT	跟单信用证形式
41A	AVAILABLE WITH...BY...	指定的有关银行及信用证兑付的方式
42A	DRAWEE	汇票付款人
42C	DRAFTS AT...	汇票付款日期
43P	PARTIAL SHIPMENTS	分装条款
43T	TRANSSHIPMENT	转运条款
44A	LOADING ON BOARD/DISPATCH/TAKING IN CHARGE AT/FORM	装船、发运和接收监管的地点
44B	FOR TRANSPORTATION TO...	货物发运的最终地
44C	LATEST DATE OF SHIPMENT	最后装船期
44D	SHIPMENT PERIOD	船期
45A	DESCRIPTION OF GOODS AND/OR SERVICES	货物描述
46A	DOCUMENTS REQUIRED	单据要求
47A	ADDITIONAL CONDITIONS	特别条款
48	PERIOD FOR PRESENTATION	交单期限
49	CONFIRMATION INSTRUCTIONS	保兑指示
50	APPLICANT	开证申请人
51A	APPLICANT BANK	开证银行

续表

代号	英文	中文含义
59	BENEFICIARY	受益人
71B	CHARGES	费用情况
72	SENDER TO RECEIVER INFORMATION	附言
78	INSTRUCTION TO THE PAYING/ACCEPTING/NEGOTIATING BANK	给付款行、承兑行、议付行的指示

任务实施

单证员根据"任务导航"提供的信息，阅读理解图 2.6 所示信用证，找出"任务要求"中所提出的以下内容。

（1）信用证号：DER260635　　开证日期：150817

（2）信用证有效期及到期地点：151030，CHINA

（3）开证人名称和地址：

WLL MARKETING ENGINEERING MATERIALS LTD

PO BOX6747，SHARJAH，U.A.E.

（4）受益人名称和地址：

GUANGDI MACHINERY IMPORT AND EXPORT CO. ,LTD.

726 DONGFENG ROAD EAST，GUANGZHOU，CHINA

（5）信用证金额：USD 58 605.00

（6）汇票期限：AT SIGHT 即期付款

汇票付款人：HBZUAEADA×××

　　　　　　HABIB BANK AG ZURICH

　　　　　　DUBAI

（7）装运港：CHINA 港口

目的港：DUBAI，UNITED ARAB EMIRATES 阿联酋迪拜

装运期限：151009

分批装运：不允许；转运：允许

（8）商品名称：HYDRAULIC HOSE FITTINGS

数量：货号 S91-001　　　　3 000SETS

　　　　F91-002　　　　460SETS

H 91-003	22SETS
991-006	3000SETS
合计：	6482 SETS

贸易术语：CIF DUBAI

（9）合同号及日期：NO.HF60809 DATED AUGUST 09，2015。

（10）要求的单据：①商业发票；②装箱单；③原产地证书（国际贸易促进委员会签发）；④清洁已装船海运提单；⑤保险单/保险凭证；⑥装船通知书（装船日后 5 个工作日内发出）；⑦受益人证明（证明装运后已立即传真副本单据）。

（11）交单期限：提单日期后 21 天内，但须在信用证的有效期内。

法兰

任务再现

帝美工业有限公司向以色列 YAMIT FILTRATION AND WATER TREATMENT LTD. 公司出口法兰（FLANGES）一批。2015 年 1 月 10 日，帝美公司收到通知行转来该笔合同项下的即期信用证一份，全文如图 2.8 所示。

Issue of a Documentary Credit

Sender: POALILIT×××

　　　　BANK HAPOALIM B.M.

　　　　TEL-AVIV IL

Receiver: CMBCCNBS182

　　　　CHINA MERCHANTS BANK(DALIAN BRANCH)

　　　　DALIAN CN

27: Sequence of Total

　　1/1

40A: Form of Doc. Credit

IRREVOCABLE

20: Doc. Credit Number

167-01-000795-7

31C: Date of Issue

150102

40E: Applicable Rules

UCP LATEST VERSION

图 2.8　帝美公司收到的信用证

31D: Date and Place of Expiry

150430 CHINA

50: Applicant

YAMIT FILTRATION AND WATER TREATMENT LTD.

MOSHAV SHAAR EFRAIM DN LEV HASHARON, 42855 ISRAEL

59: Beneficiary

DIM INDUSTRIES CO. LTD.

1708 CITY TOP ZONE NO.233 YOUHAO ROAD DALIAN, CHINA

32B: Currency Code, Amount

USD44032.90

39A: Percentage Credit Amt Tolerance

10/10

41A: Available with/By

CMBCCNBS182

CHINA MERCHANTS BANK(DALIAN BRANCH)

DALIAN CN

BY DEF PAYMENT

42P: Deferred Payment Details

PAYMENT TO BE EFFECTED 90 DAYS AFTER TRANSPORT DOC. DATE

43P: Partial Shipments

　　　PROHIBITED

43T: Transshipment

　　　ALLOWED

44E: Port of Loading

ANY PORT IN CHINA

44F: Port of Discharge

HAIFA PORT

45A: Description of Goods

FLANGES

Flange(thin)BSTD SO 4"	2 149PCS	USD5.92/PC	USD12 722.08
Flange(thin)DIN PN16 SO 14"	500PCS	USD34.81/PC	USD17 405.00
Flange(thin)ASA 150 SO 3"	156PCS	USD4.02/PC	USD627.12
Flange(thin)ASA 150 SO 8"	1 070PCS	USD12.41/PC	USD13 278.70

TRADE TERM: CIF HAIFA，INCOTERMS 2010

AS PER P.O.440024 DATED 17/12/14

46A: Documents Required

　　　+ORIGINAL COMMERCIAL INVOICE HAND SIGNED BY THE BENEFICIARY IN 4 COPIES CERTIFING THAT
GOODS ARE OF CHINESE ORIGIN.

图 2.8　帝美公司收到的信用证（续）

+ 3/3 ORIGINAL PLUS 3 NON NEGOTIABLE COPIES OF CLEAN SHIPPED ON BOARD OCEAN BILLS OF LADING, MADE OUT THE ORDER OF BANK HAPOALIM B.M.,NOTIFY: APPLICANT, MARKEWD "FREIGHT PREPAID".

+ ORIGINAL INSURANCE POLICY/CERTIFICATE IN 2 COPIES, DATED NOT LATER THAN TRANSPORT DOCUMENTS DATE，MADE OUT TO THE ORDER OF BANK HAPOALIM B.M., FOR AT LEAST 110 PERCENT OF CIF VALUE, COVERING INSTITUTE CARGO CLAUSES(A), INSTITUTE WAR CLAUSES AND STRIKES CLAUSES, ALSO CLAUSED CLAIMS PAYABLE IN ISRAEL.

+ PACKING LIST IN 3 FOLDS.

+ CERTIFICATE OF ORIGIN IN 1 ORIGINAL AND 1 COPY，ISSUED BY COMPETENT AUTHORITY.

47A: Additional Conditions

+ ALL DOCUMENTS MUST BE ISSUED IN ENGLISH.

+OUR DISCREPANT DOCUMENTS FEES，IF ANY，FOR USD60.00（FOR EACH PRESENTATION）PLUS SWIFT CHARGES FOR USD15.00 FOR EACH SWIFT(OR EQUIVALENT AMOUNT IN L/C CURRENCY) ARE FOR BENEFIARY'S ACCOUNT.

71B: Charges

ALL BANKING CHARGES OUTSIDE ISRAEL INCL YOUR SWIFT/TELEX/MAIL/COURIER ARE FOR BENEFIARY'S ACCOUNT.

49: Confirmation

WITHOUT

53A: REIMBURSING BANK

IRVTUS3N

THE BANK OF NEW YORK MELLON

NEW YORK, NY US

图 2.8 帝美公司收到的信用证（续）

补充交易资料如下：

发票号：DIM15032649　　　　　　　发票日期：MAR.27，2015

提单号：DLCHFA15040263　　　　　提单日期：APR.04，2015

船名航次：MSC BARI V.FD314R　　　装运港：DALIAN PORT，

　　　　　　　　　　　　　　　　　　　　　　CHINA

合同号：DIM140598　　　　　　　　合同日期：2014.12.20

集装箱：1×20′GP CONTAINER CY-CY

　　　　SHIPPER'S LOAD，COUNT& SEAL

　　　　MEDU6220047　SEAL3928238

生产厂家：大连新诚机械制造有限公司

原材料情况：完全中国产，不含任何进口成分

保单号：ADAL20324213　　　　　　原产地证号：131898566

HS CODE：73079100　　　　　　　　唛头：DIM/HAIFA/C NO.

货物装箱情况：TOTAL IN 24 CASES

                 G.W. 22867KGS   N.W.22387KGS

                 尺码：（66×66×72）CM/CASE

出口口岸：大连开发区海关   运费：USD1 350.00

保费：USD485.00   杂费：USD150.00

参考答案

试以帝美公司单证员的身份，将信用证内容翻译成中文。

任务三　审核和修改信用证

女士针织
连衣裙

任务导航

    粤汇进出口有限公司于 2014 年 4 月 15 日与加拿大 FFQ 贸易公司签订了一份女士针织连衣裙的出口合同，如图 2.9 所示。

    2014 年 7 月 15 日，加拿大 FFQ 贸易公司根据合同的规定开出了以粤汇进出口有限公司为受益人的编号为 CBL-GO123 的信用证，如图 2.10 所示。

合　同
CONTRACT

卖方
SELLER: YUEHUI IMPORT AND EXPORT CO.,LTD

合同号码
CONTRACT NO.: GGZ2014036

地址
ADDRESS: 256 HONGLI EAST ROAD SHENZHEN，CHINA

日期
DATE: APR.15,2014

电话　　　　　　　传真
TELEPHONE: 83550835　　　FAX: 83556688

签约地点
SIGNED AT: SHENZHEN, CHINA

买方
BUYER: FFQ TRADING CORPORATION

地址
ADDRESS: 112 ST. GEORGE STREET TORONTO, CANADA

电话　　　　　　　传真
TELEPHONE: 7366588　　　　FAX: 7366352

经买卖双方确认根据下列条款订立本合同：

This contract is made out by the Seller and Buyer as per the following terms and conditions mutually confirmed:

图 2.9　合同

（1）货物名称及规格 Name of commodity and Specification	（2）数量 Quantity	（3）单价 Unit Price	（4）金额 Amount
LADIE'S 65% SILK 20% LAMBSWOOL 10%ANGORA 5%NYLON KNITTED DRESS ART.NO.S1203 ART.NO.T1204	1 000 PCS 2 000 PCS	USD 15.00/PC USD 10.00/PC	USD15 000.00 USD20 000.00
Total 合计	3 000 PCS	CIF TORONTO	USD35 000.00

数量及总值允许有 5%的增减。

5 % more or less both in amount and quantity allowed.

（5）合同总值（大写）：

Total Value in Word: SAY US DOLLARS THIRTY FIVE THOUSAND ONLY.

（6）包装及唛头：

Packing and Shipping Marks:

EACH IN ONE PLASTIC BAG,15 PCS TO A CARTON,TOTAL200 CARTONS

SHIPPING MARK: FFQ

      TORONTO

      NO.1-200

（7）装运期：

Time of Shipment: Within 45 days of receipt of Letter of Credit and not later than the end of AUG. 2014 with partial shipments and transshipment allowed.

（8）装运口岸和目的地：

Loading Port & Destination: From SHENZHEN CHINA to TORONTO CANADA

（9）保险：由按发票全部金额110%投保险，按中国海洋运输保险条款办理。

Insurance: To be effected by the Seller for 110% of the CIF invoice value covering ALL RISKS AND WAR RISK only as per China Insurance Clauses.

（10）付款条件：

Terms of Payment: By 100% Irrevocable Sight Letter of Credit opened by the Buyer to reach the Seller not later than JULY 25TH, 2014 and to be available for negotiation in China until the 15TH day after the date of shipment. In case of late arrival of the L/C, the Seller shall not be liable for any delay in shipment and shall have the right to rescind the contract and /or claim for damages.

买方确认：   卖方：

Confirmed by The Buyer: **The Seller:**

FFQ TRADING CORPORATION   YUEHUI IMPORT AND EXPORT CO., LTD.

  JOHN   张利波

图 2.9　合同（续）

ISSUE OF A DOCUMENTARY CREDIT

ISSUING BANK: COMMERCIAL BANK LTD., TORONTO CANADA

SEQUENCE OF TOTAL	27: 1/1	
FORM OF DOC. CREDIT	40A: IRREVOCABLE	
DOC.CREDIT NUMBER	20: CBL-GO123	
DATE OF ISSUE	31C: 20140715	
EXIPRY	31D: DATE 20140915 IN CANADA	
APPLICANT	50: FFQ TRADING CORPORATION	
	112 ST. GEORGE STREET TORONTO, CANADA	
BENEFICIARY	59: YUEHUI IMPORT AND EXPORT CO., LTD.	
	256 HONGLI EAST ROAD SHENZHEN, CHINA	
AMOUNT	32B: USD30 500.00 (SAY US DOLLARS THIRTY THOUSAND FIVE HUNDRED ONLY.)	
AVAILABLE WITH/BY	41A: ANY BANK BY NEGOTIATION	
DRAFTS AT…	42C: DRAFTS AT 15 DAYS' SIGHT FOR FULL INVOICE VALUE	
DRAWEE	42A: COMMERCIAL BANK LTD., TORONTO CANADA	
PARTIAL SHIPMENTS	43P: ALLOWED	
TRANSSHIPMENT	43T: PROHIBITED	
LOADING IN CHARGE	44A: SHENZHEN	
FOR TRANSPORT TO …	44B: MAIN PORTS, CANADA	
LATEST DATE OF SHIP	44C: 20140831	
DESCRIPT OF GOODS	45A: LADIE'S 65% SILK 20% LAMBSWOOL 15% ANGORA 5% NYLON KNITTED	

DRESS AS PER S/C NO. GZ2014036

ART NO.	QUANTITY	UNIT PRICE
S1203	1 000 PIECES	USD15.00
T1013	2 000 PIECES	USD10.00

PRICE TERM：CFR TORONTO

DOCUMENTS REQUIRED 46A:

1. 3/3 SET OF ORIGINAL CLEAN ON BOARD OCEAN BILLS OF LADING MADE OUT TO ORDER OF SHIPPER AND BLANK ENDORSED AND MARKED "FREIGHT PREPAID" NOTIFY APPLICANT （WITH FULL NAME AND ADDRESS）.

2. ORIGINAL SIGNED COMMERCIAL INVOICE IN 5 FOLD INDICATING FOB VALUE，FREIGHT CHARGE AND INSURANCE COSTS SEPARATELY.

图 2.10　加拿大 FFQ 公司开来的信用证

3. INSURANCE POLICY OR CERTIFICATE IN TWO FOLD ENDORSED IN BLANK, FOR 120PCT OF THE INVOICE VALUE COVERINGING THE INSTITUTE CARGO CLAUSES(A), THE INSTITUTE WAR CLAUSES AS PER INSTITUTE CARGO CLAUSE, INSUANCE CLAIMS TO BE PAYABLE IN CANADA IN THE CURRENCY OF THE DRAFTS.

4. CERTIFICATE OF ORIGIN GSP FORM A IN 1 ORIGINAL AND 1 COPY,ISSUED BY COMPETENT AUTHORITY.

5. PACKING LIST IN 3 FOLDS.

6. BENEFICIARY'S CERTIFICATE STATING THAT ONE SET OF ORIGINAL SHIPPING DOCUMENTS HAS BEEN SENT DIRECTLY TO THE APPLICANT.

ADDITIONAL COND.   47A:

1. T.T.REIMBURSEMENT IS PROHIBITED.

2. THE GOODS TO BE PACKED IN EXPORT STRONG COLORED CARTONS.

3. SHIPPING MARKS: FFQ

TORONTO

NO.1-200

DETAILS OF CHARGES   71B: ALL BANKING CHARGES OUTSIDE CANCDA INCLUDING REIMBURSEMENT COMMISSION，ARE FOR ACCOUNT OF BENEFICIARY.

PRESENTATION PERIOD 48: DOCUMENTS TO BE PRESENTED WITHIN 15 DAYS AFTER THE DATE OF SHIPMENT，BUT WITHIN THE VALIDITY OF THE CREDIT.

CONFIRMATION   49: WITHOUT

INSTRUCTIONS   78: THE NEGOTIATION BANK MUST FORWARD THE DRAFTS AND ALL DOCUMENTS BY REGISTERED AIRMAIL DIRECT TO US IN TOW CONSECUTIVE LOTS, UPON RECEIPT OF THE DRAFTS AND DOCUMENTS IN ORDER, WE WILL REMIT THE PROCEEDS AS INSTRUCTED BY THE NEGOTIATING BANK.

图 2.10　加拿大 FFQ 公司开来的信用证（续）

要求：

以粤汇进出口有限公司单证员小杨的身份，根据合同审核信用证，指出不符之处并提出修改意见。

知识准备

信用证的审核是银行（通知行）和出口商（受益人）的共同任务，但银行和出口商对信用证的审核却各有侧重。通知行着重审核信用证表面真实性及开证行政治背景、资信能力、付款责任和索汇路线等。而卖方（受益人）收到信用证后，则必须以货物买卖合同为依据，审核信用证内容与买卖合同条款是否一致，必要时及时修改信用证，以确保合同能够顺利进行，货款安全收回。

■ 课堂思考 ■

出口公司审核信用证的主要依据有哪些？

参考答案

一、审核信用证

在实际业务中，由于各种原因，买方开来的信用证时有与合同条款不符的情况，单证员应对照合同对信用证进行认真核对和审查，及早发现问题，及时采取相应的补救措施，以确保收汇安全和合同顺利履行。受益人审核信用证的基本要点如表 2.4 所示。

表 2.4 信用证审核的基本要点

审证要点	注意事项
信用证种类	必须与合同规定一致，且应为"不可撤销（IRREVOCABLE）信用证"；若合同规定可转让信用证，则须注明"TRANSFERABLE"字样
信用证有效期和到期地点	所有信用证都要规定有效期，没有规定有效期的信用证视为无效信用证；到期地点尽量要求在我国（受益人所在国）
受益人和开证人名称、地址	必须完整、准确，与合同一致；如果有误，应及时修改更正，否则可能会因单证不符遭拒付，直接影响收汇
付款时间	应与合同中付款条件的规定一致，如是即期信用证，则汇票付款期限必须规定"DRAFT AT SIGHT"
信用证金额、币制	信用证金额不能低于合同金额，货币种类要与合同规定一致，金额的大小写要一致
装运条款	检查装期、装运港、目的港、是否允许分批装运和转运等与合同规定一致
货物描述	包括货物的名称、规格、数量、单价、总值、包装等，这部分必须与合同规定一致，否则履行合同将无所适从。还要核对信用证所列的合同号码是否正确
价格条款	不同的价格条款涉及费用，如运费、保险费由谁负担。价格条款必须与合同规定相符
单据要求	检查信用证要求的单据能否提供或及时提供。注意点如下：以 FOB 交易，提单应注明 FREIGHT COLLECT，如误开为 FREIGHT PREPAID，应要求改证；要求保险单中的保险条款、险别、保险加成等内容应与合同一致；要求出具的受益人证明书应是受益人实际已完成或受益人力所能及的任务的证明；指定某种格式或编号的海关发票，应核查能否提供，否则应改证

续表

审证要点	注意事项
交单期限	检查能否在信用证规定的交单期交单。信用证有规定交单期的，应按规定的交单期向银行交单；信用证没有规定交单期的，向银行交单的日期不得迟于提单日期后 21 天，但无论如何不得迟于信用证有效期
有无陷阱条款	检查信用证中有无陷阱条款，如有则必须要求改证。如"1/3 正本提单直接寄送进口方"，受益人将随时面临货、款两空的风险；"将客检证作为议付文件"，受益人正常处理信用证业务的主动权很大程度上掌握在对方手里，影响安全收汇
有无矛盾之处	检查信用证中有无自相矛盾之处，如空运方式，却要求提供海运提单；价格条款为 FOB，保险本应由买方办理，而信用证中却要求提供保险单

二、修改信用证

1. 信用证修改的程序

出口方（受益人）审证发现信用证与买卖合同不符而又不能接受的条款，或者信用证某些条款不符合《跟单信用证统一惯例》等要求的，应以函电方式向进口方（开证申请人）提出修改要求。修改信用证的流程如图 2.11 所示。

改证流程
示意图

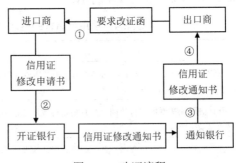

图 2.11　改证流程

小贴士

要让国外客户修改信用证，单证员要做的一项重要工作就是拟写改证函。一份规范的改证函通常包括以下三个方面内容。

（1）感谢对方通过银行开来信用证。

（2）列明证中不符点、不能接受的条款，并说明如何改正。

（3）感谢对方的合作，提醒信用证修改书应于某日前到达，以便按时装运等。

改证函范例如图 2.12 所示。

Dear Sirs,

　　While we thank you for your L/C No.123456, we regret to say that we have found some discrepancies. You are, therefore, requested to make the following amendments:

　　1. The amount both in figures and in words should respectively read "USD 25000.00"(Say U.S. Dollars twenty five thousand only).

　　2. "From Rotterdam to China port " should read "from China port to Rotterdam".

　　3. The bill of lading should be marked "Freight Prepaid" instead of "Freight to Collect".

　　4. Delete the clause "Partial shipment and transshipment prohibited".

　　5. "This L/C is valid at our counter" should be amended to read "This L/C is valid at your counter".

　　Please see to it that L/C amendment reach us not later than Aug.8,2015.

Yours sincerely

图 2.12　改证函范例

2．改证时注意事项

改证时应注意以下事项。

（1）一份信用证如有多处需要修改，应集中一次性通知开证人办理修改，避免一改再改，既增加双方的费用又浪费时间，而且还会引起不良影响。

（2）修改信用证的要求一般应用电信通知开证人，同时应规定修改书的到达时限。

（3）收到信用证修改后，应及时检查修改内容是否符合要求，并分别情况表示接受或重新提出修改。

（4）对于修改内容要么全部接受，要么全部拒绝，部分接受修改中的内容是无效的。

（5）有关信用证修改必须通过原信用证通知行才具真实、有效。经由开证人直接寄送的修改申请书或修改书复印件不是有效的修改。

（6）明确修改费用由谁承担，一般按照责任归属来确定改证费用的负担。

 小 贴 士

修改信用证的两点原则如下：

原则 1：信用证条款规定比合同条款严格时，应当作为信用证中存在的问题提出修改。

原则 2：当信用证的规定比合同条款宽松时，往往可不要求修改。

职业判断

参考答案

案例资料：

鹏远公司与国外一进口商订立销售合同，出口长毛绒玩具一批。合同规定，5月30日前开出信用证，6月20日前装船。4月28日买方按期开来信用证，有效期为6月30日。由于卖方按期装船发生困难，故书面向买方申请将信用证中装船期延至7月5日，买方回函表示同意，但并未通知开证银行修改信用证。7月3日货物装船后，卖方7月4日到银行议付时遭到拒付。

思考：

银行是否有权拒绝议付？为什么？

任务实施

粤汇公司单证员小杨经审核信用证，提出需要修改的内容如下：

（1）EXIPRY PLACE 到期地点：CANADA 改为 CHINA。

（2）AMOUNT 金额：USD30 500.00 (SAY US DOLLARS THIRTY ONE THOUSAND FIVE HUNDRED ONLY.) 改为 USD35 000.00(SAY US DOLLARS THIRTY FIVE THOUSAND ONLY.)。

（3）DRAFTS AT 汇票期限：DRAFTS AT 15 DAYS', SIGHT 改为 DRAFTS AT SIGHT。

（4）TRANSSHIPMENT 是否允许转运：PROHIBITED 改为 ALLOWED。

（5）FOR TRANSPORT TO 目的港：MAIN PORTS 改为 TORONTO, CANADA。

（6）DESCRIP. OF GOODS 货物描述中的合同号：SC NO. 改为 GGZ2014036。

（7）DESCRIP. OF GOODS 货物描述中的货号：ART NO. T1013 改为 T1204。

（8）PRICE TERM 价格条件：CFR TORONTO 改为 CIF TORONTO。

（9）DOCUMENTS REQUIRED 单据要求中的保险金额：INSURANCE POLICY FOR 120PCT OF THE INVOICE VALUE 改为 FOR 110PCT OF THE INVOICE VALUE。

（10）单据要求中的保险险别改为 COVERING ALL RISKS AND WAR RISK ONLY AS PER CHINA INSURANCE CLAUSES。

任务再现

2014 年 1 月 7 日，广州利维进出口公司和日本 ITOCHU 公司签订了一份销售全棉围裙的出口合同，2014 年 4 月 7 日 ITOCHU 公司根据合同的规定开出了以广州利维进出口公司为受益人的编号为 AB-AN250-2 的信用证（见图 2.13 和图 2.14）。

围裙

试以广州利维进出口公司单证员的身份，根据合同内容审核信用证，指出不符之处并提出修改意见。

SALES CONTRACT

The Seller:

GUANGZHOU LIWEI IMP.& EXP. CO.LTD

NO.168 LONGDONG ROAD TIANHE GUANGZHOU, CHINA

The Buyer:

ITOCHU CORPORATION, OSAKA, JAPAN

Contract No.: AN107

Date: JAN.07,2014

Signed at : GUANGZHOU

The undersigned Seller and Buyer have agreed to close the following transactions according to the terms and conditions stipulated below:

（1）货号、品名及规格 Name of Commodity and specifications	（2）数量 Quantity	（3）单价 Unit Price	（4）金额 Amount
100% PURE COTTON APRON			
ART. NO. 49394	3 600PCS	USD2.00/PC	USD7 200.00
ART. NO. 49393	3 900PCS	USD2.00/PC	USD7 800.00
ART. NO. 55306	1 500PCS	USD1.25/PC	USD1 875.00
5% more or less both in amount and quantity allowed	CIF OSAKA USD16 875.00		

(5) Packing: 12PCS/CARTON

(6) Delivery: From GUANGZHOU to OSAKA with partial shipment and transshipment allowed.

(7) Shipping Marks: ITOCHU/OSAKA/NOS.1-750

(8) Time of Shipment: Within ___30___ days after receipt of L/C .

(9)Terms of Payment: By 100% Confirmed irrevocable Letter of Credit in favor of the Seller to be available by sight draft to reach China before ___APRIL 15 ,2014___ and to remain valid for negotiation in China until 21 days after the foresaid Time of Shipment.

(10) Insurance: To be effected by Seller for 110% of full invoice value covering ___FPA　AND WAR RISK___ only as per CIC.

图 2.13　合同

(11) Arbitration: All dispute arising from the execution of or in connection with this contract shall be settled by the friendly negotiation. In case of settlement can be reached through negotiation the case shall then be submit China International Economic & Trade Arbitration Commission In Shenzhen (or in Beijing) for arbitration in act with its sure of procedures. The arbitral award is final and binding upon both parties.

The Seller:

GUANGZHOU LIWEI IMP.& EXP. CO., LTD.

何伟文

The Buyer:

ITOCHU CORPORATION

Asaoka Megumi

图 2.13　合同（续）

Issue of a Documentary Credit

Sequence of Total	*27: 1/1
Issuing Bank	51A: ASAHI BANK LTD.,TOKYO
Form of Doc. Credit	*40A: IRREVOCABLE
Credit Number	*20: AB-AN250-2
Date of Issue	31C: 140407
Expiry	*31D: 140607 IN JAPAN
Applicant	*50: ITOCHO CORPORATION, OSAKA, JAPAN
Beneficiary	*59: GUANGZHOU LIWEI　IMP.& EXP. CO., LTD. 　　　NO.168 LONGDONG ROAD TIANHE GUANGZHOU, CHINA
Amount	*32B: USD16875.00（SAY U.S. DOLLARS SIXTEEN THOUSAND EIGHT　HUNDRED AND SEVENTY FIVE ONLY）
Pos./ Neg. Tol. (%)	39A: 5/5
Available with/by	*41A: ANY BANK IN ADVISING COUNTRY BY NEGOTIATION
Draft at…	42C: DRAFTS AT 30 DAYS' SIGHT FOR FULL INVOICE VALUE
Partial Shipments	43P: PERMITTED
Transshipment	43T: PROHIBITED
Loading in Charge	44A: GUANGZHOU
For Transport to	44B: OSAKA
Shipment Period	44C: AT THE LATEST MAY 31，2014
Descript. of Goods	45A: 100% PURE COTTON APRON　AS PER S/C NO.AH107

ART. NO. 49394　　　　3 960PCS　　USD2.00/PC

ART. NO. 49393　　　　3 900PCS　　USD2.00/PC

ART. NO. 55306　　　　1 500PCS　　USD1.25/PC

图 2.14　日本 ITOCHU 公司开来的信用证

	CFR OSAKA
Documents Required	46A:
	+ COMMERCIAL INVOICE 1 SIGNED ORIGINAL AND 5 COPIES.
	+ PACKING LIST IN 2 COPIES.
	+ FULL SET OF CLEAN ON BOARD MARINE BILLS OF LADING, MADE OUT TO ORDER OF SHIPPER AND ENDORSED IN BLANK，MARKED "FREIGHT PREPAID" AND NOTIFY APPLICANT.
	+ GSP CERTIFICATE OF ORIGIN FORM A,CERTIFYING GOODS OFORIGIN IN CHINA, ISSUED BY COMPETENT AUTHORITIES.
	+ INSURANCE POLICY/CERTIFICATE IN TWO FOLDS COVERING ALL RISKS AND WAR RISKS OF CIC WITH CLAIMS PAYABLE IN JAPAN FOR AT LEAST 120 PCT OF CIF-VALUE.
	+SHIPPING ADVICES MUST BE SENT TO APPLICANT WITH 2 DAYS AFTER SHIPMENT ADVISING NUMBER OF PACKAGES,GROSS & NET WEIGHT,VESSEL NAME,BILL OF LADING NO. AND DATE,CONTRACT NO.,VALUE.
Additional Conditions	47A:
	+T/T REIMBURSEMENT IS PROHIBITED.
	+THE GOODS TO BE PACKED IN EXPORT STRONG COLORED CARTONS.
	+ALL DOCUMENTS MENTIONING THIS L/C NO.
Presentation Period	48: 3 DAYS AFTER ISSUANCE DATE OF SHIPPING DOCUMENT.
Confirmation	*49: WITHOUT
Instructions	78: THE NEGOTIATION BANK MUST FORWARD THE DRAFTS AND ALL DOCUMENTS BY REGISTERED AIRMAIL DIRECT TO US IN TOW CONSECUTIVE LOTS, UPON RECEIPT OF THE DRAFTS AND DOCUMENTS IN ORDER，WE WILL REMIT THE PROCEEDS AS INSTRUCTED BY THE NEGOTIATING BANK.

参考答案

图 2.14　日本 ITOCHU 公司开来的信用证（续）

项目小结

技能强化训练

技 能 提 高

在线同步测试 及参考答案

1. 根据合同资料和有关业务资料，指出开证申请书中的错误之处。
2015 年 6 月 20 日，青岛范氏皮革制品有限公司（QINGDAO FANS LEATHER GOODS CO., LTD. 156 CHANGXING ROAD, QINGDAO, CHINA）向 EEN DESIGN PLUS CO.,LTD. 1-509 HANNAMDONG YOUNGSAN-KU, SEOUL, KOREA 出口头层牛皮皮料一批，达成主要合同条款（合同号 FS20150315），如图 2.15 所示。

EEN DESIGN PLUS CO.,LTD. 单证员李承敏于 2015 年 6 月 23 日向

KOOKMIN BANK, SEOUL, KOREA 办理申请电开信用证手续（见图 2.16），通知行是 BANK OF CHINA, QINGDAO BRANCH。

Commodity: FIRST LAYER LEATHER SKIN MATERIAL COLOUR DARK BROWN

Quantity: 3175.25SQFT（平方英尺）

PACKING: IN CARTONS

Unit Price: USD 7.40/SQFT CIF SEOUL

Amount: USD 23496.85

Time of shipment: During NOV, 2015

Port of Loading: QINGDAO,CHINA

Port of Destination: SEOUL, KOREA

Partial shipment: ALLOWED

Transshipment: PROHIBITED

Insurance: TO BE COVERED BY THE SELLER FOR 110% INVOICE VALUE COVERING ALL RISK AND WAR RISK AS PER CIC OF THE PICC DATED 01/01/1981.

Payment: BY IRREVOCABLE LETTER OF CREDIT AT 45 DAYS SIGHT TO REACH THE SELLER NOT LATER THAN JUNE 24,2015, VALID FOR NEGOTIATION IN CHINA UNTIL THE 15TH DAY AFTER TIME OF   SHIPMENT.

Document: 1. SIGNED COMMERCIAL INVOICE IN 3 FOLDS.

2. SIGNED PACKING LIST IN 3 FOLDS.

3. FULL SET OF CLEAN ON BOARD OCEAN B/L IN 3/3 ORIGINAL SISSUED TO ORDER AND BLANK ENDORSED MARKED"FREIGHTPREPAID"AND NOTIFY THE APPLICANT.

4. CERTIFICATE OF ORIGIN IN 1 ORIGINAL AND 1 COPY ISSUED BY THE CHAMBER OF COMMERCE IN CHINA.

5. INSURANCE POLICY/CERTIFICATE IN DUPLICATE ENDORSED IN BLANK FOR 110% INVOICE VALUE, COVERING ALL RISKS AND WAR RISKS OF CIC OF PICC (1/1/1981). SHOWING THE CLAIMING CURRENCY IS THE SAME AS THE CURRENCY OF CREDIT.

图 2.15   合同主要条款

IRREVOCABLE DOCUMENTARY CREDIT APPLICATION

TO: BANK OF CHINA	DATE: JUNE 25，2015
Beneficiary(full name and address)	L/C No.
EEN DESIGN PLUS CO.,LTD. 1-509 HANNAMDONG YOUNGSAN-KU, SEOUL, KOREA	Ex-Card No. S/C NO. FS20150315
	Date and place of expiry of the credit NOV. 15, 2015 in CHINA

图 2.16   开证申请书

Partial Shipments not allowed	Transshipment allowed	Issue by teletransmission (which shall be the operative instruction)
Loading on board/dispatch/taking in charge at/from SEOUL, KOREA not later than OCT. 31,2015		Amount(both in figures and words) EUR 23496.85
For transport to QINGDAO, CHINA		SAY EURO TWENTY THREE THOUSAND FOUR HUNDRED NINETY SIX POINT EIGHTY FIVE ONLY.
Description of goods: FIRST LAYER LEATHER SKIN MATERIAL COLOUR DARK BROWN 3175.25PCS Packing: IN GUNNY BAGS		Credit available with ANY BANK IN CHINA by negotiation against the documents detailed herein and beneficiary's draft for 100 % of the invoice value At SIGHT on US CFR

Document required:(marked with x)

1. (×) Signed Commercial Invoice in__5__copies indicate L/C No. and Contract No.

2. (×) Full set of clean on board ocean Bills of Lading made out ___TO APPLICANT___ and (×) blank endorsed, marked "freight" (×) to collect/ ( ) prepaid. showing freight amount" notifying the applicant.

3. (×) Insurance Policy / Certificate in__2__copies for 120% of the invoice value showing claims payable in KOREA in currency of the draft , blank endorsed, covering (×) Ocean Marine Transportation / ( ) Air Transportation / ( ) Over Land Transportation (×) All risks.

4. (×) Packing List / Weight Memo in__5__copies indicating quantity / gross and net weights of each package and packing conditions as called for by the L/C.

5. ( ) Certificate of Quantity / Weight in copies issued by an independent surveyor at the loading port, indicating the actual surveyed quantity / weight of shipped goods as well as the packing condition.

6. ( ) Certificate of Quality in 1 copies issued by ( ) manufacturer / ( ) public recognized surveyor / ( ).

7. ( ) Beneficiary's Certified copy of cable / fax dispatched to the accountee within____days after shipment advising ( ) name of vessel / ( ) flight No. / ( ) wagon No. , date, quantity, weight and value of shipment.

图 2.16　开证申请书（续）

2. 根据下述合同内容审核信用证（见图 2.17 和图 2.18），指出不符之处，并提出修改意见。

SALES CONTRACT

Contract No. MT15008
Date: Dec. 6，2015
Signed At: Shanghai China

The Seller: SUSANG INTERNATIONAL CO., LTD.
NO.329 JIANGNING ROAD, SHANGHAI, CHINA
The Buyer: DESEN EUROPE GMBH
GIRARDETSTRASSE 2-38,EINGANG.4 D-45131 ESSEN, GERMANY

This Sales Contract is made by and between the Seller and the Buyer, whereby the Seller agree to sell and the Buyer agree to buy the under-mentioned goods according to the terms and conditions stipulated below:

Description of Goods	Quantity	Unit Price	Amount
"SUSANG"		CIF Hamburg	
Home wear			
RH1140 Blue	400PCS	@€ 5.88	€ 2 352.00
RH1150 Pink	400PCS	@€ 6.08	€ 2 432.00
DRRW005 Gray	400PCS	@€ 5.38	€ 2 152.00
DRRW008 Purple	400PCS	@€ 5.18	€ 2 072.00
AS PER ORDER NO.MY1501			
TOTAL	1 600PCS		€ 9 008.00

Total Amount: Say Euro Nine Thousand and Eight Only

Packing: 40pcs are packed in one export standard carton

Shipping Mark: SUSANG /MT13008/HAMBURG/C/No.1-40

Time of Shipment: NOT LATER THAN FEB. 15,2016

Loading Port and Destination: From Shanghai, China to Hamburg, Germany.

Partial Shipment: Not Allowed

Transshipment: Allowed

Insurance: To be effected by the seller for 110% invoice value covering All Risks and War Risk as per CIC of PICC dated 01/01/1981.

Terms of Payment: By L/C at sight, reaching the seller before Dec. 31，2015, and remaining valid for negotiation in China for further 15 days after the effected shipment. L/C

must mention this contract number. L/C advised by BANK OF CHINA. All banking Charges outside China (the mainland of China) are for account of the Drawee.

Documents:

+ Signed commercial invoice in triplicate.

+ Full set (3/3) of clean on board ocean Bill of Lading marked "Freight Prepaid" made out to order blank endorsed notifying the applicant.

+ Insurance Policy in duplicate endorsed in blank for 110% of invoice value covering All Risks and War Risk as per CIC dated 01/01/1981.

+ Packing List in triplicate.

+ Certificate of Origin issued by China Chamber of Commerce.

Signed by:

THE SELLER: THE BUYER:

SUSANG INTERNATIONAL CO., LTD.   DESEN EUROPE GMBH

顾青云   Giovanie

图 2.17　合同

27: SEQUENCE OF TOTAL: 1/1

40A: FORM OF DOCUMENTARY CREDIT: IRREVOCABLE

20: DOCUMENTARY CREDIT NUMBER: 00150010018208A1

31C: DATE OF ISSUE: 150101

40E: APPLICABLE RULES: UCP LATEST VERSION

31D: DATE AND PLACE OF EXPIRY: 150220 GERMANY

50: APPLICANT: DESEN EUROPE GMBH GIRARDETSTRASSE 2-38,EINGANG.4 D-45131ESSEN, GERMANY

59: BENEFICIARY: SUSIANG INTERNATIONAL CO., LTD.

      NO.329 JIANGNING ROAD, SHANGHAI, CHINA

32B: CURRENCY CODE, AMOUNT: USD9008.00

41A: AVAILABLE WITH…BY…: BANK OF CHINA

                           BY NEGOTIATION

42C: DRAFTS AT…: 30 DAYS AFTER SIGHT

42A: DRAWEE: DESEN EUROPE GMBH

43P: PARTIAL SHIPMENTS: NOT ALLOWED

43T: TRANSHIPMENT: NOT ALLOWED

44E: PORT OF LOADING/AIRPORT OF DEPARTURE: ANY CHINESE PORT

44F: PORT OF DISCHARGE/AIRPORT OF DESTINATION: HAMBURG BY SEA.

44C: LATEST DATE OF SHIPMENT: 150210

45A: DESCRIPTION OF GOODS AND/OR SERVICES:

      1600PCS BABYWEAR

      AS PER ORDER NO.MY1501 AND S/C NO.MT15008

      CFR HAMBURG

      PACKED IN CARTON OF 20PCS EACH

46A: DOCUMENTS REQUIRED

   + SIGNED COMMERCIAL INVOICES IN TRIPLICATE INDICATING LC NO. AND CONTRACT NO.

   + FULL SET (3/3) OF CLEAN ON BOARD OCEAN BILL OF LADING MADE OUT TO APPLICANT AND BLANK ENDORSED MARKED "FREIGHT TO COLLECT" NOTIFYING THE APPLICANT.

   + SIGNED PACKING LIST IN TRIPLICATE SHOWING THE FOLLOWING DETAILS: TOTAL NUMBER OF PACKAGES SHIPPED; CONTENT(S) OF PACKAGE(S); GROSS WEIGHT, NET WEIGHT AND MEASUREMENT.

   + CERTIFICATE OF ORIGIN ISSUED AND SIGNED OR AUTHENTICATED BY A LOCAL CHAMBER OF COMMERCE LOCATED IN THE EXPORTING COUNTRY.

   + INSURANCE POLICY/CERTIFICATE IN DUPLICATE ENDORSED IN BLANK FOR 120% INVOICE VALUE, COVERING ALL RISKS OF CIC OF PICC (1/1/1981).

71B: CHARGES: ALL CHARGES AND COMMISSIONS ARE FOR ACCOUNT OF BENEFICIARY INCLUDING REIMBURSING CHARGES.

参考答案

图 2.18　信用证（部分）

项目三

商业发票实训

知识目标

1. 理解商业发票的含义和特点;
2. 明确商业发票的用途;
3. 熟悉商业发票的基本内容和条款;
4. 掌握信用证和销售合同项下商业发票的填制规则。

能力目标

1. 能根据信用证缮制商业发票;
2. 能根据销售合同缮制商业发票;
3. 能掌握商业发票缮制的注意事项。

任务一　根据信用证制作商业发票

任务导航

　　2015 年 2 月，宁波慈溪颖光制衣厂与日本大阪 TOSHU 公司因业务发展需要，签订了一笔男士 T 恤（Men's T-shirt）出口合同。业务员小王如期收到 TOSHU 公司开来的信用证，如图 3.1 所示。

BASIC HEADER　　F 01 BKCHCNBJA5×9109 069905	
APPL. HEADER　　O 700 1332990223 SMITJPJSA××× 4956 850438 9902231232 N	
+ SUMITOMO BANK LTD OSAKA JAPAN	
(BANK NO : 2632001　　+ OSAKA, JAPAN	
USER HEADER　　　　BANK. PRIORITY 113:	
MSG USER REF. 108: G/FO- 7752807	
: MT:700--------------------ISSUE OF A DOCUMENTARY CREDIT--------------------	
SEQUENCE OF TOTAL	27: 1/1
FORM OF DOCUMENTARY CREDIT	40: IRREVOCABLE
DOCUMENTARY CREDIT NUMBER	20 : G/FO-7752807
DATE OF ISSUE	31C:150223
DATE AND PLACE OF EXPIRY	31D: 150610CIXI CHINA
APPLICANT	50: TOSHU CORPORATION OSALM 12-36, KYUTARO- MACHI 4- CHOME CHUO- KU, OSAKA 561-8177 JAPAN
BENEFICIARY	59: NINGBO YINGGUANG GARMENT CO., LTD. NO.2373DEVEL OPMENT ROAD, HUSHAN, CIXI, CHINA
CURRENCY CODE, AMOUNT	32B: USD201780.00
AVAILABLE WITH… BY…	41D: ANY BANK BY NEGOTIATION
DARFTS AT…	42C: AT SIGHT
DRAWEE	42D: THE SUMITOMO BANK, LTD. OSAKA
PARTIAL SHIPMENT	43P: ALLOWED
TRANSHIPMENT	43P: PROHIBITED
LOADING/ DISPATCH/ TAKING/ FROM	44A: NINGBO
FOR TRANS[PRTATION TO…	44B: YOKOHAMA
LATEST DATE OF SHIPMENT	44C: 150531
DESCRPT OF GOODS/ SERVICES	45A:

图 3.1　TOSHU 公司开来的信用证

CIF YOKOHAMA

MAN'S SHIRT(CONTRACT NO.99JA7031KL)

ST/NO. Q'TY UNIT PRICE

71-800 67 200PCS USD 1.43/PC

71-801 48 000PCS USD 1.46/PC

71-802 27 600PCS USD 1.29/PC

DOCUMENTS TRQUIRED

+ COMMERCIAL INVOICE IN QUINTUPLICATE.

+ FULL SET LESS ONE ORIGINAL CLEAN ON BOARD OCEAN BILL OF LADING MARKED FREIGHT PREPAID MADE OUT TO ORDER OF THE SHIPPER BLANK ENDORSED NOTIFY APPLICANT.

+ PACKING LIST IN 3 COPIES.

+ G.S.P. CERTIFICATE OF ORIGIN FORM A IN 3 COPIES.

+ INSURANCE PLOICY OR CERTIFICATE IN DUPLICATE ENDORSED IN BLANK WITH CLAIM PAYABLE IN JAPAN IN THE CURRENCY OF THE DRAFT COVERING 110 PERCENT OF INVOICE VALUE INCLUDING INSTITUTE WAR CLAUSES.

+ BENEFICIARY'S CERTIFICATE STATING THAT ONE SET OF ORIGINAL SHIPPING DOCUMENTS INCLUDING CERTIFICATE OF ORIGIN FORM A ARE TO BE SENT WITHIN TWO DAYS AFTER SHIPMENT BY AIR COURIER.

ADDITIONAL CONDITIONS   47A: THIS CREDIT IS SUBJECT TO UNIFORM CUSTOMS AND PRACTICE FOR DOCUMENTARY CREDITS (1993 REVISION) I. C. C. PUBLICATION NO. 500.

T. T. REIMBURSEMTNT: UNACCEPTABLE

X) THE GOODS SHOULD BE CONTAINERIZED.

X) A COPY OF CABLE ADVISING SHIPPING DETAILS FAX TO THE ACCOUNTEE WITHIN 2 DAYS AFTER SHIPMENT.

X) CLEAN ON BOARD COMBINED TRANSPORT B/L OF ITOCHU EXPRESS CO. LTD IS ACCEPTABLE.

CHARGES   71B: ALL BANKING CHARGES AND COMMIS-SIONS INCLUDING REIMBURSEMENT COMM. OUTSIDE JAPAN ARE FOR A/C OF BENEFICIARY.

PERIOD FOR PRESENTATIONS   48 : DOCUMENTS TO BE PRESENTED WITHIN 10 DAYS AFTER THE DATE OF SHIPMENT BUT WITHIN THE VALIDITY OF THE CREDIT.

CONFIRMATION INSTRUCTION   49 : WITHOUT

INSTRUCTION TO BANK   78 :

TO NEGOTIATING BANK:

图 3.1　TOSHU 公司开来的信用证（续）

> ALL SHIPPING DOCUMENTS TO BE SENT DIRECT TO THE OPENING OFFICE BY REGISTERED AIRMAIL IN ONE LOT.
>
> UPON RECEIPT OF THE DRAFTS AND DOCUMENTS IN ORDER, WE WILL REMIT THE PROCEEDS TO YOUR ACCOUNT WITH THE BANK DESIGNATED BY YOU.
>
> TRAILER
>
> MAC: 51EF556 CHK: D3A3848E00C NNNN

图 3.1　TOSHU 公司开来的信用证（续）

在完成了信用证审核修改的一系列流程后，业务员小王需要针对信用证内容制作商业发票。在缮制发票之前，小王必须对信用证内容详细分析，熟悉商业发票的填制规则，以便更好地开展履约工作。

制单参考资料如下：

(1) CIF YOKOHAMA

(2) SHIPPED BY S.S. HONG V26 ON MAY 28TH, 2015

(3) B/L NO.1505358

(4) INVOICE NO. JYS698　DATE：150305

(5) C/S NO. : TIT49087/R8907677

(6) G.W.: 35KGS/CTN　N.W.: 30KGS/CTN　MEASURMENT：（20×30×35）CM/CTN

(7) PACKING:100PCS/CTN

(8) H.S. NO.: 4983.3900

(9) FORM A NO.: 98766898

(10) 法人代表：李磊

要求：

请以业务员小王的身份，根据信用证内容，向日本大阪 TOSHU 公司开具一份商业发票。

知识准备

一、商业发票的含义与使用

商业发票（commercial invoice）简称"发票"，是卖方对装运货物的全面情况（包括品质、数量、价格，有时还有包装）详细列述的一种价目清单，是所有单据的核心。信用证项下商业发票的缮制必须与信用证相关内容保持一致。

发票可由出口商自行设计制作，无固定统一的格式，因此有一定灵活性。但不管格式如何变化，商业发票的内容必须符合信用证和合同的相关规定。

小 贴 士

在国际贸易中，不同的用途使用不同的发票，不同的发票名称表示不同的发票种类，缮制时应严格按信用证的规定。常见的发票有以下几种。

（1）形式发票：一种非正式发票，是卖方对潜在的买方报价的一种形式。买方常常需要形式发票，以作申请进口和批准外汇之用。

（2）厂商发票：出口货物的制造厂商所出具的以本国货币计算，用来证明出口国国内市场出厂价格的发票。要求提供厂商发票的目的是检查出口国出口商品是否有销价倾销行为，供进口国海关估价、核税以及征收反倾销税之用。

（3）领事发票：由进口国驻出口国的领事出具的一种特别印就的发票，是出口商根据进口国驻在出口地领事所提供的特定格式填制，并经领事签证的发票。

（4）海关发票：进口商向进口国海关报关的证件之一。海关发票是根据某些国家海关的规定，由出口商填制的供进口商凭以报关用的特定格式的发票，要求国外出口商填写，供本国商人（进口商）随附商业发票和其他有关单据，办理进口报关手续。

二、商业发票的填制

商业发票是我国出口贸易中使用的主要单据，是出口全套单据的核心，更是出口企业制作其他单据的中心（见图 3.2）。出口企业在制单过程中，通常是先缮制好商业发票，然后才制作其他单据。

以信用证结算方式为基础，商业发票的缮制应符合信用证和合同的相关规定，并且注意信用证中对佣金和折扣、加注声明文句等特殊要求以及有关国家对发票的特殊规定。具体内容及填制方法如表 3.1 所示。

COMMERCIAL INVOICE

ORIGINAL

TO M/S:

发票号码 INVOICE NO.

日期 DATE.

合约号码 S/C NO.

图 3.2　商业发票样本

信用证号码				
L/C NO.				
装运口岸	目的地	转运地	运输方式	
FROM:	TO:	W/T	BY	
唛头号码 Marks and Numbers	货物描述 Description of goods	数量 Quantity	单价 Unit Price	金额 Amount
TOTAL IN WORDS:				
			(Signature)	

图 3.2 商业发票样本（续）

表 3.1 商业发票内容及填制方法一览

项目名称	填制方法
EXPORTER	出票人（出口商）的名称、地址、信用证中的受益人（BENEFICIARY）
TO M/S （收货人）	信用证支付方式下一般是开证申请人（APPLICANT）
INVOICE NO. （发票号码）	由出口公司根据本公司的实际情况自行编制，一般在制单资料中可找
DATE （日期）	发票的日期就是发票的制作日期，也可理解为发票的签发日期。一般情况下，发票的日期应在运输单据出单日期之前，同时不能迟于信用证的有效期。根据《跟单信用证统一惯例》的规定，信用证没有特殊规定，银行可以接受签发日期早于信用证开证日期的发票
S/C NO. （合同编号）	按实际合同号填写，有时会用 CONTRACT NO.表示。合同是一笔业务的基础，内容较完善的发票应包括合同号。合同号应与信用证上列明的一致，一笔交易有几份合同的，都应打在发票上
L/C NO. （信用证号码）	信用证支付方式下填写信用证号码
FROM…TO （航线）	填写实际具体装运港和目的港名称，不能笼统。如需转运，应把转运港名称表示出来，如有重名应打上国别；若无转运，则应在 W/T 或 V/A 后打上***表示无转船
SHIPPED BY 运输方式	填实际运输工具的名称和航次，如无运输工具、航次则填写 BY SEA
Marks and Numbers （唛头及件号）	发票上的唛头应与信用证中规定的唛头完全一致，如无则填 N/M
Description of Goods （货物描述）	信用证下，货物描述必须与信用证的货物描述完全一致。其他单据中可以使用统称，但不得与信用证规定的抵触
Quantity （数量）	根据信用证规定填写具体的数量或重量
Unit Price （单价）	完整的单价包括计价货币、单位价格金额、计量单位和贸易术语，如有佣金折扣应扣除（小数点后保留两位小数）

续表

项目名称	填制方法
Unit Price （单价）	如 1. CIFC3 TOKYO　USD20.00　　2. CIFD5 TOKYO　USD 50.00 　　LESSC3　　　USD6.00　　　　LESSD5　　　USD2.50 　　————————————　　　———————————— 　　CIF TOKYO　　USD19.40　　　CIF TOKYO　　USD47.50
Amount （总值）	根据信用证规定填写，但不能超过信用证总金额。当金额为整数时，小数点后仍要保留两位小数
TOTAL （总计）	在多种商品规格的情况下，为了使商品的总数量以及总金额更加清晰明了，都要在发票中予以总计
TOTAL AMOUNT IN WORDS （大写总金额）	大写总金额应由小写金额翻译而成，用英文表示，以 SAY 提示开始，货币名称写在数额前，最后以 ONLY 结束。如 USD50 200 可写成 SAY U.S. DOLLARS FIFTY THOUSAND TWO HUNDRDED ONLY
SPECIAL CONDITIONS 声明文句(特殊 说明)	有来证要求填写各种费用金额、特定号码、有关证明文句的，可在发票商品栏目下的空白处注明。大致有这样几种：加注运费、保险费和 FOB 金额；注明如进口证号、配额许可证号码等特定号码；缮打证明句等
SIGNATURE 出票人签章	通常在发票的右下角打上出口公司的名称，并由负责人签名或盖章。《跟单信用证统一惯例》：商业发票无须签署。但如果信用证要求提交已签署的商业发票（SIGNED COMMERCIAL INVOICE）就必须签署；而要求手签商业发票 (MANUAL LY /HAND SIGNED COMMERCIAL INVOICE)，如发票上有证明的字句如 "WE CERTIFY THAT…"，对此也必须签署

┃▌课堂思考

买方开来信用证规定：about 80 M/T 大米，每 M/T 500.00 美元，信用证总金额为 44 000 美元。卖方最多交货多少？最少交货多少？

参考答案

三、商业发票填制的注意事项

填制商业发票时应注意以下事项。

（1）发票是弹性很大的单据。在发票上加注"原产地：中华人民共和国"之类的文句，并让出入境检验检疫机构或者贸促会加注日期和签章，这样发票就有了产地证的功能。

（2）在"D/P AT SIGHT"或"BY PAYMENT" / L/C 等即期见单付款的条件下，发票兼代汇票的功能，并加打"PAYMENT:D/P AT SIGHT"字样，或加注开证行名、证号和开证日期、大写的英文发票总额等。

（3）发票等单据上往往加有不少附注，如合同号、进口许可证号、L/C 号、"PROFO RMA"号、提单号、船名航次、柜号等，这是在单据间建立"证据链"的需要。

（4）发票是所有单据中要求最严格与信用证一致的单据。发票上出现的开证人及受益人名称，如与 L/C 所示不一致，构成不符的，单位地址等细节填写"单证不符"则无碍。

职业判断

案例资料：

宁波天一贸易公司与韩国三星服装公司签订进口女士毛衣，开出信用证中将"NINGBO TIANYI TRADE COMPANY"写成"NINGBO TIANY TRADE COMPANY"。

韩国三星公司在开具商业发票时发现开证人名称错误。

思考：

商业发票上如何填制进口商名称？

参考答案

业务员小王填制的商业发票，如图 3.3 所示。

NINGBO YINGGUANG GARMENT CO., LTD.
NO.2373 DEVELOPMENT ROAD,HUSHAN,CIXI,CHINA

COMMERCIAL INVOICE
ORIGINAL

TO M/S: TOSHU CORPORATION OSALM	发票号码 INVOICE NO.		JYS698
12-36, KYUTARO- MACHI 4- CHOME	日期 DATE.		MAR.05,2015
CHUO- KU, OSAKA 561-8177 JAPAN	合约号码 S/C NO.		99JA7031KL
	信用证号码 L/C NO.		G/FO-7752807

装运口岸	目的地	转运地	运输方式
FROM: NINGBO,CHINA	TO: YOKOHAMA,JAPAN	W/T: ***	BY: S.S. HONG V26

图 3.3　商业发票

唛头号码 Marks and Numbers	货物描述 Description of goods	数量 Quantity	单价 Unit Price	金额 Amount
N/M	MAN'S SHIRT		CIF YOKOHAMA	
	71-800	67200PCS	USD1.43/PC	USD96 096.00
	71-801	48 000 PCS	USD1.46/PC	USD70 080.00
	71-802	27 600PCS	USD1.29/PC	USD35 604.00
	TOTAL:	142800PCS		USD201 780.00
TOTAL IN WORDS: SAY U.S. DOLLARS TWO HUNDRED AND ONE THOUSAND SEVEN HUNDRED AND EIGHTY ONLY.				
			NINGBO YINGGUANG GARMENT CO., LTD. 李磊	

图 3.3　商业发票（续）

2014 年 12 月，宁波丝绸纺织品公司与日本 WILL GOOD 公司签订了一批针织服装（KNITT ED GARMENT）出口合同，日本 WILL GOOD 公司已开来信用证（见图 3.4）。

```
ISSUING BANK:THE BANK OF TOKYO-MITSUBISHI,LTD.
            NO.4 KITAHAMA STREET TOKYO, JAPAN
FORM OF CREDIT: IRREVOCABLE
CREDIT NUMBER: S-510-2033
DATE OF ISSUE:JAN.10，2015
DATE OF EXPIRY:MARCH 25，2015
APPLICANT: WILL GOOD CO. ,LTD
            7-54，6-CHOME,CHOU-KU,TOKYO,JAPAN
BENEFICIARY: NINGBO SILK GARMENTS GROUP
            NO.112DONGSAN EAST ROAD, NINGBO CHINA
AMOUNT: USD30500.00
LOADING IN CHARGE: NINGBO, CHINA
FOR TRANSPORT TO: TOKYO, JAPAN
DESCRIPTION OF GOODS: CFR TOKYO 10 000 PCS KNITTED GARMENTS AT USD 3.05/PC
```

图 3.4　日本 WILL GOOD 公司开来的信用证（部分）

其他资料：

发票号码：FDG5678

发票日期：JAN.25，2015

合同号码：SG201278

唛头：WILL
SG201278
TOKYO/JAPAN
C/NO.1-100
试为宁波丝绸纺织品公司缮制商业发票。

参考答案

任务二　根据销售合同制作商业发票

任务导航

2014年12月，上海申江进出口有限公司与日本SAKULA公司签订了一笔皮带（BELT）销售合同（见图3.5），合同约定 CIF KOBE PORT 交易条件，D/P 即期付款交单支付，金额为 USD123 000.00。

在 D/P 付款方式下，业务员小李需要根据销售合同制作商业发票。在缮制发票前，小李必须对合同内容进行详细分析，在合同项下制单的基础上，更好地行使履约责任。

上海申江进出口有限公司
SHANGHAI SHENJIANG IMP.AND EXP.CO., LTD.
NO.27, ZHONGSHAN ROAD(E.1), SHANGHAI, CHINA
售货确认书
SALES CONFIRMATION

Tel: 0086-21-66080888
Fax: 0086-21-66081888

编号：
No.:　SC0701260
日期：
Date:DEC.1,2014

TO Messrs:

SAKULA CO., LTD.

ITC BUILDING,6TH FLOOR,SUITE602

1-8-4CHOME ISOBE-DORI　　CHUO-KU,KOBE,JAPAN

Tel: 0081-78-362-1444

Fax: 0081-78-362-1445

谨启者：兹确认售予你方下列货品，其成交条件如下：

Dear Sirs: We hereby confirm having sold to you the following goods on the terms and conditions as specified below:

图3.5　销售合同

（1）货物名称及规格 Name of Commodity and Specification	（2）数量 Quantity	（3）单价 Unit Price	（4）总价 Amount
FASHION BELT		CIF KOBE	
(1)SIZE:100×4.8cm OUTER PACKING:150PCS/CTN	3 000PCS	USD12.00	USD36 000.00
(2)SIZE:105×8cm OUTER PACKING:120PCS/CTN	4 800PCS	USD15.00	USD72 000.00
(3)SIZE:105×3.8cm OUTER PACKING:100PCS/CTN	500PCS	USD30.00	USD15 000.00
TOTAL	8 300PCS		USD123 000.00

TOTAL AMOUNT IN WORDS: SAY US DOLLARS ONE HUNDRED AND TWENTY THREE THOUSAND ONLY

（5）装运期限：

Time of Shipment: LATEST DATE OF SHIPMENT Feb.28,2015 BY S.S.CHANGJIAN

（6）装运港：

Port of Loading: SHANGHAI PORT

（7）目的港：

Port of Destination: KOBE PORT

（8）分批装运：

Partial Shipment: ALLOWED

（9）转船：

Transshipment: ALLOWED

（10）付款条件：

Terms of Payment: D/P AT SIGHT

（11）运输标志：

Shipping Marks: WILL LAT/KOBE/GHCY0239-12/NO.1-65

（12）保险：

Insurance: The seller should cover insurance for 110％of the total invoice value against ALL Risks as per Ocean Marine Cargo Clauses of PICC dated Jan.1,1981.

THE BUYER   THE SELLER

高岛秀行   赵函轩

图3.5 销售合同（续）

其他制单资料：

（1）发票日期：DEC.5，2014

（2）发票号码：HJKF-09

要求：

以单证员小李的身份，根据以下销售合同内容，向日本 SAKULA 公司开具一份商业发票。

国际贸易合同在国内又被称为外贸合同或进出口贸易合同，即营业地处于不同国家或地区的当事人就商品买卖所发生的权利和义务关系而达成的书面协议。国际贸易合同对于双方当事人具有法律约束力。

商业发票没有统一规定的格式，每个出具商业发票的单位都有自己的发票格式。虽然格式各有不同，但是，商业发票填制的项目大同小异，其样式及填制方法在任务一中已做详细介绍，此处不再赘述。

小贴士

形式发票虽然内容和合同比较相近，但是一般地不能代替合同来使用，是作为进口商用来申请进口许可证书以及进口备案使用，不具备约束力。但是经过买卖双方确认以形式合同成交的，形式发票可充当合同使用。

任务实施

单证员小李填制的商业发票，如图3.6所示。

SHANGHAI SHENJIANG IMP.AND EXP.CO.,LTD.
NO.27, ZHONGSHAN ROAD(E.1),SHANGHAI,CHINA

COMMERCIAL INVOICE
ORIGINAL

TO M/S: SAKULA CO., LTD.
ITC BUILDING,6TH FLOOR,
SUITE602 1-8-4CHOME ISO
BE-DORI CHUO-KU,KOBE,
JAPAN

发票号码 INVOICE NO.	HJKF-09
日期 DATE.	DEC.05,2014
合约号码 S/C NO.	SC0701260

装运口岸 FROM:SHANGHAI,CHINA	目的地 TO: KOBE,JAPAN	转运地 W/T: ***	运输方式 BY: S.S.CHANGJIAN

唛头号码 Marks and Numbers	货物描述 Description of Goods	数量 Quantity	单价 Unit Price	金额 Amount
WILL LAT KOBE GHCY0239-12	FASHION BELT SIZE:100cm×4.8cm	3 000PCS 4 800 PCS 500PCS	CIF USD12.00/PC USD15.00/PC	KOBE USD36 000.00 USD72 000.00
NO.1-65	SIZE:105cm×8cm SIZE:105cm×3.8cm		USD30.00/PC	USD15 000.00

图3.6 小李填制的商业发票

NO.1-65	TOTAL:	8 300PCS		USD123 000.00
TOTAL IN WORDS: SAY U.S. DOLLARS ONE HUNDRED AND TWENTY-THREE THOUSAND ONLY.				
			SHANGHAI SHENJIANG IMP.AND EXP.CO.,LTD 赵函轩	

图 3.6　小李填制的商业发票

任务再现

2014 年 6 月 20 日，温州宝康集团与日本 NICHI 公司签订一批男士皮鞋（MEN'S LEATHER SHOES）出口合同，合同约定 CIF YOKOHAMA 交易条件，即期付款信用证支付，金额 USD42 000。

合同相关资料如下：

参考答案

出口商温州宝康集团 WENZHOU BAOKANG GROUP（地址：252 ZHONGSHAN RO AD, WENZHOU, ZHEJIANG, CHINA）与进口商 NICHI CO., LTD.（地址：NO.241-8, CHIN ASAKI CHUO,TSUZUKI-KU, YOKAHAMA,JAPAN）达成一笔交易，交易货物为男士皮鞋（MEN'S LEATHER SHOES）。其中，型号为 1122 的出口 1000 双，单价为每双 20 美元；型号 1123 的出口 1000 双，单价每双 22 美元，贸易术语 CIF。起运港为宁波，目的港为 YOKOHAMA，经香港转船，船名航次 V.V.JANNI-9。于 2014 年 6 月 20 日签订合同（编号 FG-0985），结算方式为不可撤销即期信用证（编号 LC-1267J），发票编号（HM35-TY）。

试为温州宝康集团缮制商业发票。

技能强化训练

技 能 提 高

项目小结

在线测试及
参考答案

根据图 3.7 所示信用证资料填制商业发票。

```
ISSUING BANK: THE SAKURA BANK, LIMITED
          56, NANIWA – CHO, CHUO – KU, KOBE, JAPAN
20/ DOCUMENTATY CREDIT NUMBER: KUW25847
31C/ DATE OF ISSUE: MAY 15, 2014
31D/ DATE AND PLACE OF EXPIRY: JUNE 30, 2014 BENEFICIARIES' COUNTRY
50/ APPLICANT: MOMO CO., LTD.
          NO. 215 NADA – KU, KOBE, JAPAN
```

图 3.7　信用证资料

59/BENEFICIARY: HUNAN TEA IMPORT & EXPORT CORPORATION

WUYI ROAD, CHANGSHA, HUNAN, CHINA

32/ CURRENCY CODE AMOUNT: USD 26 640.00

39A/ PERCENT CREDIT AMT TOLERANCE: 05/05

41D/ AVAILABLE WITH …BY… ： ANY BANK IN CHINA BY NEGOTIATON

45A/ DESCRIPT. OF GOODS AND / OR SERVICES:

AS PER S/C No. HNT(04)021

APPLICANT'S REF NO. 3 – 1190

12,000 KGS PU-ERH TEA AT USD2.22 PER KG. CIF KOBE

PACKED: IN 50 KGS PER CARTON

46A/DOCUMENTS REQUIRED:

+COMMERCIAL INVOICE IN ONE ORIGINAL PLUS 6 COPIES, SHOWING THAT THE GOODS EXPORTED ARE OF CHINESE ORIGIN, ALL OF WHICH MUST BE MANUALLY SIGNED.

47A/ ADDITIONAL CONDITIONS:

+ALL DOCUMENTS REQUIRED UNDER THIS CREDIT MUST MENTION THIS L/C NUMBER AND THE ISSUING BANK NAME.

图 3.7　信用证资料

参考资料如下：

（1）2014 年 6 月 12 日装 "FENCQING V. 25" 从广州出运。

（2）唛头自行设计。

（3）发票日期：APR.25，2014；号码自行设计。

参考答案

项目四

装箱单实训

知识目标

1. 理解装箱单的含义和作用;
2. 熟悉装箱单的内容;
3. 掌握装箱单的填制方法。

能力目标

1. 能根据信用证制作装箱单;
2. 能根据销售合同制作装箱单。

任务一 根据信用证制作装箱单

任务导航

2013年4月宁波乾湖日用品有限公司（NINGBO QIANHU HOME PRODUCT CO.,LTD）以 CIF 条件出口 4500 条地毯（Rugs）至日本大阪，即期信用证方式付款，金额为 USD 30 150.00，客户（ABC CORPPORATION）开来信用证，如图4.1所示。

ISSUE OF DOCUMENTARY CREDIT

ISSUING BANK:	ASAHI BANK,TOKYO
FORM OF DOC.CREDIT	IRREVOCABLE
DOC.CREDIT NUMBER	ABL-AN108
DATE OF ISSUE	20130405
DATE AND PLACE OF EXP. :	20130616 PLACE CHINA
APPLICANT	ABC CORPPORATION,123 RED FLOWER STREET,
	OSAKA, JAPAN
BENEFICIARY	NINGBO QIANHU HOME PRODUCT CO.,LTD
	88 QIANHU ROAD YINZHOU NINGBO CHINA
CURRENCY CODE AMOUNT:	USD30150.00
AVAILABLE WITH/BY	ANY BANK BY NEGOTIATION
DRAFS AT…	DRAFT AT SIGHT FOR FULL INVOICE VALUE
DRAWEE	ASAHI BANK，TOKYO
PARTIAL SHIPMENT	ALLOWED
TRANSSHIPMENT	ALLOWED
LOADING IN CHARGE	NINGBO, CHINA
FOR TRANSPORT TO …	OSAKA, JAPAN
LATEST DATE OF SHIP	MAY, 30, 2013

DESCRIPTION OF GOODS:

4500PCS RUGS 127×152cm USD6.9 PER PC AS PER S/C　NO. SH117le

PACKING:	30PCS/CTN
PRICE TERM:	CIF OSAKA

DOCUMENT REQUIRED:

（1）3/3 SET OF CLEAN ON BOARD OCEAN BILLS OF LADING　MADE OUT TO ORDER OF SHIPPER AND BLANK ENDORSED AND MARKED "FREIGHT PREPAID" NOTIFY ACCOUNTEE (WITH FULL NAME AND ADDRESS).

图4.1　日本公司开来的信用证

（2）ORIGINAL SIGNED COMMERCIAL INVOICE IN 5 FOLD CERTIFYING THE GOODS ARE OF CHINA ORIGIN.

（3）INSURANCE POLICY OR CERTIFICATE IN 2 FOLD ENDORSED IN BLANK FOR 110 PCT OF FULL TOTAL INVOICE VALUE COVERING THE INSTITUE CARGO (A) ,THE INSTITUTE WAR CLAUSE ,INSURANCE CLAIM TO BE PAYABLE IN JAPAN IN THE CURRENCY OF THE DRAFT.

（4）CERTIFICATE OF ORIGIN IN DUPLICATE.

（5）BENEFICIARY'S CERTIFICATE TO THE EFFECT THAT THEY HAVE COMPLIED ALL. TERMS AND CONDITIONS OF THEIR PROFORMA INVOICE NO.2004CTHS02008 DT.01-05-2004.

（6）PACKING LIST IN TRIPLICATE ADDITIONAL COND.

ALL DOUCUMENTS SHOULD BE INDICATED L/C NUMBER AND MUST BE FORWARDED DIRECTLY TO US IN ONE LOT BY COURIER SERVICES.

SHIPPING MARKS : ITOCHU/OSAKA/NO.1-150

PRESENTATION PERIOD: DOCUMENTS MUST BE PRESENTED WITHIN 15 DAYS OF SHIPMEENT, BUT WITHIN THE VALIDITY OF THE CREDIT.

图 4.1　日本公司开来的信用证（续）

要求：

试以单证员小方的身份，根据信用证及其他业务资料（见表 4.1）制作装箱单。

表 4.1　相关业务资料

发票号码	SH-25757	发票日期	2013 年 4 月 29 日	C/O 编号	GZ8/27685/1007
单位毛重	18KGS/CTN	单位净重	15KGS/CTN	单位尺寸	153cm×15cm×128cm/CTN
船名	DIEK335 V.007	地毯 H.S.编码	57029200	集装箱号码	1×40'MAKU5879524/2973385 CY/CY
提单号码	KFT2582588	提单日期	2013 年 5 月 15 日	保险单号码	PIC00178141
卖方法人代表	何一山	承运公司	ABC OCEAN AGENT COMPANY	承运人	周星
单证员	陈明	保险单签发人	李萍	买方法人代表	王立

知识准备

一、认识装箱单

装箱单（packing list）是商业发票的一种补充单据，通过对商品包装件数、规格、唛头、重量等项目的填制，明确阐明商品的包装情况，便于买方对进口商品包装及数量、重量等的了解和掌握，也便于买方在货物到达目的港时，供海关检查和核对货物（见图 4.2）。

PACKING LIST

EXPORTER			INVOICE NO.			
			DATE			
TO			S /C NO.			
			FROM			
			TO			
MARKS	DESCRIPTION OF GOODS	QTY	PKGS	NW	GW	MEAS

图 4.2　装箱单样本

小　贴　士

　　包装单据既是商业发票的补充单据，也是商业发票和提单之间的桥梁。在出口业务中，一般由出口企业自行缮制签发装箱单，无统一格式，但包含的栏目大致相同，主要包括买卖双方信息、货物名称规格、数量、重量和体积。

二、装箱单填制要点

装箱单填制要点如下。

（1）单据名称：常见的名称有 PACKING LIST,WEIGHT LIST（重量单），MEASUREMENT LIST（尺码单）。

（2）数量表达：装箱单要体现货物的包装情况，一般包括计价单位的数量（Quantity）（即内包装、小包装的数量）和运输包装（Package）（即外包装、大包装的数量）。若包装单据里只有一个包装数量，即 Quantity 或者 Package，一般显示为大包装的数量。

（3）净/毛重、体积。注意：净/毛重是以千克为单位，保留两位小数；体积以立方米为单位，保留三位小数。

（4）包装数的大写：由 SAY 开始，大写数量加包装单位，ONLY 结尾。

（5）特殊条款：根据信用证要求，应充分体现在单据上。

▌课堂思考

（1）信用证中规定包装采用 "SEAWORTHY PACKING"，受益人在制作装箱单时应如何填制？

（2）受益人在制作相关单据时，是否必须将运输包装上的标志都注明在单据上？

参考答案

三、装箱单填制注意事项

在填制装箱单时，应注意以下事项。

（1）当信用证要求做成中性装箱单（neutral packing）时，装箱单上不应显示出口商的名称，也不得签章。

（2）装箱单作为发票的附属单据，填写时应注意与发票内容的一致性。

（3）装箱单着重表现货物的包装情况，一般不显示货物价格，因为进口商在转移这些单据给实际买方的时候大多不愿泄露其购买的实际成本。

职业判断

案例资料：

某公司出口货物，从宁波港发运，运往纽约，在香港转船，在装箱单中 "TRANSPORT DETAILS" 一栏中填写的是 "FROM NINGBO TO HONGKONG AND THENCE TO NEWYORK"。

思考：

该公司的此栏填写内容是否正确？如不正确应该如何填写？

参考答案

单证员小方填写的装箱单如图 4.3 所示。

宁波乾湖日用品有限公司

NINGBO QIANHU HOME PRODUCT CO., LTD

88 QIANHU ROAD YINZHOU NINGBO CHINA

PACKING LIST

| EXPORTER
NINGBO QIANHU HOME PRODUCT CO., LTD
88 QIANHU ROAD YINZHOU NINGBOCHINA | INVOICE NO.
SH-25757 |
| | DATE
APRIL 29,2013 |

| TO
ABC CORPPORATION,123 RED FLOWER STREET, OSAKA,JAPAN | S /C NO
SH117 |
| | FROM NINGBO CHINA
TO OSAKA, JAPAN |

MARKS	DESCRIPTION OF GOODS	QTY	PKGS	NW	GW	MEAS
ITOCHU OSAKA NO.1-150	RUGS 127×152cm TOTAL	4500PCS 4500PCS	30PCS/CTN 150CTNS	15.00KGS/CTN 2250.00KGS 2250.00KGS	18.00KGS/CTN 2700.00KGS 2700.00KGS	(153×15×128)CM/CTN 44.064CMB 44.064CMB
L/C NO.:ABL-AN108 PACKING: 30PCS/CTN						

TOTAL PACKAGE IN WORDS: SAY ONE HUNDRED AND FIFTY CARTONS ONLY.

宁波乾湖日用品有限公司
NINGBO QIANHU HOME PRODUCT CO.,LTD
何一山

图 4.3 小方填写的装箱单

任务再现

2014 年 8 月天津红燕贸易有限公司（TIANJIN REDSWALLOW TRADING CO., LTD.）以 CIF 条件出口 5000 件女式夹克至日本东京，见票 30 天信用证方式付款，金额为 USD52 500.00，客户（MARUBENI CORPORATION）开来信用证，如图 4.4 所示。

A DOCUMENTARY CREDIT

ISSUING BANK: BANK OF CHINA, TOYKO BRANCH
ADVISING BANK: BANK OF CHINA, TIANJIN BRANCH

图 4.4 日本客户开来的信用证

SEQUENCE OF TOTAL	* 27: 1/1
FORM OF DOC. CREDIT	* 40A: IRREVOCABLE
APPLICABLE RULES	*40E: UCP LATEST VERSION
DOC.CREDIT NUMBER	* 20: A-08-0058
DATE OF ISSUE	* 31 C: 20140815
EXPIRY	* 31 D: DATE: 20141031 PLACE: CHINA
APPLICANT	* 50: MARUBENI CORP.HOMMACHI CHOME CHUO-KU,
	TOKYO, JAPAN
BENEFICIARY	* 53: REDSWALLOW TRADING CO., LTD.
	NO.86, ZHUJIANG ROAD
	TIANJIN, CHINA
AMOUNT	* 32B: CURRENCY USD AMOUNT USD52 500.00
AVAILABLE WITY/BY	* 41D: NEGOTIATION WITH ADVISING BANK
DRAFTS AT	* 42C: AT 30 DAYS AFTER SIGHT
	FOR FULL INVOICE VALUE
DRAWEE	* 42D: ISSUING BANK
PARTLAL SHIPMENNTS	* 43P: PROHIBITED
TRANSSHIHPMENT	* 43T: PROHIBITED
LOADING IN CHARGE	* 44A: TIANJIN, CHINA
FOR TRANSPORT TO	* 44B: TOKYO, JAPAN
LATEST DATE OF SHIP.	* 44C: 20141015
DESCRIP. OF GOODS	* 45A:

5000PCS OF GIRL JACKETS, SHELL: 100% COTTON, LINING: 100% POLYESTER

UNIT PRICE:USD10.50/PC CIF TOKYO DETAILS AS PER S/C NO. 08TF0858

PACKING: 1PC TO A PLASTIC BAG, 20BAGS TO A CARTON

DOCUMENTS REQURIED   * 46A :

+ SIGNED COMMERCIAL INVOICE IN TRIPLICATE CERTIFYING THE GOODS ARE OF CHINESE ORIGIN AND SHOWING HS CODE 6396875601

+ 3/3 SET OF CLEAN ON BOARD OCEAN BILLS OF LADING MADE OUT TO ORDER AND BLANK ENDORSED NOTIFY APPLICANT WITH FULL NAME,ADDRESS AND TEL NO.8745 9986 AND INDICATING THE NAME OF CARRYING VESSEL'S NAME AND TEL NO. AT THE PORT OF DESTIATION MARKED "FREIGHT PREPAID "

+ PACKING LIST IN DUPLICATE SHOWING THE GOODS HAVE BEEN PACKED IN CARTONS OF 20PCS EACH AND CERTIFYING EACH ITEM HAS BEEN MARKED THE LABEL "MADE IN CHINA"

+ INSURANCE POLICY OR CERTICATE IN THE NAME OF APPLICANT FOR 120% OF INVOICE VALUE AGAINST ALL RISKS AND WAR RISK AS PER CIC, CLAIM, IF ANY, PAYABLE AT PORT OF DESTINATION

ADDITIONAL COND.   * 47A:

SHIPPING MARKS:MARUBENI/ S/C 08TF0858/ TOKYO/ NO.1-UP

DETAILS OF CHARGES   * 71B:

图 4.4 日本客户开来的信用证（续）

ALL BANKING CHARGES OUTSIDE TOKYO ARE FOR ACCOUNT OF BENEFICLARY.

PRESENTATION PERIOD　　　* 48:

DOCUMENTS TO BE PRESENTED WITHIN 14 DAYS AFTER THE DATE OF SHIPMENT BUT WITHIN THE VALIDITY OF THE CREDIT

CONFIRMATION　　　* 49: WITHOUT

图 4.4　日本客户开来的信用证（续）

补充业务资料如下：

发票号：TFINV0815　　　发票日期：2014 年 10 月 2 日

毛重：38.00KGS/CTN　　　净重：35.00KGS/CTN

体积：0.08CBM/CTN　　　公司法人代表：赵龙

试以单证员小方的身份，根据信用证及其他业务资料制作装箱单。

参考答案

任务二　根据销售合同制作装箱单

任务导航

厦门新世纪进出口贸易公司（XIAMEN NEW CENTURY IMPORT AND EXPORT TRADE COMPANY）与韩国釜山 TKAMLA 公司签订棉男士裤子（COTTON MEN'S TROUSERS）的外销合同，如图 4.5 所示。

厦门新世纪进出口贸易公司

XIAMEN NEW CENTURY IMPORT AND EXPORT TRADE　COMPANY

666 ZHONGYUAN ROAD XIAMEN CHINA

销售合同

SALES CONTRACT

电话	合同号码
TEL:0592-67213256	S/C NO.:HX050264
传真	合同日期
FAX:0592-67213258	DATE: JAN.01,2013
买方名称地址	
TO MESSERS:	

图 4.5　销售合同

TKAMLA CORPORATION

6-(7)KAWARA MACH

BUSAN, KOREA

经买卖双方同意按下列条款成交：

Dear Sirs,

    We hereby confirm having sold to you the following goods on terms and conditions as specified below:

货物描述 DESCRIPTIONS OF GOODS	数量 QUANTITY	单价 U/PRICE	总价 AMOUNT
COTTON MEN'S TROUSERS		FOB XIAMEN	
ART NO.A556	1 200PCS	USD5.00	USD6 000.00
ART NO.SH90	1 600PCS	USD4.50	USD7 200.00
ART NO.BN88	2 200PCS	USD4.00	USD8 800.00
TOTAL	_____		_____
	5 000PCS		USD22 000.00

包装条件：纸箱装，每箱 20 条，共 250 箱。

PACKING: Packed in cartons of 20pcs each, total 250 cartons.

装运口岸：中国厦门

LOADING PORT: Xia Men, China

目的口岸：韩国釜山

DESTINATION: Busan, Korea

装运期限：在 3 月底前装运，不允许分批装运和转运。

TIME OF SHIPMENT: Before the end of Mar.2013. Partial shipment and transshipment are not allowed.

付款条件：电汇方式支付，预付货款。

PAYMENT: By T/T payment in advance.

    THE BUYER   THE SELLER

TKAMLA CORPORATION   XIAMEN NEW CENTURY IMPORT AND EXPORT

                                      TRADE   COMPANY

       朴书仁   王国清

图 4.5 销售合同（续）

要求：

以单证员小方的身份，根据合同及其他业务资料制作装箱单（以汇付为例）。

补充业务资料如下：

发票号：TA06885   发票日期：JAN.15,2013

毛重：32.00KGS/CTN   净重：28.00KGS/CTN   体积：（40×40×50）CM/CTN

无唛头规定

知识准备

根据合同即在非信用证业务项下填制装箱单，此时单据虽然没有在信用证项下的制作要求严格，但也要求正确、准确、精确。外贸单据是记录整笔外贸业务的见证，应该与合同和实际相符合。

小贴士

非信用证业务项下即是在汇付或托收项下填制装箱单。不管是在汇付或是托收方式下，出口商都必须按出口销售合同的规定及时制单，内容要做到正确、简洁，排列要行次整齐，重点项目要突出醒目。包装单据的种类和份数应根据实际业务的需要出具。

课堂思考

（1）汇付项下出口商如何制单、进口商如何付款？

（2）托收方式下如何交单？

（3）某出口商与进口商采用汇付方式达成交易，进口商为减少预付风险要求使用凭单付汇。出口商可否答应？为什么？

（1）（2）参考答案

任务实施

单证员小方填写的装箱单如图4.6所示。

（3）参考答案

<table>
<tr><td colspan="2" align="center">厦门新世纪进出口贸易公司
XIAMEN NEW CENTURY IMPORT AND EXPORT TRADE　COMPANY
666 ZHONGYUAN ROAD XIAMEN CHINA

PACKING　LIST</td></tr>
<tr><td rowspan="2">EXPORTER
　XIAMEN NEW CENTURY IMPORT AND EXPORT TRADE COMPANY 666 ZHONGYUAN ROAD XIAMEN CHINA</td><td>INVOICE NO.
TA06885</td></tr>
<tr><td>DATE
JAN.15,2013</td></tr>
</table>

图4.6　小方填制的装箱单

续表

MARKS	DESCRIPTION OF GOODS	QTY	PKGS	NW	GW	MEAS
N/M	COTTON MEN'S TROUSERS			28.00KGS/CTN	32.00KGS/CTN	0.08CBM/CTN
	ART NO.A556	1 200PCS	60CTNS	1680.00KGS	1920.00KGS	4.800CBM
	ART NO.SH90	1 600PCS	80CTNS	2240.00KGS	2560.00KGS	6.400CBM
	ART NO.BN88	2 200PCS	110CTNS	3080.00KGS	3520.00KGS	8.800CBM
	PACKED IN 20PCS EACH					
	TOTAL	5000PCS	250CTNS	7000.00KGS	8000.00KGS	20.000CBM
SAY TWO HUNDRED AND FIFTY CARTONS ONLY.						

厦门新世纪进出口贸易公司

XIAMEN NEW CENTURY IMPORT AND

EXPORT TRADE COMPANY

王国清

图 4.6   小方填制的装箱单（续）

上海天泰进出口有限公司（SHANGHAI TIANTAI EXP. AND IMP. CO.）与加拿大温哥华 ASADE 贸易公司达成一笔运动套装（JOGGING SUIT）的出口交易，双方签订的销售合同如图4.7所示。

上海天泰进出口有限公司

SHANGHAI TIANTAI EXP.AND IMP.CO.

FLOOR 3RD NO.115 MINGGUANG RD.SHANGHAI CHINA

销售合同

SALES CONTRACT

合同号码

S/C NO.: SC468001

买方

BUYER: ASADE TRADING COMPANY

地址

ADRESS: RM 1008-1011 101HARBOR ROAD, VANCOUVER CANADA

电话

TEL: 507-25192334

合同日期

DATE.: JUNE 30 2013

图 4.7   销售合同

传真

FAX: 507-25192334

经买卖双方同意按下列条款成交：

Dear Sirs:

　　We hereby confirm having sold to you the following goods on terms and conditions as specified below:

唛头 SHIPPING MARK	货物描述 NAME OF COMMODITY SPECIFICATION	数量 QUANTITY	单价 UNIT PRICE	总价 TOTAL AMOUNT
ASADE VANCOUVER SC468001 NO.1-150	JOGGING SUIT ART NO.12 ART NO.13 TOTAL	 1 000SETS 2 000SETS 3 000SETS	CFR VANCOUVER USD16.00 USD20.00	 USD16 000.00 USD40 000.00 USD56 000.00

装运：不迟于 2013 年 8 月 25 日，允许转运和分批装运

SHIPMENT: NOT LATER THAN AUG 25 2013ALLOWING TRANSHIPMENT AND PARTIALSHIPMENT

装运港：中国上海

PORT OF LOADING: SHANGHAI CHINA

目的港：加拿大温哥华

PORT OF DESTINATION: VANCOUVER CANADA

支付方式：即期付款交单

TERMS OF PAYMENT: BY D/P AT SIGHT

包装：20 套装一个纸箱，共 150 纸箱

PACKING: 20SETS TO BE PACKED IN ONE CARTON TOTAL 150 CARTONS

　　　THE SELLER　　　　　　　　　　　　　　　THE BUYER

　　上海天泰进出口有限公司

SHANGHAI TIANTAI EXP.AND IMP.CO.　　　　　ASADE TRADING COMPANY

　　　张开明　　　　　　　　　　　　　　　　　MIKE

图 4.7　销售合同（续）

其他业务资料如下：

IVVOICE NO: IY20130710　　　DATE: JULY 10 2013

GW: 16.00KGS/CTN　　　　　NW:14.00KGS/CTN

MEAS (CBM): 0.09/CTN

试根据合同及其他业务资料制作装箱单。

参考答案

项目小结

在线测试及
参考答案

技能强化训练

技 能 提 高

（一）填单题

1. 根据下列信用证资料填制装箱单。

ISSUING BANK: NANYANG COMMERCIAL BANK LTD.,HONGKONG

L/C NO.: KRT2899302

L/C DATE: 20140515

EXPIRY: DATE 20140622 IN BENEFICIARY COUNTRY

BENEFICIARY: NINGBO IMP.AND EXP.CO.

NO.18 ZHONGXING ROAD NINGBO CHINA

APPLICANT: CURRENT FUNDS CO.

NO.88 MODY ROAD KOWLOON HONGKONG

AMOUNT: CURRENCY USD AMOUNT 15250.00

PARTIAL SHIPMENTS: ALLOWED

TRANSSHIPMENT: ALLOWED

LOADING IN CHARGE: NINGBO CHINA

FOR TRANSPORT TO: SANTOS BRAZIL

LATEST DATE OF SHIPMENT: 20140615

DESCRIPTION OF GOODS: 3050PCS KNITTED GARMENTS AT USD6.00/PC AS PER CONTRACT NO.00568 CFR SANTOS

DOCUMENTS REQUIRED:

+ SIGNED CERTIFIED INVOICE IN TRIPLICATE

+ PACKING LIST IN TRIPLICATE

+ FULL SET OF CLEAN ON BOARD OCEAN BILLS OF LADING MADE OUT TO ORDER OF SHIPPER AND MARKED FREIGHT PREPAID NOTIFY APPLICANT

+ CERTIFICATE OF ORIGIN IN 3 COPIES

ADDITIONAL CONDITIONS:

1. INSURANCE EFFECTED BY BUYER

2. ALL DOCUMENTS MUST MENTION THE ORIGIN OF GOODS

其他资料如下：

发票号码：SG689

每箱毛重：20.00KGS

每箱净重：18.00KGS

每箱尺码：0.05CBM

业务经理：刘平

唛头：CF/00568/SANTOS/NO.1-305

货物产地：CHINA

2. 根据合同（见图4.8）及其他资料填制装箱单。

上海工具进出口公司

SHANGHAI TOOL IMPORT AND EXPORT TRADE CORPORATION

108 BEIJING ROAD SHANGHAI CHINA

销售合同

SALES CONTRACT

合同号码   合同日期

S/C NO.ST22699   DATE:AUG.10,2015

买方

THE BUYER:

TAKAMRA TRADING CORPORATION

地址

ADRESS:

82-324 OTOLI MACHI TORONTO CANADA

电话

TEL: 028-548-742

传真

FAX: 028-548-743

经买卖双方确认根据下列条款订立本合同：

THE SELLER AND THE BUYER HAVE CONFIRMED THIS CONTRACT WITH THE TERMS AND CONDITIONS STIPULATED BELOW:

货物描述 DESCRIPTIONS OF GOODS	数量 QUANTITY	单价 U/PRICE	总价 AMOUNT
HAND TOOLS		CFR TORONTO	
6PC Combination Spanner	1 000SETS	USD15.00	USD15 000.00
4PC Extra Long Hex Key Set	1 500SETS	USD18.00	USD27 000.00
TOTAL	5 000PCS		USD42 000.00

图4.8 合同

装运港:
LOADING PORT:SHANGHAI CHINA
目的港:
PORT OF DESTINATION: TORONTO CANADA
分批装运:
PARTIAL SHIPMENT:ALLOWED
转运:
TRANSSHIPMENT: ALLOWED
装运时间:
TIME OF SHIPMENT: LATEST DATE OF SHIPMENT 151031
付款条件:
PAYMENT TERMS: BY T/T
包装:
PACKING: PACKED IN 1 CARTON 50 SETS EACH TOTAL 50 CARTONS
唛头:

SHIPPING MARK: SHANGHAI

C/NO.1-50

MADE IN CHINA

THE SELLER	THE BUYER
上海工具进出口公司	TAKAMRA TRADING CORPORATION
SHANGHAI TOOL IMPORT AND EXPORT	
TRADE CORPORATION	
张大军	MIKE

图 4.8　合同（续）

参考答案

其他业务资料如下:
发票号码：TS00698　　　　　　发票日期：20150831
6PC Combination Spanner　　　毛重：18.00KGS/CTN
净重：17.00KGS/CTN　　　　　　体积：0.250CBM/CTN
4PC Extra Long Hex Key Set　　毛重：19.00KGS/CTN
净重：18.00KGS/CTN　　　　　　体积：0.250CBM/CTN

（二）审单改错题

根据给出的合同（见图 4.9）和其他业务资料审查图 4.10 所示装箱单，改正其中的错误之处。

ISSUE OF DOCUMENTARY CREDIT

ISSUING BANK: DRESDNER BANK,BREMEN GERMANY

DOC.CREDIT: IRREVOCABLE

CREDIT NUMBER: CND13789

DATE OF ISSUE: 130621

EXPIRY: DATE 130816 PLACE FINLAND

APPLICANT: W.T.G CO.

AKEKSANTERINK AUTO

P.O.BOX 30,BREMEN GERMANY

BENEFICIARY: YINZHOU TRADING CO.LTD

RM504,YINZHOU BUILIDING SHANGHAI P.R. CHINA

AMOUNT: USD18000.00

AVAILABLE WITH/BY : ANY BANK IN ADVISING COUNTRY BY NEGOTIATION

DARFT AT: 30 DAYS SIGHT FOR FULL INVOICE VALUE

PARTIAL SHIPMENT: NOT ALLOWED

TRANSHIPPMENT: ALLOWED

LOADING IN CHARGE: SHANGHAI CHINA

FOR TRANSPORT TO: BREMEN GERMANY

SHIPMENT PERIOD: AT THE LATEST JUL 30,2013

DESCRIP. OF GOODS:

4000 PCS OF BELTS LB104 USD 4.50PER PC AS PER SALES CONTRACT YZ20130501 DATED MAY 23,2013 CIF BREMEN GERMANY

DOCUMENTS REQUERED:

+ COMMERCIAL INVOICE 1 SIGNED ORIGINAL AND 5 COPIES

+ PACKING LIST IN 2 COPIES

+ FULL SET OF CLEAN ON BOARD MARINE BILLS OF LADING MADE OUT TO ORDER MARKED FREIGHT PREPAID AND NOTIFY APPLICANT (AS INDICATED ABOVE)

+ GSP CERTIFICATE OF ORIGIN FORM A CERTIFYING GOODS OF ORIGIN IN CHINA ISSUED BY COMPETENT AUTHORITIES

+ INSURANCE POLICY CERTIFICATE COVERING ALL RISKS AND WAR RISK OF PICC INCLUDING WAREHOUSE TO WAREHOUSE CLAUSE UP TO FINAL DESTINATION AT BREMEN GERMANY FOR AT LEAST 120PCT OF CIF VALUE

+ SHIPPING ADVICES MUST BE SENT TO APPLICANT WITHIN 2 DAYS AFTER SHIPMENT ADVISING NUMBER OF PACKAGES, GROSS AND NET WEIGHT, VESSEL NAME, BILL OF LADING NO. AND DATE.CONTRACT NO. VALUE.

PRESENTATION PERIOD: 16 DAYS AFTER ISSUANCE DATE OF SHIPPING DOCUMENTS

CONFERMATION: WITHOUT

INSTRUCTION: THE NEGOTIATION BANK MUST FORWARD THE DRAFTS AND ALL DOCUMENTS BY REGISTERED AIRMAIL DIRECT TO US IN TWO CONSECUTIVE LOTS UPON RECEIPT OF THE DRAFTS AND DOCUMENTS IN ORDER. WE WILL REMIT THE PROCEEDS AS INSTRUCTED BY THE NEGOTIATING BANK.

图 4.9　合同

补充业务资料如下：

包装方式：20 根装一纸箱，每箱毛重 30KGS，每箱净重 25KGS，每箱尺码 0.120CBM

唛头：W.T.G/BREMEN/NO.1-UP

发票号：YZL3453

参考答案

PACKING LIST

EXPORTER YINZHOU TRADING CO.LTD RM504,YINZHOU BUILIDING SHANGHAI P.R. CHINA			INVOICE NO. YZ20130501			
			DATE JUNE.20,2013			
TO W.T.G CO. AKEKSANTERINK AUTO P.O.BOX 30,BREMEN GERMANY			S /C NO YZ20130501			
			FROM SHANGHAI CHINA TO BREMEN GERMANY			
MARKS	DESCRIPTION OF GOODS	QTY	PKGS	NW	GW	MEAS
N/M	BELTS LB104	200CTNS	4 000PCS	@25.00KGS	@30.00KGS	@0.120CBM
				5 000.00KGS	6 000.00KGS	24.000CBM
TOTAL		200CTNS	4 000PCS	5 000.00KGS	6 000.00KGS	24.000CBM

SAY TWO HUNDRED CARTONS ONLY

鄞州贸易有限公司

YINZHOU TRADING CO.LTD

夏天林

图 4.10　装箱单

项目五

运输单据实训

知识目标

1. 理解出口货物托运的含义和程序；
2. 明确提单的种类和特点；
3. 掌握托运单、提单的实例及缮制。

能力目标

1. 能根据所给内容填制托运单；
2. 能对照信用证相关内容进行提单缮制和审核。

任务一　填制托运单

任务导航

2015 年 4 月，浙江纺织品进出口有限公司根据需要，与新加坡 CHANG LIN COMPANY 签订了一笔儿童羽绒服（children's down jacket）的出口口合同。

作为出口方的浙江纺织品进出口有限公司在备妥货物、落实信用证后，需填制出口货物托运单，委托货运代理办理订舱、报关出运等事宜。小李是浙江纺织品进出口有限公司的单证员，他必须对出口托运及托运单清楚了解，以便顺利完成货物的出口。

要求：

以单证员小李的身份，根据信用证的部分内容（见图 5.1），填制托运单。

APPLICANT: CHANG LIN COMPANY LTD., SINGAPORE

BENEFICIARY: ZHEJIANG TEXTILE IMPORT AND EXPORT CORPORATION

PORT OF SHIPMENT: SHANGHAI

PORT OF DISCHARGE: SINGAPORE

PARTIAL SHIPMENT: NOT ALLOWED

TRANSHIPMENT: NOT ALLOWED

S/S: EAST WIND V.123 FREIGHT PREPAID

MARKS&NOS.: CHANGLIN/MADE IN CHINA/NO.1-UP

L/C NO.ZJ278 DATED MAY 5, 2015

LATESET DATE OF SHIPMENT :JUN.1, 2015

EXPIRY DATE :JUN 29, 2015

DESCRIPTION OF GOODS: CHILDREN'S DOWN JACKET

UNIT PRICE: USD10.OO/PC CIF SINGAPORE

FULL SET OF CLEAN ON BOARD OCEAN BILLS OF LADING MADE OUT TO ORDER, MARKED FREIGHT PREPAID AND NOTIFY APPLICANT.

QUANTITY OF GOODS: 1000DOZS

PACKING: 30PCS/CTN

GROSS WEIGHT:@18.00KGS/CTN

NET WEIGHT:@16.OOKGS/CTN

MEASUREMENT: @(50×30×20)CM/CTN

图 5.1　信用证（部分）

知 识 准 备

一、托运流程

（一）托运的概念

托运，是指托运人或其代理人将货物委托承运人代为送至收货人或其代理人处时所办理的委托承运手续。在我国，不同的运输方式所对应的货物托运的程序和内容是不同的。

（二）海运货物的托运流程

运输货物时有一种主要的运输方式，即海运货物。一般出口企业通过海洋运输方式运输货物时，如果货物的数量不是非常大，都通过班轮运输出运。班轮运输，指的是班轮公司将船舶按事先制订的船期表，在特定航线的各既定挂靠港口之间，经常地为非特定的众多货主提供规则的、反复的货物运输服务，并按运价成本或协议运价的规定计收运费的一种营运方式。

这里介绍的海运货物的托运流程，主要是指通过班轮公司运输杂货时的托运流程，具体如图 5.2 所示。

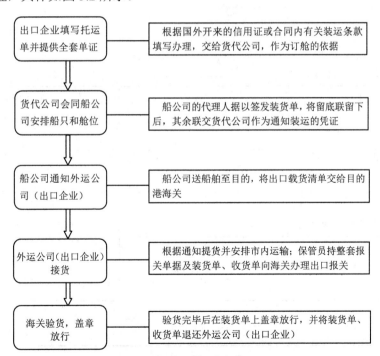

图 5.2　海运货物的托运流程

外贸单证实训

> **小 贴 士**
>
> 全球主要的班轮公司名称如下：中国远洋运输集团（COSCO）、中国海运集团公司（CHINA SHIPPING）、中国对外贸易运输公司（SINOTRANS）、马士基-海陆公司（MAERSK LINE）、地中海航运公司（MSC）、日本邮船（NYK）、韩进航运（HANJIN）、商船三井（M.O.S.K）、铁行渣华（P&O）、东方海外（OOCL）、海皇/总统轮船（NOL/APL）、长荣（EVERGREEN）、法国达飞（CMA）、德国胜利航运（SENATOR LINES）。

二、托运单的填制

托运单（shipping order 或 booking note，B/N）是指由托运人根据买卖合同和信用证的有关内容向承运人或其代理人办理货物运输的书面凭证（见图 5.3）。经承运人或其代理人对该单的签认，即表示已接受这一托运，承运人与托运人之间对货物运输的相互关系即告建立。

托运人 Shipper:				重量（千克）Weight （Kilos）	
编号 No.:		船名 S/S:			
目的港 For:					
标记及号码 Marks & Nos.	件数 Quantify	货名 Description of goods		净 Net	毛 Gross
共计件数（大写）Total Number of Packages in Writing				运费付款方式 Mode of Freight Payment	
运费计算 Freight Charges	尺码 Measurement				
备注 Remarks					

图 5.3　托运单样本

续表

抬头 Order of		可否 转船		可否 分批	
通知人 Notify		装运期		有效期	提单张数
		金额			
收货人 Consignee		银行 编号		信用 证号	

制单 月 日

图 5.3 托运单样本（续）

目前，我国各个港口使用的装货联单的组成不尽相同，但主要都是由以下各联组成：托运单及其留底；装货单，此联经船公司代理盖章后即确认货已配定船只，船上工作人员凭以收受货物；收货单（即大副收据），货物装上船后，大副在此联上签收，凭此向船公司或船公司代理换取全套正本提单。托运单内容及填制方法如表 5.1 所示。

表 5.1 托运单内容及填制方法一览

序号	项目名称	填制方法
1	托运人（Shipper or Consignor）	填写出口公司的名称和地址
2	托运单编号（No.）	填写商业发票的号码
3	目的港（For）	由出口企业按信用证的目的港填写，填写时注意重名港口的现象，一般将目的港所在国家名称一起填写在这一栏中；如果目的港是内陆城市，则应该在这一栏内填写货物卸下最后一艘海轮时的港口名称。在船方或其代理人计算运费时，是根据托运单的本项内容计算航程
4	唛头（Marks & Nos.）	信用证或买卖合同都规定了唛头，要求填写内容和形式与所规定的完全一致；如果信用证和买卖合同中没有规定唛头，可填写"N/M"（无唛头）；在选择唛头时，要充分考虑买方提货方便、买方利益和买方所在国家要求，包括商业习惯、港口规定、文化传统以及政府的有关政策
5	件数（Quantity）	托运单的最大件数指最大包装的件数；例如，出口 5 万码布，分别捆成 50 捆，填写这一栏时应是 50 捆而不是 5 万码
6	货名（Description of Goods）	对这一栏的填写允许只写大类名称或统称，应和信用证要求一致；如果同时出口几种不同的商品，应分别填写，而不允许只填写其中一种数量较大或金额较大的商品
7	重量（Weight）	重量应分别计算毛重和净重；如果一次装运的货物中有几种不同的包装材料或完全不同的货物，那么在填写这一栏时，应分别计算并填写每一种包装或每一种货物的毛重或净重，然后合计全部的毛重和净重。在计算重量时，要求使用统一的计量单位。常用的计量单位是公吨或千克
8	运费付款方式	托运单上一般不显示具体运费，只填写"运费待付"或"运费预付/已付"
9	尺码（Measurement）	该栏填写一批货的尺码总数，一般单位为立方米

续表

序号	项目名称	填制方法
10	收货人（Consignee）	在信用证支付的条件下，对收货人的规定常用以下两种表示方法： ① 记名收货人，是直接将收货人的名称、地址完整地表示出来的方法。这时，收货人一般是合同的买方。但记名收货人的单据不能直接转让，这给单据的买卖流通设下了障碍。故记名收货人的表示方法不常使用 ② 指示收货人，是将收货人以广义的形式表示出来，常用空白指示和记名指示两种表达方式。指示收货人掩饰具体的收货人的名称和地址，使单据可以转让。指示收货人的方法补充了记名收货人方法的缺陷，但也给船方通知货主提货带来了麻烦。对此由被通知人栏作出补充
11	通知（Notify）	这一栏中应填写接受船方所发货到通知的人的名称和地址。被通知人由合同的买方选择与确定，根据信用证的要求填写。有时买方确定本人为被通知人，有时将自己的代理人或其他与买方联系较为密切的人确定为被通知人。被通知人的职责是及时接受船方发出的到货通知并将该通知转告真实的收货人。被通知人无权提货
12	可否分批（Partial Shipment）	应严格按照合同和信用证条款填写。填写的内容限在"允许""不允许"两者中取其一。如果合同和信用证规定分为若干批，或对分批有进一步说明。不要将这些说明填入本栏，而应将这些说明填入"备注"类一栏中
13	可否转船（Transshipment）	填写要求与分批一致，只能在"允许"和"不允许"两者中取其一
14	装运期（Time of Shipment）	装运期的表示可以全部使用阿拉伯数字，也可以用英文与阿拉伯数字一起表示，如6/5/2015, MAY 10, 2003；装运期限还可以表示为一段时间，如2015年9～10月，或"装运期不迟于……"
15	有效期（Expiry Date）	该栏的填写一般按信用证规定，但如果装运期空白不填，这一栏也可不填
16	提单份数（Copies of B/L）	需要船公司提供的提单数应考虑信用证和合同的要求以及自己的需要，包括正本提单份数和副本提单份数。例如，要求"3 ORIGINAL BILLS OF LADING"，指3份正本提单。"ORIGNAL BILLS OF LADING IN 3"，指3份正本提单：提单副本份数=出口企业留底份数+寄单所需份数+信用证对副本提单要求的份数
17	信用证号（L/C No.）	填写此次托运货物所属的信用证号码
18	备注（Remarks）	填写信用证或合同有关运输方面的特殊要求

参考答案

▌▌ 课堂思考 ▬▬▬▬▬▬▬▬▬▬▬▬▬▬▬▬▬▬▬▬▬▬▬▬

（1）装货单（shipping order，俗称下货纸）与大副收据（mate's receipt)有什么异同？

（2）大副收据的作用是什么？

职业判断

案例资料:

2015 年 10 月,江苏华一纺织品进出口有限公司与芝加哥 POWER STAR 公司达成了一笔纺织品交易,其中由于货物有若干种,包装方式和材料完全不同:20 个托盘,20 捆布匹。

思考:

小敏是华一纺织品进出口有限公司的单证员,她应如何填写托运单中"件数"一栏?

参考答案

任务实施

单证员小李填制的海运托运单如图 5.4 所示。

托运人
Shipper: ___ZHEJIANG TEXTILE IMPORT AND EXPORT CORPORATION___

编号　　　　　　　　　　　　船名
No.: _____ S/S: ___EAST WIND V.123_____

目的港_____
Fo: ___SINGAPORE_____

标记及号码 Marks & Nos.	件数 Quantify	货名 Description of goods	重量(千克) Weight (Kilos)	
			净 Net	毛 Gross
CHANGLIN MADE IN CHINA　400CTNS OF CHILDREN'S DOWNJACKET NO.1-400			6 400.00KGS	7 200.00KGS

共计件数(大写) Total Number of Packages in Writing SAY FOUR HUNDRED CARTONS ONLY.		运费付款方式 Mode of Freight Payment FREIGHT PREPAID
运费计算 Freight Charges	尺 码 Measurement	0.012m³

图 5.4　海运托运单

备注 Remarks	1. 海关报关文件包括：发票、装箱单、报关单及出口报关委托书					
	2. 付款方式：核销单在出口后 4 周内退回					
	3. 提单电放，请速开票。					
抬头 Order of		可否 转船	NO	可否 分批	NO	
通知人　CHANG LIN COMPANY 　　　　LTD. Notify SINGAPORE		装运期	JUN.1，2015	有效期	JUN.25，2015	提单 张数　THREE
		金额	USD120 000.00			
收货人 Consignee　　TO ORDER		银行 编号		信用 证号	ZJ278	

制单　　月　　日

图 5.4　海运托运单（续）

任务再现

2015 年 2 月，青岛东越进出口有限公司与日本 TOSHU 公司签订一笔卤钨灯的交易,已于 2 月 23 日收到日本 TOSHU 公司开来的信用证(见图 5.5)。

```
BASIC HEADER      F 01 BKCHCNBJA5× 9109 069905
APPL. HEADER      O 700 1532990223 SMITJPJSA××× 4956 850438 9902231232 N
                  + SUMITOMO BANK LTD OSAKA JAPAN
(BANK NO :2632001)    + OSAKA, JAPAN
USER HEADER         BANK. PRIORITY 113:
MSG USER REF. 108: G/FO- 7752807
:MT:700---------------------ISSUE OF A DOCUMENTARY CREDIT---------------------
SEQUENCE OF TOTAL           27: 1/1
FORM OF DOCUMENTARY CREDIT   40: IRREVOCABLE
DOCUMENTARY CREDIT NUMBER   20 : G/FO-7752807
DATE OF ISSUE               31C: 150223
DATE AND PLACE OF EXPIRY     31D: 150610 QINGDAO CHINA
APPLICANT                   50 : TOSHU CHEMICAL IMPORT AND EXPORT CORPORATION
                  12-36, KYUTARO- MACHI 4- CHOME
                  CHUO- KU, OSAKA 561-8177 JAPAN
BENEFICIARY                 59 : DONGYUE    IMPORT AND EXPORT CORPORATION
                  197 ZHONGHUA ROAD, QINGDAO, CHINA
CURRENCY CODE, AMOUNT       32B: USD4380.00
```

图 5.5　日本 TOSHU 公司开来的信用证

AVAILABLE WITH… BY…   41D: ANY BANK BY NEGOTIATION

DARFTS AT…   42C: AT SIGHT

DRAWEE   42D: THE SUMITOMO BANK, LTD. OSAKA

PARTIAL SHIPMENT   43P: PROHIBITED

TRANSHIPMENT   43P: PROHIBITED

LOADING/ DISPATCH/ TAKING/ FROM: 44A: QINGDAO

FOR TRANSPRTATION TO…   44B: YOKOHAMA

LATEST DATE OF SHIPMENT   44C: 150531

DESCRPT OF GOODS/ SERVICES   45A:

   CFR YOKOHAMA

   HALOGEN LAMP (CONTRACT NO.13JA7031KL)

   ST/NO. Q'TY UNIT PRICE

   HB3   W55 1000PCS USD 1.45/PC

   HB4   W60 1000PCS USD 1.46/PC

   HB5   W65 1000PCS USD 1.47/PC

DOCUMENTS TRQUIRED

   + COMMERCIAL INVOICE IN QUINTUPLICATE

   + FULL SET LESS ONE ORIGINAL CLEAN ON BOARD OCEAN BILL OF LADING

MARKED FREIGHT PREPAID MADE OUT TO ORDER OF THE SHIPPER BLANK

ENDORSED NOTIFY APPLICANT

   + PACKING LIST IN 3 COPIES

   + G.S.P. CERTIFICATE OF ORIGIN FORM A IN 3 COPIES

PERIOD FOR PRESENTATIONS   48 : DOCUMENTS TO BE PRESENTED WITHIN

10 DAYS AFTER THE DATE OF SHIPMENT BUT WITHIN THE VALIDITY OF THE CREDIT.

CONFIRMATION INSTRUCTION   49 : WITHOUT

INSTRUCTION TO BANK   78 :

   TO NEGOTIATING BANK:

   ALL SHIPPING DOCUMENTS TO BE SENT DIRECT TO THE OPENING OFFICE BY

   REGISTERED AIRMAIL IN ONE LOT.

   UPON RECEIPT OF THE DRAFTS AND DOCUMENTS IN ORDER, WE WILL REMIT

   THE PROCEEDS TO YOUR ACCOUNT WITH THE BANK DESIGNATED BY YOU.

图 5.5   日本 TOSHU 公司开来的信用证（续）

其他业务资料如下：

NET WEIGHT:@20.00KGS/CTN

GROSS WEIGHT:@22.00KGS/CTN

PACKING: 25PCS/CTN

MEASUREMENT: 50×40×30CM/CTN

试为青岛东越进出口公司填写托运单。

参考答案

任务二 填制（审核）海运提单

任务导航

2015年1月，上海欧肯五金制品有限公司与加拿大 LIGHT SKY HOLDING LTD. 达成了一笔关于铜质拉手（COPPER HANDLE）的交易。

此批铜质拉手已于2015年3月10日由 ABC 外运公司委托中国远洋运输集团顺利装船运往温哥华。当晚，ABC 外运公司的工作人员 John 传真了一份海运提单复印件请欧肯五金制品有限公司的单证员小李审核确认（见图5.6）。

PACKING:TO BE PACKED IN PLASTIC BAGS,SIX BAGS IN A CARTON

TOTAL:950 CARTONS

UNIT PRICE: U.S.D11.40 PER CARTON CIF VANCOUVER

TOYAL AMOUNT: U.S.D10830.00

SHIPPING PER S,S"DEWEI V.213"FROM HUANGPU TO VANCOUVER B.C.,

MARKS: W.F.L.\VANCOUVER\C\NO.:1-UP

B\L DATE:20150310   B\L NO.6180

GROSS WEIGHT:17138 KGS NET WEIGHT:16188KGS MEAS:18.365CBM

NEGOTIATING BANK:BANK OF CHINA,HUNAN BRANCH

S\C NO.:P.O.2007-018 INV.DATE: 20150201 INV.NO.:CFF-016

CARRIER:ABC CO.,LTD,FOR THE AGENT,COSCO AS THE CARRIER

Shipper SHANGHAI OUKEN HARDWARE PRODUCTS IMPORT & EXPORT CORPORATION 38 WUYI RD.,SHANGHAI, CHINA	COSCO B/L NO. 中国远洋运输公司 CHINA OCEAN SHIPPING COMPANY
Consignee TO ORDER	Original Bill of Lading
Notify Party LIGHT SKY HOLDING LTD. RUA DE GREENLAND STREET,68-A 1260-297 WELL D.COQUITLAM,B.C. CANADA	

Pre-carriage by	Place of receipt	Ocean Vessel Voy. No. DEWEI V.213	port of loading SHANGHAI, CHINA	Port of Discharge VANCOUVER, CANADA	place of Delivery

图5.6 提单复印件

Container No.	Seal No. Marks & Nos. N/M	No. of Containers of Pkgs 950 CARTONS	Kind of Packages; Description of Goods	Gross Weight	Measurement
			Final Destination for the Goods-not the Ship		
			COPPER HANDLE FREIGHT PREPAID ON BOARD : MAR 10, 2003	17 138.00 KGS	18.365 CBM

TOTAL NUMBER OF CONTAINERS OR PACKAGES (IN WORDS)	SAY NINE HUNDRED AND FIFTY CARTONS ONLY				
FREIGHT & CHARGES	Revenue Tons	Rate	Per	Prepaid	Collect

Ex.Rate:	Prepaid at	Payable at	Place and date of Issue SHANGHAI, CHINA MAR. 10, 2006
	Total Prepaid	No. of Original B(S)L	Signed for the Carrier
Date	By_____		

图 5.6 提单复印件（续）

要求：

请帮助上海欧肯五金制品有限公司的单证员小李，根据所给的信用证部分内容（见图 5.7），认真审核修改这份有误的海运提单，缮制一份正确的海运提单。

```
:MT:700    -------------ISSUE A DOCUMENTARY CREDIT ---------------
FORM OF CREDIT              40A:IRREVOCABLE
DOC. CREDIT NUMBER          20:078230CDI1117LC
DATE OF ISSUE              31C:20150118
DATE AND PLACE OF EXPIRY    31D:20150310 CHINA
APPLICANT                  50: LIGHT SKY HOLDING LTD.
                               RUA DE GREENLAND STREET,68-A
                               1260-297 WELL D.COQUITLAM,
                               B.C. CANADA
BENEFICIARY                59: SHANGHAI OUKEN HARDWARE PRODUCTS IMPORT & EXPORT
                               CORPORATION
                           38: WUYI RD.,SHANGHAI, CHINA
```

图 5.7 信用证（部分）

CURRENCY CODE AND AMOUNT	32B: USD10830.00
AVAILABLE WITH…BY…	41A:ANY BANK IN CHINA BY NEGOTIATION
PARTIAL SHIPMENT	43P:PROHIBITED
TRANSSHIPENT	43T:PERMITTED
LODING\DISPATCH \FROM	48B:VANCOUVER B.C.
FOR TRANSPOTATION TO	44C:20150310
LATEST DATE OF SHIPMENT	45A: COPPER HANDLE AS PER P\I NO.CF07018
DESCRIPTION OF	44A:MAIN CHINESE PORT
DOCS REQUIERD:	46A:

+ MANUALLY SIGNED COMMERCIAL INVOICE ONE ORIGINAL AND FOUR COPIES CERTIFYING GOODS ARE OF CHINESE ORIGIN AND INDICATING P\I NO.

+FULL SET(3\3) OF CLEAN ON BOARD OCEAN BILLS OF LADING, MADE OUT TO ORDER OF SHIPPER, BLANK INDORSED NOTIFYING APPLICANT, STATING FREIGHT PREPAID OR COLLECT.

+SHIPPING ADVICE SHOULD BE SENT BY FAX TO APPLICANT IN FORMING VESSEL'S NAME AND VOY.NO.,GR.WT, MEAS, PACKING, TOTAL AMOUNT AND ETD.

图 5.7 信用证（部分）（续）

一、海运提单简介

（一）海运提单的概念

海运提单是由船长或承运人（或其代理人）签发的，证明收到特定货物，允诺将货物运至指定目的地并交付收货人的书面凭证。

（二）海运提单的性质

海运提单的性质表现为以下几个方面。

（1）海运提单是承运人或其代理人签发的货物收据（receipt for the goods），证明承运人已经按海运提单所列内容收到货物。

（2）海运提单是物权凭证（documents of title），即海运提单的合法持有人凭此可在目的港向轮船公司提取货物，也可在载货船舶到达目的港之前，通过转让海运提单而转移货物所有权；或凭此在银行办理抵押贷款。

（3）海运提单是运输合同的证明（evidence of contract of carrier），是承运人与托运人处理双方在运输中的权利和义务问题的主要依据。

二、海运提单的种类

（一）根据货物是否已装船分类

根据货物是否已装船，海运提单可分为已装船提单和备运提单。

1. 已装船提单

已装船提单（shipping B/L 或 on board B/L）是指提单上载明货物"已由某轮船装运"的字样和装运日期的提单。

该类提单是承运人或船长或其代理人将货物装上指定船只后凭大副收据（收货单）向托运人所签发的提单。

2. 备运提单

备运提单（received for shipment B/L）又称收讫待运提单，指承运人或船长或其代理人收妥所托运的货物，待装船期间签发给托运人的提单。

该类提单上一般无载货的具体船名亦无装船的具体日期，银行一般不予接受。

待运的货物一旦装运后，在备运提单上加上"已装船"字样，这样的备运提单就成了"已装运提单"。

（二）根据对货物外表状况有无不良批注分类

根据货物是否已装船，海运提单可分为清洁提单和不清洁提单。

1. 清洁提单

清洁提单（clean B/L）指货物装船时表面状况良好，承运人签发提单时未加注有任何货损、包装有缺陷的条文或批注的提单。

如信用证规定"清洁已装船"提单，那么提单上不出现"清洁"字样也是可以接受的。

2. 不清洁提单

不清洁提单（unclean B/L）指承运人或他们的代理人收到货物后，在所签发的提单上明确声明（或在正面加注了）货物存在缺陷或包装破损的条文或批注的提单。

如提单上有类似"unprotected machinery""wet cartons""damaged Crafts"的批注，银行一般不能接受。

（三）根据收货人抬头不同分类

海运提单可分为记名提单、不记名提单和指示提单。

1. 记名提单

记名提单（straight B/L）是指在提单的"收货人"栏内具体写明了收货人名称的提单。

2. 不记名提单

不记名提单（open B/L 或 bearer B/L）是指记载应向提单持有人交付货物的提单，又称空白提单或来人提单，在提单"收货人"栏内不填明收货人或指示人的名称的提单，这种提单在国际贸易中很少应用。

3. 指示提单

指示提单（order B/L）是指按照记名人（named person）的指示或非记名人（to order）的指示交货的提单。

在提单的"收货人"栏内填"to order"（凭指示）或"to order of ××"（凭某人指示）。

该类提单经背书后便可流通转让，因此指示提单在国际贸易中经常被贸易商所采用。指示提单又可分为记名式与不记名式两种。

（四）根据运输过程中是否转船分类

海运提单可分为直达提单和转船提单。

1. 直达提单

直达提单（direct B/L）是指承运人、船长或其代理人所签发的，货物自装运港装船后，中途不换船只而直驶卸货港的全程运输提单。

2. 转船提单

转船提单（transshipment B/L）是指船舶自装运港装货后，不直接驶往卸货港而在中途的某一港口转船后再将货物运至指定卸货港的提单。在上述情况下，由第一程承运人或船长或其代理人所签发的包括全程运输的提单为转船提单。

（五）根据提单格式不同分类

海运提单可分为全式提单和略式提单。

1. 全式提单

全式提单（long form B/L）也称繁式提单，提单的正面各项目齐全，背面详细载明承运人和托运人的权利、义务的详细条款。全式提单在实务中运用较广。

2. 略式提单

略式提单（short form B/L）也称简式提单，该类提单仅保留全式提单下面的必要项目，而略去提单背面全部条款，或仅摘其中重要条款扼要列出。

（六）根据签发提单的时间分类

海运提单可分为倒签提单、顺签提单、预借提单、过期提单。

1. 倒签提单

倒签提单（anti-dated B/L）是指承运人或其代理人应托运人的要求，在货物装船完毕后，以早于货物实际装船日期为签发日期的提单。

2. 顺签提单

顺签提单（post-date B/L）是指在货物装船完毕后，应托运人的要求，由承运人或其代理人签发的提单。但是该提单上记载的签发日期晚于货物实际装船完毕的日期。

3. 预借提单

预借提单（advanced B/L）是指货物尚未装船或尚未装船完毕的情况下，信用证规定的结汇期（即信用证的有效期）即将届满，托运人为了能及时结汇，而要求承运人或其代理人提前签发的已装船清洁提单，即托运人为了能及时结汇而从承运人那里借用的已装船清洁提单。

4. 过期提单

过期提单（stale B/L）有两种含义，一是指出口商在装船后延滞过久才交到银行议付的提单；二是指提单晚于货物到达目的港，这种提单也称为过期提单。

三、关于海运提单的背书

背书是实现提单转让的一种手段。提单经过背书后，提单本身所代表的物权便产生变化，转让提单，也就是转让了货物所有权。

（一）背书的类型

背书可分为空白背书和记名背书。

（1）空白背书：当"收货人"一栏填写"凭指示"（to order）时，背书人仅在提单的背面签字盖章，而不注明被背书人的名称。

（2）记名背书：当"收货人"一栏填写"记名指示"（to ×××'s order 或 to order of ×××）时，由记名的一方背书，背书人除在提单的背面签字盖章以外，还须列明被背书人的名称。

（二）背书的方法

《关于审核跟单信用证项下单据的国际标准银行实务》（以下简称《ISBP》）第85段规定，如果提单做成指示式抬头或做成凭托运人指示式抬头，则该提单必须由托运人背书。代理人代表托运人所作的背书是可以接受的。

（1）空白背书：书写背书人的名称、地址。

（2）记名背书：既书写背书人的名称、地址，又书写被背书人的名称和地址。

四、海运提单的填制

海运提单样本如图5.8所示。

Shipper		B/L NO.
		COSCO
Consignee		中国远洋运输（集团）总公司
		CHINA OCEAN SHIPPING (GROUP) CO.
Notify Party		ORIGINAL
		COMBINED TRANPORT BILL OF LADING
Place of Receipt	Ocean Vessel	
Voyage NO.	Port of Loading	
Port of Discharge	Place of Delivery	
Marks Nos.&Kinds of Pkgs Description of Goods G.W.（kg）Meas（m³）		
TOTAL NUMBER OF CONTAINERS OR PACKAGES（IN WORDS）		

图5.8　海运提单样本

Freight & Charges	Revenue TONS	Rate	Per	Prepaid	Collect
Prepaid at	Payable at		Place and Date of Issue		
Total Prepaid	Number of Original B(S)L				
Loading on Board The Vessel Date			By		

图 5.8　海运提单样本（续）

海运提单内容及填制方法如表 5.2 所示。

表 5.2　海运提单内容及填制方法一览

项目名称	填制方法
托运人（Shipper）	托运人是指委托运输的人，在国际贸易中是合同的卖方。一般情况下，如果信用证没有特别规定，提单发货人就是信用证下的受益人。根据《跟单信用证统一惯例》（UCP500）第 31 条的规定，除非信用证特别规定不得以第三方为发货人，否则提单允许由受益人以外的第三方作为发货人。在托收结算方式下，提单的发货人可以是发票的签发人也可以是发票的签发人以外的第三方
收货人（Consignee）	此栏按照信用证规定，"按不同的抬头形式"分别填制。例如，信用证或合同对提单的要求如下： 1. FULL SET OF B/L CONSIGNED TO ABC CO. 2. FULL SET OF B/L MADE OUT TO ORDER 3. B/L ISSUED TO ORDER OF APPLICANT 4. FULL SET OF B/L MADE OUT TO ORDER OF SHIPPER 提单"收货人"填写如下： 1. CONSIGNED TO ABC CO. 2. TO ORDER 3. TO ORDER OF ABC CO. 4. TO ORDER OF SHIPPER
被通知人（Notify Party；Notify；Addressed to）	第一种情况：信用证已规定该栏填写内容，根据信用证规定填写 第二种情况：信用证要求两个或两个以上的公司为被通知人，则两个或两个以上的公司都要填写 第三种情况：来证没有具体说明被通知人，正本此栏留白（即不填）
前段运输（Pre-carriage by）	第一种情况：运输过程中有转运，在这一栏中填写第一程船的名称 第二种情况：直达运输。空白这一栏（即不填） 第三种情况：货物用驳船拉到大船上，然后才到达目的港（不构成转运），在提单中的"Pre-carriage by"这栏用"Lighter"字样填入此栏目。注意：在日本、美国，则把驳船船号写出来，不能只写 Lighter

续表

项目名称	填制方法
收货地点（Place of Receipt）	如果货物需转运，填写收货的港口名称或地点，即转运港的名称或地点；如果货物不需转运，空白这一栏不填
海运船只、航次（Ocean Vessel、Voyage No）	如果货物需转运，填写第二程船的船名；如果货物不需转运，填写第一程船的船名
装运港（Port of Loading）	如果货物需转运，填写装运港/中转港名称。如：货物在广州装运，需在香港转船，则在此栏填写"GUANGZHOU/ HONGKONG"。如果直达运输，则填写装运港名称
卸货港（Port of Discharge）	直达运输，填写卸货港（指目的港）名称。若货物须转运，装运港后面没有注明中转港，填目的港 W/T 转运港，如"SINGAPORE W/T HONGKONG"（目的港新加坡，在香港转船）；若货运目的港装运内陆某地，或利用邻国港口过境，填目的港"IN TRANSIT TO 某地"，如 KUWAIT IN TRANSIT SAUDI ARABIA（目的港科威特转运沙特阿拉伯）
交货地点（Place of Delivery）	填写最终目的地名称。如果货物的目的地就是目的港的话，空白该栏
集装箱号（Container No.）	填写集装箱箱号（有关资料里面查找）
封箱号和唛头（Seal No. Marks & Nos.）	填写集装箱封箱号和唛头（有关资料里面查找）。注意：以上两个项目通常汇成一个项目，填写的时候要逐一填齐资料
商品描述（Description of Goods）	商品描述使用文字：在没有特别说明时全部使用英文。若来证要求使用中文填写时，应遵守来证规定，用中文填写
数量（No. of Package /Nos. Kinds of Pkgs.）	指本海运提单项下的商品总包装件数： ① 对于包装货物，本栏应注明包装数量和单位，例如"1000 BALES"，"250 DRUMS"等。提单下面应加大写数量，大小写数量应一致 ② 如是散装货，如煤炭、原油等，此栏可加"IN BULK"，数量无须加大写 ③ 如是裸装货物，应加件数，如一台机器或一辆汽车，填"1 UNIT"，两架飞机应填"TWO PLANES"，100 头牛应填"100 HEADS"等，并加大写数量 ④ 如是托盘装运，此栏应填托盘数量，同时用括号加注货物的包装件数，如"5 PALLETS（60 CARTONS）"。提单内还应加注"SHIPPER'S LOAD AND COUNT" ⑤ 如是两种或多种包装，如"5 CARTONS"、"10 BALES"、"12 CASES"等，件数栏内要逐项列明，同时下面应注明合计数量，如上述包装数量可合计为"27 PACKAGES"，在大写栏内应加大写合计数量 ⑥ 如是集装箱运输，由托运人装箱的整箱货可只注集装箱数量，如"2 CONTAINERS"等。只要海关已对集装箱封箱，承运人对箱内的内容和数量不负责任，提单内应加注"SHIPPER'S LOAD & COUNT"（托运人装货并计数）。如须注明集装箱箱内小件数量时，数量前应加"SAID TO CONTAIN…"
毛重（Gross Weight）	填写承运货物得总毛重，该数据是船公司计算运费的根据之一
尺码（Measurement）	填写承运货物得总尺码

续表

项目名称	填制方法
运费缴付方式	除非信用证有特别要求，几乎所有海运提单都不填写以下运费的数额，只需要填写"FREIGHT & CHARGES"这一项： 运费已付——FREIGHT PAID； 运费预付——FREIGHT PREPAID； 运费到付——FREIGHT PAYABLE AT DESTINATION； 运费待付——FREIGHT COLLECT； 如信用证规定加注运费，则需填运费总金额；如信用证规定要填写详细运费，则需根据实际产生的费用如实填写各项目
签发地点和时间（Place and Date of Issue）	签发时间：填（有关资料中）的提单日期 签发地点：填走货地点
签发地点和时间（Place and Date of Issue）	实务中，填写货物实际装运的时间或已经接受船方、船代理的有关方面监管的时间
正本的签发份数 No. of Original B(S)/L	承运人一般签发海运提单正本两份，也可应收货人的要求签发两份以上。签发的份数，应用大写数字（TWO、THREE）在栏内标明
有效的签章（Stamp & Signature）	海运提单必须经装载船只的船长签字才能生效，在没有规定非船长签字不可的情况下，船方代理可以代办。按照上述规定，提单签字应根据签字人的不同情况批注不同内容： ① 承运人签字。如果承运人为 COSCO，则提单签字处显示： COSCO （承运人签字）As Carrier（或 The Carrier） ② 代理人签字。如果承运人为 COSCO，代理人为 ABC SHIPPING CO.，则提单签字处显示： ABC SHIPPING CO. （代理人签字）As agent for the Carrier COSCO ③ 代表船长签署提单（船长姓名为 XYZ）。如果船长姓名为 XYZ，代理人为 ABC SHIPPING CO.，则提单签字处显示： ABC SHIPPING CO. （代理人签字）As agent for the Master XYZ ④ 船长签字。如果承运人为 COSCO，则提单签字处显示： COSCO（不注或注船名） （船长签字）As Master 或 The Master
已装船批注	如果提单上没有事先印制"SHIPPED ON BOARD"等类似意思的字眼，制单时，应加注"SHIPPED ON BOARD"和实际装船日期。实务中，常采用盖"SHIPPED ON BOARD"印章加注日期处理

▌ 课堂思考 ▌

海运提单在国际贸易中具有非常重要的地位和作用，谁控制了提单，

参考答案

谁就拥有了该批货物的所有权。然而，在国际贸易中，提单的使用也存在种种风险，如倒签提单和预借提单有何风险？又该如何预付？

小 贴 士

当填制好的提单需要修改或变更时，可以进行相应的更改，但必须经过证实。《ISBP》第94段规定，提单上的修正和变更必须经过证实。证实从表面看来必须是由承运人、船长或其代理人所为（该代理人与可以出具或签署提单的代理人不同），只要表明其作为承运人或船长的代理人身份。

《ISBP》第95段又规定，对于正本可能已做的任何修改或变更，不可转让提单副本无须任何签字或证实。

职业判断

案例资料：

2015年8月众良棉麻制品进出口有限公司与西班牙的一家纺织品公司达成了一笔交易，在收到对方开来的信用证中有这一条款"ADDITIONAL CONDITIONS 47A:1/3 ORIGINAL B/L MUST SENT TO THE APPLICANT DIRECTLY AFTER SHIPPMENT"，要求2/3提单提交银行，1/3正本提单在装船后直接寄送给开证申请人。

参考答案

思考：

此信用证中的1/3提单条款对出口商来说安全吗？试说明理由。

单证员小李对收到的提单复印件进行审核并作出修改，如图5.9所示。

Shipper SHANGHAI OUKEN HARDWARE PRODUCTS IMPORT & EXPORT CORPORATION 38 WUYI RD.,SHANGHAI, CHINA	COSCO　　B/L NO. 6180 中国远洋运输公司 **CHINA OCEAN SHIPPING COMPANY**

图5.9　修改后的海运提单

Consignee 　　TO ORDER OF SHIPPER					
Notify Party LIGHT SKY HOLDING LTD. RUA DE GREENLAND STREET,68-A 1260-297 WELL D.COQUITLAM,B.C. CANADA					
Pre-carriage by	Place of Receipt	Ocean Vessel Voy. No. DEWEI V.213	port of loading SHANGHAI, CHINA	Port of Discharge VANCOUVER, CANADA	place of Delivery
Container No.	Seal No. Marks & Nos. W.F.L. VANCOUVER C/NO.:1-950	No. of containers Of Pkgs 950 CARTONS	Kind of Packages; Description of Goods Final Destination for the goods-not the ship COPPER HANDLE FREIGHT PREPAID ON BOARD: MAR 10, 2003	Gross Weight 17 138.00 KGS	Measurement 18.365m^3
TOTAL NUMBER OF CONTAINERS OR PACKAGES（IN WORDS）			SAY NINE HUNDRED AND FIFTY CARTONS ONLY		
FREIGHT & CHARGES	Revenue Tons		Rate	Per	Prepaid	Collect

(table continues)

FREIGHT & CHARGES	Revenue Tons	Rate	Per	Prepaid	Collect
			ON BOARD		
Ex.Rate:	Prepaid at		Payable at	Place and date of Issue SHANGHAI, CHINA　MAR. 10, 2006	
	Total Prepaid		No. of Original B(s)L THREE（3）	Signed for the Carrier COSCO AS THE CARRIER	
Date	By_____				

图 5.9　修改后的海运提单（续）

任务再现

2015 年 2 月，青岛岳东家纺针织品出口公司与日本 SHUTO 公司签订一笔男士 T 恤衫的交易合同，已于 2 月 25 日收到日本 SHUTO 公司开来的信用证（见图 5.10）。

Issue of Documentary Credit

BASIC HEADER   F 01 BKCHCNBJA5X 9109 069905

APPL. HEADER   O 700 1332990223 SMITJPJSAXXX 4956 850438 9902231232 N

             + SUMITOMO BANK LTD OSAKA JAPAN

             (BANK NO :2632001)   + OSAKA, JAPAN

USER HEADER   BANK. PRIORITY 113:

             MSG USER REF. 108: G/FO- 7752807

:MT:700--------------------ISSUE OF A DOCUMENTARY CREDIT--------------------

SEQUENCE OF TOTAL	27: 1/1
FORM OF DOCUMENTARY CREDIT	40: IRREVOCABLE
DOCUMENTARY CREDIT NUMBER	20 : G/FO-7752807
DATE OF ISSUE	31C: 150225
DATE AND PLACE OF EXPIRY	31D: 150610QINGDAO CHINA
APPLICANT	50 : SHUTO CORPORATION OSALM
	12-36, KYUTARO- MACHI 4- CHOME
	CHUO- KU, OSAKA 561-8177 JAPAN
BENEFICIARY	59 : YUEDONG KNITWEARS AND HOMETEX-
	TILESIMPORT AND EXPORT CORPORATION
	197 ZHONGHUA ROAD, QINGDAO, CHINA
CURRENCY CODE, AMOUNT	32B: USD201 780.00
AVAILABLE WITH... BY...	41D: ANY BANK
	BY NEGOTIATION
DARFTS AT...	42C: AT SIGHT
DRAWEE	42D: THE SUMITOMO BANK, LTD. OSAKA
PARTIAL SHIPMENT	43P: ALLOWED
TRANSHIPMENT	43P: PROHIBITED
LOADING/ DISPATCH/ TAKING/ FROM	44A: QINGDAO
FOR TRANS[PRTATION TO...	44B: YOKOHAMA
LATEST DATE OF SHIPMENT	44C: 150531
DESCRPT OF GOODS/ SERVICES	45A:

CIF YOKOHAMA

MAN'S SHIRT(CONTRACT NO.99JA7031KL)

ST/NO. Q'TY UNIT PRICE

71-800 67 200PCS USD 1.43/PC

71-801 48 000PCS USD 1.46/PC

71-802 27 600PCS USD 1.29/PC

DOCUMENTS REQUIRED

图 5.10 日本 SHUTO 公司开来的信用证

```
+ COMMERCIAL INVOICE IN QUINTUPLICATE.
+ FULL SET LESS ONE ORIGINAL CLEAN ON BOARD OCEAN BILL OF LADING MARKED FREIGHT PREPAID
  MADE OUT TO ORDER OF THE SHIPPER BLANK ENDORSED NOTIFY APPLICANT.
+ PACKING LIST IN 3 COPIES
ADDITIONAL CONDITIONS          47A:
THIS CREDIT IS SUBJECT TO UNIFORM CUSTOMS AND PRACTICE FOR DOCUMENTARY CREDITS(1993
REVISION) I. C. C. PUBLICATION NO. 500.
T. T. REIMBURSEMTNT: UNACCEPTABLE
X) THE GOODS SHOULD BE CONTAINERIZED.
X) CLEAN ON BOARD COMBINED TRANSPORT B/L OF ITOCHU EXPRESS CO. LTD
IS ACCEPTABLE.
CHARGES                        71B: ALL BANKING CHARGES AND COMMIS SIONS INCLUDING REIMBUR
                               SEMENT COMM. OUTSIDE JAPAN ARE FOR A/C OF BENEFICIARY.
PERIOD FOR PRESENTATIONS       48 : DOCUMENTS TO BE PRESENTED WITHIN 10 DAYS AFTER THE DATE
                               OF SHIPMENT BUT WITHIN THE VALIDITY OF THE CREDIT.
CONFIRMATION INSTRUCTION       49 : WITHOUT
TRAILER
MAC: 51EF556 CHK: D3A3848E00C
```

图 5.10 日本 SHUTO 公司开来的信用证（续）

补充业务资料如下：

（1）SHIPPED BY S.S. HONG V26 ON MAY 28TH, 2015

（2）B/L NO. 9905358

（3）C/S NO. : TIT49087/R8907677

（4）G.W.: 35KGS/CTN   N.W.: 30KGS/CTN

MEASURMENT: 20×30×35CM/CTN

（5）PACKING:100PCS/CTN

（6）SHIPPING MARKS:

    F.V.

    492-12

    F.V.

    492-13

    F.V.

    492-14

（7）法定代表人：Make   单证员：Jack

（8）提单签发单位：CHINA OCEAN SHIPPING AGENCY QINGDAO CO., LTD.

（9）提单签发人：Sue

试为青岛岳东家纺针织品出口公司审核已填制好的提单（见图5.11），
如有不符之处提出并修改。

Shipper DONGYUE KNITWEARS AND HOMETEX- TILESIMPORT AND EXPORT CORPORATION 197 ZHONGHUA ROAD, QINGDAO, CHINA				COSCO B/L NO. 9905358 中国远洋运输公司 CHINA OCEAN SHIPPING COMPANY	
Consignee TO ORDER					
Notify Party TOSHU CORPORATION OSALM 12-36, KYUTARO- MACHI 4- CHOME CHUO- KU, OSAKA 561-8177 JAPAN				**Original Bill of Lading**	
Pre-carriage by		Place of Receipt			
Ocean Vessel S.S. HONG	Voy. No. V26	Port of Loading QINGDAO,CHINA			
Port of Discharge		Place of Delivery **JAPAN**			

Container No.	Seal No. Marks & Nos.	No. of Containers Of P kgs	Kind of Packages; Description of Goods	Gross Weight	Measurement
TIT49087/R8 907677	F.V. 492-12 F.V. 492-13 F.V. 492-14	**1428CTNS**	Final Destination for the goods- not the ship MAN'S SHIRT FREIGHT PREPAID	42 840KGS	29.988CBM

TOTAL NUMBER OF CONTAINERS
OR PACKAGES (IN WORDS)   SAY TWO HUNDRED PAPERSACKS ONLY

FREIGHT & CHARGES	Revenue Tons	Rate	Per	**ON BOARD**	Prepaid	Collect

Ex.Rate:	Prepaid at	Payable at	Place and date of Issue QINGDAO MAY 28TH, 2015
	Total Prepaid	No. of Original B(s)L	Signed for the Carrier

Date	By _____	CHINA OCEAN SHIPPING AGENCY QINGDAO CO., LTD. **SUE** AS AGENT FOR THE CARRIER, COSCO

图 5.11   海运提单

参考答案

任务三 填制（核对）国际航空运单

任务导航

2015 年 3 月，世格贸易公司（DESUN TRADING CO. LTD.）与 NEO GENERAL TRADING CO.达成了关于罐装蘑菇（CANNED MUSHROOM）的贸易。

对于此批货物，世格贸易公司已委托货运代理向某航空公司订机配舱，于 4 月 7 日从南京起运，航班为 FX0910。小季是该航空公司新进员工，他必须掌握国际航空运单的填制方法，以便顺利完成货物的出运。

DOC. CREDIT NUMBER	*20: 0011LC123756
DATE OF ISSUE	31C:150322
DATE/PLACE EXP.	*31D:
	DATE 150515 PLACE CHINA
APPLICANT	*50: NEO GENERAL TRADING CO.
	P.O. BOX 99552, RIYADH 22766, KSA
BENEFICIARY	*59: DESUN TRADING CO., LTD.
	HUARONG MANSION RM2901 NO.85 GUANJIAQIAO, NANJING 210005, CHINA
AMOUNT	*32B: CURRENCY USD AMOUNT 13 260,
AVAILABLE WITH/BY	*41D: ANY BANK IN CHINA,
	BY NEGOTIATION
PARTIAL SHIPMTS	43P: NOT ALLOWED
TRANSSHIPMENT	43T: NOT ALLOWED
LOADING ON BRD	44A: NANJING, CHINA
	44B: DAMMAM PORT, SAUDI ARABIA
LATEST SHIPMENT	44C: 150430
GOODS DESCRIPT.	45A: ABOUT 1 700 CARTONS CANNED MUSHROOM PIECES & STEMS 24 TINS X 425 GRAMS NET WEIGHT (D.W. 227 GRAMS) AT USD7.80 PER CARTON.
DOCS REQUIRED	46A: DOCUMENTS REQUIRED:
	+ SIGNED COMMERCIAL INVOICE IN TRIPLICATE ORIGINAL AND MUST SHOW BREAK DOWN OF THE AMOUNT AS FOLLOWS: FOB VALUE, FREIGHT CHARGES AND TOTAL AMOUNT C AND F.
	+ FULL SET AIR WAYBILL EVIDENCING NEO GENERAL TRADING CO., MARKED FREIGHT PREPAID.
	+ INSPECTION (HEALTH) CERTIFICATE FROM C.I.Q. (ENTRY-EXIT INSPECTION AND QUARANTINE OF THE PEOOPLES REP. OF CHINA) STATING GOODS ARE FIT FOR HUMAN BEING.
	+ THE PRODUCTION DATE OF THE GOODS NOT TO BE EARLIER THAN HALF MONTH AT TIME OF SHIPMENT. BENEFICIARY MUST CERTIFY THE SAME.

图 5.12 信用证（部分）

其他业务资料如下：

商品毛重：19074.44KGS　体积：36.85CBM

Rate Class 运价分类代号：N Rate/Charge 费率：20.61　Other Charge 其他费用：AWC（运单费）50.00

要求：

以小季的身份，根据信用证部分内容（见图5.12）及相关资料，填制航空运单。

知识准备

一、国际航空运单简介

航空运单（air waybill，AWB），是航空运输公司及其代理人签发给发货人表示已收妥货物并接受托运的货物收据。航空运单不是物权凭证，不能通过背书转移货物的所有权。航空运单不可转让，持有航空运单并不能说明可以对货物要求所有权。

（一）航空运单的作用

1. 航空运单是航空运输承运人与托运人之间的运输合同

海运提单只是运输合同的证明，它本身不是运输合同。但航空运单不仅是航空运输合同的证明，而且航空运单本身就是托运人与航空运输承运人之间签订的货物运输合同。

2. 航空运单是航空公司或其代理人收运货物的证明文件

在托运人将货物托运后，航空公司或其代理人就会将其中一份交给托运人，作为已按航空运单所列内容收妥货物的证明。

3. 航空运单是承运人核收运费的依据

航空运单分别记载着属于收货人负担的费用，属于应支付给承运人的费用和应支付给代理人的费用，并详细列明费用的种类、金额，因此可作为运费账单和发票。承运人往往也将其中的承运人联作为记账凭证。

4. 航空运单是进出口货物办理清关的证明文件

当货物通过航空运输，出口报关时必须提交航空运单。在货物到达目的地机场进行进口报关时，海关也是根据航空运单查验放行货物的。

5. 航空运单是承运人处理货物运输过程情况的依据

航空运单中的一份随货同行，用于记载有关该票货物发送、转运、交付的事项，是承运人处理货物运输过程情况的依据。

6. 航空运单是收货人核收货物的依据

航空运单的正本一式三份，其中一份交给托运人，是承运人或其代理人接收货物的依据；第二份由承运人留存，作为记账凭证；最后一份随货同行，用于记载有关该票货物发送、转运、交付的事项，在货物到达目的地时，交付给收货人作为核收货物的依据。

（二）航空运单的种类

航空运单可分为出票航空公司（issue carrier）标志的航空货运单和无承运人任何标志的中性货运单两种。

二、国际航空运单的填制

航空运单与海运提单类似，也有正面、背面条款之分，不同的航空公司也会有自己独特的航空运单格式。但各航空公司所使用的航空运单大多借鉴国际航空运输协会（International Air Transport Association，IATA）所推荐的标准格式，差别并不大，在此介绍一下主要栏的填制。

国际航空运单样本如图 5.13 所示，其内容及填制方法如表 5.3 所示。

航空货运单

999				

NOT NEGOTIABLE **中国民航**　　　**CAAC**

Shipper's Name and Address | Shipper's Account Number

AIR WAYBILL AIR CONSIGNMENT NOTE
ISSUED BY: THE CIVIL AVIATION ADMINIASTRATION OF CHINA
BEIJING CHINA
Copies 1, 2 and 3 of this Air Waybill are originals and have the same validity.

Consignee's Name and Address | Consignee's Account Number

It is agreed that the goods described herein are accepted in apparent good order and condition （except as noted) for carriage SUBJECT TO THE CONDITIONS OF CONTRACT ON THE REVERSE HEREOF. THE SHIPPER'S ATTENTION IS DRAWN TO THE NOTICE CONCERNINC CARRIER'S LIMITATION OF LIABILITY. Shipper may increase such limitation of liability by declaring a higher value for carriage and paying a supplemental charge if required.

ISSUING CARRIER MAINTAINS CARGO ACCIDENT LIABILITY INSURANCE

Issuing Carrier's Agent Name and City | Accounting Information

Agent's IATA Code | Account No.

Airport of Departure(Addr. of First Carrier) and Requested Routing

to	By First Carrier \ Routing and Destination /	to	by	to	by	Currency	CHGS Code	WT/NAL		Other		Declared Value for Carriage	Declared Value for Customs
								PPD	COLL	PPD	COLL		

Airport Destination	Flight/Date	For Carrier Use only	Flight/Date	Amount of Insurance	INSURANCE if carrier offers insurance, and such insurance is requested in accordance with conditions on reverse here of, indicate amount to be insured in figure in box marked amount of insurance.

Handling Information

(for USA only)Those commodities licensed by U.S. for ultimate destination...Diversion contray to U.S. law is prohibited.

No. of Pieces RCP	Gross Weight	Kg Lb	Rate Class Commodity Item No.	Chargeable Weight	Rate / Charge	Total	Nature and Quantity of Goods (incl. Dimensions or Volume)

Prepaid \ Weight Charge / Collect	Other Charges
Valuation Charge	AWA:50
Tax	

	Total Other Charges Due Agent	Shipper certifies that the particulars on the face hereof are correct and that insofar as any part of the consignment contains dangerous goods, such part is properly described by name and is in proper condition for carriage by air according to the applicable Dangerous Goods Regulations.
50	Total Other Charges Due Carrier	

....
Signature of Shipper or his Agent

Total Prepaid	Total Collect	
Currecncy Conversion Rates	CC Charges in Dest. Currency	Executed on (date)　　at (place)　　Signature of Issuing carrier or its Agent
For Carrier's use only at Destination	Charges at Destination	Total Collect Charges

999

图 5.13　国际航空运单样本

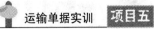

表5.3 国际航空运单的内容及填制方法一览

项目名称	填制方法
航空公司数字代号 （Airline Code Number）	填写由 IATA 统一编制的航空公司代码，如中国民航的代码为 999，日本航空公司的代号为 131 等
始发站机场（Airport of Departure）	填写 IATA 统一制定的始发站机场或所在城市的三字代码
货运单序号及检验号 （Serial Number）	填写货运单号及检验号共 8 位数字，前 7 位为顺序号，第 8 位为检查号
托运人名称和地址 （Shipper's Name and Address）	填写托运人的全名，地址填写国家名称、城市、街道的名称、门牌号码及托运人的电话、传真、电传号码。托运人的名称依据不同的支付方式确定填写内容。信用证结算方式，当信用证有特殊规定时按信用证要求填写，否则，一般填写受益人名称；托收结算方式，一般填写合同中卖方的名称。必须注意的是，一张航空运单只能用于一个托运人在同一时间、同一地点托运的由承运人承运的，运往统一目的站同一收货人的一件或多件货物
托运人账号（Shipper's Account Number）	除非承运人需要，此栏一般空白不填
收货人名称和地址 （Consignee's Name and Address）	填写收货人的全名，地址填写国家名称、城市、街道的名称、门牌号码及托运人的电话、传真、电传号码。收货人的名称依据不同的支付方式确定填写内容。信用证结算方式，根据信用证的规定填写，有时以买方为收货人，有时以开证行为收货人；托收结算方式下，一般填写合同中的买方
收货人账号 （Consignee's Account Number）	除非承运人需要，此栏一般空白不填
签发航空运单的承运人 的代理人名称和城市 （Issuing Carrier's Agent Name and City）	如果航空运单由承运人的代理人签发时，填写收取佣金的代理人名称及城市名称；如果航空运单直接由承运人本人签发，此栏空白不填
代理人的国际航协代号（Agent's IATA Code）	IATA 的代号为 7 位数，实务中本栏一般不需填写
代理人账号（Account No.）	除非承运人需要（供承运人结算时使用），此栏一般空白不填
始发站机场和指定航线 （Airport of Departure and Requested Routing）	一般仅填写起航机场名称或所在城市的全称
to（By First Carrier）	填写目的站或者第一中转站机场的 IATA 三字代码，当该城市有多个机场，不知道机场名称时，可填写该城市代号
By First Carrier	填写第一承运人的全称或者 IATA 两字代码
to（By Second Carrier）	填写目的站或者第二中转站机场的 IATA 三字代码，当该城市有多个机场，不知道机场名称时，可填写该城市代号
by（Second Carrier）	填写第二承运人的全称或者 IATA 两字代码
to（By Third Carrier）	填写目的站或者第三中转站机场的 IATA 三字代码，当该城市有多个机场，不知道机场名称时，可填写该城市代号
by（Third Carrier）	填写第三承运人的全称或者 IATA 两字代码

续表

项目名称	填制方法
目的地机场 （Airport of Destination）	填写货物运输的最终目的地机场全称，当该城市有多个机场，不知道机场名称时，可填写该城市代号
航班/日期（仅供承运人使用） （Flight /Date for Carrier's Use only）	飞机航班号及其实际起飞日期，本栏一般不需填写。本栏即使填写，所填内容只能供承运人使用，该起飞日期不能作为货物的装运日期，货物的装运日期一般以航空运单的签发日期为准
财务说明 （Accounting Information）	填写运费缴付方式及其他财务说明事项。如 FREIGHT PREPAID（运费预付）、FREIGHT COLLECT（运费到付）或托运人结算使用信用卡号、账号。货物到达目的站无法交付收货人而需退运的，应将原始货运单号码填入新货运单的本栏内
货币 （Currency）	填写始发站所在国家的货币的三字代码（由国际标准化组织，即 ISO 规定），如 USD、HKD 等
费用代码（CHGS CODE）	此栏一般空白不填，仅供电子传送货运单信息时使用
航空运费 / 声明的价值及其他费用 （WT/VAL and Other）	WT（Weight Charge）航空运费是指根据货物计费重量乘以适用的运价收取的运费 VAL（Valuation Charge）声明的价值费是指承运人声明了价值时，必须与运费一起交付声明价值费。在相应的栏目"PPD"（预付）、"COLL"（到付）内填写"×"；Other（Other Charge at Origin）其他费用是指在始发站的其他费用预付或到付。在相应的栏目"PPD"（预付）、"COLL"（到付）内填写"×"
运输申报价值 （Declared Value for Carriage）	填写托运人向承运人办理货物声明价值的总金额。托运人未办理货物声明价值，必须填写"NVD"（No Value Declaration）
海关申报价值 （Declared Value for Customs）	填写托运人向海关申报的货物价值。此栏所填价值是指提供给海关的征税依据。当以出口货物报关或商业发票征税时，本栏可空白不填或填写"AS PER INVOICE"，若货物没有商业价值（如样品），必须填写"NCV"（No Commercial Value）
保险金额 （Amount of Insurance）	中国民航不代理国际货物的保险业务，此栏填写"NIL"或者"×××"等字样；如有代办，此栏填写货物的保险金额
运输处理注意事项 （Handling Information）	① 当货物为危险货物时，分两种情况处理：一是需要托运人的危险品申报单，则填写"DANGEROUS GOODS AS PER ATTACHED SHIPPER'S DECLARATION"，对于要求装货上机的危险货物，还应再加填"CARGO AIRCRAFT ONLY"；二是不要求附危险品申报单的危险货物，则填写"SHIPPER'S DECLARATION NOT REQUIRED" ② 当一批货物既有危险又有非危险货物时，危险货物必须填写在第一栏。一般情况下，此类危险货物应属于不要求托运人附危险品申报单、不是放射性物质且数量有限的危险货物
运输处理注意事项 （Handling Information）	③ 其他注意事项：包装情况如唛头、包装方法等；飞机随带的有关商业单据名称如商业发票、装箱单等；被通知人的名称、地址、国家、电话；托运人对货物在途时的某些特别处理规定等；海关规定等

续表

项目名称	填制方法
件数 （No. of Pieces RCP）	填写货物的总包装件数。"RCP"（Rate Combination Point）即运价组合点，如果使用非公布直达运价计算运费时，在件数的下面应填写运价组合点城市的 IATA 三字代号
毛重（Gross Weight）	填写托运货物的实际毛重。以千克为单位时可保留小数后一位
千克/磅 （kg/lb）	填写重量的计量单位。"kg"或者"lb"分别表示"千克"或者"磅"
运价等级 （Rate Class）	填写所采用的货物运价种类代号： M——minimum charge，最低运费 N——normal rate，普通货物标准运价 Q——quantity over 45kg rate，45kg 以上普通货物的运价，45kg 被称为重量分界点 C——specific commodity rate，特种货物运价 R——class rate reduction，折扣运价 S——class rate surcharge，加价运价 U——unit load device basic charge or rate，集装化设备基本运费或运价
商品编号 （Commodity Item No.）	使用指定商品运价时，按运价等级填写指定商品编号，填写时应注意商品编号应于运价代号保持水平。使用等级货物运价时，填写所适用的普通货物运价的代号及百分比数。填写"R"（表示附减等级运价）、"S"（表示附加等级运价）。当托运的货物是集装货物时，填写集装货物运价等级
计费重量 （Chargeable Weight）	填写托运货物的实际毛重，若属于"M"运价等级和以尺码计费者，则可空白此栏
运价/运费 （Rate/Charge）	填写实际计费的运价，对折扣运价或加价运价，此栏与运价等级对应填写附加或附件后的运价
运费总额 （Total）	填写根据货物运价和货物计费重量计算出的航空运费额。如果分别填写时，将航空运费总额填写在内
货物品名及数量（包括尺寸或体积） [Nature and Quantity Goods（incl. Dimensions or Volume）]	填写合同或信用证中规定的货物名称、数量及尺码等内容应注意以下几方面的内容： ① 当托运货物中含有危险货物时，应分别填写，并把危险货物列在第一项 ② 当托运货物为活动物时，应根据 IATA 活动物运输规定进行填写 ③ 对于集合货物，填写"Consolidation as Per Attached List" ④ 货物的体积，表示为"长×宽×高"，"DIMS:30×30×20"
计重运费 （Weight Charge）	根据付款方式对应填写预付或者到付，其运费额与上面"运费总额（Total）"中的金额一致
声明价值附加费 （Valuation Charge）	填写按规定收取的声明价值，则在对应的"预付"或"到付"栏内填入声明价值附加金额，其公式为：声明价值附加费金额=（声明价值－实际毛重×最高赔偿额）×0.5%

续表

项目名称	填制方法
税款 （Tax）	根据付款方式对应在"预付"或者"到付"栏内填入适用的税款
由代理人收取的其他费用 （Total Other Charges Due Agent）	根据付款方式对应在"预付"或者"到付"栏内填入由代理人收取的其他费用总额
由承运人收取的其他费用 （Total Other Charges Due Carrier）	根据付款方式对应在"预付"或者"到付"栏内填入由承运人收取的其他费用总额。一般填写"AS ARRANGED"
预付费用总额 （Total Prepaid）	前面37、38、39、40、41等栏有关预付费用总和，也可在对应栏内填列"AS ARRANGED"
到付费用总额 （Total Collect）	前面37、38、39、40、41等栏有关到付费用总和，也可在对应栏内填列"AS ARRANGED"
货币兑换比价 （Currency Conversion Rates）	填写目的站国家货币代号及兑换比率
用目的站国家货币付费 （CC Charge in Dest. Currency）	填写目的站国家货币到付的费用总金额
仅供承运人在目的站使用 （For Carrier's use only at Destination）	本栏一般不填写
在目的站的费用（Charges at Destination）	填写最后承运人将在目的站发生的货物运费金额包括利息等
到付费用总额（Total Collect Charges）	填写到付费用总和
其他费用 （Other Charges）	填写始发站运输中发生的其他费用，应以代号表示，具体如下： AC——animal container，动物容器费 AS——assembly service fee，集装服务费 AT——attendant，押运员服务费 AW——air waybill fee，货运单费 BR——bank release，银行放行 DB——disbursement fee，代垫付款手续费 DF——disbursement service，分发服务费 FC——charge collect fee，货物运费到付手续费 GT——government tax，政府税 HR——human remains，尸体、骨灰附加费 IN——insurance premium，代办保险手续费 LA——live animal，活体动物处理费 MA——miscellaneous——due agent，代理人收取的杂项费 MZ——miscellaneous——due issuing carrier，制单承运人收取的杂项费 PK——packaging，货物包装费 RA——dangerous goods fee，危险物品处理费 SD——surface charge——destination，目的站地面运输费 SO——storage——origin，始发站仓储费 TR——transit，过境费 TX——taxes，税款

续表

项目名称	填制方法
其他费用 （Other Charges）	UH——ULD—handling，集装设备处理费 SR——surface charge—origin，始发站地面运费 SU——storage—destination，目的站仓储费 其他费用代号后加"C"表示该项费用由承运人收取，加"A"表示该项费用由代理人收取
托运人或其代理人签名 （Signature of shipper or his Agent）	签名后以示保证所托运的货物并非危险品
运单日期 [Executed on（date）]	签单以后正本航空运单方能生效。本栏所示的日期为签发日期，也就是本批货物的装运日期。如果信用证规定运单必须注明实际起飞日期，则以所注明的实际起飞日期作为装运日期。本栏的日期不得晚于信用证规定的装运日期
（签发运单）地点 （Executed）[at（place）]	填开证地点
承运人或其代理人签名 （Signature of Issuing carrier or its Agent）	以代理人身份签章时，如填制提单一样，需在签章处加注"AS AGENT"；承运人签章则加注"AS CARRIER"

小 贴 士

关于航空运单日期

《ISBP》第 151 段规定，如果信用证不要求单据显示实际的发运日期，则航空运单的出具日期将被视为发运日期，即使单据在"仅供承运人使用"或类似用于的栏位中标明了航班日期及/或航班号。如果实际的航班日期在单据上被单独批注，但信用证并未要求，则该日期将不被用来确定装运日期。

课堂思考

在"航空运单"的"收货人"栏内，能不能做成指示性抬头？试说明理由。

参考答案

 职业判断

案例资料：

2015年2月16日，江苏通福纺织品进出口有限公司与纽约道齐公司签订了一份金额为100万美元的纺织品出口合同。委托江苏外运代理人小张向来航空公司进行订机配舱，在填制航空运单的最后需要签名盖章。

思考：

最后答案是由代理人小张完成还是由承运人航空公司完成？试说明理由。

参考答案

任务实施

单证员小季填制的航空运单，如图5.14所示。

999			999—	
Shipper's Name and Address	Shipper's Account Number	Not Negotiable Air waybill Issued by	**AIR CHINA** 中国国际航空公司 **BEIJING CHINA**	
DESUN TRADING CO., LTD. HUARONG MANSION RM2901 NO.85 GUANJIAQIAO, NANJING 210005, CHINA TEL: 0086-25-4715004 FAX: 0086-25-4711363		Copies 1, 2 and 3 of this Air Waybill are originals and have the same validity.		
Consignee's Name and Address	Consignee's Account Number	It is agreed that the goods described herein are accepted for carriage in apparent good order and condition (except as noted) and SUBJECT TO THE CONDITIONS OF CONTRACT ON		
NEO GENERAL TRADING CO. P.O. BOX 99552, RIYADH 22766, KSA TEL: 00966-1-4659220 FAX: 00966-1-4659213		THE REVERSE HEREOF. ALL GOODS MAY BE CARRIED BY AND OTHER MEANS INCLUDING ROAD OR ANY OTHER CARRIER UNLESS SPECIFIC CONTRARY INSTRUCTIONS ARE GIVEN HEREON BY THE SHIPPER. THE SHIPPER'S ATTENTION IS DRAWN TO THE NOTICE CONCERNING CARRIER'S LIMITATION OF LIABILITY. Shipper may increase such limitation of liability by declaring a higher value for carriage and paying a supplemental charge if required.		
Issuing Carrier's Agent Name and City		Accounting Information		

图5.14 小季填制的航空运单

Agent's IATA Code		Account No.										

FREIGHT PREPAID

Airport of Departure (Addr. of First Carrier) and Requested Routing

NANJING

To	By First Carrier Routing and Destination	to	by	to	by	Currency	CHGS Code	WT/VAL		Other		Declared Value for Carriage	Declared Value for Customs
								PPD	COLL	PPD	COLL		
						USD		×		×			

Airport of Destination	Flight/Date For carrier Use Only Flight/Date	Amount of Insurance	INSURANCE If Carrier offers insurance, and such insurance is requested in accordance with the conditions thereof, indicate amount to be insured in figures in box marked "Amount of Insurance."
DAMMAM PORT	FX0910 APRIL 7, 2015		

Handing Information

(For USA only) These commodities licensed by U.S. for ultimate destination···Diversion contrary to U.S. law is prohibited.

No. of Pieces RCP	Gross Weight	kg lb	Rate Class	Commodity Item No.	Chargeable Weight	Rate	Charge	Total	Nature and Quantity of Goods (incl. Dimensions or Volume)
1700 CTNS	19 074.44	K	N		19 074.44	20.61		393 124.21	CANNED MUSRHOOM PIECES & STEMS 24 TINS × 425 GRAMS

Prepaid	Weight Charge	Other Charges
393 124.21		
Valuation Charge		
		AWC: 50.00
Tax		

Total other Charges Due Agent	Shipper certifies that the particulars on the face hereof are correct and that insofar as any part of the consignment contains dangerous goods, such part is properly described by name and is in proper condition for carriage by air according to the applicable Dangerous Goods Regulations.

图 5.14 小季填制的航空运单（续）

Total other Charges Due Carrier				
50.00		Signature of Shipper or his Agent		
Total Prepaid	Total Collect	7/APRIL/2001	NANJING	DESUN TRADING CO., LTD.
393 174.21				
Currency Conversion Rates	CC Charges in Dest. Currency			
		Executed on (date)　　at(place)　　Signature of Issuing Carrier or its Agent		
For Carrier's Use only at Destination	Charges at Destination	Total Collect Charges		999—

图 5.14　小季填制的航空运单（续）

任务再现

2015 年 6 月，宁波花森工艺品制造有限公司与韩国 DAYU 公司谈妥了一笔关于皮质仿真花（CORIACEOUS EMULATION FLOWER）的交易，在收到韩国进口商开来的信用证后，宁波出口商备妥货物后，委托宁波中外货运空运公司代理人小方向中国民航订机配舱，于 7 月 20 日装运完毕。

负责填写本次航空运单的中国民航员工 Lisa 已完成了填写，根据所学知识结合所示信用证相关资料及其他资料对此航空运单认真核对，找出是否有不符之处，如有提出并改正。

（1）信用证相关资料：

APPLICANT: DAYU IMPORT AND EXPORT TRADE CO.,LTD.

　　　　　564-9，SUNMAN-DONG,NAM-KU ULSAN KOREA

BENEFICIARY: HUASENG HANDICRAFT MANUFACTURING CO., LTD

　　　　　NO.266 ZHONGSHAN ROAD NINGBO CHINA

AMOUNT: USD 15 000.00

LOADING IN CHARGE:NINGBO AIRPORT

FOR TRANSPORT TO:PUSAN AIRPORT

DESCRIPTION OF GOODS: 15 000PCS OF CORIACEOUS

EMULATION FLOWER

（2）其他资料：

① 收货人为 PUSAN CENTRALBANK 釜山中央银行

② 装运日期：JUL.20，2015

③ PACKING:75 PCS IN A CARTON　G.W.:650.00KGS N.W.:600.00 KGSMEAS:20.56M³

④ SHIPPING MARK:DAYU/PUSAN/NO.1-200

⑤ 航班号：CA983　运价等级：Q　费率：CNY20

⑥ 空运单签发人：SINOAIR NINGBO COMPANY,NINGBO

（3）Lisa 填写完成的空运提单如图 5.15 所示。

999	SHA	1488 7574		999—	1488 7574
Shipper's Name and Address	Shipper's Account Number	Not Negotiable Air waybill Issued by	**AIR CHINA** 中国国际航空公司 BEIJING CHINA		
HUASENG HANDICRAFT MANUFACTURING CO., LTD NO.266 ZHONGSHAN ROAD NINGBO CHINA		Copies 1, 2 and 3 of this Air Waybill are originals and have the same validity.			
Consignee's Name and Address	Consignee's Account Number	It is agreed that the goods described herein are accepted for carriage in apparent good order and condition (except as noted) and SUBJECT TO THE CONDITIONS OF CONTRACT ON THE REVERSE HEREOF. ALL GOODS MAY BE CARRIED BY AND OTHER MEANS INCLUDING ROAD OR ANY OTHER CARRIER UNLESS SPECIFIC CONTRARY INSTRUCTIONS ARE GIVEN HEREON BY THE SHIPPER. THE SHIPPER'S ATTENTION IS DRAWN TO THE NOTICE CONCERNING CARRIER'S LIMITATION OF LIABILITY. Shipper may increase such limitation of liability by declaring a higher value for carriage and paying a supplemental charge if required.			
TO ORDER OF SHIPPER					
Issuing Carrier's Agent Name and City		Accounting Information			
SINOAIR NINGBO COMPANY,NINGBO					
Agent's IATA Code	Account No.				
Airport of Departure (Addr. of First Carrier) and Requested Routing					
NINGBO					

to	By First Carrier	Routing and Destination	to	by	to	by	Currency	CHGS Code	WT/VAL PPD	WT/VAL COLL	Other PPD	Other COLL	Declared Value for Carriage	Declared Value for Customs
PUSAN							USD		×		×			

图 5.15　空运提单

Airport of Destination	Flight/Date	For carrier Use Only Flight/Date	Amount of Insurance	INSURANCE - If Carrier offers insurance, and such insurance is requested in accordance with the conditions thereof, indicate amount to be insured in figures in box marked "Amount of Insurance."
PUSAN	**CA983 JUL.20,2015**			

Handing Information

NOTIFY DAYU IMPORT AND EXPORT TRADE CO.,LTD. 564-9，SUNMAN-DONG,NAM-KU ULSAN KOREA

(For USA only) These commodities licensed by U.S. for ultimate destination ...Diversion contrary to U.S. law is prohibited

No of Pieces RCP	Gross Weight	kg lb	Rate Class	Commodity Item No.	Chargeable Weight	Rate / Charge		Total	Nature and Quantity of Goods (incl. Dimensions or Volume)
15 000 PCS	**650.00**	**K**			**650.00**		**20**	**13 000.00**	**CORIACEOUS EMULATION FLOWER** **DAYU** **PUSAN** **NO.1-200** **20.56CBM**

Prepaid Weight Charge		Other Charges
13000.00	Collect	
Valuation Charge		
Tax		

Total other Charges Due Agent	Shipper certifies that the particulars on the face hereof are correct and that insofar as any part of the consignment contains dangerous goods, such part is properly described by name and is in proper condition for carriage by air according to the applicable Dangerous Goods Regulations.
Total other Charges Due Carrier	
	.... Signature of Shipper or his Agent

Total Prepaid	Total Collect	
Currency Conversion Rates	CC Charges in Dest. Currency	
		.... Executed on (date) at(place) Signature of Issuing Carrier or its Agent
For Carrier's Use only at Destination	Charges at Destination	Total Collect Charges 999－1488 7574

参考答案

图 5.15　空运提单（续）

项目小结

在线测试及
参考答案

技能强化训练

技能提高

（一）填单题

根据以下部分信用证资料及补充资料缮制托运单。

ISSUING BANK: NATIONAL BANK, SINGAPORE

L/C NO.: ZJ489　DATE:140620

EXPORY DATE: JULY. 25, 2014

BENEFIGIARY: ZHEJIANG TEXTILE IMPORT AND EXPORT CORPORATION

NO. 124 QINGCHUN ROAD HANGZHOU , CHINA

APPLICANT：CHANG LIN HAI COMPANY, LTD., SINGAPORE NO.111 AVENUE , SINGAPORE

SHIPMENT: FROM SHANGHAI TO SINGAPORE , NOT LATER THAN JUN. 25, 2015

PARTIAL SHIPMENT: NOT ALLOWED

TRANSSHIPMENT: ALLOWED

DESCRIPTION OF GOODS: 1000 DOZS 100% COTTON SHIRTS USD3.80 PER PC

DOCUMENTS REQUIRED:

......

+3/3 CLEAN ON BOARD OCEAN BILLS OF LADING MADE OUT TO ORDER OF SHIPPER BLANK ENDORSED AND MARKED FREIGHT PREPAID AND NOTIFY APPLICANT.

补充资料如下：

PACKING: 20DOZS/CTN

GROSS WEIGHT: @14KGS/CTN

NET WEIGHT:@12KGS/CTN

MEASUREMENT: @(50×30×20)CM/CTN

MARKS&NOS: CLA/08998/SINGAPORE

参考答案

（二）审单改错题

根据下述信用证（见图 5.16）及补充业务资料审核修改提单（见图 5.17）。

Issue of Documentary Credit

Issuing Bank   : METTTABANK LTD., FINLAND

Form of DOC. Credit: IRREVOCABLE

Credit Number   : LRT9802457

Date of Issue   : 110428

Expiry   : Date 110416 Place FINLAND

Applicant   : F. T. C. CO.

                     AKEKSANTERINK AUTO

                     P. O. BOX 9, FINLAND

Beneficiary   : GREAT WALL TRADING CO., LTD.

                     RM201, HUASHENG BUILDING, NINGBO, P. R. OF CHINA

Amount   : USD 36480.00 (SAY U. S. DOLLARS THIRTY SIX THOUSAND FOUR HUNDRED AND EIGHTY ONLY)

Available with / by: ANY BANK IN ADVISING COUNTRY

                     BY NEGOTIATION

Draft at …   : DRAFTS AT 30 DAYS SIGHT FOR FULL INVOICE VALUE

Partial Shipment : NOT ALLOWED

Transshipment   : ALLOWED

Loading in Charge : NINGBO

For Transport to   : HELSINKI

Shipment Period : AT THE LATEST MAY 30, 2011

Descrip. of Goods : 9600PCS OF HALOGEN FITTING W 500, USD3.80 PER PC

                     AS PER SALES CONTRACT GW2005M06 DD 22. 4. 2011

                     CIF HESINKI

Documents required : * COMMERCIAL INVOICE 1 SIGNED ORIGINAL AND 5 COPIES

                     * PACKING LIST IN 2 COPIES

      * FULL SET OF CLEAN ON BOARD MARINE BILL OF LADING, MADE OUT TO ORDER, MARKED "FREIGHT PREPAID" AND NOTIFY APPLICANT(AS INDICATE ABOVE)

      * GSP CERTIFICATE OF ORIGIN FORM A, CERTIFY GOODS OF ORIGIN IN CHINA, ISSUED BY COMPETENT AUTHORITIES

      * INSURANCE POLICY/ CERTIFICATE COVERING ALL RISKES AND WAR RISK OF PICC. INCLUDING WAREHOUSE TO WAREHOUSE CLAUSE UP TO FINAL DESTINATION AT HELSINKI, FOR AT LEAST 120 PCT OF CIF VALUE

Presentation Period : 6 DAYS AFTER ISSUANCE DATE OF SHIPPING DOCUMENT

Confirmation   : WITHOUT

图 5.16　信用证

补充业务资料如下：

INVOIVE NO. : TAR20057149   INVOICE DATE: MAR. 2, 2006

B/L NO.: GSG05-723   B/L DATE: MAR. 15, 2006

FORM A NO. :   GZ7/80067/0589

ISSUING DATE OF FORM A AND POLICY : MAR. 10, 2006

POLICY NO.:   TES3478921   单证员：李丽

SHIPPING MARK: N/M PORT OF LOADING: NINGBO

PACKING: 40KGS IN EACH PAPERSACKS

交单日期: MAR.

25, 2006

NEGOTIATING BANK: BANK OF CHINA, NINGBO BRANCH

CONTAINER, SEAL NO.: TEXU3730336/KHS487605/20'

NAME OF STEAMER: DONGFANG SENATOR V.743

WEIGHT: N. W. @40.00KGS   G. W. @40.70KGS

MEASUREMENT: @50CM×50CM×40CM

法定代表人：王立

参考答案

Shipper NINGBO TEA IMP. & EXP. CORP . NO. 200, DAHE ROAD, NINGBO,CHINA						
Consignee TO ORDER						
Notify Party ARELLA AND C. SPA PIAZZA COLLEGIO CAIROLI N. 3 27100 PAVIA, ITALY				COSCO B/L NO. 中国远洋运输公司 **CHINA OCEAN SHIPPING COMPANY**		
Pre-carriage by			Place of Receipt			
Ocean Vessel DONGFANG SENATOR	Voy. No. V.743		port of Loading NINGBO PORT			
Port of Discharge LA SPEZIA PORT			Place of Delivery			
Container No. TEXU3730336/ KHS487605/20'	Seal No. Marks & Nos. N/M	No. of Containers of Pkgs 200PAPERSACKS	Kind of Packages; Description of Goods	Gross Weight	Measurement
			Final Destination for the goods-not the ship		
			TEA FREIGHT COLLECT	8140.00KGS	20.00 M³
TOTAL NUMBER OF CONTAINERS OR PACKAGES (IN WORDS) SAY TWO HUNDRED PAPERSACKS ONLY						
FREIGHT & CHARGES	Revenue Tons	Rate	Per	Prepaid	Collect
			ON BOARD		
Ex.Rate:	Prepaid at		Payable at	Place and date of Issue NINGBO, CHINA MAR. 15, 2006	
	Total Prepaid		No. of Original B(s)L 3	Signed for the Carrier	
Date By--------------------				中国远洋运输公司宁波分公司 许 利 明	
(COSCO STANDARD-FORM 02)				(TERMS CONTINUED ON BACK HERE OF)	

图 5.17　已填制好的海运提单

项目六

保险单据实训

知识目标

1. 理解保险单与投保单的含义;
2. 了解保险单的种类及特点;
3. 掌握信用证下常见的保单条款;
4. 熟悉出口海运货物的基本险别及特别险别。

能力目标

1. 掌握保单的内容、缮制保单的方法;
2. 掌握保单缮制过程中的要领和应注意的事项;
3. 能对照合同或信用证审核、修改保单。

任务一 填制投保单

汇丰银行

上海华美轻工业进出口公司在2015年3月与英国的MTY(UK) LIMITED公司达成一项合作，从上海出口一批不同型号的牙具用品（MOUTHWASH PRODUCTS）。双方协商后决定采用信用证方式达成交易，7月，香港汇丰银行开来了信用证（见图6.1）。

上海华美轻工业进出口公司阅读信用证后了解了信用证中有关保险单的条款。因为在 CIF 贸易术语下出口到英国的产品需要卖方办理投保，所以需要出口公司准备好所需材料，向保险公司办理投保。

Issue of a Documentary Credit

HSBC BANK PLC, TRADE SERVICES,
51 DE MONTFORT STREET, LEICESTER LE17BB
11 JUL, 2015

SHANGHAI HUAMEI LIGHT INDUSTRIAL PRODUCTS I.&E. COMPANY
NO.210 BEIJING EAST RD
SHANGHAI 200221 CHINA

27	SEQUENCE OF TOTAL	1/1
40A	FORM OF DOC. CREDIT	IRREVOCABLE
20	DOC. CREDIT NUMBER	TR-MHLCO1
31C	DATE OF ISSUE	11JUL2015
31D	DATE AND PLACE OF EXPIRY	09SEP2015 CHINA
50	APPLICANT	MTY(UK)LIMITED
		566,BOROUGH HIGH STREET,LONDON,
		SE1 1HR,UNITED KINGDOM
		TEL:+44 207 407 4035
		FAX:+44 207 407 4080
59	BENEFICIARY	SHANGHAI HUAMEI LIGHT INDUSTRIAL PRODUCTS
		I.&E.COMPANY
		NO.210 BEIJING EAST RD
		SHANGHAI 200221,P.R. CHINA
32B	CURRENCY CODE, AMOUNT	USD74 380.00
41A	AVAILABLE WITH ... BY ...	ANY BANK BY NEGOTIATION
42C	DRAFTS AT ...	60 DAYS AFTER SIGHT
42A	DRAWEE	ISSUING BANK

图 6.1 香港汇丰银行开立的信用证

43P	PARTIAL SHIPMENTS	NOT ALLOWED
43T	TRANSHIPMENT	NOT ALLOWED
44A	LOADING ON BOARD/DISPATCH / TAKING IN CHARGE AT/FROM ...	SHANGHAI
44B	FOR TRANSPORTATION TO...	FELEXSTOWE
44C	LATEST DATE OF SHIPMENT	25AUG2015
45A	DESCRIPTION OF GOODS AND/OR SERVICES	CIF FELEXSTOWE MOUTHWASH PRODUCTS ASSORTED ITEMS AS PER SC NO.HMSC2005321 OF 21MAR2015.
46A	DOCUMENTS REQUIRED	1. ORIGINAL SIGNED COMMERCIAL INVOICE AND 2 COPIES, INDICATING F.O.B.VALUE, FREIGHT CHARGES AND INSURANCE PREMIUM SEPARATELY.AND CERTIFYING THE GOODS ARE OF CHINESE ORIGIN
		2. FULL SET OF ORIGINAL CLEAN MARINE BILLS OF LADING MADE OUT TO ORDER, ENDORSED IN BLANK MARKED FREIGHT PREPAID AND NOTIFY MTY(UK)LIMITED566, BOROUGH HIGH STREET, LONDON, SE1 1HR, UNITED KINGDOM AND US
46A	DOCUMENTS REQUIRED	3. INSURANCE POLICEIES OR CERTIFICATES IN DUPLICATE, ENDORSED IN BLANK FOR 110 PCT OF INVOICE VALUE COVERING INSTITUTE CARGO CLAUSES (A).
		4. BENEFICIARY'S CERTIFICATE CERTIFYING THAT ONE SET OF COPIES OF SHIPPING DOCUMENTS HAS BEEN SENT TO APPLICANT WITHIN 7 DAYS AFTER SHIPMENT.
47A	ADDITIONAL CONDITIONS	1. DOCUMENTS ARE NOT TO BE PRESENTED PRIOR TO 15 DAYS AFTER SHIPMENT.
		2. DRAFTS/DOCUMENTS MUST BE DRAWN AT TENOR STATED ABOVE.
		3. NOT WITHSTANDING THE PROVISIONS OF UPC500, IF WE GIVE NOTICE OF REFUSAL OF DOCUMENTS PRESENTED UNDER THIS CREDIT WE SHALL HOWEVER RETAIN THE RIGHT TO NOT WITHSTANDING THE PROVISIONS OF UPC500, IF WE GIVE NOTICE OF REFUSAL OF DOCUMENTS PRESENTED UNDER THIS CREDIT WE SHALL HOWEVER RETAIN THE RIGHT TO ACCEPT A WAIVER OF DISCREPANCIES FROM THE APPLICANT AND, SUBJECT TO SUCH WAIVER BEING ACCEPTABLE TO US, TO RELEASE THE DOCUMENTS AGAINST THAT WAIVER WITHOUT REFRENCE TO THE PRESENTER PROVIDED THAT NO WRITTEN INSTRUCTIONS TO THE CONTRARY HAVE BEEN RECEIVED BY US FROM THE PRESENTER BEFORE THE RELEASE OF THE DOCUMENTS.
		4. ANY SUCH RELEASE PRIOR TO THE RECEIPT OF CONTRARY INSTRUCTIONS SHALL NOT CONSTITUTE A FAILURE ON OUR PART TO HOLD DOCUMENTS AT THE PRESENTERS RISK AND DISPOSAL, AND WE SHALL HAVE NO LIABILITY TO THE PRESENTER IN RESPECT OF ANY SUCH RELEASE.

图 6.1 香港汇丰银行开立的信用证（续）

47A	ADDITIONAL CONDITIONS	5. UNLESS OTHERWISE EXPRESSLY STATED, ALL DOCUMENTS MUST BE IN ENGLISH. EXCEPT SO FAR AS OTHERWISE EXPRESSLY STATED, THIS DOCUMENTARY CREDIT IS SUBJECT TO UNIFORM CUSTOMS AND PRACTICE FOR DOCUMENTARY CREDIT ICC PUBLICATION NO.500. 6. ANY PROCEEDS OF PRESENTATIONS UNDER THIS DC WILL BE SETTLED BY TELETRANSMISSION AND A CHARGE OF GBP40.00 (OR CURRENCY EQUIVALENT) WILL BE DEDUCTED.
71B	CHARGES	ALL CHGS OUTSIDE COUNTRY OF ISSUE FOR ACCOUNT OF BENEFICIARY /EXPORTER AND ALL DISCOUNT CHARGES ARE FOR THE ACCOUNT OF THE BENEFICIARY.
48	PERIOD FOR PRESENTATION	WITHIN 21 DAYS AFTER THE DATE OF SHIPMENT BUT WITHIN THE VALIDITY OF THE CREDIT
49	CONFIRMATION INSTRUCTIONS	WITHOUT
78	INSTRUCTIONS TO THE PAYING/ ACCEPTING/NEGOTIATING BANK	1. WE UNDERTAKE TO REIMBURSE YOU IN ACCORDANCE WITH YOUR INSTRUCTIONS WHICH SHOULD INCLUDE YOUR UID NUMBER AND THE ABA CODE OF THE RECEIVING BANK ON THE MATURITY DATE, WHICH WE SHALL ADVISE. 2. WE ARE PREPARED TO DISCOUNT ALL BILLS DRAWN UNDER THIS CREDIT AT OUR PREVAILING DISCOUNT RATE ON THE DATE OF ACCEPTANCE OF THE DOCUMENTS COMPLYING WITH THE CREDIT ON THE SPECIFIC INSTURCTIONS OF THE NEGOTIATING BANK, WHO SHOULD STATE ON THEIR SCHEDULE THAT THEY REQUIRE US TO DO SO.
57A	"ADVISE THROUGH"BANK	BANK OF CHINA SHANGHAI JIN MAO TOWER SUB-BRANCH
72	SENDER TO RECEIVER INFORMATION	DOCUMENTS TO BE DESPATCHED BY COURIER SERVICE IN ONE LOT TO HSBC BANK PLC, TRADE SERVICES,51 DE MONTFORT STREET, LEICESTER LE17BB

图 6.1 香港汇丰银行开立的信用证（续）

补充资料如下：

商品名称：MOUTHWASH PRODUCTS

货 号	交易数量	单 价	包装数量	包装方式	毛 重	净 重	尺 码
S4950	4600PCS	USD6.50	20	CTNS	25KGS	23KGS	30cm×25cm×30cm
S4728	2000PCS	USD5.20	8	CTNS	18KGS	16KGS	25cm×25cm×40cm
S4101	2500PCS	USD12.80	10	CTNS	15KGS	13KGS	29cm×50cm×30cm

发票号码：HMINV2585　　发票日期：2015-8-5　　汇票日期：2015-9-9
装运船名：ANGLAIS　　航次：V.296　　装船日：2015-8-23
提单号码：TD359790　　海运费：USD1400.00
保单号码：ICC610426057　　保单日期：2015-8-20　　保险费：USD656.00

运输代理：MTY

HMSC2005321

FELEXSTOWE

C/NO.1-780

要求：

请以上海华美轻工业进出口公司业务员小李的身份，根据英国公司提供的信用证，填制一份符合规定的投保单。

知识准备

一、投保单的定义及作用

（一）投保单的含义

投保单又称投保书、要保书，是投保人向保险人申请订立保险合同的书面要约。投保书是由保险人事先准备的、具有统一格式的书据。投保人必须依其所列项目一一如实填写，以供保险人决定是否承保或以何种条件、何种费率承保。

（二）投保单及其作用

投保单本身并非正式合同的文本，但一经保险人接受后，即成为保险合同的一部分。在保险实物中，投保人提出保险要约时，均需填写投保单。如投保单填写的内容不实或故意隐瞒、欺诈，都将影响保险合同的效力。

投保单是日后制作保险单据的背景材料，故务必正确缮制，尤其在信用证支付条件下更应严格按照信用证条款来制作。

二、关于投保单的法律政策

投保单是进出口企业向保险公司对运输货物进行投保的申请书，也是保险公司据以出具保险单的凭证，保险公司在收到投保单后即缮制保险单。投保单是投保人的书面要约。投保单经投保人据实填写交付给保险人就成为投保人表示愿意与保险人订立保险合同的书面要约。

三、填写投保单时的注意事项

出口企业制单人员在填写投保单时应注意以下事项。

（1）投保人的姓名或名称。应当用投保时的法定姓名或名称，户口

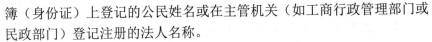

簿（身份证）上登记的公民姓名或在主管机关（如工商行政管理部门或民政部门）登记注册的法人名称。

（2）投保人的地址要详细写清地址全称。如果住所地（户籍所在地或法人注册地）与其居所地（居住地或法人营业地）不一致时，应当分别填写清楚。

（3）投保人的职业或经营范围，应当填写投保人在投保时，所从事的职业或主管机关批准的经营范围。具体的职业，不要用工、农、商、学、兵等简单写法，而应当写出具体的工作性质，如司机、教师、纺织工、大学生等。

（4）投保人欲投保何种险种险别，是否已就同一保险标的、保险风险向其他保险人投保同一险种及其投保人的保险金额。

（5）投保的保险标的应当填写清楚。例如，投保财产保险标的的名称、种类、数量及其坐落地点等均应分项填写。而人身保险的投保单，则应就投保生存、死亡、伤残、劳动能力、疾病及其医药费支出等标的予以明确填写。

（6）投保人身保险时，投保人还必须如实填写被保险人的姓名、年龄（出生年月日），从事的职业或工作岗位等。其中，被保险人的年龄应当采用公元纪年的实足年龄。不足一年的、大于 6 个月的计算为上一年，不足 6 个月的计为下一年。例如，被保险人年龄为 20 岁又 7 个月的，则填写为 21 岁。

（7）投保人身保险时，投保人应当根据被保险人出于真实意志所指定的受益人，在投保单中填写受益人的姓名、住址。如果该受益人在国外或其他地方工作或居住的，还应当将其通讯地址予以填写。如果被保险人未指定受益人时，投保人可在"受益人"一栏内暂填"法定继承人"。

（8）填写投保金额时，投保人应当根据投保标的的具体情况和自己寻求保险保障的需要，以及保险人在有关保险条款中的要求，填写适当的数额。

（9）投保人应当在投保单上亲自签名或盖章。如果是文盲的，可用拇指画押，不要用手指模来替代。

四、海洋运输保险的种类

海洋运输货物保险条款所承保的险别，分为基本险别和附加险别两类。

（一）基本险别

基本险别有平安险（Free from Particular Average，F.P.A.）、水渍险（With Average or With Particular Average，W.A. or W.P.A.）和一切险

（All Risk，A.R.）三种。

平安险的责任范围包括以下几个方面。

（1）被保货物在运输过程中，由于自然灾害造成整批货物的全部损失或推定全损。被保货物用驳船运往或远离海轮的，每一驳船所装货物可视为一整批。

（2）由于运输工具遭受意外事故造成货物全部或部分损失。

（3）在运输工具已经发性意外事故的情况下，货物在此前后又在海上遭受自然灾害落海造成的全部或部分损失。

（4）在装卸或转运时，由于一件或数件货物落海造成的全部或部分损失。

（5）被保险人对遭受承保范围内的货物采取抢救、防止或减少货损的措施而支付的合理费用，但以不超过该批被救货物的保险金额为限。

（6）运输工具遭难后，在避难港由于卸货所引起的损失以及在中途港、避难港由于卸货、存仓以及运送货物所产生的特别费用。

（7）共同海损的牺牲、分摊和救助费用。

（8）运输合同订有"船舶互撞责任条款"，根据该条款规定应由货方偿还船方的损失。

水渍险的责任范围：除平安险的各项责任外，还负责被保货物由于自然灾害造成的部分损失。

一切险的责任范围：除平安险和水渍险的各项责任外，还负责被保货物在运输途中由于一般外来原因所造成的全部或部分损失。

（二）附加险别

附加险别是基本险别责任的扩大和补充，它不能单独投保，附加险别有一般附加险和特别附加险。

（1）一般外来风险，是指货物在运输途中由于偷窃、下雨、短量、渗漏、破碎、受潮、受热、霉变、串味、沾污、钩损、生锈、碰损等原因所导致的风险。

（2）特殊外来风险，是指由于战争、罢工、拒绝交付货物等政治、军事、国家禁令及管制措施所造成的风险与损失。如因政治或战争因素，运送货物的船只被敌对国家扣留而造成交货不到；某些国家颁布的新政策或新的管制措施以及国际组织的某些禁令，都可能造成货物无法出口或进口而造成损失。

五、投保单据的缮制

投保单样本如图 6.2 所示。

海洋货物运输险投保单			
投保人			
发票号码及标记	件数	货物名称	保险金额
运输工具、航次（及转载工具）		约启运于	赔付地及币别
运输路程	自　　　经到		提单号码
承保险别		投保单位签章： 投保日期：	

图 6.2　投保单样本

投保单内容和填制方法如表 6.1 所示。

表 6.1　投保单内容及填制方法一览表

序号	项目名称	填制方法
1	投保人名称	按可保利益的实际有关人填写。由买方或卖方投保的则分别填写其规范名称。如信用证另有规定，按来证要求办理
2	发票号码及标记	填发票号码及装船标记唛头，与提单上同一栏及外包装上的实际标记相一致
3	件数	此项写明包装方式以及包装数量。如果一次投保有数种不同包装时，可以件（packages）为单位。散装货应填写散装重量。如果采用集装箱运输，应予注明（IN CONTAINER）
4	保险货物名称	应填写保险货物的名称，按发票或信用证填写，不必过于具体
5	保险金额	按照贸易合同或信用证规定的加成计算得出的保险金额数值填写，计算时一般按发票的金额加成。保险金额货币名称要与发票一致
6	装载运输工具	海运时应写明具体的船名。如果中途需转船，已知第二程船时应打上船名；如果第二程船名未知，则只需打上转船字样。集装箱运输应打用集装箱
7	开航日期	一般应注明"按照提单"或注明船舶的大致开航日期
8	赔付地及币别	通常在目的地支付赔款。如果被保险人要求在目的地以外的地方赔款，应予注明
9	运输路线	填写起始地和目的地名称。中途如需转船，则应注明转船地；若到目的地后，需转运内陆，应注明内陆地名称；如果到达目的地路线不止一条，要填写经过的中途港（站）的名称
10	提单号码及运单号码	提单或运单号码也应填明，以便保险公司核查
11	承保险别	按信用证和买卖合同约定的承保险别填写。如对保险条款有特殊要求，也应在此栏注明
12	投保单位签章	由投保单位签章并注明投保日期。投保日期应早于船舶开航日期或运输工具开航日期

参考答案

课堂思考

投保单和保险单有何区别？

小 贴 士

什么是电子保单？为什么电子保单不能篡改？

电子保单是指保险公司借助遵循 PKI（public key infrastructure，公钥基础设施）体系的数字签名软件和企业数字证书为客户签发的具有保险公司电子签名的电子化保单。

电子保单是经过数字签名的一组数据块，该数据块中包含了原始保单，即用户可以通过浏览器看得见的保单内容、签发方的电子签名和签发时所使用的数字证书，这些内容通过符合 PKI 体系的数学算法计算后组合在一起。因此对该数据块进行任何修改都会在验证的时候被发现，被篡改的电子保单是不可能通过验证的。

职业判断

案例资料：

浙江某进出口公司向韩国出口一批茶叶，投保了平安险，船舶在途中遭遇恶劣天气，雨水灌进船舱，造成部分茶叶变质，三天后船上又发生爆炸。

思考：

对于这种情况，保险公司是否给予赔偿？试说明理由。

参考答案

任务实施

上海华美轻工业进出口公司业务员小李根据英国公司提供的信用证填制的一份符合规定的投保单，如图 6.3 所示。

海洋货物运输险投保单

投保人 SHANGHAI HUAMEI LIGHT INDUSTRIAL PRODUCTS I&.E COMPANY

发票号码及标记	件数		货物名称	保险金额
HMINV2585 MTY HMSC2005321 FELEXSTOWE C/No.1-780	780CTNS		MOUTHWASH PRODUCTS	USD81 818.00
运输工具、航次 （及转载工具）	ANGLAIS V.296	约启运于	AS PER B/L	赔付地及币别	UK IN USD
运输路程	自 SHANGHAI, CHINA 经到 FELEXSTOWE, UK			提单号码	TD359790

承保险别

COVERING INSTITUTE CARGO CLAUSES(A)

AS PER INSTITUTE CARGO CLAUSES OF

THE INSURANCE INSTITUTE OF LONDON DATED 1/1/1982

(WAREHOUSE TO WAREHOUSE CLAUSE INCLUDED)

投保单位签章：

SHANGHAI HUAMEI LIGHT INDUSTRIAL

PRODUCTS I&.E COMPANY

×××

投保日期：

2015 年 8 月 19 日

图 6.3　小李填制的投保单

任务再现

　　宁波明空贸易有限公司于 2015 年 6 月与巴西服装进口公司签订一笔棉裤的出口合同，CIF SAN PAULO 成交，合同金额为 96 000 美元。9 月，GARMENTS IMPORTING 公司开来信用证（见图 6.4），宁波明空贸易有限公司业务员小李按照信用证要求准备好所需材料，向保险公司办理了投保手续。

棉裤

Issue of a Documentary Credit

APPLICATION HEADER: BANK OF CHINA, SAN PAULO,BRAZIL

USER HEADER　103：BANK OF CHINA,NINGBO

SEQUENCE OF TOTAL　　*27:　1/1

FORM OF DOC.CREDIT　*40A: IRREVOCABLE

DOC.CREDIT NUMBER:　*20: LC-09112

图 6.4　中国银行圣保罗分行开立的信用证

DATE OF ISSUE   *31C: 150918
EXPIRY   *31D: DATE 151105 PLACE IN CHINA
APPLICANT   *50:   BRAZIL GARMENTS IMPORTING COMPANY
                              01404 SAN PAULO, SP, BRAZIL
BENEFICIARY   *59:   NINGBO BRIGHT SKY TRADE CO., LTD
                              NO.1299 YINXIAN WEST ROAD,NINGBO,CHINA
AMOUNT   *32B: CURRENCY USD AMOUNT USD 96000.00
AVAILABLE WITH/BY   *41D: PNBPERSHXXX
                              BY DEF PAYMENT
                       42P: DEFERRED PAYMENT DETAILS
                              AT 60 DAYS AFTER SHIPMENT DATE
PARITIAL SHIPMENTS   43P: NOT ALLOWED
TRANSSHIPMNET   43T: ALLOWED
LOADING IN CHARGE   44A: CHINESE MAIN PORT
FOR TRANSPORT TO   44B: SAN PAULO,BRAZIL
LATEST DATE OF SHIP.   44C:151025
DESCRIPT OF GOODS   45A: CIF SAN PAULO,BRAZIL USD 9.60 PER PC 10000 PCS 100% COTTON TROUSERS AS
                            PER CONTRACT NO.: RN622 PACKING:PACKED IN STRONG WOODEN CASES

DOCUMENTS REQUIRED   46A:

+MANUALLY SIGNED COMMERCIAL INVOICE IN DUPLICATE.

+PACKING LIST IN DUPLICATE.

+FULL SET OF CLEAN ON BOARD OCEAN BILLS OF LADING MADE OUT TO OUR ORDER AND ENDORSED IN BLANK, MARKED FREIGHT COLLECT NOTIFY APPLICANT.

+INSURANCE POLICY IN DUPLICATE BLANK ENDORSED COVERING ALL RISKS AND WAR RISK FOR 10% INVOICE VALUE. CLAIMS,IF ANY,PAYABLE AT DESTINATION IN THE CURRENCY OF THE DRAFT.

+GSP CERTIFICATE OF ORIGIN FORM A, CERTIFYING GOODS OF ORIGIN IN CHINA, ISSUED BY COMPETENT QUTHORITIES

+COPY OF TELEX/FAX ADVICE, ADDRESSED TO APPLICANT BY BENEFICIARY, WITHIN 2 DAYS AFTER SHIPMENT BEARING NUMBER OF PACKAGES,GROSS AND NET WEIGHT,VESSEL NAME,BILL OF LADING NO.AND DATE, CONTRACT NO.,VALUE

+ONE SET OF NON-NEGOTIABLE SHIPPING DOCUMENTS MUST BE AIRMAILED TO APPLICANT AFTER SHIPMENT AND A CERTIFICATE TO THIS EFFECT MUST ACCOMPANY THE DOCUMENTS FOR NEGOTIATION.

ADDITIONAL COND   47A:

1. A DISCREPANCY HANDLING FEE OF USD50.00(OR EQUIVALENT)AND THE RELATIVE TELEX/SWIFT COST WILL BE DEDUCTED FROM THE PROCEEDS NO MATTER THE BANKING CHARGES ARE FOR WHOEVER ACCOUNT.

2. B/L TO EVIDENCE SHIPMENT EFFECTED BY CONTAINER VESSEL ONLY.

图 6.4　中国银行圣保罗分行开立的信用证（续）

DETAILS OF CHARGES   71B:

ALL BANKING CHARGES ARE FOR ACCOUNT OF BENEFICIARY INCLUDING OUR REIMBURSEMENT CHARGES.

PRESENTATION PERIOD   48:

WITHIN 10 DAYS AFTER THE DATE OF SHIPMENT BUT WITHIN THE CREDIT VALIDITY.

CONFIRMATION   49：WITHOUT

INSTRUCTIONS   78:

1. DOCUMENTS MUST BE SENT THROUGH NEGOTIATING BANK TO US IN 1 LOT BY COURIER SERVICE.

2. UPON RECEIPT OF COMPLIANT DOCUMENTS,WE SHALL REIMBURSE YOU AS INSTRUCTED.

图 6.4　中国银行圣保罗分行开立的信用证（续）

补充资料如下：

（1）INVOICE NO.: RST1008/007

（2）INVOICE DATE:150922

（3）B/L NO.: COSU2010351001

（4）B/L DATE:151101

（5）提单签发单位：CHINA OCEAN SHIPPING AGENCY NINGBO CO., LTD

　　提单签发人：王晓

（6）船名航次：RED WIND V.113

（7）POLICY NO.: POSTER567

（8）GSP NO.: 2010NB34899

（9）手签员：李丽

（10）工厂完货时间：OCT.23,2015

（11）集装箱号码和封箱号：COSU58763/30654

（12）实际装运港：宁波

参考答案

以宁波明空贸易有限公司业务员小李的身份，根据巴西服装进口公司提供的信用证，填制一份符合规定的投保单。

任务二　填制（审核）保险单

任务导航

　　上海运动商品进出口公司在 2015 年 11 月与加拿大的 PETRRCO 公司达成合作意向，从中国出口一批不同型号的运动球类（Ball Of

Sporting）。双方协商后决定采用信用证方式达成交易，2016 年 1 月，对方公司开来了信用证（见图 6.5）。

上海运动商品进出口公司首先要阅读信用证，了解信用证中有关保险单的条款。因为在 CIF 贸易术语下出口到加拿大的产品需要卖方办理投保，所以需要根据信用证的内容准备好所需材料，向保险公司办理投保。

加拿大皇家银行开立的信用证如图 6.5 所示。

Issue of a Documentary Credit

USER HEADER	SERVICE CODE 103:
	BANK PRIORITY 113:
	MSG USER REF 108:
	INFO FROM CI 115:
SQUENCE OF TOTAL	27: 1/1
FROM OF DOC.CREDIT	40A: IRREVOCABLE
DOC CREDIT NUMBER	20: BL120197
DATE OF ISSUE	31C: 150130
APPLICABLE RULES	40E: UCP LATEST VERSION
DATE AND PLACE OF EXP.	1D: DATE 010415 PLACE IN APPLICANT' S COUNTRY
APPLICANT BANK	51D: THE ROYAL BANK OF CANADA, BRITISH, COLUMBIA

INTERNATIONAL CANTER.1055 WEST GEORGIA STREET, VANCOUVER, B.C. V6E 3P3

APPLICANT	50 : PETRRCO INTERNATONAL TRADING

CORPORATION 1100 SHEPPARD AVENUE EAST SUITE 406 WILLOWDALE ONTARIO, CANADA M2K 2W2

BENEFICIARY	59: SHANGHAI SPORTING GOODS IMP&EXP.CO.
	215 HUQIU ROAD SHANGHAI,CHINA
AMOUNT	32B: CURRENCY USD AMOUNT 88710.00
AVAILABLE WITH/BY…	41D: ANY BANK IN APPLICANT'S COUNTRY BY NEGOTIANTION
DRAFTS AT…	42C: 30DAYS AFTER SIGHT
DRAWEE	42D: THE ROYAL BANK OF CANADA,BRITISH
PARTIAL SHIPMENT	43P: ALLOWED
TRANSSHIPMENT	43T: ALLOWED
LOADING/DISPATCHING/TAKING	44A: SHANGHAI,CHINA
TRANSPORTATION TO	44B: VANCOUVER,CANADA
LATEST DATE OF SHIPMENT	44C: 150331
DESCRIP OF GOODS	45A: BALL OF SPOTING AS PER S/C NO:SPT-211
	2000PCS OF SBW32 BASKETBALL AT USD16.95/ PC
	2000PCS OF GBW322 FOOTBALL AT USD21.33/PC

图 6.5 加拿大皇家银行开立的信用证

1000PCS OF ERVS VOLLEYBALL AT USD 12.15/PC

GOODS TO BE PACKED IN CARTONS OF 50PCS EACH, TOTAL 100

CARTONS TERMS OF DELIVERY: CIF VANCOUVE

DOCUMENTS REQUIRED

46A: +MANUALLY SIGNED COMMERCIAL

INVOICE IN 5 COPIES SHOWING SEPARATELY FOB VALUE, FREIGHT CHARGE , INSURANCE PREMIUM, CIF VALUE AND COUNTRY OF ORIGIN.

+FULL SET OF CLEAN ON BOARD OCEAN BILLS OF LADING TO ORDER OF BENEFICIARY MARKED FREIGHT PREPAID PLUS TWO NON-NEGOTIABLE COPIES, NOTIFY: APPLICANT AND ISSUING BANK AND SHOWING THIS DOCUMENTARY CREDIT NUMBER.

+MARINE INSURANCE POLICY OR CERTIFICATE IN DUPLICATE, ENDORSED IN BLANK, FOR FULL INVOICE VALUE PLUS 10 PERCENT STATING CLAIM PAYABLE IN CANADA COVERING ALL RISKS AND WAR RISKS AS PER THE RELEVANT OCEAN MARINE CARGO CLAUSES OF THE PEOPLE'S INSURANCE COMPANY OF CHINA DATED01/01/1981.

+PACKING LIST IN 5 COPIES.

+ONE FULL SET OF NON-NEGOTIABLE SHIPPING DOCUMENTS MUST BE SENT TO THE APPLICANT BY AIR COURIER WITHIN 3 DAYS AFTER SHIPMENT AND BENEFICIARY'S CERTIFICATE TO THIS EFFECT IS REQUIRED.

+BENEFICIARY'S CERTIFICATE CERTIFYING THAT ONE COPY EACH OF INVOICE , N/N B/L HAVE BEEN FAXED TO BUYER TO FAX NO.662-225 WITHIN 3 DAYS AFTER SHIPMENT.

+CERTIFICATE OF ORIGIN GSP CHINA FORM A, ISSUED BY THE CHAMBER OF COMMERCE OR OTHER ARTHOUITY DULY ENTITLED FOR THIS PURPOSE.

ADDITIONAL CONDITION   47A:

+MAKING SHIPPING MARK AS P I T C/SPT-211/VANCOUVER/NO.1-UP

+ALL DOCUMENTS MENTIONING THIS L/C NO.

+BOTH AMOUNT AND QUANTITY PLUS OR MINUS SPCT ACCEPTABLE.

+IF ANY DISCREPANCY,WE SHALL DEDUCT USD50.00 BEING OUR FEE FROM THE PROCESS.

+THE NAME , ADDRESS, TELEPHONE NUMBER OF SHIPPING AGENT IN VANCOUVER MUST BE MENTIONED ON B/L.

DERAILS OF CHARGES   71B: ALL BANKING CHARGES OUTSIDE CANADA

                                                INCLUDING COST OF WIRE AND REIM CHARGE

                                                ARE FOR BENEFICIARY'S ACCOUNT.

PRESENTATION PERIOD   48: WITHIN 15 DAYS AFTER THE DATE OF SHIPMENT

CONFIRMATION   49:CONFIRMED

INSRTUCT. TO NEGOTATING   78:

+UPON RECEIPT YOUR SHIPPING DOCUMENTS IN STRICT CONFORMITY WITH L/C TERMS,WE WILL COVER YOUR   ACCOUNT

+DRAFT(S) AND DOCUMENTS TO BE SENT TO US BY COURIER SERVICE MAILING ADDRESS   COLUMBIA INTERNATIONAL CANTER.1055 WEST GEORGIA STREET, VANCOUVER, B.C. V6E 3P3

+THIS ADVICE IS OPERATIVE WITH NO CONFIRMATION TO FOLLOW AND SUBJUCT TO ICC1993 REVISION PUB 500.

图 6.5　加拿大皇家银行开立的信用证（续）

补充业务资料如下：

(1) INVOICE NO. 01A30676-032A　　INVOICE DATE:MAR.05,2015

(2) FREIGHT: USD300/CONTAINER

(3) G.W:25KGS/CARTONS　　　　　N.W:22KGS/CARTONS

(4) MEAS:80×55×30CMS /CTN

(5) VESSEL: CHAO HE V.02386　　　集装箱：TINU3112933(20')SEAL062472

　　　　　　　　　　　　　　　　　(20GP)FCL

(6) B/L NO.: COSU298000081　　　B/L DATE:MAR.23,2015

(7) 保单号码：01-78963　　　　　保单日期：MAR.20,2015

(8) 买方经办人：MARY

(9) 上海运动用品进出口公司

　　卖方负责人：华海红　　　制单员：李玲

(10) FORMA NO.:ZJ01698

(11) 船代资料：KAWA THAI SHIPPING AGENCY

　　　　　　　55-8 MAITRICHITR RD, VANCOUVER,CANADA

　　　　　　　TEL NO:2667893

要求：

请以上海运动商品进出口公司业务员小王的身份，根据加拿大公司提供的信用证，填制一份符合规定的保险单。

知识准备

一、保险单的定义及作用

（一）保险单的定义

保险单（insurance policy）简称保单，是保险人与被保险人订立保险合同的正式书面证明。保险单必须完整地记载保险合同双方当事人的权利义务及责任。保险单是保险合同成立的证明，是被保险人索赔与保险人进行理赔的依据。

（二）保险单的内容及作用

保险单必须明确、完整地记载有关保险双方的权利义务，保单上主要载有保险人和被保险人的名称、保险标的、保险金额、保险费、保险期限、赔偿或给付的责任范围以及其他规定事项。

保险单根据投保人的申请，由保险人签署，交由被保险人收执。保险单是被保险人在保险标的遭受意外事故而发生损失时，向保险人索赔的主要凭证，同时也是保险人收取保险费的依据。在 CIF 保险合同中，保险单是出口方向进口方提供的结汇单据之一，经过背书后，可以随货物所有权的转移而进行转让。

二、保险单的种类

保险单的种类有以下几种。

（1）保险单。一般外贸企业所称的大保单就是保险单。它是保险人根据被保险人的要求，表示已接受承保责任而出具的一种独立文件。在保险单正面有双方约定保险标的物的有关内容。背面印有海洋运输货物保险条款，其中包括基本险的责任范围，还有除外责任、责任起讫、被保险人的义务和索赔期限等。它是一种正规的保险单据，是被保险人在货物发生损失时进行索赔的主要依据。

（2）保险凭证（insurance certificate），俗称小保单。保险凭证是保险人为了简化手续，把保险单的条款作了简略，对背面条款并不作详细记载的一种文件，所以它是保险单的一种简化形式的凭证。保险单与保险凭证具有同等法律效力。

（3）联合保险凭证（combined insurance certificate）。保险公司不另出保险单，利用商业发票在上面加盖章戳，注明保险编号、承保险制、金额、装载船名、开船日。

（4）预约保险单（open policy）。预约保险单是进口贸易中，被保险人（一般为进口人）与保险人之间订立的总合同。订立这种合同既可以简化保险手续，又可以使货物一经装运即可取得保障。

（5）保险声明（insurance declaration）。预约保险单项下的货物一经确定装船，要求被保险人立即以保险声明书的形式，将该批货物的名称、数量、保险金额、船名、起讫港口、航次、开航日期等通知保险人，银行可将保险声明书当作一项单据予以接受。

（6）批单。保险单出立后，如需变更其内容，可由保险公司另出的凭证注明更改或补充的内容，称为批单。其须粘在保险单上并加盖骑缝章，作为保险单不可分割的一部分。

三、保险合同的当事人

保险合同的当事人就是在保险合同中享有权利、承担义务的人，包括保险人和投保人。保险人是指与投保人订立保险合同，并承担赔偿或者给付保险金责任的保险公司。投保人是指与保险人订立保险合同，并按照保险合同负有支付保险费义务的人。另外，在保险合同中还存在两种关系人，这就是被保险人和受益人。被保险人，是以其财产、生命或者身体作为保险标的，受到保险合同保障的人。当投保人为自己的利益订立保险合同时，投保人就是被保险人，二者是同一人。受益人，是指人身保险合同中由被保险人或者投保人指定的享有保险金请求权的人。

四、信用证中有关保险单据条款的举例

信用证中有关保险单据条款的情形有以下两种。

（1）MARINE INSURANCE POLICY OF CERTIFICATE IN DUPLICATEINDORSED IN BLANKFOR FULL INVOICE VALUE PLUS 10 PERCENT STATING CLAIM PAYABLE IN JAPAN COVERING FPA AS PER OCEAN MARINE CARGO CLAUSE OF THE PEOPLE'S INSURANCE COMPANY OF CHINA DATED 1/1/1981.

保险单或保险凭证一式二份，空白背书，按发票金额加 10%投保，声明在日本赔付，根据中国人民保险公司 1981 年 1 月 1 日的海洋运输货物保险条款投保平安险。

（2）INSURANCE PLOICIES OR CERTIFICATE IN DUPLICATE ENDORSED IN BLANK OF 110% OF INVOICE VALUE COVERING ALL RISKS AND AR RISKS AS PER CIC WITH CLAIMS PAYABLE AT CANADA IN THE CURRENCY OF DRAFT (IRRESPECTIVE OF PERCENTAGE), INCLUDING 60 DAYS AFTER DISCHARGES OFTHE GOODS AT PORT OF DESTINATION SUBJECT TO CIC.

保单或保险凭证做成空白背书，按发票金额的 110%投保中国保险条款的一切险和战争险，按汇票所使用的货币在加拿大赔付（无免赔率），并根据中国保险条款，保险期限在目的港卸船后 60 天为止。

五、保险单据的缮制

保险单样本如图 6.6 所示，其内容及填制方法如表 6.2 所示。

中国人民保险公司

THE PEOPLE'S INSURANCE COMPANY OF CHINA

总公司设于北京		一九四九年创立
Head Office：BEIJING		Established in 1949

发票号码	保险单	保险单号次
Invoice No.＿＿＿＿	INSURANCE POLICY	Policy No.＿＿＿＿

中国人民保险公司（以下简称本公司）

This Policy of Insurance witnesses that The People's Insurance Company of China（hereinafter called "the Company"）

图 6.6　保险单样本

根据 NAME OF INSURED

At the request of _____

（以下简称保险人）的要求，由被保险人向本公司缴付约定的保险费，按照本保险单承保险别和背面所载条款与下列特款承保下述货物运输保险，特立本保险单。（hereinafter called the "insured"）and in consideration of the agreed premium paying to the Company by the Insured undertakes to Insure the undermentioned goods in transportation subject to the conditions of this Policy .As per the clauses printed overleaf and other special clauses attached hereon.

标记 Marks and Nos.	包装及数量 Quantity	保险货物项目 Description of Goods	保险金额 Amount Insured

总保险金额

Total Amount Insured：_____

保费   费率   装载运输工具

Premium   AS ARRANGED   Rate   AS ARRANGED   Per conveyance S.S _____

开航日期

Slg.on or abt _____   From _____to _____

承保险别

Conditions   SPECIAL CONDITIONS IN INSURANCE POLICY_____

所保货物，如遇出险，本公司凭本保险单及其他有关证件给付赔款。

Claims, if any, payable on surrender of this   Policy together with other relevant documents.

所保货物，如发生本保险单项下负责赔偿的损失或事故应立即通知本公司下述代理人查勘。

In the event of accident whereby loss or damage may result in a claim under this Policy immediate notice applying for Survey must be given to the Company's Agent as mentioned hereunder.

赔款偿付地点

Claim payable at_____

日期

DATE _____   ADDRESS _____

图 6.6 保险单样本（续）

表 6.2 保险单内容及填制方法一览表

序号	项目名称	填制方法
1	发票号码（Invoice No.）	此处填写发票号码
2	保险单号次（Policy No.）	填写保险公司指定号码
3	被保险人（Insured）	如信用证无特别规定，保险单的被保险人应是信用证的受益人。 按照习惯，被保险人一栏中填写出口公司的名称

续表

序号	项目名称	填制方法
4	唛头（Marks and Nos.）	保险单唛头应与发票、提单等一致，也可只填"AS PER INVOICE NO …"，并填写最大外包装数量
5	包装及数量（Quantity）	如以包装件数计价者，则将最大包装的总件数填入，如以毛重 或净重计价，可填件数及毛重或净重，如果是裸装货物，则表示其件数即可；散装货物则表示其重量，并在其后注明"IN BULK"字样
6	保险货物项目（Description of Goods）	填写货物名称，此栏允许填写货物总称
7	保险金额（Amount Insured）	一般按照发票总金额的 110%投保。信用证项下的保险单必须按信用证规定办理。此栏保险金额使用的货币应与信用证使用的货币相一致，大小写保持一致
8	总保险金额（Total Amount Insured）	即保险金额的大写数字，以英文表示，末尾应加"ONLY"，以防涂改
9	保费（Premium）	一般已由保险公司印就"AS ARRANGED"（如约定）字样。除非信用证另有规定，每笔保费及费率可以不具体表示
10	费率（Rate）	一般已由保险公司印就"AS ARRANGED"（如约定）字样。无须填制
11	装载工具（Per Conveyance S.S）	填写装载船的船名。当运输由两程运输完成时，应分别填写一程船名和二程船名
12	开航日期（Slg.on or abt）	一般填写提单的签发日期，也可填写提单签发日前后各 5 天之内任何一天的日期，或填"AS PER B/L DATE"
13	起运地和目的地（From…to…）	此栏填写起运地和目的地名称。当货物经转船到达目的港时，可填写 FROM 装运港 TO 目的港 W/TAT 转运港（WITH TRANSIMENT AT ×××），也可打成 VIA 转运港 ANDTHENCETO 投保最终目的地
14	承保险别（Conditions）	一般应包括具体投保险别、保险责任起始时间、适用保险条款的文本及日期
15	赔付地点（Claim Payable at）	此栏按合同或信用证要求填制。如果信用证中并未列明确，一般将目的港作为赔付地点。赔款货币一般为投保额相同的货币
16	日期（Date）	日期指保险单的签发日期。由于保险公司提供仓至仓（WAREHOUS-ETOWAREHOUSE）服务，所以要求保险手续在货物离开出口方仓库前办理。保险单的日期也应是货物离开出口方仓库前的日期
17	投保地点（Place）	一般为装运港（地）的名称
18	签章（Authorized）	由保险公司签字或盖章以示保险单正式生效

参考答案

课堂思考

（1）保险单中的被保险人一般情况下究竟是卖方还是买方？

（2）为什么保险单的签发日期不得迟于装运单据的签发日期？

小 贴 士

保险单据可按信用证的要求和需要将由被保险人在单据上背书（endorsement）。

保险单据的背书根据信用证规定和被保险人的不同情况分为以下几种。

（1）持单人是被保险人（出口商）时，做成空白背书。

（2）按信用证规定做成记名背书。

（3）被保险人是买方/进口商，则卖方/出口商不须背书，保险单如需转让，应由买方被保险人背书。

（4）被保险人是第三者、中性名称（to whom it may concern），若保险单转让时，不须背书。

（5）被保险人是bearer，在赔付地点写明"claim payable at（place）to bearer or holder"，保险单若转让时，不必背书。

职业判断

案例资料：

2015年3月，上海华东食品有限公司与加拿大H&N公司达成交易，出口瓜子100公吨，CIF术语下每公吨100美元。华东食品公司的单证员与H&N公司联系后，H&N公司开来信用证。华东食品公司的业务员审核信用证时发现，信用证中要求B/L签发日期为5月15日，而保单日期为5月17日。

思考：

信用证中涉及的提单与保单日期是否符合规定？

参考答案

任务实施

上海运动商品进出口公司小王根据加拿大皇家银行开立的信用证，填制了一份符合规定的保险单，如图6.7所示。

中国人民保险公司
THE PEOPLE'S INSURANCE COMPANY OF CHINA

总公司设于北京	一九四九年创立
Head Office: BEIJING	Established in 1949

发票号码	保险单	保险单号次
Invoice No.01A30676-032A	INSURANCE POLICY	Policy No. 01-78963

中国人民保险公司（以下简称本公司）

This Policy of Insurance witnesses that The People's Insurance Company of China（hereinafter called "the Company"）

根据 NAME OF INSURED

At the request of SHANGHAI SPORTING GOODS IMP.& EXP.CO.

（以下简称保险人）的要求，由被保险人向本公司缴付约定的保险费，按照本保险单承保险险别和背面所载条款与下列特款承保下述货物运输保险，特立本保险单。

（hereinafter called the "insured"）and in consideration of the agreed premium paying to the Company by the Insured undertakes to Insure the undermentioned goods in transportation subject to the conditions of this Policy .As per the clauses printed overleaf and other special clauses attached hereon.

标记 Marks and Nos.	包装及数量 Quantity	保险货物项目 Description of Goods	保险金额 Amount Insured
PITC SPT-211 VANCOUVER NO.1-100	100 CTNS	BALL OF SPORTING L/C No.: BL 120197	USD97 581.00

总保险金额

Total Amount Insured : SAY U.S.DOLLARS NINTY-SEVEN FIVE HUNDRED AND EIGHTY-ONE ONLY

保费	费率	装载运输工具
Premium AS ARRANGED	Rate AS ARRANGED	Per conveyance S.S CHAO HE V.02386

开航日期

Slg.on or abt MAR.23,2015   From SHANGHAI PORT   to VANCOUVER ,CANADA

承保险别 SPECILA CONDTIONS IN INSURANCE POLICY

Conditions ALL RISKS AND WAR RISKS AS PER THE RELEVANT OCEAN MARINE CARGO CLAUSES OF THE PEOPLE'S INSURANCE COMPANY OF CHINA DATED 01/01/1981.

所保货物，如遇出险，本公司凭本保险单及其他有关证件给付赔款。

Claims, if any, payable on surrender of this   Policy together with other relevant documents.

所保货物，如发生本保险单项下负责赔偿的损失或事故应立即通知本公司下述代理人查勘。

In the event of accident whereby loss or damage may result in a claim under this Policy immediate notice applying for Survey must be given to the Company's Agent as mentioned hereunder.

赔款偿付地点

Claim payable at VANCOUVER ,CANADA

日期

DATE MAR.20,2015   ADDRESS SHANGHAI CHINA

图 6.7 小王签发的中国人民保险公司保险单

上海盛大进出口公司于2015年1月与孟加拉国ALFAGA公司签订一笔不同型号的卷尺出口合同，即期信用证付款，CIF CHITTAGONG 成交，合同金额为 9300 美元。2 月末，ALFAGA 公司开来信用证（见图 6.8），上海盛大进出口公司业务员按照信用证要求准备好所需材料，向保险公司办理了投保手续。

Issue of a Documentary Credit

SQUENCE OF TOTAL	27: 1/1
FROM OF DOC.CREDIT	40A: IRREVOCABLE
DOC CREDIT NUMBER	20: 11660801
DATE OF ISSUE	31C: FEBRUARY 24,2015
APPLICABLE RULES	40E: UCP LATEST VERSION
DATE AND PLACE OF EXP.	31D: MAY 23,2015 IN CHINA
APPLICANT	50: ALFAGA ENTERPRISE
	28,IMAMCONJ
	DHAKA,BANGLADESH
ISSUING BANK:	52A: AB BANK ;LIMITED
	IMAMGANJ BRANCH, 40
	IMAMGANJ,DHAKA-1211,BANGLADESH
BENEFICIARY	59: SHANGHAI SHENG DA CO. LTD.
	UNIT C 5/F JINGMAO TOWER
	SHANGHAI,CHINA
AMOUNT	32B: CURRENCY USD AMOUNT 9300.00
AVAILABLE WITH/BY…	41D: ANY BANK IN CHINA BY NEGOTITAION
DRAFTS AT…	42C: DRAFTS AT SIGHT FOR 100PCT INVOICE VALUE
DRAWEE	42D: AB BANK LIMITED, IMAMGANJ BRANCH
PARTIAL SHIPMENT	43P: ALLOWED
TRANSSHIPMENT	43T: ALLOWED
LOADING/DISPATCHING/TAKING	44A: ANY CHINESE PORTS
TRANSPORTATION TO	44B: CHITTAGONG SEA PORT, BANGLADESH
LATEST DATE OF SHIPMENT	44C: MAY 31,2015
DESCRIP OF GOODS	45A: TAPE RULES
	(1) 2000 DOZ PAIR MODEL: JH-392WSIZE: 3M X16 MM @USD3.60 PER DOZEN CIF CHITTAGONG
	(2) 500 DOZ PAIR MODEL:JH-380WSIZE:3M

图 6.8　孟加拉国 AB 银行开立的信用证

	X16 MM @USD4.20 PER DOZEN CIF CHITTAGONG
	PACKING: EXPORT STANDARD SEAWORTHY PACKING
DOCUMENTS REQUIRED	46A: +SINGED COMMERCIAL INVOICE IN TRIPLICATE
	+SINGED PACKING LIST IN TRIPLICATE
	+BENEFICIARY'S CERTIFICATE STATING THAT ONE SET OF ORIGINAL SHIPPING DOCUMENTS INCLUDING ORIGINAL C/O HAS BEEN SENT DIRECTLY TO THE APPLICANT AFTER THE SHIPMENT.
	+INSURANCE POLICY / CERTIFICATE ENDORSED IN BLANK FOR 130 PCT OF CIF VALUE, COVERING ALL RISKS AS PER OCEAN MARINE CARGO CLAUSES OF THE P.I.C.C.
	+3/3 PLUS ONE BILLS OF LADING MADE OUT TO ORDER AND BLANK ENDORSED MARKED "FREIGHT PREPAID " AND NOTIFY APPLICANT .
	+CERTIFICATE OF ORIGIN ISSUED BY AUTHORITY PARTY IN CHINA IN THREE COPIES.
ADDITIONAL CONDITION	47A:
	+ ALL DRAFTS DRAWN HERE UNDER MUST BE MARKED "DRAWN UNDER AB BANK LIMITED,IMAMGANJ BRANCH CREDIT NO. 11660801 DATED FEB.24,2015".
	+ T/T REIMBURSEMENT IS NOT ACCEPTABLE.
DERAILS OF CHARGES ACCOUNT	71B: ALL BANKING CHARGES OUTSIDE BANGLADESH ARE FOR BENEFICIARY'S
PRESENTATION PERIOD	48: DOCUMENTS MUST BE PRESENTED WITHIN 15 DAYS AFTER THE DATE OF ISSUANCE OF THE SHPPING DOCUMENTS BUT WITHIN THE VALIDITY OF THE CREDIT.
CONFIRMATION	49: WITHOUT
INSRTUCT. TO NEGOTATING	78: THE AMOUNT AND DATE OF NEGOTIATION OF EACH DRAFT MUST BE ENDORSED ON THE REVERSE OF THIS CREIDIT, ALL DOCUMENTS INCLUDING BENEFICIARY'S DRAFTS MUST BE SENT BY COUTIER SERVICE DIRECTLY TO US IN ONE LOT. UPON OUR RECEIPT OF THE DRAFTS AND DOCUMENTS WE SHALL MAKE PAYMENT AS INSRTUCTED BY YOU

图 6.8　孟加拉国 AB 银行开立的信用证（续）

其他业务资料如下：

（1）INVOICE NO. ：NBSM11022

（2）INVOICE DATE：MARCH.1,2015

（3）PACKING：TO BE PACKED IN CARTONS OF 50DOZS

（4）GW：15KGS/CARTONS

（5）NW：13KGS/CARTONS

（6）MEAS：100CM×100CM×50CM=0.5CBM /CTN

（7）VESSEL：GOLDEN　BRIDGE　V.988

　　集装箱号码：COSCC28272/9889

（8）B/L NO.：COSU66089803

（9）B.L DATE：MAR.10,2015

（10）C/O 号码：S082827709

（11）保单号码：HJ29877677　　保单日期：2015-3-9

（12）买方经办人：KATE

（13）上海盛大有限公司

　　卖方负责人：李明　　报检员：王一

（14）H.S.编码：92870088

上海盛大进出口公司业务员小王收到保险公司签发的保险单以后，发现保险单上多处内容与信用证中的内容不符合（见图 6.9）。根据信用证，以业务员小王的身份修改收到的错误保险单，缮制一份正确的保险单。

中国人民保险公司
THE PEOPLE'S INSURANCE COMPANY OF CHINA

总公司设于北京	一九四九年创立
Head Office: BEIJING	Established in 1949

发票号码	保险单	保险单号次
Invoice No. NBSM11022	INSURANCE POLICY	Policy No. HJ29877677

中国人民保险公司（以下简称本公司）

This Policy of Insurance witnesses that The People's Insurance Company of China(hereinafter called "the Company")

根据 NAME OF INURED

At the request of ALFAGA ENTERPRISE CO.,LTD.

（以下简称保险人）的要求，由被保险人向本公司缴付约定的保险费，按照本保险单承保险别和背面所载条款与下列特款承保下述货物运输保险，特立本保险单。

（hereinafter called the "insured"）and in consideration of the agreed premium paying to the Company by the Insured undertakes to Insure the under-mentioned goods in transportation subject to the conditions of this Policy .As per the clauses printed overleaf and other special clauses attached hereon.

标记 Marks and Nos.	包装及数量 Quantity	保险货物项目 Description of Goods	保险金额 Amount Insured
A.E. CHITTAGONG	2 500DOZ PAIR	TAPE RULES	USD9 300.00

图 6.9　保险公司签发的保险单

总保险金额

Total Amount Insured : <u>SAY U.S. DOLLARS NINE THOUSAND THREE HUNDRED ONLY</u>

保费　　　　　　　　费率　　　　　　　　装载运输工具

Premium <u>AS ARRANGED</u>　　Rate <u>AS ARRANGED</u>　　Per conveyance S.S <u>GOLDEN</u>　　<u>BRIDGE</u>　　<u>V.988</u>

开航日期

Slg.on or abt <u>AS PER B/L DATE</u>　　From <u>SHANGHAI PORT</u>　　to　<u>CHITTAGONG SEA PORT,BANGLADESH</u>

承保险别　SPECILA CONDTIONS IN INSURANCE POLICY

Conditions <u>W.P.A RISK AND WAR RISK AS PER CIC DATED 1/1/1981.</u>

所保货物，如遇出险，本公司凭本保险单及其他有关证件给付赔款。

Claims, if any, payable on surrender of this　Policy together with other relevant documents.

所保货物，如发生本保险单项下负责赔偿的损失或事故应立即通知本公司下述代理人查勘。

In the event of accident whereby loss or damage may result in a claim under this Policy immediate notice applying for Survey must be given to the Company's Agent as mentioned hereunder.

赔款偿付地点：

Claim payable at　<u>BANGLADESH</u>

日期

DATE <u>MAR10,2015</u>　　　　　　　ADDRESS <u>CHITTAGONG</u>

参考答案

图 6.9　保险公司签发的保险单（续）

技能强化训练

项目小结

技 能 提 高

1. 根据信用证（见图 6.10）和有关资料，填制一份完整的保险单。

在线测试及
参考答案

Issue of a Documentary Credit		
MT700		ISSUE OF A DOCUMENTARY CREDIT
SENDER		HSBC BANK PLC,MONTREAL, CANADA
RECEIVER		HANGZHOU CITY COMMERCIAL BANK, HANGZHOU,CHINA
SEQUENCE OF TOTAL	27 :	1/1
FORM OF DOC.CREDIT	40A :	IRREVOCABLE
DOC.CREDIT NUMBER	20 :	044/3075989
DATE OF ISSUE	31C :	150811

图 6.10　信用证

APPLICABLE RILES	40E :	UCP LATEST VERSION
DATE AND PLACE OF EXPIRY	31D:	DATE 081210 PLACE IN CHINA
APPLICANT	50 :	KU TEXTILE CORPORATION 430 VTRA MONTREAL CANADA
BENEFICIARY	59 :	ZHEJIANG JINYUAN IMPORT & EXPORT CORPORATION 118 XUEYUAN STREET , HANGZHOU , P.R.CHINA
AMOUNT	32B :	CURRENCY USD AMOUNT 31 800.00
AVAILABLE WITH/BY	41D:	ANY BANK IN CANADA, BY NEGOTIATION
DRAFTS AT…	42 C:	AT SIGHT
DRAWEE	42A :	HSBC BANK PLC , MONTREAL , CANADA.
PARTIAL SHIPMTS	43P :	PROHIBITED
TRANSSHIPMENT	43T :	ALLOWED
PORT OF LOADING/	44E :	CHIENESE MAIN PORT
PORT OF DISCHARGE	44F :	CANADA MAIN PORT
LATEST DATE OF SHIPMENT	44C :	151031
DESCRIPTION OF GOODS AND/OR SERVICES.	45A :	10000PCS MEN'S80% DOWN AND 20% FEATHER JACKETS, STYLE NO.UK858 , AS PER S/C NO.920131 AT USD3.18/PCS CIF MONTREAL
DOCUMENTS REQUIRED	46A :	
		+SIGNED INVOICE IN TRIPLICATE , MADE OUT"WOODLAND LIMITED"AND INDICATE L/C NO. AND FREIGHT AND INSUR-ANCE FREE
		+PACKING LIST IN TRIPLICATE.
		+INSURANCE POLICY/CERTIFICATE IN DUPLICATE MADE OUT " TO ORDER OF HSBC BANK PLC, MONTREAL,CANADA." FOR 110% INVOICE VALUE, COVERING ALL RISKS AND WAR RISK. WAREHOUSE TOWAREHOUSE AND I.O.P. AND SHOWING THE CLAIMING CURRENCY IS THE SAME AS THE CURRENCY OF CREDIT.
		+FULL SET OF CLEAN ON BOARD BILL OF LADING MARKED "FEIGHT PREPAID" MADE OUT TO ORDER OF APPLICANT BLANK EDDORSED NOTIFYING "WOODLAND LIMITED".
		+SHIPPING ADVICE SHOWING THE NAME OF THE CARRYING VESSEL , DATE OF SHIPMENT , MARKS , QUANTITY , NET WEIGHT AND GROSS WEIGHT OF THE SHIPMENT TO APPLICANT WITHIIN 3 DAYS AFTER THE DATE OF BILL OF LADING.
		+CUSTOMS INVOICE MUST BE OFFERED IN DUPLICATE.
ADDITIONAL CONDITION	47A :	
		+DOCUMENTS DATED PRIOR TO THE DATE OF THIS CREDIT ARE NOT ACCEPTABLE.
		+TRANSSHIPMENT ALLOWED AT HONGKONG ONLY.
		+SHORT FORM/CHARTER PARTY/THIRD PARTY BILL OF LADING ARE NOT ACCEPTABLE.

图 6.10　信用证（续）

		+SHIPMENT MUST BE EFFECTED BY 1*20'FULL CONTAINER LOAD. B/L TO SHOW EVIDENCE OF THIS EFFECT IS REQUIRED.
		+BENEFICIARY'S CERTIFIED COPY OF FAX DISPACHED TO THE APPLICANT WITHIN 2 DAYS AFTER SHIPMENT.
		+ALL PRESENTATIONS CONTAINING DISCREPANCIES WILL ATTRACT A DISCREPANCY FEE OF USD40.00 PLUS TELEX COSTS OR OTHER CURRENCY EQUIVALENT. THIS CHARGE WILL BE DEDUCTED FROM THE BILL AMOUNT WHETHER OR NOT WE ELECT TO CONSULT THE APPLICANT FOR A WAIVER
PERIOD FOR PRESENTATION	48 :	WITHIN 7 DAYS AFTER THE DATE OF SHIPMENT, BUT WITHIN THE VALIDITY OF THIS CREDIT.
CONFIRMATION INSTRUCTION	49 :	WITHOUT
REIMBURSING BANK	53A :	HSBC BANK PLC, NEW YORK
INFORMATION TO PRESENTING BANK	78 :	ALL DOCUMENTS ARE TO BE REMITTED IN ONE LOT BY COURIER TO HSBC BANK PLC, MONTREAL, CANADA. ,TRADE SERVICES, MONTREAL BRANCH , P O BOX 108, HSBC BANK BUILDING 5/32 BRIGHT ROAD, MONTREAL, CANADA.

图 6.10　信用证（续）

其他业务信息如下：

发票号码：044/3077351

发票日期：150820

提单号码：WS

提单日期：150901

船名：SHIPPED BY REDSTAR001 ON AUG.31,2015

集装箱：TEXJZ3521(40')

H.s.编码：321123

Form A：001002

保单号码：6272155

运费：360 美元　　　保费：150 美元

G/W：15KGS/CTN　　NW：13KGS/CTN

MEASURMENT：25×30×35CMS/CTN

PACKING：10PCS/CTN

2. 根据信用证（见图 6.11）和有关资料审核错误的保险单（见图 6.12），并填制一份正确的保险单。

Issue of a Documentary Credit

APPLICATION HEADER	*ASAHI BANK LTD
	*TOKYO
SEQUENCE OF TOTAL	*27: 1/1
APPLICABLE RULES	*40 : IRREVOCABLE
DOC, CREDIT NUMBER	*20 : LC-429-393536
DATE OF ISSUE	*31C : 141225
EXPIRY	*31D :DATE 150316
	PLACE IN THE COUNTRY OF THE BENEFICIARY
BENEFICIARY	*59: SHAOXING TEXTILE& GARMENT CO., LTD
	NO.1005 ZHONGSHAN ROAD(E-1),SHAOXING CHINA
APPLICANT	*50 : SHINORMAN CO.,LTD.
	NAKANOMACHI 2-20-16,MIYAKOJIMA-KU OSAKA JAPAN
AMOUNT	*32B : CURRENCY USD AMOUNT 39600.00
MAX. CREDIT AMOUNT	*39: UP TO USD39600.00
AVAILABLE WITH/BY	*41D : ANY BANK BY NEGOTIATION
DRAFTS AT ...	*42C: DRAFTS AT SIGHT FOR FULL INVOICE VALUE
DRAWEE	*42A : *ASAHI BANK LTD, <FORMERLY THE
	*KYOWA SAIYAMA BANK, LTD.>
	*TOKYO
PARTIAL SHIPMENTS	*43P: ALLOWED
TRANSSHIPMENT	*43T: NOT ALLOWED
PORT OF LOADING	*44E: SHANGHAI，CHINA
PORT OF DISCHARGE	*44F: OSAKA，JAPAN
LATEST DATE OF SHIP.	*44C: 150301
DESCRIPT. OF GOODS	*45A :
	(1)3000PCS OF APRON ART NO.96837 @USD4.00
	(2)4000PCS OF APRON ART NO.96838 @USD6.00
	PRICE TERM: CIF KOBE
DOCUMENTS REQUIRED	*46A :

+ 3/3 SET OF ORIGINAL CLEAN ON BOARD OCEAN BILLS OF LADING MADE OUT TO ORDER OF SHIPPER AND BLANK ENDORSED, MARKED "FREIGHT PREPAID" AND NOTIFY APPLICANT.

+ ORIGINAL SIGNED COMMERCIAL INVOICE IN 5 FOLD INDICATING CONTRACT NO.

+ PACKING LIST IN 3 FOLD

+ FORM A IN 1 ORIGINAL AND 1 COPY.

图 6.11　信用证

+INSURANCE POLICY/CERTIFICATE IN DUPLICATE FOR 110% INVOICE VALUE , COVERING FPA. WAREHOUSE TOWAREHOUSE

+SHIPPING ADVICE SHOWING THE NAME OF THE CARRYING VESSEL , DATE OF SHIPMENT , MARKS , QUANTITY , NET WEIGHT AND GROSS WEIGHT OF THE SHIPMENT TO APPLICANT WITHIIN 3 DAYS AFTER THE DATE OF BILL OF LADING.

ADDITIONAL COND.   *47A :

1.   T.T. REIMBURSEMENT IS PROHIBITED.

2.   5PCT MORE OR LESS IN QUANTITY ACCEPTABLE.

DETAILS OF CHARGES *71B: ALL BANKING CHARGES OUTSIDE JAPAN INCLUDING REIMBURSEMENT COMMISSIONS ARE FOR ACCOUNT OF BENEFICIARY.

PRESENTATION PERIOD *48 : DOCUMENTS TO BE PRESENTED WITHIN 15 DAY AFTER THE DATE OF SHIPMENT, BUT WITHIN THE VALIDITY OF THE CREDIT.

CONFIRMATION   *49 : WITHOUT

INSTRUCTIONS   *78: THE NEGOTIATION BANK MUST FORWARD THE DRAFTS AND ALL DOCUMENTS BY REGISTERED AIRMAIL DIRECT TO US (INT'L OPERATIONS CENTER MAIL ADDRESS: C.P.O.BOX NO. 800 TOKYO 100-91 JAPAN) IN TWO CONSECUTIVE LOTS, UPON RECEIPT OF THE DRAFTS AND DOCUMENTS IN ORDER, WE WILL REIMBURSE THE NEGOTIATING BANK IN ACCORDANCE WITH THEIR INSTRUCTIONS.

图 6.11　信用证（续）

其他业务资料如下：

（1）INVOICE NO：INV081222

（2）INVOICE DATE：DEC.15,2014

（3）G.W：20KGS/CARTONS

（4）N.W：15KGS/CARTONS

（5）MEAS:40×40×50CM/CTN

（6）VESSEL：DONGFENG V.188　C/S NO：COSCO23435/8866

（7）B/L NO.：AB007

（8）B/L DATE：FEB.28,2014

（9）FORM A 号码：095678

（10）保单号码：IL35678

（11）H.S. NO：12567893

中国人民保险公司
THE PEOPLE'S INSURANCE COMPANY OF CHINA

总公司设于北京   一九四九年创立
Head Office:BEIJING   Established in 1949

发票号码	保险单	保险单号次
Invoice No. INV081222	INSURANCE POLICY	Policy No. IL35678

中国人民保险公司（以下简称本公司）

This Policy of Insurance witnesses that The People's Insurance Company of China(hereinafter called "the Company")

根据 NAME OF INURED

At the request of   SHINORMAN CO.,LTD

(以下简称保险人)的要求，由被保险人向本公司缴付约定的保险费，按照本保险单承保保险险别和背面所载条款与下列特款承保下述货物运输保险，特立本保险单。

（hereinafter called the "insured"）and in consideration of the agreed premium paying to the Company by the Insured undertakes to Insure the undermentioned goods in transportation subject to the conditions of this Policy .As per the clauses printed overleaf and other special clauses attached hereon.

标记（4） Marks and Nos.	包装及数量（5） Quantity	保险货物项目（6） Description of Goods	保险金额（7） Amount Insured
SN SC0801260 OSAKA NO1-7000	7 000CTNS	APRON	USD39 600.00

总保险金额（8）
Total Amount Insured：SAY U.S.DOLLARS THIRTY NINE THOUSAND SIX HUNDRED ONLY

保费（9）	费率（10）	装载运输工具（11）
Premium AS ARRANGED	Rate AS ARRANGED	Per conveyance S.S DONGFENG V.188

开航日期（12）   （13）

Slg.on or abt AS PER B/L   From SHANGHAI CHINA   to   OSAKA JAPAN

承保险别（14）

Conditions   COVERING FPA.

所保货物，如遇出险，本公司凭本保险单及其他有关证件给付赔款。

Claims, if any, payable on surrender of this   Policy together with other relevant documents.

所保货物，如发生本保险单项下负责赔偿的损失或事故应立即通知本公司下述代理人查勘。

In the event of accident whereby loss or damage may result in a claim under this Policy immediate notice applying for Survey must be given to the Company's Agent as mentioned hereunder.

赔款偿付地点：

Claim payable at   OSAKA JAPAN IN USD

日期（16）   （17）

DATE FEB.28 2015   ADDRESS SHANGHAI CHINA

参考答案

图 6.12　存在错误的保险单

项目七

原产地证书实训

知识目标

1. 理解原产地证书的含义和特点;
2. 理解原产地证书的分类;
3. 熟悉信用证中关于原产地证书的条款。

能力目标

1. 能够根据信用证分析原产地证书条款;
2. 能够根据信用证及相关资料制作常见原产地证书;
3. 能够根据信用证及相关资料制作原产地证书申请书。

任务一 填制一般原产地证书

三通

任务导航

　　宁波金铸阀门有限公司在 2015 年 7 月与印度的 CASTER LOS 公司达成合作意向，从中国出口一批型号为 MD519 的 T 型三通（TEE）。双方协商后决定采用信用证方式达成交易，8 月初，对方公司开来了信用证。

　　金铸阀门有限公司首先要阅读信用证，了解信用证中有关原产地证书的条款。因为出口到印度的产品需要提供一般原产地证书，所以需要根据信用证内容申请原产地证书，取得由贸促会或出入境检验检疫部门签发的一般原产地证书。

　　印度国家银行（State Bank of India）开立的信用证如图 7.1 所示。

Issue of a Documentary Credit

27/ Sequence of Total: 1/1

40A/ Form of Doc. Credit: IRREVOCABLE

20/ Doc. Credit Number: 300290ML

31C/ Date of Issue: 150810

31D/ Date of Place of Expiry: 151008

50/Applicant: CASTER LOS CO.

　　　　　　 JASON RD. 113

59/Beneficiary: JINZHU VALVE CO. LTD

　　　　　　 ZHONGSHAN RD. 108 NINGBO, CHINA

32B/ Currency Code, Amount: USD 9 900.00

41D/ Available with /by; ANY BANK BY NEGOTIATION

42C/ Drafts at…: AT SIGHT FOR 100PCT OF INCOIVE VALUE

42A/ Drawee: BANK OF CHINA, NINGBO BRANCH

43P/ Partial Shipments: ALLOWED

43T/ Transshipment: ALLOWED

44E/ Port of Loading: ANY PORT IN CHINA

44F/ Port of Discharge: NEW DELHI

44C/ Latest Date of Shipment: 150925

45A/ Description of Goods and / or Services:

MD519 T-TEE　　1800PCS　　AT USD5.50/PC　　AS PER S/C NO. 102

FOB CHINESE PORT (INCOTERMS 2010)

46A/ Documents Required:

图 7.1　印度国家银行开立的信用证

1. COMMERCIAL INVOICE IN 3 FOLDS INDICATING S/C NO.

2. FULL SET OF CLEAN ON BOARD BILL OF LADING MADE OUT TO ORDER OF SHIPPER, MARKED FREIDHT COLLECT, NOTIFY APPLICANT.

3. PACKING LIST IN 3 FOLDS.

4. CERTIFICATE OF ORIGIN ISSUED BY RELATIVE AUTHORITY.

47A/ Additional Conditions:

DRAFTS MUST BEAR OUR NAME, THE CREDIT NUMBER AND DATE.

SHIPMENTS MUST BE EFFECTED BY CONTAINER.

B/L MUST SHOWING SHIPPING PLUS ANY INCCURED MARKS: CL/ SC102/NEW DELIH/C/NO. FOR DOCS WHICH OD NOT COMPLY WITH OLC TERMS AND CONDITIONS, WE SHALL DECUCT FROM THE PROCEEDS A CHARGE OF EUR 60.00 PAYABLE IN USD EQUIVALENT PLUS ANY INCCURED SWIFT SHARGES IN CONECTION WITH.

71B/ Details of Charges: ALL BANKING COMM/CHRGS OUTSIDE INDIA ARE ON BENEFICIARY'S ACCOUNT.

48/ Presentation Period: 20 DAYS AFTER THE DATE OF B/L, BUT WITHIN THE L/C VALIDITY.

49/ Confirmation: WITHOUT

72/ Send to Rec. Info. : CREDIT SUBJECT TO ICC PUBL. 600

图 7.1　印度国家银行开立的信用证（续）

其他业务资料如下：

（1）发票号码：JZ20151201

（2）发票日期：20150902

（3）H.S.编码：7307.9900

（4）包装方式：10PCS TO A CARTON，　TOTAL 180 CARTONS

（5）申请单位注册号：8667410

（6）出运日期：20150926

要求：

以金铸阀门公司单证员王丽的身份协助报检员周小蕾，根据印度公司提供的信用证，填写原产地申请书和一般原产地证书。

知 识 准 备

一、原产地证书的含义及作用

（一）原产地证书的含义

原产地证书是出口商应进口商的要求，向出口国政府有关机构申请而签发的证明货物原产地或制造地的法律文件。

（二）原产地证书的作用

原产地证书的作用表现在以下几个方面。

（1）作为征税的依据。根据所提供的原产地证书，进口国所征收的税率也有所不同。如我国出口至普惠制给惠国，需提交普惠制原产地证书格式 A（GSP FORM A）以获得给惠国所给予的普惠制优惠关税。

（2）作为允许进口的文件之一。

（3）作为进口贸易统计的依据。

（4）作为商品内在品质和结算货款的依据。

二、原产地证书的分类

原产地证书可以分为一般原产地证书、普惠制原产地证书、区域性优惠原产地证书和专用原产地证书四种。我国目前主要签发和使用的是前三类原产地证书。

三、一般原产地证书

（一）一般原产地证书的含义

一般原产地证书（CERTIFICATE OF ORIGIN，C/O）是由出入境检验检疫局或各地国际贸易促进委员会（简称贸促会）及分支机构签发的，主要用于征收关税和贸易统计等方面的证明文件。它是一种非优惠的原产地证书，进口国海关对此类证书下的货物征收最惠国税。

（二）一般原产地证书的填制规则

一般原产地证书样本如图7.2所示，其内容与填制方法如表7.1所示。

ORIGINAL	
1. Exporter	Certificate No.
2. Consignee	**CERTIFICATE OF ORIGIN OF** THE PEOPLE'S REPUBLIC OF CHINA

图 7.2　一般原产地证书样本

3.Means of transport and route	5.For certifying authority use only			
4.Country / region of destination				

6. Marks and number	7. Number and kind of packages; description of goods	8.H.S.Code	9.Quantity	10.Number and date of invoices

11.Declaration by the exporter The undersigned hereby declares that the above details and statements are correct, that all the goods were produced in China and that they comply with the Rules of Origin of the People's Republic of China. Place and date, signature and stamp of authorized signatory	12.Certification It is hereby certified that the declaration by the exporter is correct. Place and date, signature and stamp of certifying authority

图 7.2　一般原产地证书样本（续）

表 7.1　一般原产地证书内容及填制方法一览表

序号	项目名称	填制方法
1	Exporter （出口商）	出口商全称、详细地址及国家（地区）。若需要填写中间商或者转口商，可在出口商后面加"VIA"或者"C/O"
2	Consignee （收货人）	最终收货方名称、详细地址及国家（地区），一般为合同中的买方或信用证上规定的运输单据的被通知人。由于贸易的需要，可以填"TO ORDER"
3	Means of transport and route （运输方式和路线）	此栏填写两项内容：运输路线和运输方式。运输路线以起运地（港）和目的地（港）表示，如果需要转运，还应注明转运地（港）；运输方式填写海运、空运或陆运，如 FORM NINGBO, CHINA TO NEW YORK, JAPAN BY VESSEL VIA HONGKONG
4	Country/region of destination （目的地国/地区）	货物最终运抵目的地的国家或地区的名称，一般与最终收货人或最终目的地（港）所在国家或地区一致，不能填写中间商国家名称
5	For certufying authority use only （仅供签证机构使用）	此栏为签证机构使用栏，签证机构根据需要再次加注。如证书更改、丢失、重新补发等情况。证书申领单位此栏留空不填
6	Marks and numbers （运输标志）	按照商业发票上所列唛头完整填写，不可简单地填写"按照发票（AS PER INVOICE NO.）"或"按照提单（AS PER B/L NO.）"；如无唛头，填写 NO MARK 或 N/M，不得留空。如果内容过长，可填在第 7、第 8、第 9、第 10 栏空白处
7	Number and kind of packages; description of goods （包装种类和件数、货物描述）	填写货物的数量、包装种类及商品名称。填写时应注意： ① 商品名称要具体详细，应详细到可以准确判定该商品的 H.S.编码。不得用概括性描述，如衣服（GARMENT）等 ② 如果信用证中品名笼统或拼写错误，必须在括号内加注具体描述或正确品名

续表

序号	项目名称	填制方法
7	Number and kind of packages; description of goods （包装种类和件数、货物描述）	③ 包装数量及种类要按具体单位填写，并在包装数量的英文数字描述后面用括号加上阿拉伯数字。如 ONE HUNDRED（100）CARTONS OF LEATHER SHOES。如是散装货，则在商品名称后面加注"散装（IN BULK）"，所列内容必须与信用证或其他单据保持一致 ④ 该内容填写完后在后面加结束符号"**********"以防伪造或添加 ⑤ 有时信用证要求在所有单证上加注合同及信用证号码、生产厂商名称、地址等，可加在此栏
8	H.S. Code （商品编码）	填写 8 位数的 H.S.编码，与报关单一致。若同一证书包含多种商品，则应将相应的 H.S.编码全部填写，此栏不得留空，与第 7 栏品名一一对应
9	Quantity （量值）	填写出口货物的量值（即数量或重量）及商品的计量单位，若以重量计算的则要注明毛重或净重
10	Number and date of invoice （发票号码和发票日期）	按商业发票中的号码和日期填写，必须与商业发票的内容完全一致
11	Declaration by the exporter （出口商声明）	① 签字人为报检员，即在签证机构注册的原产地证手签员签名，并加盖申请单位在签证机构备案的中英文印章，手签人的签名与印章不得重合 ② 此栏还须填写申报地点和日期，申报日期不得早于发票日期
12	Certification （签证机构证明）	① 经签证机构审核人员审核无误后，由授权的签证人在此栏手签姓名并加盖签证机构印章；注明签署地点和日期。签名和印章不能重合 ② 注意此栏签发日期不得早于发票日期（第 10 栏）和申报日期（第 11 栏）
13	Certificate No. （证书编号）	此栏在证书的右上角，必须填写证书的编号，不能留空，否则证书无效

（三）申请一般原产地证书的程序

1. 申请签证

企业最迟应于货物报关出运前三天向签证机构申请办理原产地证书，申请单位领证时要严格按签证机构要求，真实、完整、准确地填制并提交如下资料。

（1）原产地证明书申请书一份。

（2）一般原产地证明书（C/O）一套（一正三副）。

（3）正式出口商业发票正本一份，如发票内容不全，另附装箱单（盖章，不得涂改）。

（4）含有进口成本的产品，必须提交含有进口成分产品成本明细单。

（5）签证机构需要的其他单据。

2. 签发证书

商检机构在调查或抽查的基础上，逐一审核申请单位提交的有关单证，无误后签发一般原产地证书，交申请单位。

3. 电子签证流程

（1）与软件公司联系，安装企业端软件。

（2）在签证机构开通注册邮箱。

（3）通过网络，将原产地证书传输到签证机构。

（4）企业待收到正确回执后，由申报员提交有关单据到签证机构取证。

（四）填写一般原产地证书申请书

在申请一般原产地证书前，需要先填写一般原产地证书申请书，在经过相关部门在网上的初步审核通过后再填制一般原产地证书，并办理相关手续，支付费用。

一般原产地证书申请书如图7.3所示，其内容及填制方法如表7.2所示。

中国贸促会宁波分会
中国国际商会宁波分会
一般原产地证书/加工装配证明书
申 请 书

申请单位注册号_____	证书号_____	全部国产填上 P
申请人郑重声明：_____	发票号_____	含进口成分填上 W

本人被正式授权代表企业办理和签署本申请书。

本申请书及一般原产地证明书/加工装配证明书所列内容正确无误，如发现弄虚作假，冒充证书所列货物，擅改证书，愿按《中华人民共和国出口货物原产地规则》有关规定受惩处并承担法律责任。现将有关情况申报如下：

商品名称		H.S.编码（八位数）	
商品生产、制造、加工单位、地点			
含进口成分产品主要制造加工工序			
商品 FOB 总值（以美元计）		最终目的地国家/地区	
拟出口日期		转口国（地区）	
包装数量或毛重或其他数量			
贸易方式和企业性质			

图 7.3　一般原产地证书申请书样本

贸易方式	企业性质

现提交中国出口货物商业发票副本一份，报关单一份或合同/信用证影印件，一般原产地证明书/加工装配证明书一正三副，以及其他附件____份，请予审核签证。

申领人（签名）：

电话：

申请单位盖章：   日期：

图 7.3　一般原产地证书申请书样本（续）

表 7.2　一般原产地证书申请书内容及填制方法一览

序号	项目名称	填制方法
1	申请单位注册号	企业在出证机构的注册备案登记号码
2	证书号	按出证机构的编码规律顺序（网上申请时系统会自动生成）
3	发票号	出口货物商业发票的号码，并与随附发票一致
4	商品成分确认	关系到关税问题，全部国产填"P"，有进口成分填"W"
5	商品名称	必须与信用证或合同上商品名称完全一致
6	H.S.编码	商品的八位 H.S.编码，海关统计编码
7	商品生产、制造、加工单位、地点	企业名称，申请原产地证的出口企业
8	商品 FOB 总值（以美元计）	根据申报的出口货物出口发票上所列的金额以 FOB 价格填写（以美元计），如出口货物不是以 FOB 价格成交的，应换算成 FOB 价格
9	最终目的地国家/地区	即货物即将运抵的最终销售国
10	拟出口日期	如实准确填写货物离开启运口岸的当天日期（年、月、日），但此日期不得超过申请产地证的前七天
11	转口国（地区）	填写本批货物的转口国家，如无转运港的填写"***"
12	包装数量或毛重或其他数量	填写该批出口货物的箱数、毛重或个数等
13	贸易方式	主要分为一般贸易、三来一补、其他贸易方式三种，根据实际情况填写，有些申请书的格式只需要打"√"做选择就可以了
14	企业性质	根据实际情况，如"国有企业"或"三资企业"，有些申请书的格式只需要打"√"做选择就可以了
15	申请单位盖章	申请原产地证书的出口企业盖章
16	申领人签章及电话	填写领证人姓名，多为报检员
17	申领日期	一般为装运前三天

课堂思考

（1）申请一般原产地证书时，不需要提交一般原产地证书，只需要提交申请书就可以了。因为原产地证书是由贸促会签发的。这种说法对吗？试说明理由。

（2）一般原产地证书中商品名称一栏可以写统称。这种说法对吗？试说明理由。

参考答案

小 贴 士

产地证电子签证是指与检验检疫机构联网后，通过企业端软件或以 Web 方式进行一般原产地证书或普惠制原产地证书的申请，从而完成原产地证远程申请工作。签证机构以电子方式审核原产地证书，实现远程办理出入境检验检疫报检的行为。图 7.4 为电子签证系统。

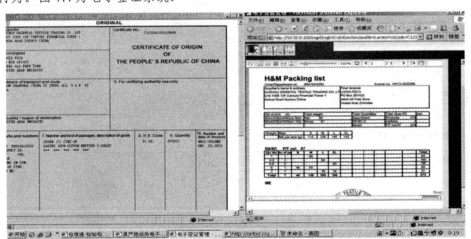

图 7.4　电子签证系统

 职业判断

案例资料：

2014 年 3 月，上海茂城食品有限公司与加拿大 BUSHER 公司达成交易，出口绿茶 50 公吨，CIF 价每公吨 3000 美元。茂城公司的单证员与 BUSHER 公司联系后，确定货物出运日期为 4 月 15 日。

思考：

茂城公司的报检员应在什么时间向什么机构申请签发一般原产地证书？

参考答案

任务实施

（1）单证员王丽协助报检员周小蕾填制的一般原产地证书如图 7.5 所示。

ORIGINAL	
1.Exporter JINZHU VALVE CO. LTD ZHONGSHAN RD. 108 NINGBO, CHINA	Certificate No. **CERTIFICATE OF ORIGIN** **OF** **THE PEOPLE'S REPUBLIC OF** **CHINA**
2.Consignee CASTER LOS CO. JASON RD. 113	
3.Means of transport and route FROM NINGBO, CHINA TO NEW DELIH BY VESSEL	5.For certifying authority use only
4.Country / region of destination INDIA	

6.Marks and numbers	7.Number and kind of packages; description of goods	8.H.S.Code	9.Quantity	10.Number and date of invoices
CL SC102 NEW DELIH C/NO.1-180	ONE HUNDRED AND EIGHTY (180) CARTONS OF T-TEE **************************	7307.9900	1800PCS	JZ20151201 SPET. 02，2015

11.Declaration by the exporter The undersigned hereby declares that the above details and statements are correct, that all the goods were produced in China and that they comply with the Rules of Origin of the People's Republic of China.	12.Certification It is hereby certified that the declaration by the exporter is correct.
JINZHU VALVE CO. LTD NINGBO SEPT. 02，2015　　　周小蕾 --- Place and date, signature and stamp of authorized signatory	CCPIT NINGBO SEPT. 02，2015 --- Place and date, signature and stamp of certifying authority

图 7.5　填制的一般原产地证书

（2）单证员王丽又协助报检员周小蕾填制了一般原产地证书申请书，如图7.6所示。

中国贸促会宁波分会

中国国际商会分会

一般原产地证书/加工装配证明书

申 请 书

申请单位注册号 8667410　　证书号 JZ20151201 　　　　　　　　　发票号＿＿＿＿	全部国产填上 P 含进口成分填上 W	P

申请人郑重声明：

本人被正式授权代表企业办理和签署本申请书。

本申请书及一般原产地证明书/加工装配证明书所列内容正确无误，如发现弄虚作假，冒充证书所列货物，擅改证书，愿按《中华人民共和国出口货物原产地规则》有关规定受惩处并承担法律责任。现将有关情况申报如下：

商品名称	T型三通	H.S.编码（八位数）	7307.9900
商品生产、制造、加工单位、地点		宁波金铸阀门有限公司　宁波市中山路108号	
含进口成分产品主要制造加工工序			
商品FOB总值（以美元计）	9 900美元	最终目的地国家/地区	印度
拟出口日期	2015年9月26日	转口国（地区）	***
包装数量或毛重或其他数量		180箱	

贸易方式和企业性质

贸易方式	企业性质
一般贸易	国有企业

现提交中国出口货物商业发票副本一份，报关单一份或合同/信用证影印件，一般原产地证明书/加工装配证明书一正三副，以及其他附件　份，请予审核签证。

申领人（签名）：周小蕾

电话：87871101

申请单位盖章：（宁波金铸阀门有限公司章）

日期：2015年9月2日

图7.6　填制的一般原产地证书申请书

儿童木质吉他

任务再现

上海利雪进出口公司于2014年3月与加拿大MONDA公司签订一笔仿真儿童木质吉他的出口合同，即期信用证付款（见图7.7），CFR MONTREAL成交，合同金额为15 000美元。

```
BASIC HEADER          F 01BKCHCNBJAXXX0205090946
APPLICATION HEADER
15051725911114BMOBK22BXXXD146251 5499111151037N
                                        *BANK OF MONTREAL
                                        *MONTREAL, CANADA


USER HEADER           BANK. PRIORITY        113:
                      MSG USER REF          108:
FORM OF DOC. CREDIT   *40A: IRREVOCABLE TRANSFERABLE
DOC. CREDIT NUMBER    *20: 086/3075989
DXPIRY                *31D: DATE 150403 PLACE CHINA
APPLICANT             *50: MONDA CO.
                         119 RUE ST-JACQUES
                         MONTREAL, CANADA
BENEFICIARY           *59: SHANGHAI LIXUE IMPORT & EXPORT
                         CORPORATION,60, HUAHAI ROAD
                         SHANGHAI, CHINA
AMOUNT                *32B: CURRENCY USD AMONT 1, 5000.00
MAX. CREDIT AMOUNT    39B: MAXIMUM
AVAILABLE WITH/BY     41D: FREELY NEGOTIABLE AT ANY BANK
                         BY NEGOTIATION
42D/DR: 42C/DRAFT        : AT SIGHT
DRAWEE-NAME AND ADDRESS:  DRAWN ON US FOR FULL INVOICE VALUE
LOADING IN CHARGE     44A: CHINA
FOR TRANSPORT TO…     44B: MONTREAL, CANADA
LATEST DATE OF SHIP.  44C: 150516
DESCRIPT. OF GOODS    45A:
600 SETS OF SIMULATION CHILDREN SMALL GUITAR TOYS STYLE NO. 2089
AT USD 25.00/SET
COLOUR ASSORTMENT AS PER CONTRACT NO. 207731 CFR MONTREAL
                      46A: DOCUMENTS REQUIRED:
                         + FULL SET OF CLEAN ON BOARD OCEAN BILL OF LADING, MADE OUT
                            TO THE ORDER OF BANK OF MONTREAL, CANADA, MARKED FREIGHT
                            PREPAID NOTIFY ACCOUNTEE.
                         +SIGNED COMMEERCIAL INVOICE IN TRIPLICATE SHOWING ORDER NO.
                            WW65-3.
                         +PACKING LIST IN TRIPLICATE.
+CERTIFICATE OF ORIGIGIN IN 1 ORIGINAL PLUS 2 COPIES SIGNED BY CCPIT.
```

图 7.7　加拿大蒙特利尔银行开立的信用证

	47A: ADDITIONAL CONDITIONS
	+INSURANCE IS TO BE EFFECTED GY BUYER.
	+ALL DOC. MUST BE MAILED IN ONE LOT TO THE ISSUING BANK BY
	COURIER SERVICE.
	78: INSTRUCTIONS TO PAY/ ACCOUNT/ NEG BK:
	+ THE AMOUNT OF EACH DRAFT MUST BE ENDORSED ON THE REVERSE
	OF THIS CREDIT.
	456, EASTCHEPT ST., LONDON, UK
SENDER TO RECEIVER INFO	72: THIS CREDIT IS SUBJECT TO THE UNIFORM
	CUSTOMS AND PRACTICE FOR DOCUMENTARY
	CREDITS, 2007 REVISION,
	ICC
	PUBLICATION NO. 600

图 7.7　加拿大蒙特利尔银行开立的信用证（续）

其他业务资料如下：

（1）发票号码：LX039489

（2）发票日期：5 月 6 日

（3）H.S.编码：9202.9090

（4）包装方式：五台装一纸箱

（5）申请单位注册号：7449002

（6）出运日期：5 月 12 日　出口口岸：上海

（7）运输标志：M.D./SC207731/MONTREAL/NO.1-UP

（8）贸易方式：一般贸易　企业性质：三资企业

试为上海利雪进出口公司向贸促会申请一般原产地证书，填写一般原产地证书和原产地证书申请书。

任务二　填制普惠制原产地证书

任务导航

广州隆兴进出口有限公司与德国 LIEHU 贸易公司达成交易，出口女士衬衫型号 203 的 5 000 件，型号 303 的 6 000 件（TEE）。双方协商后决定采用 30 天远期信用证方式达成交易，4 月初，对方公司开来了信用证（见图 7.8）。

出口到德国的产品需要提供普惠制原产地证书，广州隆兴进出口有限公司首先要阅读信用证，根据信用证内容申请普惠制原产地证书，取得由商检机构签发的普惠制原产地证书。

BASIC HEADER   F 01 BKCHCNBJA5×× 1528 157873

APPL. HEADER   O 700 1630000731 DUTCHS6LA××× 1809 042841 0008010730 N

+ DEUTSCHE BANK

+ BERLIN, GERMANY

MT: 700----------------ISSUE OF A DOCUMENTARY CREDIT----------------------

SEQUENCE OF TOTAL	27 : 1/1
FORM OF DOCUMENTARY CREDIT	40A: IRREVOCABLE
DOCUMENTARY CREDIT NUMBER	20 : DB01413
DATE OF ISSUE	31C: 150406
DATE AND PLACE OF EXPIRY	31D: 150615CHINA
APPLICANT	50 : LIEHU TRADING CO.
	129 HAYW ARD WAY
	BERLIN, GERMANY
BENEFICIARY	59 : LONGXING IMP. & EXP. CO. LTD.
	NO. 369 XIANGYANG STREET
	GUANGDONG, CHINA
CURRENCY CODE, AMOUNT	32B: USD133 500.00
AVAILABLE WITH… BY…	41D: ANY BANK
	BY NEGOTIATION
DRAFTS AT…	42C: 30 DAYS AFTER SIGHT
DRAWEE	42D: DEUTSCHE BANK
	BERLIN, GERMANY
PARTIAL SHIPMENT	43P: NOT ALLOWED
TRANSHIPMENT	43T: NOT ALLOWED
LOADING/DISATCH/TAKING/FROM	44A: GUANGZHOU PORT, CHINA
FOR TRANSPORTATION TO…	44B: HAMBURG, GERMANY
LATEST DATE OF SHIPMENT	44C: 150527
DESCRPT OF GOODS/ SERVICES	45A:

STYLE NO.	ITEM	UNIT PRICE	QUANTITY
203	100% COTTON BLOUSE	USD 12.00	5000
303	100% COTTON BLOUSE	USD 12.25	6000

图 7.8 德意志银行开立的信用证

AS PER S/C NO. 90/1/8832

CIF HAMBURG, GERMANY

DOCUMENTS REQUIRED   46A:

  + COMMERCIAL INVOICE IN DUPLICATE

  + PACKING LIST IN DUPLICATE

  + FULL SET (3/3) OF CLEAN ON BOARD OCEAN BILLS OF LADING MADE OUT TO

  ORDER AND BLANK ENDORSED, MARKED FREIGHT PREPAID AND NOTIFY APPLICANT

 + ASSORTMENT LIST IN 2 ORIGINALS PLUS 1 COPY

 + GSP CERTIFICATE OF ORIGIN IN 3 ORIGINALS

 + MARINE INSURANCE POLICY IN THE CURRENCY OF THE CREDIT ENDORSED IN

  BLANK FOR CIF VALUE PLUS 10 PCT COVERING ALL RISKS OF PICC CLAUSES

  INDICATING CLAIMS PAYABLE IN GERMANY

ADDITIONAL CONDITIONS   47A:

  + ALL DOCS. MUST BE ISSUED IN ENGLISH

  + A DISCRIPENCY FEE BF USD50.00 WILL BE DEDUCTED FROM PROEEDS ON EACH SET OF DISCREPANT

    DOCUMENTS PRESENTED.

  + ALL DOCS. MUST SHOW THIS L/C NO.

  + B/L MUST SHOWING SHIPPING MARKS: LH, S/C 90/1/8832, HAMBURG, C/NO.

CHARGES   71B: ALL BANKING CHARGES OUTSIDE OF OUR COUNTER

                                   ARE FOR ACCOUNT OF THE BENEFICIARY.

PERIOD FOR PRESENTATIONS   48 : DOCUMENTS MUST BE PRESENTED TO

                                   PAY/NEGO. BANK WITHIN 15 DAYS

                                   AFTER DATE OF SHIPMENT BUT WITHIN

                                   VALIDITY OF THE L/C.

      CONFIRMATION INSTRUCTION   49 : WITHOUT

      ADVICE THROUGH BANK   57D: YOUR PINGDU SUB-BRANCH

                                   98 ZHENGYANG RAOD

                                   PINGDU SIDTRICT

                                   GUANGZHOU, CHINA

      SENDER TO RECEIVER INFO   72 : THIS TREDIT IS SUBJECT TO THE

                                   UNIFORM CUSTONS AND PRACTICE

                                   FOR DOCUMENTARY CREDITS,2007

                                   REVISION, ICC PUBLICATION NO. 600.

图 7.8   德意志银行开立的信用证（续）

其他业务资料如下：

（1）装箱方式：Cartons of 20 pcs each

（2）船名和开行日期：S. S CaiHong V125 on 25th May 2015

（3）每箱净重：30KGS　每箱毛重：40KGS　每箱体积：30cm×40 cm×50 cm

（4）发票开立日期及号码：2015 年 5 月 18 日　DK903498

（5）出口商申请地点及日期：广州，2015 年 5 月 20 日

（6）签证机构签证地点及日期：广州，2015 年 5 月 21 日

（7）生产厂商及联系电话：广东东莞明丽服装厂　0769-81866120

（8）全棉女式衬衫 H.S.编码：6206.3009

产品原材料全部原产于中国。

要求：

以隆兴进出口有限公司单证员小沈的身份协助报检员袁燕，根据德国 LIEHU 公司开来的信用证，填写普惠制原产地证书及申请书。

知识准备

一、普惠制原产地证书的含义

普惠制原产地证书（GSP CERTIFICATE OF ORIGIN FORM A）是一种优惠原产地证书，出口商在出口商品到给惠国时，需向进口国提供此类证书，以获得普遍优惠制的关税待遇。

二、普惠制原产地证书的填制规则

普惠制原产地证书样本如图 7.9 所示，其内容及填制方法如表 7.3 所示。

ORIGINAL	
1. Goods consigned from (Exporter's business name, address, country)	Reference No. **GENERALIZED SYSTEM OF PREFERENCES** CERTIFICATE OF ORIGIN (Combined declaration and certificate) **FORM A** THE PEOPLE'S REPUBLIC
2. Goods consigned to (Consignee's name, address, country)	Issued in **OF CHINA** -------------------------------------- (country) See Notes overleaf

图 7.9　普惠制原产地证书样本

3. Means of transport and route (as far as known)			4. For official use		
5. Item number	6. Marks and numbers of packages	7. Number and kind of packages; description of goods	8. Origin criterion (see Notes overleaf)	9. Gross weight or other quantity	10. Number and date of invoices

11. Certification It is hereby certified, on the basis of control carried out, that the declaration by the exporter is correct. ------------------------------ Place and date, signature and stamp of certifying authority	12. Declaration by the exporter The undersigned hereby declares that the above details and statements are correct, that all the goods were **CHINA** produced in ------------------------------ (country) and that they comply with the origin requirements specified for those goods in the Generalized System of Preferences for goods exported to .... ------------------------------ Place and date, signature and stamp of authorized signatory

图 7.9　普惠制原产地证书样本（续）

表 7.3　普惠制原产地证书内容及填制方法一览表

序号	项目名称	填制方法
1	Goods consigned from（出口商）	出口商全称、详细地址及国家（地区）；FORM A 不允许打上中间商的名称
2	Goods consigned to 收货人	给惠国的最终收货方名称、详细地址及国家（地区）。欧洲、挪威、土耳其对此栏无强制要求，可以填写 TO ORDER；日本对此栏要求必须具体详细，不能写 TO ORDER，国名不能太笼统，不能只填欧洲等
3	Means of transport and route（运输方式和路线）	此栏填写两项内容：运输路线和运输方式。一般不要求填写出运日期，运输方式中不要出现 BY ROAD、BY SHIP 等
4	FOR certifying authority use only（仅供签证机构使用）	此栏为签证机构使用栏，正常情况下此栏空白；特殊情况下，系统会自动在此栏加注
5	Item number（商品顺序号）	如同一批货物有不同品种，则按不同品种、发票号等分列"1""2""3"，以此类推。顺序号应与 7、8、9 栏对应
6	Marks and numbers of packages（唛头及包装号）	① 此栏的唛头应与实际货物外包装上的唛头及发票上的唛头一致,填写完整的图案标记及包装号 ② 唛头不得出现中国以外的地区或国家制造的字样，也不能出现香港、澳门、台湾原产地字样 ③ 此栏不得留空，如货物无唛头时，应填写"无唛头"（N/M 或 NO MARK） ④ 如唛头过多，此栏不够填，可填在第 7、8、9、10 栏结束符号以下的空白处
7	Number and kind of packages, description of goods（包装种类和件数、货物描述）	填写货物的数量、包装种类及商品名称，要求同一般原产地证书
8	Origin criterion（原产地标准）	完全国产填写"P"，非完全国产时各国的填写规则不一，主要国家的非原产地填法如下： ① 欧盟、挪威、瑞士、列支敦士登公国、日本："W"并标注 H.S.编码

续表

序号	项目名称	填制方法
8	Origin criterion （原产地标准）	② 俄罗斯、乌克兰、白俄罗斯、哈萨克斯坦："Y"并标注非原产地成分价值占产品离岸价格的百分比 ③ 加拿大："F" ④ 澳大利亚、新西兰：留空 ⑤ 在一个受惠生产国生产而在另一个或一个以上受惠国制作或加工的产品："PK"
9	Gross weight or other quantities （毛重或其他数量）	填写出口货物的量值（即数量或重量）及商品的计量单位，若以重量计算的则要注明毛重或净重
10	Number and date of invoice （发票号码和发票日期）	按商业发票中的号码和日期填写，必须与商业发票的内容完全一致
11	Certification （签证机构证明）	① 经签证机构审核人员审核无误后，由授权的签证人在此栏手签姓名并加盖签证机构印章；注明签署地点和日期。签名和印章不能重合 ② 注意此栏签发日期不得早于发票日期（第10栏）和申报日期（第11栏）
12	Declaration by the exporter （出口商声明）	① 签字人为报检员，即在签证机构注册的原产地证手签员签名，并加盖申请单位在签证机构备案的中英文印章，手签人的签名与印章不得重合 ② 此栏还须填写申报地点和日期，申报日期不得早于发票日期

三、申请普惠制原产地证书的程序

普惠制原产地证书的申领与一般原产地证书的申领程序大致相同，都经过了申请签证和签发证书两个环节，电子签证流程也相似。

申报手签人在本批货物出运前5日到商检机构办理申请事宜。对首次申请签证的单位，商检机构将派员到生产现场做例行调查。对非首次申请签证的单位，商检机构对申报内容有疑问，或认为有必要时，也可派员对产品的生产企业进行抽查。做上述调查后，商检机构将填写"出口企业（或生产厂）普惠制签证调查记录"，以此作为是否同意签证的依据。

申请单位领证时需要提交如下资料。

（1）《普惠制原产地证明书申请书》一份。

（2）《普惠制原产地证明书（FORM A）》一套（英文缮制）。

（3）正式出口商业发票正本一份，如发票内容不全，另附装箱单（盖章，不得涂改）。

（4）含有进口成分的产品，必须提交"含有进口成分产品成本明细单"。

（5）复出口加拿大、澳大利亚、新西兰、日本的来料加工产品或进料加工产品申请单位还需提供该四国公司或商社签发的有关原料、零部件的出口商业发票。

（6）签证机构需要的其他单据。普惠制原产地证书申请书如图7.10

所示，其内容及填制方法如表 7.4 所示。

中华人民共和国出入境检验检疫
原产地证明书申请书

申请单位（加盖公章）：　　　　　　　　　　　　证书号＿＿＿＿＿＿＿＿＿＿

　　　　　　　　　　　　　　　　　　　　　　　注册号＿＿＿＿＿＿＿＿＿＿

申请人郑重声明：

　　本人被正式授权代表单位办理原产地证明书和签署本申请书的。

　　本人所提供原产地证明书及所付单据内容正确无误，如发现弄虚作假，冒充证书所列货物，擅改证书，自愿接受签证机关的处罚及负法律责任。现将有关情况申领如下：

生产单位		生产单位联系人电话	
商品名称 （中英文）		H.S.税目号 （以六位数码计）	

商品 FOB 总值（以美元计）			发票号	
最终销售国		证书种类划"√"	加急证书	
货物拟出运日期				

贸易方式和企业性质（请在适合处划"√"）

正常贸易 C	来料加工 L	补偿贸易 B	中外合资 H	中外合作 Z	外商独资 D	零售 Y	展卖 M

包装数量或毛重或其他数量	

原产地标准：

本项商品系在中国生产，完全符合该给惠国方案规定，其原产地情况符合以下第　　条：

（1）"P"（完全国产，未使用任何进口原材料）；

（2）"W" 其 H.S.税目号为＿＿＿＿＿＿＿（含进口成分）；

（3）"F"（对加拿大出口产品，其进口成分不超过产品出厂价的 40%）

本批产品系：1. 直接运输从＿＿＿＿＿＿＿到＿＿＿＿＿＿＿；

　　　　　　2. 转口运输从＿＿＿＿＿中转国（地区）＿＿＿＿＿到＿＿＿＿＿＿＿；

申请人说明：　　　　　　　　　　　　　　申领人（签名）：

　　　　　　　　　　　　　　　　　　　　电话：

　　　　　　　　　　　　　　　　　　　　日期：　　　年　　月　　日

　　现提交中国出口商品商业发票副本一份，普惠制产地证明书格式 A（FORM A）一正二副，以及其他附件　　份，请予审核签证。

　　注：凡有进口成分的商品，必须要求提交"含进口成分受惠商品成本明细单"。

图 7.10　普惠制原产地证书申请书样本

表7.4 普惠制原产地证书申请书内容及填制方法一览表

序号	项目名称	填制方法
1	申请单位（加盖公章）	申请原产地证书的出口企业并加盖申请单位公章
2	注册号	填写申请单位在检验检疫局产地证签证部门注册的注册号
3	证书号	根据签证机构的编号规则，对应于每批申领货物的编号；不得重号或跳号
4	生产单位	申请原产地证的出口企业
5	生产单位联系人电话	填写申请单位的联系电话
6	商品名称（中英文）	填写商品品名的中英文，并且与发票证的商品名称一致
7	H.S.税目号（以六位数码计）	商品的H.S.六位数编码，海关统计编码前六位
8	商品FOB总值（以美元计）	根据申报的出口货物出口发票上所列的金额以FOB价格填写（以美元计），如出口货物不是以FOB价格成交的，应换算成FOB价格
9	发票号	填写正式出口发票的号码，并与随附发票相一致
10	最终销售国	即货物即将运抵的最终销售国
11	证书种类	在此证书种类栏划"√"
12	货物拟出运日期	如实准确填写货物离开启运口岸的当天日期（年、月、日）
13	贸易方式和企业性质	根据实际情况选择划"√"
14	包装数量或毛重或其他数量	填写该批出口货物的箱数、毛重或个数等
15	原产地标准	根据提示及货物实际情况选择1～4项如实填写
16	本批商品系……	根据货物运输路线的启运港、中转港及目的港填写本批商品运输路线，无转运港的填写"×××"
17	申请人说明	填写具体说明，如果没有则填"×××"
18	领证人	填写领证人姓名、电话及日期

▌▌课堂思考 ▶▶▶▶▶

（1）普惠制原产地证书中"原产地标准"一栏全部原产于中国的出口商品，应填写什么？

（2）只有首次申请签证的单位，商检机构才将派员到生产现场做例行调查。非首次申请签证的企业，商检机构都不能派员进行调查。这种说法对吗？试说明理由。

参考答案

小 贴 士

所谓普遍优惠制，简称普惠制，是西方发达国家给予发展中国家的特别优惠的关税待遇，以鼓励发展中国家的商品出口，促进经济增长。与一般原产地证书不同的是，普惠制原产地证书必须由中国出入境检验检疫局签发。

给中国普惠制的给惠国分别是欧盟 27 国（即法国、英国、爱尔兰、德国、丹麦、意大利、比利时、荷兰、卢森堡、希腊、西班牙、葡萄牙、奥地利、瑞典、芬兰、匈牙利、波兰、捷克、斯洛伐克、斯洛文尼亚、爱沙尼亚、立陶宛、拉脱维亚、马耳他、塞浦路斯、罗马尼亚、保加利亚）、瑞士、挪威、日本、新西兰、澳大利亚、美国、加拿大、俄罗斯、白俄罗斯、乌克兰、哈萨克斯坦和土耳其，2007 年 8 月 22 日开始，列支敦士登被列为普惠制给惠国。目前，除了美国外，有 39 个国家给予中国普惠制待遇。

　　从 2015 年 1 月 1 日起，欧盟正全面逐步取消对中国产品的普遍优惠制。

 职业判断

参考答案

案例资料：

2015 年 5 月，广东闽齐进出口有限公司出口一批玻璃工艺品到日本，产品的一部分原料从印度进口。

思考：

闽齐进出口有限公司的报检员应如何填写普惠制原产地证书的原产地标准？

任务实施

　　（1）单证员小沈协助报检员袁燕填制的普惠制原产地证书，如图 7.11 所示。

ORIGINAL	
1. Goods consigned from (Exporter's business name, address, country) LONGXING IMP. & EXP. CO. LTD. NO. 369 XIANGYANG STREET GUANGDONG, CHINA	Reference No. **GENERALIZED SYSTEM OF PREFERENCES** CERTIFICATE OF ORIGIN (Combined declaration and certificate)
2. Goods consigned to (Consignee's name, address, country) LIEHU TRADING CO. 129 HAYW ARD WAY BERLIN, GERMANY	Issued in **THE PEOPLE'S REPUBLIC OF CHINA** (country) See Notes overleaf

图 7.11　单证员填制的普惠制原产地证书

3. Means of transport and route (as far as known) FROM GUANGZHOU ,CHINA TO HAMBURG, GERMANY			4. For official use			
5. Item number	6. Marks and numbers of packages	7. Number and kind of packages; description of goods	8. Origin criterion (see Notes overleaf)	9. Gross weight or other quantity	10. Number and date of invoices	
01	LH S/C90/1/8 832, HAMBURG, C/NO1-550	FIVE HUNDRED AND FIFTY (550) CARTONS OF 100% COTTON BLOUSE ********************************** L/C NO. DB01413	P	21 000PCS	MAY 18 2015 DK903498	

11. Certification It is hereby certified, on the basis of control carried out, that the declaration by the exporter is correct.	12. Declaration by the exporter The undersigned hereby declares that the above details and statements are correct, that all the goods produced in ————————— CHINA ————————— (country) and that they comply with the origin requirements specified for those goods in the Generalized System of Preferences for goods exported to GERMANY —————————
GUANGZHOU, CHINA MAY 21. 2015 - ————————————————— Place and date, signature and stamp of certifying authority	GUANGZHOU, CHINA MAY 20. 2015 - ————————————————— Place and date, signature and stamp of authorized signatory

图 7.11　单证员填制的普惠制原产地证书（续）

（2）单证员小沈又协助报检员袁燕填制了普惠制原产地证书申请书，如图 7.12 所示。

中华人民共和国出入境检验检疫
原产地证明书申请书

申请单位（加盖公章）：　广州隆兴进出口有限公司　　　　证书号_____
　　　　　　　　　　　　　　　　　　　　　　　　　　　注册号_____

申请人郑重声明：

本人被正式授权代表单位办理原产地证明书和签署本申请书的。

本人所提供原产地证明书及所付单据内容正确无误，如发现弄虚作假，冒充证书所列货物，擅改证书，自愿接受签证机关的处罚及负法律责任。现将有关情况申领如下：

生产单位	广东东莞明丽服装厂	生产单位联系人电话	0769-81866120
商品名称 （中英文）	全棉女士衬衫 （100% COTTON BLOUSE）	H.S.税目号 （以六位数码计）	6206.3009

图 7.12　单证员填制的普惠制原产地证书申请书

商品 FOB 总值（以美元计）		133 500.00 美元	发票号		DK903498
最终销售国	德国	证书种类划"√"	加急证书		普通证书√
货物拟出运日期		2015 年 5 月 25 日			

贸易方式和企业性质（请在适合处划"√"）

正常贸易C	来料加工L	补偿贸易B	中外合资H	中外合作Z	外商独资D	零售Y	展卖M
√							

包装数量或毛重或其他数量	550 箱

原产地标准：

本项商品系在中国生产，完全符合该给惠国方案规定，其原产地情况符合以下第　　条；

（1）"P"（完全国产，未使用任何进口原材料）；

（2）"W" 其 H.S.税目号为＿＿＿＿＿＿＿＿＿＿（含进口成分）；

（3）"F"（对加拿大出口产品，其进口成分不超过产品出厂价的40%）

本批产品系：1.直接运输从＿＿广州＿＿到＿＿汉堡＿＿；

　　　　　　2.转口运输从＿＿＿＿＿＿中转国（地区）＿＿＿＿＿＿＿＿＿到＿＿＿＿＿＿＿；

申请人说明	申领人（签名）：袁燕
	电话：
	日期：2015 年 5 月 20 日

　　现提交中国出口商品商业发票副本一份，普惠制产地证明书格式 A（FORM A）一正二副，以及其他附件一份，请予审核签证。

　　注：凡有进口成分的商品，必须要求提交"含进口成分受惠商品成本明细单"。

图 7.12　单证员填制的普惠制原产地证书申请书（续）

任务再现

水龙头

　　苏州马星发展有限公司于 2015 年 8 月与西班牙 VASARI M.R.公司达成交易，出口 7500 只水龙头。

　　试根据信用证资料（见图 7.13）和其他业务资料为苏州马星发展有限公司向出入境检验检疫机构申请普惠制原产地证书，填写普惠制原产地证书和普惠制原产地证书申请书。

MT700		ISSUE OF A DOCUMENTARY CREDIT
SENDER		HSBC BANK PLC, SPAIN
RECEIVER		XIAMEN CITY COMMERCIAL BANK, XIAMEN, CHINA
SEQUENCE OF TOTAL	27:	1/1
FORM OF DOC.CREDIT	40A:	IRREVOCABLE

图 7.13　西班牙银行开立的信用证

DOC.CREDIT NUMBER	20:	077/5675989
DATE OF ISSUE	31C:	150823
APPLICABLE RILES	40E:	UCP LATEST VERSION
DATE AND PLACE OF EXPIRY	31D:	DATE 151015 PLACE IN CHINA
APPLICANT	50:	VASARI M.R.
		CTRA. VIVER-PTO.
BENEFICIARY	59:	SUZHOU XINGMA DEVELOPING CO. LTD.
		118 XUEYUAN STREET, SUZHOU, P.R.CHINA
AMOUNT	32B:	CURRENCY USD AMOUNT 112 500.00
AVAILABLE WITH/BY	41D:	ANY BANK IN CHINA ,
		BY NEGOTIATION
DRAFTS AT…	42C:	60 DAYS AFTER SIGHT
DRAWEE	42A:	HSBC BANK PLC, SPAIN
PARTIAL SHIPMTS	43P:	PROHIBITED
TRANSSHIPMENT	43T:	ALLOWED
PORT OF LOADING/	44E:	CHIENESE MAIN PORT
PORT OF DISCHARGE	44F:	BARCELONA, SPAIN
LATEST DATE OF SHIPMENT	44C:	150923
DESCRIPTION OF GOODS AND/OR SERVICES.	45A:	7500PCS OF WATER TAPS, STYLE NO.UK858, AS PER S/C NO.920131 AT USD15.00/PCS CFR BARCELONA, SPAIN
DOCUMENTS REQUIRED	46A:	
		+SIGNED INVOICE IN TRIPLICATE, INDICATE L/C NO. AND FREIGHT AND INSURANCE FREE
		+PACKING LIST IN TRIPLICATE.
		+GSP CERTIFICATE OF ORIGIN FORM A.COUNTSIGNED BY CIQ.
		+FULL SET OF CLEAN ON BOARD BILL OF LADING MARKED "FEIGHT PREPAID" MADE OUT TO ORDER OF APPLICANT BLANK EDDORSED NOTIFYING "VASARI M.R.".
		+SHIPPING ADVICE SHOWING THE NAME OF THE CARRYING VESSEL, DATE OF SHIPMENT, MARKS, QUANTITY, NET WEIGHT AND GROSS WEIGHT OF THE SHIPMENT TO APPLICANT WITHIIN 3 DAYS AFTER THE DATE OF BILL OF LADING.
ADDITIONAL CONDITION	47A:	
		+TRANSSHIPMENT ALLOWED AT HONGKONG ONLY.
		+SHIPMENT MUST BE EFFECTED BY 1*20'FULL CONTAINER LOAD. B/L TO SHOW EVIDENCE OF THIS EFFECT IS REQUIRED.
		+BENEFICIARY'S CERTIFIED COPY OF FAX DISPACHED TO THE APPLICANT WITHIN 2 DAYS AFTER SHIPMENT.

图 7.13　西班牙银行开立的信用证（续）

		+ALL PRESENTATIONS CONTAINING DISCREPANCIES WILL ATTRACT A DISCREPANCY FEE OF USD40.00 PLUS TELEX COSTS OR OTHER CURRENCY EQUIVALENT. THIS CHARGE WILL BE DEDUCTED FROM THE BILL AMOUNT WHETHER OR NOT WE ELECT TO CONSULT THE APPLICANT FOR A WAIVER
CHARGES	71B:	ALL CHARGES AND COMMISSIONS ARE FOR ACCOUNT OF BENEFICIARY INCLUDING REIMBURSING FEE.
PERIOD FOR PRESENTATION	48:	WITHIN 15DAYS AFTER THE DATE OF SHIPMENT, BUT WITHIN THE VALIDITY OF THIS CREDIT.
CONFIRMATION INSTRUCTION	49:	WITHOUT

图 7.13   西班牙银行开立的信用证（续）

其他业务资料如下：

（1）发票号码：920100

（2）发票日期：9 月 6 日

（3）H.S.编码：8481.9090

（4）包装方式：10 只装一纸箱

（5）生产厂商及联系电话：扬州红运卫浴制造厂   0514-9973431

（6）出运日期：9 月 22 日   出口口岸：上海

（7）运输标志：卖方自定

（8）出口商申请地点及日期：上海，2015 年 9 月 19 日

（9）签证机构签证地点及日期：上海，2015 年 9 月 20 日

产品原材料全部原产于中国

参考答案

摄像头支架

任务三   填制区域性原产地证书

任务导航

2015 年 3 月，青岛鑫茂进出口公司与马来西亚舍尔公司达成交易，出口迷你电源插座（ELECTRICAL SOCKET，型号 J209 共 450 只、摄像头支架（CAMERA SUPPORT，型号 3706）共 280 只。双方协商决定采用即期信用证的方式支付货款。4 月初，双方签订了出口合同，10 月中旬马来西亚舍尔公司开来了信用证（见图 7.14）。

出口到马来西亚的产品需要提供区域性原产地证书，青岛鑫茂进出口公司将根据信用证内容，向出入境检验检疫机构申领自由贸易区原产地证书。

IRREVOCABLE DOCUMENTARY CREDIT

SEQUENCE OF TOTAL	*27: 1 / 1
FORM OF DOC，CREDIT	*40A: IRREVOCABLE
DOC. CREDIT NUMBER	*20: LOD88095
DATE OF ISSUE	31C: 2015.04.01
APPLICABLE RULES	*40E: UCP LATEST VERSION
DATE AND PLACE OF EXPIRY	*31D: DATE 2015.05.20 PLACE CHINA.
APPLICANT	*50: SHERE TRADING COMPANY
	81 WORDFORD STREET,
	MALAYSIA
ISSUING BANK	52A: MALAYAN BANKING BERHAD,
	MALAYSIA
BENEFICIARY	*59: QINGDAO XINMAO IMP. & EXP. CORP.
	NO.97 MAOMING NAN ROAD
	QINGDAO, P. R. OF CHINA
AMOUNT	*32B: USD10710.00 (SAY U. S. DOLLARS TEN THOUSAND SEVEN HUNDRED

ND TEN ONLY)

AVAILABLE WITH / BY	*41D: ANY BANK BY NEGOTIATION
DRAFTS AT …	42C: DRAFTS AT SIGHT FOR FULL INVOICE VALUE
DRAWEE	42A: DEVELOPMENT BANK OF SINGAPORE,
	SINGAPORE
PARTIAL SHIPMENTS	43P: NOT ALLOWED
TRANSSHIPMENT	43T: ALLOWED
PORT OF LOADING//AIRPORT OF DEPARTURE	*44E: QINGDAO, CHINA
PORT OF DISCHARGE/AIRPORT OF DESTINATION	*44F: PORT KELANG
LATEST DATE OF SHIPMENT	44C: 2015.05.08
DESCRIPT OF GOODS	45A:

MINI ELECTRICAL SOCKET

ART. NO. H666	260PCS	@USD15.50/PC	USD 4 030.00
ART. NO.HX88	190PCS	@USD16.00/PC	USD 3 040.00

CAMERA SUPPORT

ART. NO. HE21	280PCS	@USD13.00/PC	USD 3 640.00
TOTAL:	730PCS		USD 10 710.00

CIF KELANG

AS PER CONTRACT NO.XM2015X806

DOCUMENTS REQUIRED	46A:

*SIGNED COMMERCIAL INVOICE IN TRIPLICATE

图 7.14　马来西亚银行开立的信用证

*PACKING LIST IN TRIPLICATE

*FULL SET OF CLEAN ON BOARD MARINE BILLS OF LADING MADE OUT TO ORDER MARKED FREIGHT PREPAID NOTIFY APPLICANT

*CHINA- SINGAPORE FTA CERTIFICATE OF ORIGIN CERTIFYING THAT THE GOODS ARE OF CHINESE ORIGIN ISSUED BY COMPETENT AUTHORITIES

*INSURANCE POLICY / CERTIFICATE COVERING ALL RISKS INCLUDING WAREHOUSE TO WAREHOUSE CLAUSE UP TO FINAL DESTINATION AT SINGAPORE FOR AT LEAST 110 PCT OF CIF VALUE AS PER CIC OF PICC

CHARGES   71B : ALL BANKING CHARGES OUTSIDE MALAYSIA ARE FOR A/C OF
                                   BENEFICIARY

PERIOD FOR PRESENTATION   48 : 15 DAYS AFTER ISSUANCE DATE OF SHIPPING DOCUMENTS BUT
                                   WITHIN THE VALIDITY OF THE CREDIT

图 7.14 马来西亚银行开立的信用证（续）

其他业务资料如下：

（1）启运日期：2015.05.06

（2）船名航次：XINGYUN V.120

（3）包装情况：两只装一箱，共 365 箱

（4）发票开立日期及号码：2015 年 4 月 27 日 XM20150330

（5）出口商申请地点及日期：青岛，2015 年 4 月 29 日

（6）签证机构签证地点及日期：青岛，2015 年 4 月 29 日

（7）两种产品唛头卖方自定

（8）迷你电源插座商品编码：8536.6900 摄像头支架商品编码：9021.9009

（9）产品原材料全部原产于中国

（10）迷你电源插座的 FOB 总值为 6760 美元，摄像头支架的 FOB 总值为 3580 美元。

要求：

以鑫茂进出口公司单证员小张的身份协助报检员刘春，根据马来西亚舍尔公司开来的信用证，填写区域性原产地证书。

知 识 准 备

一、区域性原产地证书的含义

区域性原产地证书是订有区域性贸易协定的国家官方机构或民间机构签发的享受成员方关税减免待遇的凭证。自由贸易区的优惠原产地证书是区域性优惠原产地证书的主要形式。

二、区域性原产地证书的种类

目前，在我国签发的区域性原产地证书主要有以下几种：亚太自贸区原产地证书（FORM B）；中国-东盟自贸区原产地证书（FORM E）；中国-智利自贸区原产地证书（FORM F）；中国-巴基斯坦自贸区原产地证书（FORM P）；中国-新西兰自贸区原产地证书（FORM N）；中国-新加坡自贸区原产地证书（FORM X）；中国-秘鲁自贸区原产地证书（FORM R）；《海峡两岸经济合作框架协议（ECFA）》原产地证书（FORM H）；中国-哥斯达黎加自由区原产地证书。下面将重点介绍亚太自由贸易区原产地证书、中国-东盟自贸区原产地证书、中国-巴基斯坦自贸区原产地证书3种。

（一）亚太自贸区原产地证书

1. 签证国家

亚太自贸区原产地证书签证国家包括韩国、印度、斯里兰卡、孟加拉国。

2. 证书名称

证书英文名称为 CERTIFICATE OF ORIGIN ASIA-PACIFIC TRADE AGREEMENT，简称"亚太证书"。

3. 签证产品

亚太自贸区原产地证明书的签发，限于已公布的《亚太贸易协定》项下给予关税优惠的产品，这些产品必须符合《亚太贸易协定原产地规则》。

4. 填制规则

亚太自贸区原产地证书样本如图 7.15 所示，其内容及填制方法如表 7.5 所示。

1.Goods consigned form （Exporter's business name ,address ,country）	Reference No. **CERTIFICATE OF ORIGIN** **Asia-Pacific Trade Agreement** （**Combined Declaration and Certificate**） Issued in The People's Republic of China （Country）

图 7.15　亚太自贸区原产地证书样本

2.Goods consigned to （consignee's name address ,country）			3.For Official use			
4. Means of transport and route						
5.Tariff item number	6.Marks and numbers of Packages	7.Number and kind of packages/description of goods	8.Origin criterion (see notes overleaf)	9.Gross weight or other quantity	10.Number and date of invoices	
11.Declaration by the exporter The undersigned hereby declares that the above details and statement are correct; that all the goods were produced in CHINA （Country） And that they comply with the origin requirements specified for these goods in the Asia- Pacific Trade Agreement for goods exported to ------------------------------------- （Importing Country） ------------------------------------- Place and date, signature of Authorized signatory			12.Certification It is hereby certified , on the basis of control carried out ,that the declaration by the exporter is correct. ------------------------------------- Place and date, signature and stamp of certifying authority			

图 7.15　亚太自贸区原产地证书样本（续）

表 7.5　亚太自贸区原产地证书内容及填制方法一览表

序号	项目名称	填制方法
1	Goods consigned from （出口商）	出口商全称、详细地址及国家（地区），该出口商必须是在商检机构登记的公司出口代理其他公司申报时可在其名称、地址后加打"ON BEHALF OF（O/B）"、"CARE OF（C/O）"或"VIA"，然后打上被代理公司的名称（或地址）。被代理公司含境外名称、地址的不得申报
2	Goods consigned to （收货人）	给惠国的最终收货方名称、详细地址及国家（地区），最终收货人不明确时该栏可以填写"TO ORDER"
3	For official use （供签证机构使用）	官方使用栏的填写方式参考普惠制证书统一栏的填写标准
4	Means of transport and route （运输方式和路线）	运输方式与路线的填写方式参考普惠制证书统一栏的填写标准
5	Tariff item number （商品序号）	四位 H.S.码
6	Marks and numbers of packages （唛头及包装号）	唛头，如实填写，参考普惠制证书统一栏的填写标准

续表

序号	项目名称	填制方法
7	Number and kind of packages, description of goods（包装种类和件数、货物描述）	货物描述、包装数量与方式的填写方式，参考普惠制证书统一栏的填写标准
8	Origin criterion（原产地标准）	注明申报货物享受优惠待遇所依据的原产地标准： ① 如货物为完全原产，填写"A" ② 如货物含进口成分，非国产价值成分＜55%，填写字母"B"和原产于非成员国或原产地不明的材料、部件或产品的总货值占出口产品离岸价的百分比，如"B" 40% ③ 如货物含进口成分，国产及成员国累计价值成分≥60%，填写"C"家原产于成员国的累计含量的总值与出口产品离岸价的百分比 ④ 符合特定原产地标准的产品，填写字母"D"（该项主要针对不发达国家出口申报的产品）
9	Gross weight or other quantities（毛重或其他数量）	填写货物数量的计量单位。计量单位应依据发票所列的销售单位为准，如"公斤""台""件""双""套"等
10	Number and date of invoice（发票号码和发票日期）	按商业发票中的号码和日期填写，必须与商业发票的内容完全一致
11	Declaration by the exporter（出口商声明）	申报日期，申报员签名，加盖公章。申报日期不得早于发票日期
12	Certification（签证机构证明）	应在货物出口前，或出口后的3个工作日内申请办理。预期签证机构不再接受证书的签发申请。已出货3个工作日内的证书采用倒签的形式，申请日期和签证日期可与实际出货日期一致，无须加盖后发印章。倒签时不需提供提单等有关单证

（二）中国-东盟自贸区原产地证书

1. 签证国家

中国-东盟自贸区原产地证书签证国家有文莱、柬埔寨、印度尼西亚、老挝、马来西亚、缅甸、菲律宾、新加坡、泰国、越南。

2. 证书名称

证书英文名称为ASEAN- CHINA FREE TRADE AREA PREFERENTIAL TARIFF CERTIFICATE OF ORIGIN FORM E，简称"FORM E"或"东盟证书"。

3. 签证产品

中国-东盟自贸区优惠原产地证书的签发，限于已公布的《货物贸易协定》项下给予关税优惠产品，这些产品必须符合《中国-东盟自由贸易区原产地规则》。

4. 填制规则

中国-东盟自贸区原产地证书样本如图 7.16 所示，内容及填制方法如表 7.6 所示。

ORIGINAL	
1. Products consigned form（Exporter's business name, address,country）	Reference No. **ASEAN-CHINA FREE TRADE AREA** **PREFERENTIAL TARIFF** **CERTIFICATE OF ORIGIN** **(Combined Declaration and Certificate)** **FORM E** Issued in <u>THE PEOPLE'S REPUBLIC OF CHINA</u> (Country) See Overleaf Notes
2. Products consigned to（consignee's name address,country）	
3. Means of transport and route（as far as known） Departure date Vessel's name/Aircraft etc. Port of Discharge	4. For Official Use ☐Preferential Treatment Given ☐Preferential Treatment Not Given(Please state reasons) -- Signature of Authorized Signatory of the Importing Party

5.Item number	6.Marks and numbers of packages	7. Number and type of packages, description of products（including quantity where appropriate and HS number of the importing Party）	8. Origin criteria（see overleaf notes）	9. Gross weight or other quantity and value（FOB）	10. Number and date of invoices

| 11. Declaration by the exporter
The undersigned hereby declares that the above details and statement are correct; that all the products were produced in

------------CHINA------------
（Country）

And that they comply with the origin requirements specified for these products in the rules of origin for the ACFTA for the products exported to

----
(Importing Country)

Place and date, signature of Authorized signatory | 12. Certification
It is hereby certified , on the basis of control carried out ,that the declaration by the exporter is correct.

Place and date, signature and stamp of certifying authority |

图 7.16　中国-东盟自贸区原产地证书样本

表7.6 中国-东盟自贸区原产地证书内容及填制方法一览表

序号	项目名称	填制方法
1	Products consigned from（出口商）	① 此栏带有强制性，应填写在中国境内的出口商名称、地址和国名 ② 此栏不得出现香港、台湾等中间商名称
2	Products consigned to（收货人）	① 此栏应填中国-东盟自贸区成员国最终收货人名称（即信用证上规定的提单通知人或特别声明的收货人）、地址和国名 ② 此栏不得出现香港、台湾等中间商名称
3	Means of transport and route（运输方式和路线）	此栏应填离港日期、运输工具及卸货口岸，卸货港必须是东盟的成员国之一
4	For official use（供签证机构使用）	进口国海关标准产品享受关税优惠情况，如： □根据中国-东盟自由贸易区优惠关税协议给予优惠待遇 □不给予优惠待遇（请注明原因） 此栏由进口国有权签字人签字；不论是否给予优惠待遇，进口成员国海关必须在此栏作出相应的标注
5	Item number（商品顺序号）	如同批出口货有不同品种，则按不同品种分列 1，2，3，…，以此类推。单项成品，此栏填"1"
6	Marks and numbers of packages（唛头及包装号）	唛头的填写方式参考普惠制证书统一栏的填写标准
7	Number and kind of packages, description of Products（包装种类和件数、货物描述）	货物描述、包装数量与方式的填写方式参考普惠制证书统一栏的填写标准
8	Origin criterion（原产地标准）	注明申报货物享受优惠待遇所依据的原产地标准： ① 如货物为完全原产，填写"X" ② 货物在出口成员国加工但并非完全生产，未使用原产地累计规则判断原产地标准的，填该成员国成分的百分比 ③ 货物在出口成员国加工但并非完全生产，使用了原产地累计规则判断原产地标准的，填中国-东盟累计成分的百分比 ④ 货物符合产品特定原产地标准的产品，填"PSR"（产品特定原产地标准）
9	Gross weight or other quantities and value（FOB）（毛重或其他数量及 FOB 价）	填写货物数量的计量单位，填写方式同中国-东盟原产地证书的填制标准
10	Number and date of invoice（发票号码和发票日期）	按商业发票中的号码和日期填写，必须与商业发票的内容完全一致
11	Declaration by the exporter（出口商声明）	① 签字人为报检员，即在签证机构注册的原产地证手签员签字，并加盖申请单位在签证机构备案的中英文印章，手签人的签字与印章不得重合 ② 此栏还须填写申报地点和日期，申报日期不得早于发票日期
12	Certification（签证机构证明）	① 经签证机构审核人员审核无误后，由授权的签证人在此栏手签姓名并加盖签证机构印章；注明签署地点和日期。签名和印章不能重合 ② 注意此栏签发日期不得早于发票日期（第 10 栏）和申报日期（第 11 栏）

（三）中国–巴基斯坦自贸区原产地证书

1. 签证国家

中国–巴基斯坦自贸区原产地证书的签证国家为巴基斯坦。

2. 证书名称

证书英文名称为 CERTIFICATE OF ORIGIN CHINA-PAKISTAN FTA，简称"FORM P"或"中巴证书"。

3. 签证产品

中国–巴基斯坦自贸区原产地证书的签发，限于已公布的《中国–巴基斯坦自贸协定》项下给予关税优惠产品，这些产品必须符合《中国–巴基斯坦自由贸易区原产地规则》。

4. 填制规则

中国–巴基斯坦自贸区原产地证书样本如图 7.17 所示，内容及填制方法如表 7.7 所示。

ORIGINAL					
1. Exporter's business name ,address ,country	Reference NO. **CERTIFICATE OF ORIGIN** **CHINA-PAKISTAN FTA** （**Combined Declaration and Certificate**） Issued in <u>THE PEOPLE'S REPUBLIC OF CHINA</u> （Country） See Overleaf Notes				
2.Consignee's name address ,country					
3.Producer's Name and Address, country					
4. Means of transport and route (as far as known) Departure date Vessel's name/Aircraft etc. Port of loading Port of discharge	5. For Official Use Only ☐Preferential Treatment Given Under China- Pakistan FTA Free Trade Area Preferential Tariff ☐Preferential Treatment Not Given(Please state reasons) - Signature of Authorized Signatory of the Importing Party				
6.Item number	7.Marks and numbers on packages; Number and kind of packages; description of goods; HS code of the importing country	8.Origin criterion	9.Gross weight or other quantity and FOB value	10.Number and date of invoices	11. Remarks

图 7.17　中国–巴基斯坦自贸区原产地证书样本

12.Declaration by the exporter The undersigned hereby declares that the above details and statement are correct; that all the goods were produced in ------------------------------------ (Country) and that they comply with the origin requirements specified for these products in the rules of origin for the ACFTA for the products exported to ------------------------------------ (Importing Country) ------------------------------------ Place and date, signature of Authorized signatory			13.Certification It is hereby certified, on the basis of control carried out, that the declaration by the exporter is correct. ------------------------------------ Place and date, signature and stamp of certifying authority	

图 7.17 中国-巴基斯坦自贸区原产地证书样本（续）

表 7.7 中国-巴基斯坦自贸区原产地证书内容及填制方法一览表

序号	项目名称	填制方法
1	Exporter's business name，address，country （出口人全称、详细地址及国家）	该出口人必须是在商检机构备案登记的公司
2	Consignee's name，address country （收货人的全称、详细地址和国名）	最终受货人不明确时该栏可填写"TO ORDER"
3	PRODUCER'S NAME AND ADDRESS，country （生产商的合法的全名、地址和国别）	① 如证书产品包含一个以上的生产商，应全部列出 ② 如出口人希望对该信息保密，可填写"应要求提供主管政府机构（AVAILABLE TO CUSTOMS UPON REQUEST）" ③ 如生产商与出口人相同，应填写"同上（SAME）" ④ 如生产商与出口人不同，且所填写生产商内容不能确定企业性质，需提供生产商营业执照备查
4	Means of transport and route （运输方式和路线）	此栏填写方法同普惠制原产地证书的此栏一致，但卸货港必须是巴基斯坦的港口
5	For Official Use Only （仅供签证机构使用）	进口国海关在该栏注明根据协定是否给予优惠，方式同中国-东盟自贸区原产地证书
6	Item number（商品顺序号）	如同批货物有不同品种，则按不同品种、发票号，等同普惠制原产地证书
7	Marks and numbers of packages（唛头及包装号）；Number and kind of packages, description of goods（包装种类和件数、货物描述）	填具体的唛头应与货物外包装上的唛头及发票上的唛头一致，与普惠制原产地证书填法一致
		填写货物的数量、包装种类及商品名称，要求同一般原产地证书
8	Origin criterion （原产地标准）	注明申报货物享受优惠待遇所依据的原产地标准： ① 如货物为完全原产，填写"P" ② 如货物含进口成分，国产成分≥40%，填写国产价值的百分比

续表

序号	项目名称	填制方法
8	Origin criterion（原产地标准）	③ 如货物含进口成分，中国-巴基斯坦自贸区累计价值成分≥40%，填写该累计价值的百分比 ④ 产品符合特定原产地标准，填写"PSR"
9	Gross weight or other quantity and FOB value（毛重或其他数量，货物的 FOB 价值）	填写出口货物的量值（即数量或重量）及商品的计量单位，若以重量计算的则要注明毛重或净重
10	Number and date of invoice（发票号码和发票日期）	按商业发票中的号码和日期填写，必须与商业发票的内容完全一致
11	Remarks（附注）	可注明订单号、信用证号、也可留空
12	Declaration by the exporter（出口商声明）	① 生产过的横线上应填上"CHINA"，进口国横线上的国名应填写"PAKISTAN" ② 申请单位的申报员应在此栏签字，加盖已注册的中英文合璧签证章 ③ 申报日期不得早于发票日期，不得迟于出运日期
13	Certification（签证机构证明）	填写签证机构的签证地点和签证日期，一般情况下与出口商申报日期、地址一致，签证机构授权签证人员在此栏手签，并加盖签证当局印章

三、区域性原产地证书的申领

因为区域性原产地证书的种类繁多，根据不同证书的具体情况，申领的文件也略有不同，但大致与普惠制原产地证书相似。FORM B、FORM E 和 FORM P 书面申办证书时都采用 FORM A 申请书，内容如实填写。

■ 课堂思考

（1）FORM N 是指哪种原产地证书？

（2）无论是 FORM A、FORM B、FORM P 还是 FORM E，只要是完全国产的产品，在填写原产地标准的时候，都填写"P"，这个说法对吗？试说明理由。

参考答案

小 贴 士

1. 自由贸易区

自由贸易区（Free Trade Area，FTA），通常指两个以上的国家或地区，通过签订自由贸易协定，相互取消绝大部分货物的关税和非关税壁垒，取消绝大多数服务部门的市场准入限制，开放投资，从而促进商品、服务和资本、技术、人员等生产要素的自由流动，实现优势互补，促进共同发展。

2. 亚太经合组织

　　亚太经合组织是亚洲太平洋地区最大的经济合作官方论坛。截至 2014 年 9 月，该组织共有 21 个正式成员和 3 个观察员。中国也是该组织的成员之一。组织为推动区域贸易投资自由化、加强成员间经济技术合作等方面发挥了不可替代的作用。它是亚太区内各地区之间促进经济成长、合作、贸易、投资的论坛。

3. 东南亚国家联盟

　　东南亚国家联盟简称"东盟"，是东南亚地区以经济合作为基础的政治、经济、完全一体化的合作组织，并建立起一系列合作机制。旨在促进东沿岸地区的经济增长、社会进步和文化发展，为建立一个繁荣、和平的东南亚国家共同体奠定基础，以促进本地区的和平与稳定。

职业判断

案例资料：

　　2014 年 12 月，南京博康电缆有限公司（以下简称"博康公司"）出口一批电缆到新加坡，为了能够使新加坡的 MAJIN 公司在进口商品时可以得到进口的关税优惠，于是博康公司需要在出口时申请原产地证书。

　　思考：

　　博康公司的报检员应申请哪种原产地证书？为什么？

参考答案

任务实施

　　由于进口国是马来西亚，所以单证员小张协助报检员柳春填制的应是中国-东盟自贸区原产地证书，如图 7.18 所示。

ORIGINAL

1. Products consigned form（Exporter's business name, address ,country） QINGDAO XINMAO IMP. & EXP. CORP. NO.97 MAOMING NAN ROAD QINGDAO，P. R. OF CHINA	Reference No. **ASEAN-CHINA FREE TRADE AREA** **PREFERENTIAL TARIFF** **CERTIFICATE OF ORIGIN** （**Combined Declaration and Certificate**）
2. Products consigned to　（consignee's name address ,country） LIEHU TRADING CO. 129 HAYW ARD WAY BERLIN, GERMANY	**FORM E** Issued in <u>THE PEOPLE'S REPUBLIC OF CHINA</u> （Country） See Overleaf Notes

图 7.18　单证员填制的中国-东欧自贸区原产地证书

3. Means of transport and route（as far as known）			4. For Official Use		
Departure date MAY 06，2015 Vessel's name/Aircraft etc. XINGYUN V.120 Port of Discharge KELANG FROM QINGDAO, CHINA TO KALANG BY SEA			☐Preferential Treatment Given ☐Preferential Treatment Not Given(Please state reasons) -- Signature of Authorized Signatory of the Importing Party		
5.Item number	6.Marks and numbers of packages	7. Number and type of packages, description of products(including quantity where appropriate and HS number of the importing Party)	8. Origin criteria (see overleaf notes)	9.Gross weight or other quantity and value(FOB)	10.Number and date of invoices
1 2	N/M N/M	TWO HUNDRED AND TWENTY FIVE(225) CARTONS OF MINI ELECTRICAL SOCKET ONE HUNDRED AND FORTY（140） CARTONS OF CAMERA SUPPORT ********************************	X X	450PCS USD 6760.00 280PCS USD 3580.00	XM201503 30 APR. 27, 2015
11.Declaration by the exporter The undersigned hereby declares that the above details and statement are correct; that all the products were produced in CHINA -- (Country) And that they comply with the origin requirements specified for these products in the rules of origin for the ACFTA for the products exported to MALAYSIA -- (Importing Country) （盖公司条形章，手签员签字） QINGDAO, CHINA APR. 29, 2015 -- Place and date, signature of Authorized signatory			12.Certification It is hereby certified , on the basis of control carried out ,that the declaration by the exporter is correct. （检验检疫局盖章、签字处） QINGDAO, CHINA APR. 29， 2015 -- Place and date, signature and stamp of certifying authority		

图 7.18   单证员填制的中国-东欧自贸区原产地证书

节能管

1. 天津节能管业有限公司于 2015 年 7 月 26 日与斯里兰卡 BEN PO 公司签订合同，出口节能管 10 000 只，总金额为 31 800 美元，支付方式为即期付款交单。

试代表天津节能管业有限公司的单证员小余协助报检员钟云根据合同（见图 7.19）和附加资料完成亚太自贸区原产地证书的填制。

SALES CONTRACT

NO.:yl0131   DATE:JUL.26,2015

THE SELLER: Yongliang Energy Management Co. Ltd.

NO. 118, Xiangyang Street, Tianjin, China

THE BUYER: Ben Po & Co. Ltd.

NO. 430 Circular, Road, Sri Lanka

This Contract is made by and between the Buyer and Seller, whereby the Buyer agrees to buy and the Seller agree to sell the under-mentioned commodity according to the terms and conditions stipulated below:

Commodity & specification	Quantity	Unit price	Amount
Energy Saving Tubes Art. No. 33984	10 000PCS	FOB Tianjin USD3.18/PC	USD31 800.00
TOTAL	10 000PCS		USD31 800.00

TOTAL CONTRACT VALUE: SAY U.S. DOLLARS THIRTY ONE THOUSAND EIGHT HUNDRED ONLY.

More or less 5% of the quantity and the amount are allowed.

PACKING: one pc in a plastic bag ten pcs to a carton

MARKS: Shipping mark includes BP, S/C No. port of destination and carton No.

TIME OF SHIPMENT: Within Aug. 2015.

PORT OF LOADING AND DESTINATION:

From Tianjin, China to Colombo , Sri Lanka

Transshipment is allowed and partial shipment is prohibited.

INSURANCE: To be effected by the buyer

TERMS OF PAYMENT: By D/P at sight

INSPECTION:

The certificate of Quality issued by the China Entry-Exit Inspection and Quarantine Bureau shall be taken as the basis of delivery.

FORCE MAJEURE:

The seller shall not held responsible if they , owing to force majeure cause , fail to make delivery within the time stipulated in the Contract or cannot deliver the goods . However, in such a case, the seller shall inform the buyer immediately by cable and if it is requested by the buyer, the seller shall also deliver to buyer by registered letter a certificate attesting the existence of such a cause.

ARBITRATION:

All disputes in connection with this contract or the execution thereof shall be settled amicably by negotiation. In case no settlement can be reached, the case shall then be submitted to the China International Economic Trade Arbitration Commission for

图 7.19 出口合同

settlement by arbitration in accordance with the Commission's arbitration rules. The award rendered by the commission shall be final and binding on both parties. The fees for arbitration shall be borne by the losing party unless otherwise awarded.

This contract is made in four original copies and becomes valid after signature, two copies to be held by each party.

Signed by:

THE SELLER:

YONGLIANG ENERGY MANAGEMENT CO. LTD.

王欣（经理）

THE BUYER:

BEN PO & CO. LTD.

TOHN WHITE(Manager)

图 7.19　出口合同（续）

附加资料如下：

（1）启运日期：2015.08.19

（2）船名航次：SHUNLI V.490

（3）发票开立日期及号码：2015 年 8 月 11 日　　YL4UEI4

（4）出口商申请地点及日期：天津，2015 年 8 月 11 日

（5）签证机构签证地点及日期：天津，2015 年 8 月 11 日

（6）节能管商品编码：41.40

（7）产品原材料全部原产于中国

2. 舟山海产品公司出口一批冰冻黄鱼至巴基斯坦，主要交易条件如下：

出口商：ZHOUSHAN MARINE PRODUCTS CO.

　　　　NO. 71 MINAN ROAD

　　　　ZHOUSHAN, ZHEJIANG, CHINA

进口商：PINDOCS SINO.

　　　　744 GOLDEN GATE STEET

　　　　KARACHI, PAKISTAN

生产商：出口商

运输方式和路线：海运，舟山直达卡拉奇

货名：FROZEN CROAKER

唛头：N/M

数量及包装情况：共 50 公吨，每箱 25 千克，共 2000 个木箱

毛重：每箱 30 千克

单价：每千克 4 美元，共 200 000 美元

出运日期：2015 年 3 月 6 日

船名航次：DONGFENG V.121

发票号码和日期：ZMP150215 2015 年 2 月 15 日

出口商申请地点及日期：舟山，2015 年 2 月 15 日

参考答案

签证机构签证地点及日期；舟山，2015 年 2 月 16 日

产品全部原产于中国

试代表舟山海产品公司的报检员，根据上述条件填写 FORM P 证书。

技能强化训练

项目小结

技 能 提 高

（一）填单题

根据下列资料，填制一般原产地证书及申请书。

出口商兼生产商：FUJIAN HOBBY FOOD CO. LTD.（福建好比食品有限公司）

在线测试及
参考答案

        39 NANJING ROAD   （南京路 39 号）

        FUZHOU, CHINA   （中国福建）

进口商：JERRY IMP. & EXP. CO.

       76 VICTORIA STREET

       HONGKONG

运输路线：福州直达香港，海运

唛头：自行设计

货名、货号：罐头蘑菇   CANNED MUSHROOM

商品单价：每罐 50 美元

H.S. 编码：2003.1019

数量及包装：4000 罐，每 4 罐装一个纸箱

申请单位注册号：8667410

发票号及日期：HB4842，2015 年 6 月 4 日

预计出口日期：2015 年 6 月 15 日

报检员：叶琳

出口商申请地点及日期：福州，2015 年 6 月 4 日

签证机构签证地点及日期：福州，2015 年 6 月 5 日

参考答案

（二）审单改错题

根据下列资料，审核原产地证书和申请书，指出单证中的错误。

（1）信用证，如图 7.20 所示。

	ISSUE OF A DOCUMENTARY CREDIT
TO	HANGSENG BANK LTD. SHANGHAI BRANCH
FROM	NORDEA BANK, SWEDEN
MT700	
SEQUENCE OF TOTAL	27: 1/1
FROM OF DC	40A: IRREVOCABLE
DC NO	20: 4489-4805/90
DATE OF ISSUE	31C: 140514
EXPIRY DATE AND PLACE	31D: DATE: JUL. 15，2014
	PLACE: CHINA
APPLICANT	50: JYSK CD
	FOERETA 6 Y-41952 ARLOEV SWEDEN
BENEFICIARY	59: WATLEE TRADING LTD.
	6/FL, FLATF TIANHE PLAZA
	SHANGHAI, CHINA
AMOUNT	32B: USD 26 330.40
AVAILABLE WITH/BY	41A: ANY BANK BY NEGOTIATION
DRAFT AT…	42C: AT 30 DAYS SIGHT
DRAWEE	42A: ISSUING BANK
PARTIAL SHIPMENT	43P: ALLOWED
TRANSSHIPMENT	43T: NOT ALLOWED
LOADING IN CHARGE	44A: CHINESE PORTS
FOR TRANSPORT TO	44B: GOTHENBURG, SWEDEN
LATEST DATE OF SHIPMENT	44C: JUN. 08, 2014
DESCRIPTION OF GOODS	45A: LEATHER GLOVE
	AS PER S/C NO 2014KG02350
	8 400 PCS ART NO. RE09 USD 1.25/PC
	15 520 PCS ART NO. P90 USD 1.20/PC
	FOB SHANGHAI (INCOTERMS 2010)
DOCUMENTS REQUIRED	46A: 1.SIGNED ORIGINAL COMMERCIAL INVOICE AND 5 COPIES
	2. PAKCING LIST IN 2 COPIES
	3. FULL SET OF CLEAN ON BOARD MARINE BILLS OF LADING MADE OUT TO ORDER OF ISSUING BANK, MARKED "FREIGHT PRIPAID" AND NOTIFY APPLICANT (AS INDICATED ABOVE); MENTIONING L/C NO.
	4. GSP CERTIFICATE OF ORIGIN FORM A, CERTIFIYING GOODS OF ORIGIN IN CHINA, ISSUED BY COMPETENT AUTHORITIES.
ADDITIONAL CONDITIOANS	47A: 1. ALL DOCUEMNTS MUST BE ISSUED IN ENGLISH.
	2. MULTIMODAL TRANSPORT DOCUMENTS ACCEPTALBE EVIDENCING SHIPMENT CLEAN ON BOARD ON A NAMED VESSEL BILL OF LADING MUST SHOW CONTAINER NUMBER.

图 7.20 信用证

DETAILS OF CHARGES	71B: ALL COMMISSION AND CHARGES OUTSIDE SWEDEN ARE FOR ACCOUNT OF BENEFICIARY
PRESENTATION PERIOD	48: DOCUMENTS TO BE PRESENTED WITHIN 15 DAYS AFTER THE DATE OF SHIPMENT, BUT WITHIN THE VALIDITY OF THE CREDIT.
CONFIRMATION	79: WITHOUT

图 7.20　信用证（续）

（2）制单资料：

① 装箱方式：40 件装一纸箱

② 船名和开行日期：LONGDONG V.053　2014 年 6 月 7 日

③ 发票开立日期及号码：2014 年 5 月 26 日　Z339480

④ 出口商名称及联系电话：上海沃利贸易公司

⑤ 出口商申请地点及日期：上海，2014 年 5 月 26 日

⑥ 签证机构签证地点及日期：上海，2014 年 5 月 27 日

⑦ 生产厂商及联系电话：苏州无锡真皮制品厂　0510-3943048

⑧ 真皮手套 H.S.编码：4203.2990

产品原材料全部原产于中国

（3）普惠制原产地证书，如图 7.21 所示。

ORIGINAL

1. Goods consigned from (Exporter's business name, address, JYSK CD FOERETA 6 Y-41952 ARLOEV SWEDEN	Reference No. **GENERALIZED SYSTEM OF PREFERENCES** CERTIFICATE OF ORIGIN
2. Goods consigned to (Consignee's name, address, country) WATLEE TRADING LTD. 6/FL, FLATF TIANHE PLAZA SHANGHAI, CHINA	(Combined declaration and certificate) **THE PEOPLE'S REPUBLIC OF CHINA** Issued in _____ (country) See Notes overleaf
3. Means of transport and route (as far as known)	4. For official use

图 7.21　普惠制原产地证书

FROM CHINESE PORTS TO GOTHENBURG, SWEDEN

5. Item number 01	6. Marks and numbers of packages N/M	7. Number and kind of packages; description of goods FIVE HUNDRED AND FIFTY EIGHT(598) CARTONS OF LEATHER GLOVE	8. Origin criterion (see Notes overleaf) A	9. Gross weight or other quantity 598CTNS	10. Number and date of invoices Z339480 MAY 26 , 2014

11. Certification	12. Declaration by the exporter
It is hereby certified, on the basis of control carried out, that the declaration by the exporter is correct.	The undersigned hereby declares that the above details and statements are correct, that all the goods were **SWEDEN** produced in _____ (country) and that they comply with the origin requirements specified for those goods in the Generalized System of Preferences for goods exported to CHINA -----------------
SHANGHAI, CHINA MAY 26. 2014 报检员手签签章 ------------------------------- Place and date, signature and stamp of certifying authority	SHANGHAI, CHINA MAY 27. 2014 ------------------------------- Place and date, signature and stamp of authorized signatory

图 7.21　普惠制原产地证书（续）

（4）普惠制原产地证书申请书，如图 7.22 所示。

中华人民共和国出入境检验检疫
原产地证明书申请书

申请单位（加盖公章）：上海沃利贸易公司　　　　　　　　证书号_____

申请人郑重声明：　　　　　　　　　　　　　　　　　　　注册号_____

本人被正式授权代表单位办理原产地证明书和签署本申请书的。

本人所提供原产地证明书及所付单据内容正确无误，如发现弄虚作假，冒充证书所列货物，擅改证书，自愿接受签证机关的处罚及负法律责任。现将有关情况申领如下：

生产单位	上海沃利贸易公司	生产单位联系人电话		0510-3943048
商品名称（中英文）	皮手套 （LEATHER GLOVE）	H.S.税目号(以六位数码计)		4203.2990
商品 FOB 总值（以美元计）	26 330.40 美元	发票号		Z339480
最终销售国	瑞士	证书种类划"√"	加急证书	普通证书√

图 7.22　普惠制原产地证书申请书

货物拟出运日期	2014 年 5 月 27 日						
贸易方式和企业性质（请在适合处划"√"）							
正常贸易 C	来料加工 L	补偿贸易 B	中外合资 H	中外合作 Z	外商独资 D	零售 Y	展卖 M
√							
包装数量或毛重或其他数量	23 928 只						

原产地标准：

本项商品系在中国生产，完全符合该给惠国方案规定，其原产地情况符合以下第　　条；

（1）"P"（完全国产，未使用任何进口原材料）；

（2）"W"其 H.S.税目号为＿＿＿＿＿＿＿（含进口成分）；

（3）"F"（对加拿大出口产品，其进口成分不超过产品出厂价的 40%）

本批产品系：1.直接运输从＿＿中国口岸＿＿到＿＿瑞典＿＿＿；

2.转口运输从＿＿＿＿＿＿中转国（地区）＿＿＿＿＿＿到＿＿＿＿＿＿；

申请人说明	申领人（签名）：
	电话：
	日期：2014 年　5　月 20 日

现提交中国出口商品商业发票副本一份，普惠制产地证明书格式 A（FORM A）一正二副，以及其他附件一份，请予审核签证。

注：凡有进口成分的商品，必须要求提交"含进口成分受惠商品成本明细单"。

图 7.22　普惠制原产地证书申请书

参考答案

项目八

报检报关单据实训

知识目标

1. 掌握出境货物报检流程及出境货物报检单的填写方法；
2. 掌握出口货物报关流程及出口货物报关单的填写方法；
3. 掌握进口货物报关流程及进口货物报关单的填写方法。

能力目标

1. 能熟悉出境货物报检流程并填写出境货物报检单；
2. 能熟悉出口货物报关流程并填写出口货物报关单；
3. 能熟悉进口货物报关流程并填写进口货物报关单。

任务一　填制出境货物报检单

任务导航

　　肇庆市卓瑞轻工业品有限公司与东韩公司签订如下合同，出口一批抛光机配件（减速电机）到越南，合同如图 8.1 所示。

出 口 合 同

SALES COMFIRMATION

卖方：肇庆市卓瑞轻工业品有限公司　　　　　　　No.: 1505A
Sellers:

地址：　　　　　　　　　　　　　　　　　　　　日期：2015/08/12
ADD:　　　　　　　　　　　　　　　　　　　　　Date:

买方：DONG NAM CO., LTD　　　　　　　　　　签约地：肇庆
Buyers:　　　　　　　　　　　　　　　　　　　　Signed at:

根据买卖双方同意成交下列商品订立条款如下：

The undersigned Sellers And Buyers have agreed to close the following transactions according to the terms and conditions stipulated below:

商品 Articles	规格 Specifications	数量 Quantity	单价 Price	总值 Amount
			FOB 肇庆	USD4950.00
抛光机配件（减速电机）		3 台	USD570.00/台	USD1710.00
抛光机配件（减速电机）		4 台	USD810.00/台	USD3240.00

数量及总值均得有 5 %的增减，由卖方决定。

Within 5% more or less both in amount and quantity allowed at the Seller's option.

总值　　　美元：肆仟玖佰伍拾元正
Total Value:

包装　夹板箱
Packing:

装运期　2015 年 09 月 30 日前
Time of Shipment:

装运口岸及目的地　由中国到越南
Load port & Destination:

保险　买方
Insurance:

付款条件　电汇
Terms of payment:

图 8.1　出口合同

备注	
Remark:	
卖方	买方
THE SELLERS:	THE BUYERS:

图 8.1　出口合同（续）

要求：

根据上述合同，填写出境货物报检单。

知 识 准 备

一、出境货物报检流程

出境货物报检流程：申请报检（电子申报）→受理报检→实施检验检疫→出具出境货物通关单（海关凭此单放行）。

二、出境货物报检的种类

出境货物报检的种类如下。

（1）出境一般报检。

（2）出境换证报检。

（3）出境货物预检报检。

三、出境货物报检的时间与地点

对于出境货物报检的时间与地点，我国法律、法规有以下规定。

（1）最迟在出口报关/装运前 7 天。

（2）需隔离检疫的出境动物，在出境前 60 天预报、隔离前 7 天报检。

（3）原则上产地检验、检疫。

四、报检范围

列入报检范围的商品有以下几类。

（1）《商检机构实施检验的进出口商品种类表》内的进出口商品。

（2）出口食品卫生检验和检疫，以及出口动物产品的检疫。

（3）出口危险品包装容器的性能鉴定和使用鉴定。

（4）装运出口易腐烂变质食品的船舱、集装箱等。

（5）其他法律或者行政法规规定必须经商检机构检验的进出口商品。

（6）我国与进口国主管部门协定必须凭我国商检机构证书方准进口的商品。

（7）对外贸易合同、信用证规定由商检机构检验出证的商品。

（8）对外贸易关系人申请的鉴定业务。

（9）委托检验业务。

有下列情况之一者，商检机构一般不予受理报检：①应施检验的出口商品，未经检验已装运出口的；②按分工规定，不属商检工作范围的。

五、报检时必须提供的单证

出口企业在报检时必须提供以下单证。

（1）出口商品报检时，报验人应提供外贸合同（确认书），信用证以及有关单证函电等。

（2）须向商检机构办理卫生注册及出口质量许可证的商品，必须交附商检机构签发的卫生注册证书、厂检合格单或出口质量许可证。

课堂思考

出口商品检验的内容和根据是什么？

参考答案

小　贴　士

出现在我国的报关、报检单等上面的 H. S. 编码为什么有 10 位数，也有 8 位数的呢？

H. S.采用 6 位数编码，把全部国际贸易商品分为 21 类 97 章。章以下再分为目和子目。商品编码第 1、第 2 位数码代表"章"，第 3、第 4 位数码代表"目"（heading），第 5、第 6 位数码代表"子目"（subheading）。前 6 位数是 HS 国际标准编码，H. S.有 1241 个四位数的税目、5113 个六位数子目。有的国家根据本国的实际，已分出第 7、第 8、第 9 位数码。我国进出口税则采用 10 位编码，前 8 位等效采用 H. S.编码，后两位是我国子目，它是在 H. S.分类原则和方法基础上，根据我国进出口商品的实际情况延伸的两位编码。

职业判断

案例资料：

表 8.1 为截取于《商检机构实施检验的进出口商品种类表》的部分资料。

表 8.1　商品编码资料

商品编码	商品名称	计量单位	检验别
第五类	矿产品		
25101010	未碾磨磷灰石	公斤	AB
25101090	未碾磨其他天然磷酸钙、天然磷酸铝钙及磷酸盐白垩	公斤	A
25102010	已碾磨磷灰石	公斤	AB
25111000	天然硫酸钡（重晶石）	公斤	B

思考：

"检验别"（种类）项下的 "A"、"B"、"AB" 分别表示什么？

 任务实施

 参考答案

肇庆卓瑞出具的出境货物报检单，如图 8.2 所示。

中华人民共和国出入境检验检疫
出境货物报检单

报检单位（加盖公章）：肇庆市卓瑞轻工业品有限公司				*编　号：441270216000061	
报检单位登记号：（4412960111）联系人：　　　电话：				报检日期：2015 年 08 月 23 日	
发货人	（中文）肇庆市卓瑞轻工业品有限公司				
	（外文）				
收货人	（中文）东韩公司				
	（外文）DONG NAM CO., LTD				
货物名称（中/外文）	H.S.编码	产地	数/重量	货物总值	包装种类及数量
抛光机配件（减速电机）0.75 千瓦	**8501520000**	中国 肇庆	3 台 114.0 千克		毛重：630 公斤
抛光机配件（减速电机）7.5 千瓦	**8501520000**	中国 肇庆	4 台 336.0 千克	USD4950.00	净重：450 公斤

图 8.2　出境货物报检单

运输工具名称号码		贸易方式	一般贸易	货物存放地点		
合同号	1505A	信用证号			用途	
发货日期	输往国家（地区）	越南	许可证/审批号			
启运地	肇庆	到达口岸		生产单位注册号		
集装箱规格、数量及号码						

合同、信用证订立的检验检疫条款或特殊要求	标 记 及 号 码	随附单据（划"√"或补填）	
不需通关单		☐合同 ☐信用证 ☑发票 ☐换证凭单 ☐装箱单 ☐厂检单	☐包装性能结果单 ☐许可/审批文件 ☐ ☐ ☐ ☐

需要证单名称（划"√"或补填）				*检验检疫费	
☐品质证书	__正__副	☐植物检疫证书	__正__副	总金额（人民币元）	
☐重量证书	__正__副	☐熏蒸/消毒证书	__正__副		
☐数量证书	__正__副	☐出境货物换证凭单	__正__副	计费人	
☐兽医卫生证书	__正__副	☐		收费人	
☐健康证书	__正__副	☐			
☐卫生证书	__正__副	☐		总金额（人民币元）	
☐动物卫生证书	__正__副	☐		计费人	
				收费人	

报检人郑重声明： 1. 本人被授权报检。 2. 上列填写内容正确属实，货物无伪造或冒用他人的厂名、标志、认证标志，并承担货物质量责任。 签名：____×××____	领 取 证 单	
	日期	
	签名	

注：有"*"号栏由出入境检验检疫机关填写　◆国家出入境检验检疫局制

图8.2　出境货物报检单（续）

任务再现

肇庆市富庆五金塑料有限公司和台湾金顺庆实业有限公司签订出口合同，如图8.3所示。试根据合同内容填制出境货物报检单。

合 同

日期：2015.11.28
Date：

合同号码：2015FQ022
Contract No：

卖方：（The Seller） 肇庆市富庆五金塑料有限公司
地   址：广东省肇庆市高新区文德四街 电话：86-758-3625058
买方：（The Buyer）金顺庆实业有限公司
地   址：台湾台北市基隆路 2 段 135 号

兹经买卖双方同意按照以下条款由买方购进，卖方售出以下商品：

This contract is made by and between the Buyer and the Seller；whereby the Buyer agree to buy and the Seller agree to sell the under-mentioned goods subject to the terms and conditions as stipulated hereinafter：

(1) 商品名称:车厢配件 / 工具箱锁
Name of Commodity：
(2) 数 量：1636.2 千克
Quantity：
(3) 单 价：
   Unit price：
(4) 总 值：FOB 肇庆 USD12494.5
Total Value：
(5) 包 装：纸箱
Packing：
(6) 支付条款：电汇
Terms of Payment：
(7) 起 运 港：肇庆
Port of Lading：
(8) 目 的 港：香港
Port of Destination：

卖方：肇庆市富庆五金塑料有限公司   买方：金顺庆实业有限公司

（授权签字）   （授权签字）

图 8.3　出口合同

参考答案

项目小结

任务二　填制出口货物报关单

任务导航

　　肇庆市富庆五金塑料有限公司和台湾金顺庆实业有限公司于 2015 年 11 月 28 日签订出口合同，如图 8.4 所示。

　　要求：

　　根据出口合同，填写出口货物报关单。

中华人民共和国海关出口货物报关单

预录入编号：　　　　　　进制　　　　　海关编号：

出口口岸	备案号		出口日期	申报日期
经营单位	运输方式	运输工具名称		提运单号
发货单位	贸易方式	征免性质		结汇方式
许可证号	运抵国（地区）	指运港		境内货源地
批准文号	成交方式	运费	保费	杂费
合同协议号	件数	包装种类	毛重（公斤）	净重（公斤）
集装箱号	随附单据		生产厂家	

标记唛码及备注

项号	商品编号	商品名称	规格型号	数量及单位	最终目的国（地区）	单价	总价	币制	征免

税费征收情况

录入员　录入单位 报关员 单位地址 邮编：	兹声明以上申报无讹并承担法律责任 申报单位（签章） 电话： 填制日期：	海关审单批注及放行日期（签章）
		审单　　　　审价
		征税　　　　统计
		查验　　　　放行

图 8.4　出口货物报关单样本

一、出口货物报关单的含义

出口货物报关单是由海关总署规定的统一格式和填制规范，由出口企业或其代理人填制并向海关提交的申报货物状况的法律文书，是海关依法监管货物出口、征收关税及其他税费、编制海关统计以及处理其他海关业务的重要凭证（见图8.4）。

二、出口货物报关单的作用

出口货物报关单用于确认货物是否真正出口或者进口，是海关出具的进出口的正式凭证。其作用包括以下几个方面。

（1）它是海关监管、征税、统计以及开展稽查和调查的重要依据。

（2）它是加工贸易进出口货物核销，以及出口退税和外汇管理的重要凭证。

（3）它是海关处理走私、违规案件，以及税务、外汇管理部门查处骗税和套汇犯罪活动中的重要证书。

三、出口货物报关单的填写方法

出口货物报关单，由出口货物的收发货人，或者他们委托的代理人（以下统称"报关员"），在货物进、出口的时候填写并向海关申报，同时提供批准货物出口的证件和有关的货运、商业单据，以便海关依据这些单据证件审查货物的进出口是否合法，确定关税的征收或减免事宜，编制海关统计。

出口货物报关单的填写方法具体如下所述。

（1）出口口岸：填写海关放行货物出境的中国国境口岸名称。

（2）经营单位：填写对外签订或执行出口贸易合同（协议）的中国境内企业或单位的名称。

（3）指运港（站）：填写本批货物预定最后运达港口、机场或车站。

（4）合同（协议号）：填写本批货物合同协议的详细年份、字头和编号及附件号码。

（5）贸易方式：分别填写"一般贸易"、"国家间、联合国及国际组织无偿援助物资和赠送品"、"华侨、港澳同胞及外籍华人捐赠品"、"补偿贸易"、"来料加工装配贸易"（对口合同除外）、"对口合同的来料加工配贸易"、"进料加工贸易"、"寄售、供销贸易"、"边境地方贸易及边境地区小额贸易"，或"其他"。不能简略填报为"援助"、"赠送"或"加工装配"等。

（6）贸易国（地区）：货物的售予国（地区）。填写同中国境内的企业和单位签订合同（协议）的国家或成交厂商所在地的国家（地区）。

（7）消费国（地区）：填写出口货物实际消费的国家（地区）。如果不能确定消费国的，以尽可能预知的最后运往作为消费国。如果一张报关单的货物有不同的消费国，应当分别注明。

（8）收货单位：填写国外最后收货的企业的名称和所在地。

（9）运输工具名称及号码：江海运输填船名，陆运填车号，空、邮运只填"空运"或"邮运"字样。

（10）装货单或运单号：海运填装货单号，陆运填运单号，邮运填报税清单（包裹单）号。

（11）收结汇方式：填写电汇（T/T）、信汇（M/T）、信用证（L/C）、承兑交单（D/A）或付款交单（D/P）等结汇方式。

（12）起运地点：填写出口货物的起运点和出口货物发货单位所在地区。但是经济特区、海南行政区、经济技术开发区、经济开放区的企业对外成交及发运的出口货物，不论货物原发运单位是何处，均以有关经济特区、海南行政区、经济技术开发区、经济开放区为起运地点。其他省、自治区、直辖市的企业或单位对外成交发运的出口货物，如果经过或者去经济特区、海南行政区、经济技术开发区、经济开放区暂存待运出口的，则以原省、自治区、直辖市为出口货物的起运地。

（13）海关统计商品编号：按照《中华人民共和国海关统计商品目录》的规定填写。

（14）货名规格及货号：应填写货物的中外文名称和详细规格。货号填写公司编制的商品代号。

（15）标记唛码：填写货物的实际标记唛码，如有地点名称的，也应该填写。

（16）件数及包装种类：填写包装种类指袋、箱、捆、包、桶等。一批货物有多种包装的，要分别填报件数。

（17）数量：填写货物的实际数量和数量单位（如台、个、打等）。如合同规定的数量单位同海关统计商品目录规定的计量单位不同，或者统计商品规定有第二数量单位的（如发电机除台数外，还需填千瓦数；内燃机除台数外，还需填马力），都要按照海关统计商品目录规定的数量单位填写。整套机械分批出口时，应在本栏注明"分批装运"字样。

（18）重量："毛重"填写本批货物全部重量；"净重"填写扣除外层包装后的自然净重。合同发票等单据上没有净重时，可以按照商品习惯填写公量重、净重等，也可以将毛重扣除估计外层重最后填报。对于不同品种的货物，应当分别填明净重。

（19）成交价格：填写合同规定的成交单价、总价格条件（如 CIF、FOB 等），并注明外币名称。如果价格条件为 CIF、CFR 或包括佣金、折扣时，在计算成交总价时应分别扣除运费、保险费和佣金、折扣等费用，并填明 FOB 成交总价。

（20）离岸价格：应按照国家外汇管理部门核定的各种货币对美元内部统一折算率，将第十九项的 FOB 成交总价折合为美元填报在"外币"栏。离岸价格人民币免填。邮运、空运出口货物，采用货物在启运地寄交的离岸价格。美元离岸价格计至元为止，元以下四舍五入。

（21）随附单据：填写单据的名称。

（22）申报单位（盖章）：必须加盖申报单位的公章、报关员的印章并填明申报日期。

（23）海关放行日期：由出口地海关在核放货物后填注日期，并加盖海关放行章。

出口货物报关单应当在出口货物装货前 24 小时前向海关填报。如果在递交了出口货物报关单后发生退关性事件，申报人应当在 3 天内向海关办理更改手续。

四、填写时的注意事项

报关员在填制出口货物报关单时，应注意以下事项。

（1）报关单填写的项目要准确、齐全、清楚，填报项目若有更改，应在更改项目处加盖核对章。

（2）不同合同的货物，不能填在一份报关单上。

（3）如果同一合同中包括多种商品，应注意，在一份报关单上填写的海关统计商品编号的货物一般不要超过 5 项。

（4）报关单与随附合同、发票、箱单等应相符（单单一致），报关单所申报的内容与实际出口的货物要相符（单货一致）。

▌ 课堂思考

填写出口货物报关单的根据是什么？

参考答案

报关编号的意义

每一份报关单都有一个固定的海关编号，共 18 位，如 424020090909038703。

其中，1~4 位 "4240" 代表关区，是青岛海关快件监管中心。5~8 位 "2009" 代表年份；第 9 为有两个数字 0 和 1，0 代表出口报关单，1 代表进口报关单；第 10 位相对来说是比较固定的，每个海关都不一样，用固定的两个数字分别代表进口和出口报关单；第 11 位代表的是关区 4 位数编码的最后一位数字；第 12 位代表的是年份，如例子中的 "9" 即代表 2009 年；最后 6 位数字是流水号。

任务实施

肇庆市富庆五金塑料有限公司的报关代理人出具的报关单，如图 8.5 所示。

中华人民共和国海关出口货物报关单

预录入编号：5176201607660001　　　　　　海关编号：5176201607660001

发货单位 4412940595 肇庆市富庆五金塑料有限公司	出口口岸 肇庆四会	出口日期		申报日期 2016-01-18
经营单位 4412940595 肇庆市富庆五金塑料有限公司	运输方式 水路运输	运输工具名称 5200550037/160118000000		提运单号 MFLGA0035
申报单位：肇庆顺通报关有限公司	监管方式 0110 一般贸易	征免性质 101 一般征税		备案号
贸易国（地区） 142 中国	运抵国（地区）110 香港	指运港 110 香港		境内货源地 44129 肇庆
许可证号	成交方式 FOB	运费	保费	杂费
合同协议号 2015FQ022	件数 3	包装种类 托盘	毛重（公斤） 1745	净重（公斤） 1636.20
集装箱号 CKSU2168675	随附单证			
标记唛码及备注 随附单据　肇庆四会退税				

总值：12494.5 美元　壹万贰仟肆佰玖拾肆元伍角。

项号　商品编号	商品名称、规格型号	数量及单位	最终目的国（地区）	单价	总价	币制	征免
1. 83023000.00	车厢配件	552.5 千克	香港	3.0000	1657.5	美元	照章
车厢用，铁制，脚踏板，品牌：无							
2. 83014000.00	工具箱锁	10837 千克	香港	10.0000	10837	美元	照章
工具箱用，不锈钢、锌合金，品牌：无							

图 8.5　报关代理人出具的报关单

特殊关系确认：	价格影响确认：	支付特许权使用费确认：	
录入员 000000116571	录入单位	兹申明对以上内容承担如实申报、依法纳税之法律责任	海关批注及签章
报关人员 潘伟良 肇庆顺通报关有限公司		申报单位（签章）	

图 8.5 报关代理人出具的报关单（续）

参考答案

任务再现

　　肇庆市富庆五金塑料有限公司和台湾金顺庆实业有限公司于 2015 年 11 月 28 日电约出口一批门用配件（把手、门闩）和家具用的挡片、挂钩到香港。

　　参照如图 8.6 所示的装箱单，填制相关的出口报关单。

参考答案

肇 庆 市 富 庆 五 金 塑 料 有 限 公 司
Zhaoqing Fu Qing Metal Plastics Co. Ltd
地址：肇庆市高新区迎宾大道文德四街西
装箱单
Packing List

编号	品名	箱数	数量 （个）	净重/箱 （KGS）	总净重 （KGS）	毛重/箱 （KGS）	总毛重 （KGS）	备注
90-114	车厢配件/脚踏板（无牌子，铁）	25 纸箱	1000	22.1	552.5	22.6	565	第 1 板
115-138	工具箱锁（无牌子，不锈钢）	25 纸箱	1000	23.1	577.5	23.9	597.5	第 2 板
139-169	工具箱锁（无牌子，锌合金）	31 纸箱	496	16.2	502. 5	17.2	533.2	第 3 板
170	工具箱锁（无牌子，锌合金）	1 纸箱	4	4	4	4.3	4.3	第 3 板
						托盘重	45	
合计		82	2500		1636.20		1745	

注：共 3 托盘

图 8.6 装箱单

项目小结

任务三　　填制进口报关单

任务导航

　　肇庆市五金塑料有限公司向台湾申光实业有限公司进口一批锁舌和锁头，合同、装箱单、发票如图 8.7～图 8.9 所示。

合 同

甲方：肇庆市富庆五金塑料有限公司　　　　乙方：申光实业有限公司

地址：肇庆高新技术开发区文德四街西　　　地址：板桥市大观路一段 38 巷 200 弄 79-7 号

电话：0758-3626903　　　　　　　　　　电话：886-2-23778536

合同号：2014FQ030　　　　签约日期：2014-12-28　　　　签约地点：肇庆大旺

经甲乙双方协商达成如下产品销售及条款：

（一）乙方销售产品名称：

序号	名称、规格	单位	数量	单价（USD）	总金额（USD）	装运期
1	锁舌/铁制	千克	83.8	4.34	363.69	2015-02-15～
2	锁头/锌合金制	千克	38	17.9	680.20	2015-3-15
总值			USD CIF 肇庆		1043.892	

（二）运输方式：海运。

（三）保险及保险费由乙方负责。

　　甲方签章：　　　　　　　　　　　　乙方签章：

　　日期：2014.12.28　　　　　　　　　日期：2014.12.28

图 8.7　合同

申光實業有限公司

地址：板橋市大觀路一段 38 巷 200 弄 79-7 號　　電話：886-2-22727371　　傳真：886-2-22727367

PACKING WEIGHT LIST

For account and risk of Messrs: 肇慶市富慶五金塑料有限公司

　　　　　　　　　　　　　　廣東省肇慶市高新區文德四街

Shipped by

Per S.S

sailing on or about

From _____ TAIWAN _____ to ZHAOQING CHINA

箱號	貨物描述	數量	單位	@淨重 KGS	總淨重 KGS	@毛重 KGS	總毛重 KGS
1	鎖舌/鐵制	1	紙箱	14.5	14.5	15	15
2～4	鎖舌/鐵制	3	紙箱	18.1	54.3	18.6	55.8
5	鎖舌/鐵制	1	紙箱	11.5	11.5	12	12
6	鎖舌/鐵制	1	紙箱	3.5	3.5	4	4
7	鎖頭/鋅合金制	1	紙箱	12.5	12.5	13	13
8	鎖頭/鋅合金制	1	紙箱	25.5	25.5	26	26
合計：		8	紙箱		121.80		125.80

图 8.8　装箱单

申光實業有限公司

地址：板橋市大觀路一段 38 巷 200 弄 79-7 號　　　電話：886-2-22727371　　　傳真：886-2-22727367

INVOICE

合同號　　2014FQ030

For account and risk of Messrs：肇慶市富慶五金塑料有限公司

廣東省肇慶市高新區文德四街

Shipped by

Per S.S

sailing on or about

From _____TAIWAN_____ to _____ZHAOQING CHINA_____

標嘜	貨物描述	原產地	數量	單位	單價（USD）	CIF 廣州　總價（USD）	
	鎖舌	台灣	83.8	KGS	4.34	363.69	
	鎖頭	台灣	38	KGS	17.9	680.2	
	合計：		121.8KGS		CIF 廣州 USD	1043.89	

图 8.9　发票

要求：

根据合同、装箱单和发票，填写进口货物报关单。

知识准备

一、进口货物报关单

进口货物报关单是指海关受理进口报关后，向进口单位出具的注有进口数量、成交总价并盖有验讫章的纸质凭证。

二、进口货物报关单的内容和缮制

进口货物报关单的内容和缮制方法如下所述。

（1）申报单位编号：由申报单位自己编号。

（2）进口口岸：填写货物进入我国国境的口岸名称及代码。

（3）经营单位：填写对外签订或执行进口合同的单位，不能填写收货单位或国外出口厂商。填写时应包括经营单位全称及其代码。

（4）收货单位：填写进口货物的使用单位名称及其所在省、市名称。

（5）合同（协议号）：填写进口合同（协议）的详细年份、编号及附件号码。

（6）批准机关及文号：填许可证号、特定减免号和免税表号等。

（7）运输工具名称及号码：运输工具根据货物进入我国国境时使用的运输方式加以确定。运输方式分为6类：江海运输、铁路运输、公路运输、空运、邮运和其他。海运填船名，陆运填车号，空邮运只填"空运""邮运"字样。

（8）贸易性质（方式）：贸易的性质（方式）分为16类，包括一般贸易、捐赠品、样品、个人自用品以及其他等。填写时应根据该批进口货物的实际贸易性质选择填写，并须注明代码。

（9）贸易国别（地区）：贸易国别即成交国别，填写货物直接购自国（地区）的名称。

（10）原产国别（地区）：填写进口货物生产制造的国家（地区）。如货物经过其他国家加工复制，以最后加工的国家为原产国。但若仅经简单整理如改装、涂改或加贴标签等，而并未改变货物的性质、规格的，不作加工论。原产国一般可根据货物的产地证明书加以确定。如果一张报关单上有不同的原产国的货物，应当分别注明。

（11）外汇来源：按本进口合同的实际外汇来源分别填写"中央外汇""地方外汇""贷款外汇""分成外汇""国外投资"或"其他"。

（12）进口日期：填写运载货物的运输工具申报进口日期。

（13）提单或运单号：海运填写提单号，陆运、空运填写运单号，邮运填写报税清单（包裹单）号。

（14）运杂费：填写实际支付运杂费金额。如实际支付运杂费不能确认，可按规定的定额率估算。

（15）保险费库：价格条件为FOB或CFR条件下，填写实际支付的保险金额或定额率。如实际支付保险费不能确认，可按规定的定额率估算。

（16）标记唛码：填写货物实际使用标记唛码，或按进口合同、发票载明的标记唛码填写。如有地点名称也应照填。

（17）包装种类及件数：包装种类即指袋、箱、包、捆、桶等。一批货物有多种包装种类，应分别填写件数。

（18）毛重及净重：毛重填本批货物全部重量。净重一般填毛重扣除外层包装后的自然净重。对于一批不同品种的货物，应当分别注明净重。对于有销售包装的货物，不必扣除销售包装的重量。不能取得净重时，应按进口合同或商业习惯填写。

（19）海关统计商品编号：参照《中华人民共和国海关统计商品目录》，填写商品代号。未列入商品目录的，按其用途归入0~6类。

（20）货名规格及货号：按进口合同（协议）或发票上载明的货物名称、规格填写。货名、规格填中文名称并附注外文。货号填公司自编货号。

（21）数量：此栏包括数量、单位两个小项，应按实际进口货物数量及计量单位填写。若合同中采用的计量单位与海关统计商品目录所规定的计量单位不同，应将其折算成目录规定的计量单位填写。若货物仅从一种数量单位不足以反映其性能，或海关统计规定有第二数量单位，则还须填写第二数量单位。一张报关单有不同品种的货物，应分别填写其数量。若整套机械分批进口，应在本栏注明"分批装运"字样。

（22）成交价格：填进口合同约定的成交单价、总价和价格条件（如FOB、CIF 等），并注明货币名称。若货价和其他费用为不同外币时应分别注明。分批进口货物，按每批进口货物的数量填写成交价格。

（23）到岸价格：填进口货物到达我国国境时的实际到岸价，包括货价、运抵我国卸货前的运费、保险费和其他一切费用。空运、邮运采用货物运至指运地的到岸价。到岸价格人民币一项，应将外币按照向海关申报日中国银行公布的人民币对各种货币的外汇牌价的中间价的月平均数折算成人民币填写。外币一项，按中国银行核定的各种货币对美元的内部统一折算率折合成美元。到岸价格的人民币和外币均计至元为止，元以下四舍五入。

（24）关税完税价格、税则号列及税率、关税税额：由海关分别按规定填写计算。

（25）备注：根据海关规定，有些货物必须注明有关事项，如"减免纳税""保税货物"等，属于此类进口货物应在本栏加以注明。

（26）集装箱号：采用集装箱运输的进口货物应填集装箱号。

（27）随附单据：应填写报关随附的单据名称，并注明份数。

（28）海关放行日期：由进口地海关在核放货物后填注日期，并加盖海关放行章。

（29）填制单位（盖章）：填制报关单的单位必须加盖报关单位已向海关备案的报关专用章及报关员名章或签字，并注明填制日期。

三、填写进口货物报关单的注意事项

单证员在填写进口货物报关单时，应注意以下事项。

（1）报关单的填制必须真实，不得出现差错，更不能伪报、瞒报及虚报。要做到单证相符、单货相符。

（2）报关单填报要准确、齐全，尽可能打字，如用笔写，字迹要清晰

整洁，不可用铅笔和红墨水。如有更改，必须在更改项目上加盖校对章。

（3）不同合同、不同运输工具名称、不同免征性质、不同许可证号的货物，不能填在同一份报关单上。同一张报关单上可以允许填写不超过 5 项海关统计商品编号的货物，但须逐项填报清楚。

（4）不同贸易方式的货物，须用不同颜色的报关单填报。一般贸易进口货物采用白色报关单；来料加工、补偿贸易货物采用浅绿色的专用报关单；进料加工货物采用粉红色的专用报关单；外商投资企业进口货物采用浅蓝色的专用报关单。上述报关单只是颜色有所区别，报关单中的项目和格式完全相同。

（5）报关单有关项目有海关规定的统计代码的，除填写有关项目外，还应填写有关项目的海关统计代码。

（6）预录入的报关单与手工报关单具有同样的法律效力，报关员在打印报关单上签字盖章前，应认真核对，防止出现差错。

（7）向海关申报的进口货物报关单，如事后由于种种原因，出现原来填写的内容与实际货物有出入时，须向海关办理更正手续，填写报关单更正单，对原来填写的项目进行更改，且更改内容必须清楚，一般情况下，错什么，改什么。

（8）进口货物报关单基本联一式三联，第一联海关留存，第二联供海关统计，第三联供企业留存。一般贸易进口货物填制一式四联报关单，分别供海关留存、海关统计、企业留存、进口付汇核销。

小贴士

代理报关委托书

编号：

我单位现（A. 逐票；B. 长期）委托贵公司代理_____等通关事宜。（A. 报关查验；B. 垫缴税款；C. 办理海关证明联；D. 审批手册；E. 核销手册；F. 申办减免税手续；G. 其他）详见《委托报关协议》。

我单位保证遵守《中华人民共和国海关法》和国家有关法规，保证所提供的情况真实、完整、单货相符。否则，愿承担相关法律责任。

本委托书有效期自签字之日起至　　　　　年　　月　　日止。

委托方（盖章）：

法定代表人或其授权签署《代理报关委托书》的人（签字）

年　　月　　日

委托报关协议（正面）

为明确委托报关具体事项和各自责任，双方经平等协商签订协议如下：

委托方		被委托方		
主要货物名称		*报关单编码	No.	
H.S.编码	□□□□□□□□□	收到单证日期	年月日	
进出口日期	年 月 日	收到单证情况	合同□	发票□
提单号			装箱清单□	提（运）单□
贸易方式			加工贸易手册□	许可证件□
原产地/货源地		其他		
传真电话		报关收费	人民币：	元
其他要求：		承诺说明：		
背面所列通用条款是本协议不可分割的一部分，对本协议的签署构成了对背面通用条款的同意。		背面所列通用条款是本协议不可分割的一部分，对本协议的签署构成了对背面通用条款的同意。		
委托方业务签章：		被委托方业务签章：		
经办人签章：		经办报关员签章：		
联系电话：　　　年 月 日		联系电话：　　　年 月 日		

（白联：海关留存、黄联：被委托方留存、红联：委托方留存）中国报关协会监制

委托报关协议（背面）

委托报关协议通用条款

一、委托方责任

委托方应及时提供报关报检所需的全部单证，并对单证的真实性、准确性和完整性负责。

委托方负责在报关企业办结海关手续后，及时、履约支付代理报关费用，支付垫支费用，以及因委托责任产生的滞报金、滞纳金和海关等执法单位依法处以的各种罚款。

负责按照海关要求将货物运至指定场所。

负责与被委托方报关员一同协助海关进行查验，回答海关的询问，配合相关调查，并承担产生的相关费用。在被委托方无法做到报关前提取货样的情况下，承担单货相符的责任。

二、被委托方责任

负责解答委托方有关向海关申报的疑问。

负责对委托方提供的货物情况和单证的真实性、完整性进行"合理审查"，审查内容包括：①证明进出口货物实际情况的资料，包括进出口货物的品名、规格、用途、产地、贸易方式等；②有关进出口货物的合同、发票、运输单据、装箱单等商业单据；③进出口所需的许可证件及随附单证；④海关要求的加工贸易（纸质或电子数据的）及其他进出口单证。

因确定货物的品名、归类等原因，经海关批准，可以看货或提取货样。

在接到委托方交付齐备的随附单证后，负责依据委托方提供的单证，按照《中华人民共和国海关进出口报关单填制规范》认真填制报关单，承担单单相符的责任，在海关规定和本委托报关协议中约定的时间内报关，办理海关手续。

负责及时通知委托方共同协助海关进行查验，并配合海关开展相关调查。

负责支付因报关企业的责任给委托方造成的直接经济损失，所产生的滞报金、滞纳金和海关等执法单位依法处以的各种罚款。

负责在本委托书约定的时间内将办结海关手续的有关委托内容的单证、文件交还委托方或其指定的人员（详见《委托报关协议》"其他要求"栏）。

赔偿原则：被委托方不承担因不可抗力给委托方造成损失的责任。因其他过失造成的损失，由双方自行约定或按国家有关法律法规的规定办理。由此造成的风险，委托方可以投保方式自行规避。

不承担的责任：签约双方各自不承担因另外一方原因造成的直接经济损失，以及滞报金、滞纳金和相关罚款。

收费原则：一般货物报关收费原则上按当地《报关行业收费指导价格》规定执行。特殊商品可由双方另行商定。

法律强制：本《委托报关协议》的任一条款与《中华人民共和国海关法》及有关法律、法规不一致时，应以法律、法规为准。但不影响《委托报关协议》其他条款的有效。

协商解决事项：变更、中止本协议或双方发生争议时，按照《中华人民共和国合同法》有关规定及程序处理。因签约双方以外的原因产生的问题或报关业务需要修改协议条款，应协商订立补充协议。

小 贴 士

代理报关费有哪些？可能各地不同。

深圳大部分代理进口的报关报检公司收费是按步骤收费的，具体如下。

（1）船公司收取的THC操作费及文件费用（1000～1500元人民币）。

（2）换单手续费：200～250元人民币。

（3）码头费：460～650元人民币（不同的码头，收费标准不一样）。

（4）港建费：100～300元人民币（不同的码头，收费标准不一样）。

（5）过磅费：100元人民币（如需过磅就产生费用）。

（6）吊柜费：400元人民币/次（可能会产生海关和商检机构查货吊柜）。

（7）标签备案费：450～650元人民币（根据品种的多少而定）。

（8）报检费：600元人民币/单。

（9）报关费：600元人民币/单。

（10）服务费：1500元人民币/票。

（11）经营单位抬头费：3000元人民币/票（如有进出口权，及酒类或食品流通许可证，则此项不收费）。

223

（12）商检规费：商检局，一般按货值的 3‰ 收取。

（13）商检查货费：300 元人民币（食品类货物的进口过关时必查）。

（14）海关查货费：300 元人民币（海关随机抽查，不一定会产生）。

（15）查货装卸费：根据实际情况而定，通常为数百元。

（16）送样费：300 元人民币。

（17）运输费：1000 元人民币（从码头到商检局监管仓）。

（18）仓库装卸费：50～70 元人民币/吨。

（19）仓储费：4～6 元人民币/立方米·天。

（20）印刷标签费：根据实际数量而定。

（21）加贴中文标签：0.3 元人民币/个。

（22）派车接商检局查看费：300 元人民币。

（23）派送费：根据客户仓库远近而定。

■ 课堂思考

参考答案

分析海关编号 517720160776000166。

任务实施

肇庆市富庆五金塑料有限公司之代理人出具的进口货物报关单，如图 8.10 所示。

任务再现

肇庆市富庆五金塑料有限公司从台湾申光实业有限公司电约进口一批锁舌、垫片和锁盒。

中华人民共和国海关进口货物报关单

预录入编号：514120151415019791　　　　　海关编号：514120151415019791

进口口岸 5141 广州机场		备案号		进口日期 2015-01-28	申报日期
经营单位 4412940595 肇庆市富庆五金塑料有限公司		运输方式 航空运输	运输工具名称 CZ3098	提运单号 78415254175—RTL815630	
收货单位 4412940595 肇庆市富庆五金塑料有限公司		贸易方式 一般贸易		征免性质 一般征税	征税比例
许可证号	启运国（地区） 台澎金马关税区		装货港 台湾省		境内目的地 肇庆
批准文号	成交方式 CIF	运费		保费	杂费
合同协议号 2014FQ030	件数 8	包装种类 纸箱		毛重（千克） 124	净重（千克） 121.8
集装箱号	随附单证			用途 企业自用	
标记唛码及备注 随附单证 总值：1043.89 美元					

项号	商品编号	商品名称、规格型号	数量及单位	原产国（地区）	单价	总价	币制	证免
01	83016000.00	锁舌 锁用具，铁制	83.8 千克	台澎金马关税	4.3400	363.69	美元	
02	83016000.00	锁头 锁用具，锌合金制	38 千克	台澎金马关税	17.9000	680.20	美元	

税费证收情况			
录入员　　　录入单位 　9000000049766	兹声明以上申报无讹并承担法律 责任	海关审单批注及放行日期（签章） 审单　　　　　审价	
报关员			
单位地址	申报单位（签章） 广州顶驭国际货运代理有限公司	征税　　　　　统计	
		查验　　　　　放行	
邮编　　　　电话	填制日期 2015-01-29		

图 8.10　进口货物报关单

参照如图 8.11 和图 8.12 所示的装箱单和发票，填写相关的进口货物报关单。

申光實業有限公司

地址：板橋市大觀路一段 38 巷 200 弄 79-7 號　　　電話：886-2-22727371　　　傳真：886-2-22727367

PACKING WEIGHT LIST

For account and risk of Messrs . <u>肇慶市富慶五金塑料有限公司</u>

<u>廣東省肇慶市高新區文德四街</u>

From _____ <u>TAIWAN</u> _____ to <u>ZHAOQING CHINA</u>

箱號	貨物描述	數量	單位	@淨重 KGS	總淨重 KGS	@毛重 KGS	總毛重 KGS
1	鎖舌\#2700，鐵質	1	紙箱	19.5	19.5	20	20
2	鎖舌\#2700，鐵質	1	紙箱	12.5	12.5	13	13
3	鎖舌\#2701，鐵質	1	紙箱	2.6	2.6	3.1	3.1
4	鎖舌\#2724，鐵質	1	紙箱	1.5	1.5	2	2
5～7	鎖舌\#2727，鐵質	3	紙箱	22.7	68.1	23.2	69.6
8	鎖舌\#2727，鐵質	1	紙箱	5.8	5.8	6.3	6.3
9	鎖舌\#2727，鐵質	1	紙箱	13.5	13.5	14	14
10	鎖舌\#2727，鐵質	1	紙箱	19.1	19.1	19.6	19.6
11	鎖舌\#2727，鐵質	1	紙箱	20.1	20.1	20.6	20.6
12	鎖舌\#2729，鐵質	1	紙箱	19.9	19.9	20.4	20.4
13	鎖舌\#2729，鐵質	1	紙箱	16.5	16.5	17	17
14	鎖舌\#2746，鐵質	1	紙箱	20.5	20.5	21	21
15	鎖舌\#2746，鐵質	1	紙箱	8.5	8.5	9	9
16	鎖舌\#2746，鐵質	1	紙箱	14.5	14.5	15	15
17～18	鎖舌\#2746，鐵質	2	紙箱	15.2	30.4	15.7	31.4
19～25	鎖舌\#2746，鐵質	7	紙箱	19.8	138.6	20.3	142.1
26	鎖舌\#2746，鐵質	1	紙箱	2.4	2.4	2.9	2.9
27	泡棉墊片	1	紙箱	3.03	3.03	3.53	3.53
28～29	泡棉墊片	2	紙箱	0.62	1.24	1.12	2.24
30	泡棉墊片	1	紙箱	4.5	4.5	5	5
31	橡膠墊片	1	紙箱	0.5	0.5	1	1
32	橡膠墊片	1	紙箱	3.5	3.5	4	4
33～34	鎖盒\不鏽鋼制	2	紙箱	21.5	43	22	44
35～36	鎖盒\不鏽鋼制	2	紙箱	20.5	41	21	42
37	鎖盒\不鏽鋼制	1	紙箱	8.5	8.5	9	9
合計		37	紙箱		519.27		537.77

图 8.11　集裝箱

申光實業有限公司

地址：板橋市大觀路一段 38 巷 200 弄 79-7 號　　　電話：886-2-22727371　　　傳真：886-2-22727367

INVOICE

合同號　　2014FQ029

For account and risk of Messrs: 肇慶市富慶五金塑料有限公司

廣東省肇慶市高新區文德四街

Shipped by

Per S.S

sailing on or about

From_____TAIWAN_____to_____ZHAOQING CHINA

標嘜	货物描述	原產地	數量	單位	單價（USD）	CIF 廣州 總價（USD）
	鎖舌\#2700	台灣	32	KGS	4.7	150.4
	鎖舌\#2701	台灣	2.6	KGS	5.6	14.56
	鎖舌\#2724	台灣	1.5	KGS	3	4.5
	鎖舌\#2727	台灣	126.6	KGS	3.9	493.74
	鎖舌\#2729	台灣	36.4	KGS	4.6	167.44
	鎖舌\#2746	台灣	214.9	KGS	5.7	1224.93
	泡棉墊片	台灣	8.77	KGS	21.6	189.432
	橡膠墊片	台灣	4	KGS	9.3	37.2
	鎖盒	台灣	92.5	KGS	14.3	1322.75
合計			519.27KGS		CIF 廣州 USD	3604.952

图 8.12　发票

技能强化训练

技 能 提 高

项目小结

在线测试及
参考答案

参考答案

参考答案

1. 图 8.2 所示出境货物报检单（441270216000061）的"合同、信用证订立的检验、检疫条款或特殊要求"下，填写的是"不需通关单"。既然不需要通关单，那么，为什么还要报检呢？试说明理由。

2. 肇庆市富庆五金塑料有限公司是一家没有报关资质的企业，其出口报关业务是逐票与报关公司签订代理协议进行的。2016 年 1 月，该公司有一批货物要出口，必须和肇庆市报关有限公司签订一份代理报关委托书。试为其拟订一份代理报关委托书。

项目九

其他单据实训

知识目标

1. 了解装船通知的主要内容;
2. 了解受益人证明的填制内容;
3. 了解船公司证明书的种类与缮制内容。

能力目标

1. 能根据信用证、合同及有关资料正确缮制装船通知;
2. 能根据信用证、合同及有关资料正确缮制受益人证明;
3. 能根据信用证的要求缮制(审核)船公司证明书。

任务一   制作装船通知

任务导航

上海东方国际集团与智利 TRICOT S.A. 公司签订了女装 T 恤的贸易合同，收到信用证后，上海东方国际集团组织备货、托运、报检、报关。根据信用证的规定，单证员李小丽在 2014 年 6 月 1 日确认海运提单后，需要及时缮制装运通知，以便买方尽早安排投保和接货。

其他业务资料：L/C No. K829534；合同号码：LTE20140510；发票号码：LT300210。

要求：

根据收到的海运提单（见图 9.1）及其他业务资料以李小丽的身份缮制装运通知。

Shipper ORIENT INTERNATIONAL ENTERPRISE,LTD. TOWER A,85 LOUSHANGUAN ROAD, SHANGHAI CHINA		B/L No.: NGB280189
Consignee TO THE ORDER OF BANCO SANTANDER CHILE		
Notify Party TRICOT S.A. AV.VICUNA MACKENNA 3600 SANTIAGO CHILE		中国外运上海公司 SINOTRANS SHANGHAI COMPANY OECAN BILL OF LADING
Pre-carriage by	Port of Loading SHANGHAI, CHINA	SHIPPED on board in apparent good order and condition (unless otherwise indicated) the goods or packages specified herein and to be discharged at the mentioned port of discharge or as near thereto as the vessel may safely get and be always afloat.
Ocean Vessel Voy. No. MOL PACE 0607E	Port of Transshipment	The weight, measure, marks and numbers, quality, contents and value being particulars furnished by the shipper, are not checked by the carrier on loading.
Port of Discharge VALPARAISO,CHILE	Final Destination	The shipper, consignee and the holder of this Bill of Lading hereby expressly accept and agree to all printed, written or stamped provisions, exceptions and conditions of this Bill of Lading, including those on the back hereof. IN WITNESS whereof the number of original Bills if Lading stated below have been signed, one of which being accomplished, the other to be void

图 9.1 海运提单

Container/Seal No. or Marks and Nos.	Number of Containers or Packages 480CTNS	Description of Goods	Gross Weight (KGS)	Measurement (M³) 23.04M³
TRICOT SAN ANTONIO CHILE C/NO:1-480 LOADED INTO CONTAINER NO:KKFU1528480 SEAL UBH23919		480CARTONS LADIES' T-SHIRT	2600KGS	

Total Number of Containers and/or Packages(In Words)
SAY FOUR HUNDRED AND EIGHTY CARTONS ONLY

Freight and Charges FREIGHT PREPAID	Revenue Tons	Rate	Per	Prepaid	Collect
Ex. Rate	Prepaid at	Payable at	Place and Date of Issue SHANGHAI CHINA JUN.1,2014		
	Total Prepaid	No. of Original B(S)/L THREE(3)	Signed for the Carrier: SINOTRANS SHANGHAI COMPANY ×××AS CARRIER		

图 9.1　海运提单（续）

知识准备

一、装运通知的含义

装运通知（declaration of shipment；notice of shipment），系出口商向进口商发出货物已于某月某日或将于某月某日装运某船的通知。装运通知的作用在于方便买方购买保险或准备提货手续，其内容通常包括货名、装运数量、船名、装船日期、契约或信用证号码等。这项通知，大多以电报方式为之，然而也有用航邮方式的。装运通知的作用在于方便买方投买保险、准备提货手续或转售；出口商做此项通知时，有时还附上或另行寄上货运单据副本，以便进口商明了装货内容。若遇到货运单据正本迟到的情况，仍可及时办理担保提货（delivery against letter of guarantee）。

二、注意事项

对于装运通知书，外贸机构应注意以下几点。

（1）CFR/CPT 交易条件下派发装运通知的必要性。因货物运输和保险分别由不同的当事人操作，所以受益人有义务向申请人对货物装运情况给予及时、充分的通知，以便进口商保险，否则如漏发通知，则货物越过船舷后的风险仍由受益人承担。

（2）通知应按规定的方式、时间、内容、份数发出。

（3）几个近似概念的区别：shipping advice（装运通知）是由出口商（受益人）发给进口商（申请人）的；shipping instructions 意思是"装运须知"，一般是进口商发给出口商的；shipping note/ bill 指装货通知单/船货清单；shipping order（S/O），含义是装货单/关单/下货纸（是海关放行和命令船方将单据上载明的货物装船的文件）。

三、装运通知书的格式与内容

装运通知书由出口企业根据信用证或合同自行拟制，无固定格式，但基本栏大致相同。空白装运通知书样单如图 9.2 所示。

装运通知书一般包括合同号或信用证号、品名、数量、金额、运输工具名称、开航日期、启运地和目的地、提运单号码、运输标志等，并且与其他相关单据保持一致，如信用证提出具体项目要求，应严格按规定出单。此外，通知中还可能出现包装说明、ETD（船舶预离港时间）、ETA（船舶预抵港时间）、ETC（预计开始装船时间）等内容。

NAME AND ADDRESS OF BENEFICIARY（2）

Shipping Advice(1)

To：（3）

Invoice No.：（4）

Contract No.：（5）

L/C No.：（6）

Date：（7）

Commodity：（8）

Number of Pkgs：（9）

Quantity：（10）

Total Gross weight：（11）

图 9.2　装运通知书样单

Total Value：(12)

Shipping Marks：(13)

Ocean Vessel：(14)

Date of Departure：(15)

B/L No.：(16)

Port of Loading：(17)

Port of Destination：(18)

Beneficiary's signature(19)

图 9.2   装运通知书样单（续）

四、装运通知书的缮制要点

装运通知书的缮制要点包括以下几个方面。

（1）单据名称：主要体现为 Shipping/Shipment Advice, Advice of Shipment 等，也有人将其称为 Shipping Statement/Declaration，如信用证有具体要求，从其规定。

（2）受益人的名称和地址（Name and Address of Beneficiary）：应按信用证填写卖方的名称和地址。可写，也可不写。

（3）抬头人（To）：按信用证填写买方的名称和地址，有时是买方指定的保险公司或代理人的名称和地址。

（4）发票号码（Invoice No.）：填写这笔贸易的发票号码。

（5）合同号码（Contract No. 或 S/C No.）：填写这笔贸易的合同号码。

（6）信用证号码（L/C No.）：填写这笔贸易的信用证号码。

（7）制作和发出日期（Date）：日期不能超过信用证约定的时间，常见的有以小时为准（Within 24/48 hours）和以天（within 2 days after shipment date）为准两种情形。信用证没有规定时应在装船后立即发出，如信用证规定"Immediately after shipment"（装船后立即通知），应掌握在提单后 3 天之内。

（8）货物描述（Commodity）：填写信用证要求的货物描述。

（9）包装数量（Number of Pkgs）：填写运输包装数量。

（10）数量（Quantity）：填写计价单位数量。

（11）总毛重（Total Gross.Weight）：填写货物总毛重。

（12）总值（Total Value）：填写信用证的货物总价值。

（13）唛头（Shipping Marks）：填写信用证要求的唛头。

（14）船名及航次（Ocean Vessel）：填写运输货物的船名和航次。

（15）装运日期（Date of Departure）：填写实际装运日期或海运提单。

签发日期。

（16）提单号码（B/L No.）：填写这笔贸易的海运提单号码。

（17）装运港（Port of Loading）：填写信用证要求的装运货物的港口名称。

（18）目的港（Port of Destination）：填写信用证要求的卸货的港口名称。

（19）签署（Beneficiary's signature）：填写受益人的名称和负责人签字。

▌ 课堂思考 ▬▬▬▬▬▬

为什么装船后卖方要及时向买方发出装运通知？

参考答案

小 贴 士

装运通知书的制作和发出日期不能超过信用证约定的时间，常见的有以小时为准（within 24/48 hours）和以天（within 2 days after shipment date）为准两种情形，信用证没有规定时应在装船后立即发出，如信用证规定"Immediately after shipment"（装船后立即通知），应掌握在提单后 3 天之内。

职业判断

案例资料：

中国某外贸公司以 FOB 价格条件出口棉纱 2000 包，每包净重 200 千克。装船时已经双方认可的检验机构检验，货物符合合同规定的品质条件。该外贸公司装船后因疏忽未及时通知买方，直至 3 天后才给予装船通知。但在启航 18 小时后，船只遇风浪致使棉纱全部浸湿，买方因接到装船通知晚，未能及时办理保险手续，无法向保险公司索赔。

参考答案

思考：

该合同中，货物风险是否已转移给买方？应由谁来承担赔偿责任？

任务实施

单证员李小丽根据信用证的要求及收到的海运提单，缮制装运通知书（见图 9.3），以便买方尽早安排投保和接货。

ORIENT INTERNATIONAL ENTERPRISE LTD
2301-2302 NO.1 LANE 500 ZHOJNGSHAN NAN YI RD LIDU BUILDING
SHANGHAI CHINA

SHIPPING ADVICE

TO：TRICOT　S A

　AV VICUNA MACKENNA 3600

　MACUL, SANTIAGO, CHILE

Invoice No.: LT300210

Contract No.: LTE20140510

L/C No.: K829534

Date： 140601

Dear Sir or Madam:

　We are Please to Advice you that the following mentioned goods has been shipped out, Full details were shown as follows:

Commodity:	LADIES' T-SHIRT
Bill of loading Number:	NGB280189
Ocean Vessel:	MOL PACE 0607E
Port of Loading:	SHANGHAI,CHINA
Date of Shipment:	140601
Port of Destination:	VALPARAISO,CHILE
Number of Pkgs:	480CARTONS
Shipping Marks:	TRICOT
	SAN ANTONIO
	CHILE
	C/NO：1-480
Quantity:	9600PCS
Total Value:	USD59 520.00

Thank you for your patronage. We look forward to the pleasure of receiving your valuable repeat orders.

Sincerely yours,

ORIENT INTERNATIONAL ENTERPRISE LTD

图 9.3　单证员填制的装运通知书

任务再现

　　中国矿产进出口公司广东分公司与日本大阪 SAKAI TRADING CO. LTD. 达成花岗岩石的出口贸易，根据信用证（见图 9.4）和制单参考资料，缮制装运通知。

LETTER OF CREDIT

27:SEQUENCEOF TOTAL	1/1
40A:FORMOF DOCUMENTARY CREDIT	IRREVOCABLE
20:DOCUMENTAR CREDIT NUMBER	41-1902141-003
31C:DATE OF ISSUE	NOV. 2, 2014
31D: DATE AND PLACE OF Expiry	JAN 15 2015 IN CHINA
50:APPLICANT	SAKAI TRADING CO. LTD.
	SANWA BLDG1-1 KAWARAMACH 2-CHOME CHUO-KU OSAKA 541, JAPAN
59:BENEFICIARY	CHINA NATIONAL METALS AND MINERALS I/E CORP GUANGDONG BRANCH
	774 DONG FENG EAST ROAD , GUANGZHOU , CHINA
32B:CURRENCY CODE,AMOUNT	USD 18698.16
41D:AVAILABLE WITH BY	ANY BANK BY NEGOTIATION
42C:DRAFT AT	AT SIGHT FOR FULL INVOICE VALUE
42A:DRAWEE	SANWA BANK LTD.
43P: PARTIAL SHIPMENT	NOT ALLOWED
43T: TRANSSHIPMENT	ALLOWED
44E: PORT OF LOADING	HUANGPU GUANGDONG
44F: PORT OF DISCHARGE	OSAKA/YOKOHAMA JAPAN
44C: LATEST DATE OF SHIP	JAN 15 2015
45A: DESCRIP of GOODS	CHINA GRANITE(G485 ROUGH BLOCKS)
	SHIPPING MARK: N/M
	PACKAGE:IN BULK
	TRADE TERM:FOB HUANGPU BY VESSEL
46A:DOCUMENTS REQUIRED	+SIGNED COMMERCIAL INVOICE IN 3 COPIES INDICATING L/C NO. AND CONTRACT NO.
	+PACKING LIST/WEIGHT MEMO IN 3 COPIES INDICATING QUANTITY, GROSS AND WEIGHTS OF EACH PACKAGE
	+MANUALLY SIGNED CERTIFICATE OF ORIGIN IN 3 COPIES INDICATING THE NAME OF THE MANUFACTURER
	+FULL SET OF CLEAN ON BOARD BILLS OF LADING MADE OUT TO ORDER OF SHIPPER AND BLANK ENDORSED AND MARKED FREIGHT PREPAID, NOTIFYING THE APPLICANT.
	+SHIPPING ADVICE IN 3 COPIES INDICATING L/C NO. AND CONTRACT NO.
	+BENEFICIARY'S CERTIFICATE IN TWO COPIES STATING THAT THREE SETS OF EACH NON-NEGOTIABLE B/L HAVE BEEN AIRMAILED DIRECT TO THE BUYER IMMEDIATELY AFTER SHIPMENT.

图 9.4　日本公司开来的信用证

47A: ADDITIONAL CONDITIONS	THIRD AS SHIPPER IS NOT ACCEPTABLE,SHORT FORM/BLANK B/L IS NOT ACCEPTABLE; 5 PERCENT MORE OR LESS BOTH IN QUANTITY AND AMOUNT IS ALLOWED; INSURANCE TO BE EFFECTED BY BUYERS
71B: DETAILS OF CHARGES	ALL BANKING CHARGES OUTSIDE BRAZIL ARE FOR A/C OF BENEFICIARY.
48: PRESENTATION PERIOD	DOCUMENTS TO BE PRESENTED WITHIN 21 DAYS AFTER THE DATE OF SHIPMENT，BUT WITHIN THE VALIDITY OF THE CREDIT.
49:CONFIEMATION INSTRUCTIONS	WITHOUT
57D:ADVISE THROUGH BANK	BANK OF CHINA GUANGZHOU

图 9.4　日本公司开来的信用证（续）

参考答案

制单参考资料如下：

合同号码：01MAF400-5-23

发票号码：RB-1206

毛重：167.804.KGS

船名和航次：YOUNG STAR V.231E

集装箱号码：1×40'CPIU2254836

提单号：XMVO2014

提单签发地点和日期：广东黄埔 NOV.30,2014

女装 T 恤

任务二　制作受益人证明

任务导航

　　上海东方国际集团与智利 TRICOT S.A. 签订了女装 T 恤的贸易合同，收到信用证（见图 9.5）后，上海东方国际集团组织备货、托运、报检、报关。根据信用证的规定，单证员李小丽在 2014 年 6 月 1 日确认海运提单后，开具受益人证明，证明自己是按信用证要求办理的。

LETTER OF CREDIT			
SEQUENCE OF TOTAL	*	27	1 / 1
FORM OF DOC. CREDIT	*	40 A	IRREVOCABLE TRANSFERABLE
DOC. CREDIT NUMBER	*	20	K829534
DATE OF ISSUE		31 C	140423
APPLICABLE RULES		40 E	UCP LATEST VERSION
EXPIRY	*	31 D	140616CHINA

图 9.5　信用证

APPLICANT	*	50	TRICOT S A
			AV VICUNA MACKENNA 3600
			MACUL, SANTIAGO, CHILE
BENEFICIARY	*	59	ORIENT INTERNATIONAL ENTERPRISE LTD
			2301-2302 NO.1 LANE 500 ZHOJNGSHAN NAN YI RD LIDU BUILDING
			SHANGHAI CHINA
AMOUNT	*	32 B	CURRENCY USD AMOUNT US59520.00
AVAILABLE WITH/BY	*	41 D	ANY BANK IN CHINA,
			BY NEGOTIATION
DRAFTS AT...		42 C	AT SIGHT
DRAWEE		42 A	BSCHHKHHXXX
			BANCO SANTANDER, CHILE
PARTIAL SHIPMTS		43 P	NOT ALLOWED
TRANSSHIPMENT		43 T	ALLOWED
PORT OF LOADING		44 E	SHANGHAI PORT, CHINA
PORT OF DISCHARGE		44 F	VALPARAISO CHILE
LATEST SHIPMENT		44 C	140530
GOODS DESCRIPT.		45 A	ORIGIN CHINA CIF VALPARAISO
			9600 PCS. T-SHIRTS AT USD6.20 USD59520.00
DOCS REQUIRED		46 A	
			+BENEFICIARY'S CERTIFICATE CERTIFYING THAT THEY HAVE SENT
			ONE FULL SET OF NON-NEGOTIABLE DOCUMENTS REQUIRED BY
			L/C TO TH APPLICANT VIA DHL WITHIN 2 DAYS AFTER SHIPMENT.

图 9.5   信用证（续）

制单参考资料如下：

合同号码：01TFF40-5-24

发票号码：LT-1406

受益人证明出证地点和日期：上海 JUN.1,2014

要求：

根据信用证的有关条款及具体交易情况，以单证员李小丽的身份缮制受益人证明。

知识准备

一、受益人证明的含义

受益人证明（beneficiary's certificate）是一种由受益人自己出具的书面证明，以便证明自己履行了信用证规定的任务或证明自己按信用证的要求办事，如证明所交货物的品质、证明运输包装的处理、证明按要求寄单等。一般无固定格式，内容多种多样，以英文制作，通常签发一份。

二、注意事项

在填制受益人证明的时候，应注意以下几点。

（1）单据名称应合适恰当。

（2）一般的行文规则是以所提要求为准直接照搬照抄，但有时也应做必要的修改。如信用证规定"BENEFICIARY'S CERTIFICATE EVIDENCING THAT TWO COPIES OF NON-NEGOTIABLE B/L WILL BE DESPATCHED TO APPLICANT WITHIN TWO DAYS AFTER SHIPMENT"，在具体制作单据时应将要求里的"WILL BE DESPATCHED"改为"HAVE BEEN DESPATCHED"；再如，对"BENEFICIARY'S CERTIFICATE STATING THAT CERTIFICATE OF MANUFACTURING PROCESS AND OF INGREDIENTS ISSUED BY ABC CO SHOULD BE SENT TO SUMITOMO CORP"的要求，"SHOULD BE SENT"最好改为"HAD/HAS BEEN SENT"。

（3）证明文件通常以"THIS IS TO CERTIFY"（或DECLARE、STATE、EVIDENCE 等）或"WE HEREBY CERTIFY"等开始。

三、受益人证明的格式与内容

受益人证明由出口企业根据信用证或合同自行拟制，无固定格式，但基本栏大致相同。空白受益人证明样本如图 9.6 所示。

受益人证明的内容一般包括单据名称、出单日期、发票号码和信用证号码、抬头人、证明文句、签章等。

NAME & ADDRESS OF BENEFICIARY（2）
BENEFICIARY'S CERTIFICATE（1）

DATE: （3）

INVOICE NO.: （4）

L/C NO.: （5）

TO: （6）

WE HEREBY CERTIFY THAT （7）_____

Signature（8）

图 9.6 受益人证明样本

四、受益人证明的缮制要点

受益人证明的缮制要点包括以下几个方面。

（1）单据名称（Name of Document）：按信用证规定填写。来证要求提供"BENEFICARY'S CERTIFICATE"、"BENEFICIARY'S DECLARATION"，按信用证的要求写明单证名称。

（2）受益人名称和地址（Name and Address of Beneficiary）：按信用证中受益人名称和地址填写。

（3）出证日期（DATE）：根据实际情况填写受益人证明的签发日期。

（4）发票号码（INVOICE NO.）：填写这笔贸易的发票号码。

（5）信用证号码（L/C No.）：填写这笔贸易的信用证号码。

（6）抬头人（TO）：通常填写"TO: WHOM IT MAY CONCERN"，意为"致有关当事人"。

（7）证明文句：根据信用证规定的内容填写。

（8）签单（Signature）：填写受益人名称并由经办人签单。

课堂思考

某受益人证明规定：BENEFICIARY'S CERTIFICATE TO THE EFFECT THAT ALL TERMS AND CONDITIONS HAVE BEEN COMPLIED WITH ORIGINAL DOCUMENTS。那么，受益人证明的内容是什么？

参考答案

小贴士

常见的受益人证明有以下几种。

（1）寄单证明：最常见的一种，通常是受益人根据规定，在货物装运前后一定时期内，邮寄、传真、快递给规定的收受人全套或部分副本单据，并将证明随其他单据交给银行议付。

（2）寄样证明：通常是受益人根据规定，在货物装运前后一定时期内，邮寄/快递给规定的收受人寄送船样、样品、样卡及码样等，并提供相应的证明。

（3）包装声明（Packing Declaration）：关于出口货物包装材料的一种声明，主要用于目的港清关，只需要按客户提供的格式填好打印出来，再盖章即可。有些国家担心出口国出口货物的包装材料中含有可能危害进口国当地森林资源的虫类，因此要求提供这种声明。其内容主要是描述包装材料中无稻草、树皮一类的东西。目前需要提供包装声明的国家主要是澳大利亚、新西兰、加拿大和美国等。

（4）投邮证明（Certificate of Posting）：邮局出具的证明文件，据此证实单据确已寄发或邮包确已寄出和作为邮寄日期的证明。有的信用证规定，出口商寄送有关单据、样品或包裹后，除要出具邮政收据外，还要提供投邮证明，作为结汇的一种单据。

职业判断

参考答案

案例资料：

国内 A 银行收到一份开来的信用证，证中规定必须提交一份邮局收据（postal receipt），证明受益人已将信用证所要求的单据副本通过快递方式邮寄给开证申请人。信用证通知不久，受益人向 A 银行交单，经审核无误，A 银行办理出口押汇后将单据邮寄给 H 银行。H 银行在合理期限内提出拒付：所提交的 DHL 收据系伪造。在 A 银行极力反驳的情况下，H 银行将拒付理由改为：快邮收据未经 DHL 公司签字。

思考：

（1）银行拒付理由成立吗？为什么？

（2）为什么会发生这样的情况？

 任务实施

单证员李小丽根据信用证的要求，开具受益人证明（见图 9.7），证明自己是按信用证要求办理的。

ORIENT INTERNATIONAL ENTERPRISE LTD

2301-2302 NO.1 LANE 500 ZHOJNGSHAN NAN YI RD LIDU BUILDING SHANGHAI CHINA

BENEFICIARY'S CERTIFICATE

DATE : JUN.1.2014

INVOICE NO. : LT-1406

L/C NO. : K829534

TO WHOM IT MAY CONCERN:

WE HEREBY CERTIFY THAT WE HAVE SENT ONE FULL SET OF NON-NEGOTIABLE DOCUMENTS REQUIRED BY L/C TO THE APPLICANT VIA DHL WITHIN 2 DAYS AFTER SHIPMENT.

ORIENT INTERNATIONAL ENTERPRISE LTD

×××

图 9.7 单证员开具的受益人证明

任务再现

利用本项目任务一"任务再现"中日本大阪 SAKAI TRADING CO. LTD. 开来的信用证（见图9.4）和制单参考资料，缮制受益人证明。

参考答案

任务三　　制作船公司证明

任务导航

上海东方国际集团与智利 TRICOT S.A. 签订了女装 T 恤的贸易合同，收到信用证（见图9.8）后，上海东方国际集团组织备货、托运、报检、报关。信用证规定需要出具船龄证明，单证员李小丽要求承运的中国外运公司出具相应的船龄证明书。

LETTER OF CREDIT

SEQUENCE OF TOTAL	*27：1/1
FORM OF DOC. CREDIT	*40A： IRREVOCABLE TRANSFERABLE
DOC. CREDIT NUMBER	*20： K829534
DATE OF ISSUE	31C：140423
APPLICABLE RULES	40E： UCP LATEST VERSION
EXPIRY	*31D： 140616CHINA
APPLICANT	*50： TRICOT　S. A.
	AV VICUNA MACKENNA 3600
	MACUL, SANTIAGO, CHILE
BENEFICIARY	*59： ORIENT INTERNATIONAL ENTERPRISE LTD
	2301-2302 NO.1 LANE 500 ZHOJNGSHAN NAN YI RD LIDU BUILDING
	SHANGHAI CHINA
AMOUNT	*32B： CURRENCY USD AMOUNT US59520.00
AVAILABLE WITH/BY	*41D： ANY BANK IN CHINA,
	BY NEGOTIATION
DRAFTS AT...	42C： AT SIGHT
DRAWEE	42A： BSCHHKHHXXX
	BANCO SANTANDER, CHILE
PARTIAL SHIPMTS	43P： NOT ALLOWED
TRANSSHIPMENT	43T： ALLOWED

图 9.8　智利公司开来的信用证

PORT OF LOADING	44 E: SHANGHAI PORT, CHINA
PORT OF DISCHARGE	44 F: VALPARAISO CHILE
LATEST SHIPMENT	44 C: 140530
GOODS DESCRIPT.	45 A: ORIGIN CHINA CIF SHANGHAI
	9600 PCS. T-SHIRTS AT USD6.20 USD59520.00
DOCS REQUIRED	46 A:
	+SHIP'S AGE CERTIFICATE TO EVIDENCE THE SHIP IS NOT OVER 15
	YEARS OLD.

图 9.8 智利公司开来的信用证（续）

其他资料如下：

合同号码：01TFF40-5-24

发票号码：LT-1406

船名和航次：MOL PACE 0607E

提单号码：NGB280189

承运人：中国外运上海公司 SINOTRANS SHANGHAI COMPANY

提单签发地点和日期：上海 JUN.1,2014

船龄证明出证地点和日期：上海 JUN.1,2014

要求：

根据信用证的有关条款及具体交易情况，以中国外运公司的负责人的身份缮制船公司证明。

知识准备

一、船公司证明的含义

船公司证明（shipping company's certificate）是船公司或船公司代理说明所载船舶某些特定事项的证明文件，是进口商为了了解货物运输情况或为了满足进口国当局规定而要求出口商提供的单据。

二、常见的船公司证明

实务中，常见的船公司证明包括以下几种。

（1）船龄证明：以说明船龄，一般船龄在 15 年以上的船为超龄船（保险公司不愿承保），所以进口商往往要求出具 15 年以下船龄的证明。

（2）船籍证明：用以说明载货船舶国籍。

（3）航程证明：说明航程中停靠的港口。

（4）抵制以色列证明：主要是阿拉伯国家为了对以色列进行抵制，而要求不使用以色列船只，不停靠以色列口岸，不装与以色列有业务关系的所谓"黑名单"内的船只等。

（5）运费收据：船公司向托运人收取运费而出立的证明运费已收受的收据。

（6）船长收据：目的是要求发货人装船后将一套单据交船方随船带给收货人以便货到目的港后及时提货或办理其他手续。

> **小 贴 士**
>
> 黑名单证明（Black List Certificate）是用以说明载货船舶未被阿拉伯国家（有22个国家）列入与以色列有来往船舶名单的证明。阿拉伯地区国家为了抵制以色列，常在来证中（即开给受益人的L/C）要求卖方提供此类证明。它的内容若已包含在船籍证明中，则不必单独出具。

三、船公司证明的格式与内容

船公司证明由船公司或其代理人根据信用证或合同自行拟制，无固定格式，但基本栏目大致相同，主要包括出证日期和地址、船名、提单号和证明文句等。空白船公司证明样本如图9.9所示。

船公司证明书	
Vessel Name & Voyage No.: （2）	
B/L No.:（3）	CERTIFICATE（1）
Place & Date of Issue.: （4）	
To.: （5） We hereby certify that（6）	
	SIGNITURE（7）

图9.9　船公司证明书样本

四、船公司证明的缮制要点

船公司证明的缮制要点包括以下几个方面。

（1）证明函标题：按照信用证要求提供各类证明，标题常为"Certificate of …（……证明）"或"Statement of…（……声明）"，如船龄证明（SHIP'S AGE CERTIFICATE）、船籍证明（CERTIFICATE OF REGISTRY）、航程证明（CERTIFICATE OF ITINERARY）。如果信用证未限定标题，此项可以省略。若信用证内规定了是何种证明函，则一定要加注标题。

（2）船名和航次（Vessel Name & Voyage No.）：填写运输的运载船只的名称和航次。

（3）提单号码（B/L No.）：填写提单号码。

（4）出证日期和地址（Place & Date of Issue）：一般填写签发提单的日期和地址。

（5）抬头人（To）：一般都笼统打印为"TO WHOM IT MAY CONCERN（致有关人士）"。

（6）证明文句（We hereby certify that）：按照信用证要求根据实际情况作出相应证明。

（7）出证人签章（Signature）：应与提单签单人一致，通常为承运货物的船公司或其代理人或承担联运业务的外运公司等。

课堂思考

参考答案

出口北非的利比亚的货物，其运输船只需要开具船公司证明吗？要开具哪种船公司证明？为什么？

职业判断

案例资料：

广东省土产进出口公司出口一批竹制品到巴基斯坦，收到国外发来信用证，要求交单时提交船籍（要求非印度籍）证明，而单证员由于审证遗漏或制单时忘记了向承运人要求船籍证明，到银行交单议付时，银行认为单证不符，拒付这笔业务。

参考答案

思考：
为什么银行会拒付这笔业务？

中国外运上海分公司根据上海东方国际集团的要求，对载货船只"MOL PACE 0607E"出具船龄证明书，如图 9.10 所示。

Vessel Name & Voyage No.: MOL PACE 0607E	CERTIFICATE
B/L No.: NGB280189	
Place & Date of Issue: SHANGHAI,JUNE.1,2014	
To：WHOM IT MAY CONERN： We hereby certify that MOL PACE 0607E IS NOT MORE THAN 15 YEARS.	
	SINOTRANS SHANGHAI COMPANY ×××

图 9.10　船龄证明书

上海华南家具进出口公司与阿联酋迪拜 UNITED FURNITURE CO LLC 达成办公椅的出口贸易，根据信用证（见图 9.11）和相关资料缮制船公司证明书。

办公椅

SEQUENCE OF TOTAL	*	27	1 / 1
FORM OF DOC. CREDIT	*	40A	IRREVOCABLE
DOC. CREDIT NUMBER	*	20	K3344534
DATE OF ISSUE		31C	140520
APPLICABLE RULES		40 E	UCP LATEST VERSION
EXPIRY	*	31D	1401016CHINA
APPLICANT	*	50	UNITED FURNITURE CO LLC P.O. BOX 7410, DUBAI, U.A.E. TEL: 04-3391640, FAX:04-3391650
BENEFICIARY	*	59	HUANAN FURNITURE CO.LTD 1004-1006 DA HUA RD　DAZONG BUILDING SHANGHAI CHINA

图 9.11　信用证（部分）

AMOUNT	* 32 B	CURRENCY USD AMOUNT USD32400.00
AVAILABLE WITH/BY	* 41 D	EMIRATES NBD BANK PJSC BY ACCEPTANCE
DRAFTS AT...	42 C	120 DAYS FROM THE DATE OF BILL OF LADING.
DRAWEE	42 A	EMIRATES NBD BANK PJSC
		DUBAI, U.A.E
PARTIAL SHIPMTS	43 P	ALLOWED
TRANSSHIPMENT	43 T	ALLOWED
PORT OF LOADING	44 E	SHANGHAI PORT, CHINA
PORT OF DISCHARGE	44 F	JEBEL ALI PORT, DUBAI, UAE
LATEST SHIPMENT	44 C	140630
GOODS DESCRIPT.	45 A	2000 PCS OFFICE CHAIRS AT USD16.20 USD32400.00
DOCS REQUIRED	46 A	
		+CERTIFICATE FROM THE SHIPPING COMPANY OR OWNER/MASTER OF THE VESSEL OR THEIR AGENT CERTIFYING THAT THE CARRYING VESSEL A) IS ALLOWED TO ENTER THE PORTS OF ARAB STATES. B) IS 'ISM (INTERNATIONAL SAFETY MANAGEMENT) CODE' CERTIFIED C) IS CLASSIFIED UNDER LLOYDS REGISTER AS 100A1 OR BS OR EQUIVALENT AND BELONGS TO CONFERENCE OR REGULAR LINE.

图 9.11　信用证（部分）（续）

制单资料如下：

承运人：中国外运上海公司 SINOTRANS SHANGHAI COMPANY

提单号码：HNFC221367

装船日期：JUN.25,2014

船名和航次：DONGFANG.V108

项目小结　　　技能强化训练　　　在线测试及参考答案

技能提高

根据图 9.12 信用证资料和其他业务资料缮制装运通知书、受益人证明、船公司证明。

LETTER OF CREDIT	
27:SEQUENCEOF TOTAL	1/1
40A:FORM OF DOCUMENTARY CREDIT	IRREVOCABLE
20:DOCUMENTARY CREDIT NUMBER	LC-16441688
31C:DATE OF ISSUE	140210
31D: DATE AND PLACE OF Expiry	140630 IN CHINA

图 9.12　信用证

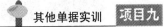

50:APPLICANT	LINKMAX INTERNATIONAL COMPANY
	ROOM 3 24/F HANG SAM HOUSE KING TIN COURT SHATIN, HONGKONG
59:BENEFICIARY	SHANGHAI MEIHUA BALL PEN CO. LTD.
	3601MEIHUA ROAD SHANGHAI CHINA
32B:CURRENCY CODE,AMOUNT	USD14109.40
41D:AVAILABLE WITH BY	ANY BANK
42C:DRAFT AT	AT SIGHT
	FOR FULL INVOICE VALUE
42A:DRAWEE	DAO HENG BANK LTD., HONGKONG
	11 QUEENS ROAD,CENTRAL, HONGKONG
43P: PARTIAL SHIPMENTS	NOT ALLOWED
43T: TRANSSHIPMENT	NOT ALLOWED
44E: PORT OF LOADING	SHANGHAI, CHINA
44F: PORT OF DISCHARGE	BANGKOK, THAILAND
44C:LATEST DATE OF SHIPMENT	140630
45A: DESCRIP OF GOODS	5740 DOZS AND 4500 BAGS OF BALL PEN
	1480 DOZS OF ROLLER PEN
	720 DOZS OF WATER COLOUR PEN
46A:DOCUMENT REQUIRED	+SIGNED COMMERCIAL INVOICE IN 3 COPIES INDICATING L/C NO. AND CONTRACTNO.
	+PACKING LIST/WEIGHT MEMO IN 3 COPIES INDICATING QUANTITY, GROSS AND WEIGHTS OF EACH PACKAGE
	+MANUALLY SIGNED CERTIFICATE OF ORIGIN IN 3 COPIES INDICATING THE NAME OF THE MANUFACTURER
	+FULL SET OF CLEAN ON BOARD BILLS OF LADING MADE OUT TO ORDER OF SHIPPER AND BLANK ENDORSED AND MARKED FREIGHT PREPAID, NOTIFYING THE APPLICANT.
	+SHIPPING ADVICE IN 3 COPIES INDICATING L/C NO. AND CONTRACT NO.
	+INSURANCE POLICY/CERTIFICATE IN 3 COPIES FOR 110% OF THE INVOICE VALUE SHOWING CLAIMS PAYABLE IN SHANGHAI IN CURRENCY OF THE DRAFT.
	+BENEFICIARY'S CERTIFICATE VERTIFYING THAT THEY HAVE SENT ONE FULL SET OF NON-NEGOTIABLE DOCUMENTS REQUIRED BY L/C TO THE APPLICANT VIA DHL WITHIN 2DAYS AFTER SHIPMENT.
	+A CERTIFICATE ISSUED BY SHIPPING COMPANY STATING THAT THE CARRYING VESSEL IS NOT MORE THAN 20 YEARS

图 9.12   信用证（续）

其他业务资料如下：
B/L NO.：CGLSHA0303088NA
发票号码：CBD2456
受益人证明的日期：2014 年 6 月 10 号
受益人单据的签发人：韩涛
VESSEL NAME：DANUBHUM/S009
承运人：COSCO CONTAINER LINES
提单签发日：2014 年 6 月 10 日

参考答案

项目十

汇票及审单、交单实训

知识目标

1. 了解汇票的含义、内容及作用;
2. 熟悉汇票运行及交单结汇的业务流程;
3. 掌握汇票缮制的方法及审核议付单据的方法。

能力目标

1. 能正确制作汇票;
2. 能做好审单、交单结汇工作。

任务一 缮 制 汇 票

秋冬针织女装

任务导航

2015年3月26日，广东肇庆丰盛贸易有限公司与日本某商社签订了一份买卖女士秋冬针织服装的合同。业务员小董在完成出货任务并取得提单后，根据合同和信用证的规定，准备缮制汇票，以完成办理结汇所需要的整套单据。

要求：

以业务员小董身份，根据如图10.1所示信用证的要求制作汇票，办理结汇。

ISSUE OF A DOCUMENTARY CREDIT	
ISSUING BANK	THE ROYAL BANK.TOKYO
SEQUENCE OF TOTAL	1 / 1
FORM OF DOC. CREDIT	NON-TRANSFERABLE
DOC. CREDIT NUMBER	JST-AB12
DATE OF ISSUE	20150405
EXPIRY	DATE 20150615 PLACE CHINA
APPLICANT	WAV GENEAL TRADING CO., LTD
	5-18 ISUKI-CHOHAKI, OSAKA, JAPAN
BENEFICIARY	FENG SHENG CO.LTD 8 XI JIANG NAN ROAD ZHAO QING , GUANG DONG , CHINA
AMOUNT	CURRENCY USD AMOUNT 10300,00
AVAILABLE WITH/BY	BANK OF CHINA BY NEGOTIATION
DRAFTS AT...	DRAFTS AT SIGHT FOR FULL INVOICE VALUE
DRAWEE	THE ROYAL BANK,TOKYO
PARTIAL SHIPMTS	ALLOWED
TRANSSHIPMENT	ALLOWED
LOADING IN CHARGE	ZHAO QING PORT
FOR TRANSPIRT TO...	OSAKA,JAPAN
LATEST SHIPMENT	20150531
GOODS DESCRIPT.	7071 PCS OF LADIES' KNITTED GARMENTS FOR DES PETITS HAUTS FALL WINTER 2015 AS PER CONTRACT NO.P11Q0152

图 10.1 日本某商社开来的信用证

DOCS REQUIRED	*3/3 SET OF ORIGINAL CLEAN ON BOARD OCEAN BILLS OF LADING MADE OUT TO ORDER OF SHIPPER AND BLANK ENDORSED AND MARKED "FREIGHT PREPAID" NOTIFY APPLICANT(WITH FULL NAME AND ADDRESS). *ORIGINAL SIGNED COMMERCIAL INVOICE IN 5 FOLD. *INSURANCE POLICY OR CERTIFICATE IN 2 FOLD ENDORSED IN BLANK,FOR 110PCT OF THE INVOICE VALUE COVERING THE INSTITUTE CARGO CLAUSES (A),THE INSTITUTE WAR CLAUSES, INSURANCE CLAIMS TO BE PAYABLE IN JAPAN IN THE CURRENCY OF THE DRAFTS. *CERTIFICATE OF ORIGIN GSP FORM A IN 1 ORIGINAL AND 1 COPY. *PACKING LIST IN 5 FOLD.
ADDITIONAL COND	1. THE GOODS TO BE PACKED IN EXPIRT STRONG COLORED CARTONS. 2. SHIPPING MARKS: ITOCHU OSAKA NO,1-200
DETAILS OF CHARGES	ALL BANKING CHARGES OUTSIDE JAPAN INCLUDING REIMBURSEMENT COMMISSION ARE FOR ACCOUNT OF BENEFICIARY.
PRESENTATION PERIOD	DOCUMENTS TO BE PRESENTED WITHIN 10 DAYS AFTER THE DATE OF SHIPMENT, BUT WITHIN THE VALIDITY OF THE CREDIT.
INSTRUCTIONS	THE NEGOTIATION BANK MUST FORWARD THE DRAFTS AND ALL DOCUMENTS BY REGISTERED AIRMAIL DIRECT TO U.S. IN TWO CONSECUTIVE LOTS,UPON RECEIPT OF THE DRAFTS AND DOCUMENTS IN ORDER,WE WILL REMIT THE PROCEEDS AS INSTRUCTED BY THE NEGOTIATING BANK.

图 10.1　日本某商社开来的信用证（续）

知识准备

一、汇票概述

汇票（bill of exchange；postal order；draft）是由出票人签发的，要求付款人在见票时或在一定期限内，向收款人或持票人无条件支付一定款项的票据（见图 10.2）。

BILL OF EXCHANGE

Place ____4.出票地点____ Date ____出票时间____

凭

Drawn under ____1.出票依据____

支取   按_____息____付款_____

Payable With Interest @._____%_____

号码   汇票金额

No. ____2.汇票号码____ Exchange for ____3.汇票金额（小写）

见票   日后（本汇票之副本未付）   付 交

At ____5.付款期限____ sight of this FIRST of Exchange（Second of Exchange being unpaid）pay to the order of ____6.收款人

金额

the sum of ____3.汇票金额（大写）____

此致

To ____7. 付款人____

                                                                    For 8. 出票人签章

图 10.2   汇票样本

汇票是国际结算中使用最广泛的一种信用工具。其流程如下：

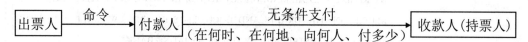

根据不同的划分依据，汇票可分为如表 10.1 所示的种类。

表 10.1   汇票的种类

划分依据	汇票种类	
按出票人不同	银行汇票	商业汇票
按付款时间不同	即期汇票	远期汇票
按承兑人不同	银行承兑汇票	商业承兑汇票
按有无随附商业单据	光票	跟单汇票

二、汇票的填写

（一）信用证项下汇票的填写

信用证项下汇票须填写的栏目内容包括以下几个方面。

1. Drawn under：出票依据

（1）开证行名称：填写全称及地址，不能填缩写和漏填地址（因知名银行在各地有分行）。

（2）信用证号码：按来证所述的填写。

（3）开证日期：按来证所述的填写。

（4）年息：按来证规定的利息率填写。若没有，留空，由银行填写。

2. No.：汇票号码

该栏目填写商业发票号码，实际业务中一般留空不填。

3. Amount：汇票金额

（1）"Exchange for"一栏填小写金额，可保留 2 位小数，由货币名称缩写和阿拉伯数字组成，如 USD1850.80。

（2）"the sum of"一栏填大写金额，习惯句首加"say"，意指"计"；句尾加"only"，意指"整"；小数点用"point"或"cents"表示。例如，Say U.S dollars one thousand eight hundred and fifty point eight only。

需注意的是，大小写金额与币制必须相符，汇票金额与发票金额也通常一致，但当信用证有要求扣除佣金时，前者就小于后者。无论如何，汇票金额不能超过信用证金额，除非信用证另有规定。

4. Place and Date：出票地点和出票时间

出票地点为出票人所在地或议付地，出票时间为议付日期，通常由议付行代填。

需注意的是，出票时间填写不能早于发票、提单等单据日期，但也不能晚于信用证有效期或提单签发日后 21 天。

5. At＿＿sight：付款期限

其有以下两种情况。

（1）即期汇票：只需在"At＿sight"间填写"*****"即可，不能留空，否则无效。

（2）远期汇票：按 L/C 规定的付款期限填写。又有下述 3 种情况。

① 见票后若干天付款。例如，Available against your drafts drawn us at 60 days after sight（见票后 60 天付款），应填写为：At 60 days after sight。

② 出票后若干天付款。例如，Available against presentation of the documents detailed herein and of your at 60 days after date of the draft（出票

253

日后 60 天付款），应填写为：At <u>60 days after date of the draft</u>，并将汇票上印就的"sight"划掉。

③ 提单日后若干天付款。例如：Available by beneficiary's drafts at 60 days after date of B/L（提单日后 60 天付款），应填写为：at <u>60 days after date of B/L</u>（注明提单日期），并将汇票上印就的"sight"划掉。

6. pay to the order：收款人

本栏目有以下 3 种情况：
（1）限制性抬头：填写为 pay to <u>A Com. Only</u>（仅付给 A 公司）。
（2）持票人抬头：填写为 pay to <u>the bearer</u>（付给来人）。
（3）指示性抬头：填写为 pay to <u>the order of A Com.</u>（根据 A 公司指示付款）。

在实务操作过程中，一般填写议付行的名称和地址，如 pay to the order of <u>×××　bank（negotiating bank）</u>。

7. To：付款人或受票人

本栏目按信用证要求填写，通常填写开证行或其指定银行。
（1）汇票条款中规定"××draw on us"或"draw on ourselves"，则付款人为开证行。
（2）汇票条款中规定"××draw on ××× bank"，则付款人为该银行（非开证行，而是付款行）。
（3）汇票条款中规定"××draw on yourselves"，则付款人为通知行或保兑行。

8. Signature of the Drawer：出票人签章

于汇票右下方填出口公司全称、盖章。如有要求，则手签法定代表人或经办人名字。

（二）托收项下汇票的填写方法

托收项下汇票的填写包括以下几个方面。
（1）出票依据（Drawn under）：填写货物名称、数量，还可加注合同号、装运港和目的港等，或仅填"for collection"。"L/C No."和"DATE"两栏空白不填。
（2）付款期（At sight）：支付方式一般为 D/P 或 D/A，填在 At 的前面，付款期限填写在 At 和 sight 之间。
① 即期付款交单：填写为"<u>D/P</u> At *** sight"。

② 远期付款交单：填写为 "<u>D/P At 60 days after sight</u>"。

③ 承兑交单：填写为 "<u>D/A At 60 days after sight</u>"。

（3）付款人（To）：应填写进口商的名称及其详细地址。

（4）收款人（pay to the order:）：一般填写代收行名称。

其余栏目填写跟信用证项下大致一样。

课堂思考

汇票、本票、支票有什么区别？

参考答案

小 贴 士

实际业务中，为何会有相同内容的汇票1和汇票2？交单时应提交哪张呢？

汇票是一种有价证券，是支付工具，有银行汇票和商业汇票两种形式，在信用证和托收业务中，多使用由出口商出具的商业汇票，为防止丢失，一般有两张正本，具同等效力，但付款人"付一不付二，付二不付一"，先到先付，后到无效。银行寄单时，一般将两张汇票分两个邮政班次向国外寄出，以防在邮程中丢失。

职业判断

案例资料：

合同规定部分货款用即期信用证结算，部分货款用30天远期付款交单结算，单证员出货后准备办理制单结汇。

思考：

单证员应如何制作汇票？付款人和金额应如何填写？

参考答案

任务实施

单证员小董根据上述信用证的规定填制好的汇票如图10.3所示。

BILL OF EXCHANGE

ZHAOQING，CHINA， May 20., 2015

凭   信用证号码   开证日期

Drawn under THE ROYAL BANK.TOKYO   L/C No. JST-AB12   Date APRIL 5. 2015

支取   按_____息____付款_____

Payable With Interest@_____%_____

号码   汇票金额

No. ZH26686   Exchange for USD10,300.00

见票_____日后（本汇票之副本未付）付交

At ***sight of this FIRST of EXCHANGE（Second of Exchange being unpaid）pay to the order of BANK OF CHINA，ZHAO QING BRANCH

金额

the sum of SAY U.S. DOLLARS TEN THOUSAND THREE HUNDRED ONLY.

此致

To THE ROYAL BANK.TOKYO

ZHAO QING FENG SHENG CO.LTD

董杨

图10.3 单证员填制的汇票

任务再现

纯棉毛巾

参考答案

2015 年 3 月，广东美和贸易公司与加拿大贸易公司签订了一份买卖纯棉毛巾合同，数量 3000 打，按 CIF VANCOUVER 成交，付款条件为见票日后 60 天付款交单，合同金额为 80 万美元。

根据下面提供的资料，缮制一份托收项下的汇票。

出口方：GUANG DOND MEI HE CO.LTD

进口方：YIMA TRADING CORPORATION 20 MARSHALL AVE DONCASTER VICOI CANADA

合同号：CONTRACT NO.2015ZH32

发票号码：ZH126323

代收行：SCOTIA BANK CANADA

托收银行：BANK OF CHINA，ZHAOQING BRANCH

出票日期：AUG. 6, 2015

任务二　　审单与交单结汇

新鲜芦笋

任务导航

　　2015 年 5 月，广东西江土产公司与日本公司签订了买卖新鲜芦笋的合同，即期信用证付款方式。业务员小王在完成汇票的制作后，对全套缮制好的单证进行审核，准备到银行办理交单结汇，如图 10.4 所示。

要求：

　　根据提供的已制作好的商业发票与汇票（见图 10.4 和图 10.5），以小王的身份对它们的准确性、完整性和一致性进行审核，如有错误，请更正。

COMMERCIAL INVOICE

To:		Invoice No.	NP6200
SHITAYA KINZOKU CO.LTD 6-126-CHOME		Invoice Date	EIGHT2,2015
UENO TAITO-KU TOKYO,JAPAN		S/C No.	NP86021
		S/C Date	JUNE2,2015

From:　ZHAO QING, GUANG DONG			To: TOKYO	
L/C No.TY28662　　Dated: JUNE20,2015			Issued By:DONTUSU COMMERCIAL BANK TOKYO,JAPAN	

Marks and Numbers	Numbers and Kind of Package Description of Goods	Quantity	Unit Price	Amount
N/M	FRESH ASPARAGUS	30M/T	CIFTOKYO USD1 800.00 PER M/T	USD54 000.00

Total:		30M/T	USD54 000.00	
Say Total	SAY US DOLLARS　　FIFTY-FOUR THOUSAND ONLY			
Remarks	XI JIANG GUANG DONG NATIVE PRODUCE CO.LTD.			

图 10.4　商业发票

BILL OF EXCHANGE

ZHAO QING CHINA，EIGHT 5. 2015

凭　　　　　　　　　信用证号码　　开证日期

Drawn under <u>DONTUSU COMMERCIAL BANK TOKYO, JAPAN L/C No.TY28662 Date JUNE20, 2015</u>

支取　　按_____息_____付款_____

Payable With Interest @._____%_____

号码　　　　汇票金额

No.__NP86021__ Exchange for___USD 54 000.00___

见票_____日 后　　(本 汇 票 之 副 本 未 付) 付 交

At____sight of this FIRST of Exchange (Second of Exchange being unpaid) pay to the order of <u>BANK OF CHINA，ZHAO</u>

<u>QING BRANCH</u>

金额

the sum of　<u>SAY U.S.DOLLARS FIFTY-FOUR THOUSAND ONLY</u>

此致

To <u>SHITAYA KINZOKU CO.LTD 6-126-CHOME UENO TAITO-KU TOKYO,JAPAN</u>

XI JIANG GUANG DONG NATIVE PRODUCE CO.LTD.

图 10.5　汇票

知识准备

一、交单结汇工作程序

交单结汇的工作程序包括以下几个方面。

（1）核算。在制单前，须将单证中很多需要计算的数据，如货物的尺码、毛重、净重、发票的单价、总价、中间商的佣金等，逐项认真加以核算。

（2）备单。根据信用证或合同的要求，把需要提供的各种空白单据及份数逐一配妥备用，既可以防止某一单据的漏制，又能提高制单工作效率。

（3）制单。完成了上述工作以后，即可以着手制单。制单一般可先从发票和装箱单开始，因为发票记载的内容比较全面，它是一切单证的中心。发票制妥后，就可以参照发票的内容缮制其他单证。

（4）审单。单据制妥后，要求制单人员自审一遍，如有差错立即更正，以保证迅速、有效地向银行交单。

（5）交单。出口商在规定时间内向银行提交信用证或合同要求的全套单据，这些单据经银行审核，按规定付汇方式办理结汇。

二、审核单据的要求

（一）单证一致

单证一致，即各种单据与信用证要求（含信用证修改书内容）一致，应仔细分辨和核对来证中对单据与货物有无特殊的规定。

（二）单单一致

单单一致，即各种单据之间必须相互一致，不能彼此矛盾。一是各种单据的填制内容在措辞和用语方面保持一致（提单用概括性的商品统称除外），二是各种单据的签发日期应保持合理，符合逻辑性及国际惯例。通常，提单日期是确定各单据日期的关键，汇票日期应晚于提单、发票等其他单据日期，但不能晚于 L/C 的有效期。各单据日期关系如下。

（1）发票日期应在各单据日期之首。

（2）提单日期不能超过 L/C 规定的装运期也不得早于 L/C 的最早装运期。

（3）保单的签发日期应早于或等于提单日期（一般早于提单 2 天），不能早于发票。

（4）装箱单签发日期应等于或迟于发票日期，但必须在提单日期之前。

（5）原产地证书签发日期不早于发票日期，不迟于提单日。

（6）商检证签发日期不晚于提单日期，但也不能过早于提单日期，尤其是鲜活货物和容易变质的商品。

（7）受益人证明：等于或晚于提单日期。

（8）装船通知：等于或晚于提单日期后 3 天内。

（9）船公司证明：等于或早于提单日期。

（三）单货一致

单货一致，即指单据上记载的内容应与实际货物内容一致。虽然信用证业务是单据业务，银行仅凭单据付款，而不管货物的实际交付情况，但信用证是依据买卖合同开立的，单货不一致，则极易造成所交货物与合同不相符合，从而导致违约情况的发生。另外，单货不一致也会在报关、检验时遇到麻烦。

（四）单同一致

单同一致，即各种单证与合同要求一致。但在信用证支付方式下，当信用证的要求与合同不一致时，单证应按信用证的要求来做。

三、各种结汇方式下的业务流程图

（1）信用证方式下交单结汇的流程如图 10.6 所示。

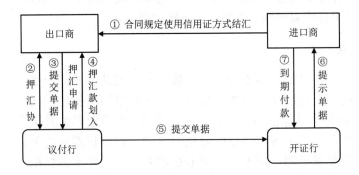

图 10.6　信用证交单结汇流程

（2）托收方式下交单结汇的流程，如图 10.7 所示。

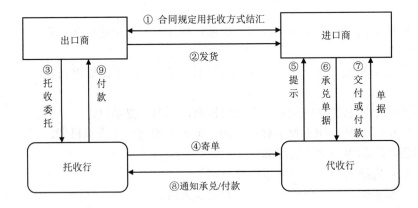

图 10.7　托收方式交单结汇流程

（3）汇付方式下交单结汇的流程。

① 电汇/信汇流程如图10.8所示。

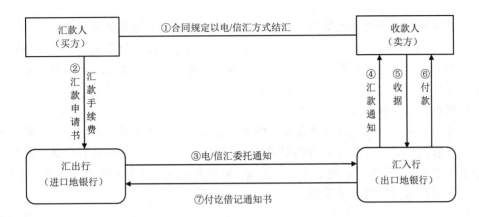

图10.8　电汇/信汇流程

② 票汇流程如图10.9所示。

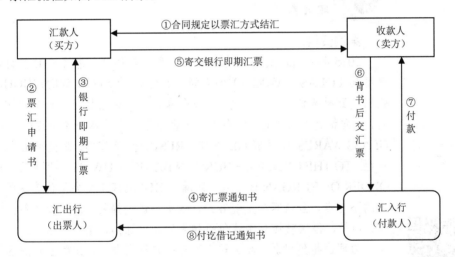

图10.9　票汇流程

课堂思考

信用证、托收、汇付3种结汇方式，哪种更好？

参考答案

小 贴 士

　　业务中如何办理结汇既安全又节省费用？方法是两种结汇方式并用。

　　一种是信用证与托收结合使用。例如，有 100 万美元货物要出口，一部分货款（如 60%）由进口商开立信用证，其余部分金额（剩下的 40%）由出口商在货物装运后，连同信用证项下的装船单据，一并交议付银行，通过开证行向进口商以托收结算方式收取剩余货款。

　　另一种是汇付与托收结合使用。例如，有 100 万美元货物要出口，卖方可先向买方收取一部分订金（如 30%货款），用 T/T 方式汇入。等货物装船后，再将全套单据（包括提单）拿到银行去做托收，要求进口商支付余下的 70%货款之后，才能取得代表货物的整套单据。

职业判断

　　案例资料：

　　2015 年 4 月广交会上某公司 A 与科威特的某位老客户 B 签订购买玻璃餐具（GLASS WARES）的合同，A 公司报价 FOB WENZHOU，从温州出运到科威特，海运费到付，支付条件为全额信用证。A 公司按期出了货，并向银行交单议付，但在审核单据过程中发现两个不符点：①发票上，GLASS WARES 错写成 GLASSWARES，即没有空格；②提单上"提货人"一栏，TO THE ORDER OF BURGAN BANK, KUWAIT 错写成了 TO THE ORDER OF BURGAN BANK，即漏写 KUWAIT。A 公司认为这两个是极小的不符点，且该客户是老客户，根本不影响提货，没有就不符点担保出单。但是，很快就接到由议付行转来的拒付通知，银行就以上述两个不符点作为理由拒绝付款。A 公司立即与客户取得联系，知悉主要原因是客户认为到付的运费太贵（原来 A 公司 5 月报给客户的是 USD1 950.00，6 月海运费价格上涨为 USD2 275.00），但客户并无预计到，因而拒绝到付运费，导致货物滞留在码头，A 公司也无法收到货款。

　　思考：

　　对于这种情况，A 公司应如何处理？

参考答案

通过审核，小王发现填制的汇票存在错漏，并作出改正（加方框部分），如图 10.10 所示。

BILL OF EXCHANGE

ZHAO QING CHINA，Aug. 5. 2015

凭　　　　　　　　　　　信用证号码　　开证日期

Drawn under <u>DONTUSU COMMERCIAL BANK TOKYO,JAPAN</u>　<u>L/C No.TY28662 Date JUNE20,2015</u>

支取　　按＿＿＿＿＿＿息＿＿＿＿付款＿＿＿＿＿

Payable With Interest@ ＿＿＿＿＿＿％＿＿＿＿＿

号码　　　汇票金额

No. NP6200　Exchange for USD 54 000.00

见票＿＿＿＿日后＿＿＿＿（本 汇 票 之 副 本 未 付）付 交

At ＿＿＿＿ sight of this FIRST of Exchange (Second of Exchange being unpaid) pay to the order of <u>BANK OF CHINA，ZHAO QING BRANCH</u>

金额

the sum of <u>SAY U.S DOLLARS FIFTY-FOUR THOUSAND ONLY.</u>

此致

To DONTUSU COMMERCIAL BANK TOKYO,JAPAN

XI JIANG GUANG DONG NATIVE PRODUCE CO.LTD.

小王

图 10.10　改正后的汇票

2015 年 7 月，广东芙蓉食品公司与印度尼西亚某公司签订了一份买卖柑橘的合同，规定用信用证方式支付，数量 150 万公斤，合同金额 70 万美元。

柑橘

根据以下信用证资料对已填制好的汇票（见图 10.11）进行审核并作出修改。

信用证号码：FHS-JWTE05

开证行：SEMARANG BANK 1286 VTRA SEMARANG ,INDONESIA

开证日期：JULY16,2015
开证人：HYCO LANGGENG PT.
受益人：FU RONG GUANGDONG FOODSTUFFS I/E (GROUP) CORPORATION
货物情况：1000KG CITRUS
总金额：USD700,000.00
付款期：AT 30 DAYS AFTER SIGHT
议付行：BANK OF CHINA ZHAOQING BRANCH

BILL OF EXCHANGE

ZHAO QING CHINA，SEP. 8. 2015

凭

信用证号码　　开证日期

Drawn under <u>SEMARANG BANK, INDONESIA</u> L/C No. FHS-JWTE05 Date JULY16,2015

支取　　按＿＿＿＿息＿＿＿付款＿＿＿＿＿＿＿＿＿＿

Payable With Interest @＿＿＿＿＿%＿＿＿＿＿＿

号码　　　　汇票金额

No.＿NP20158＿Exchange for＿USD 700 000.00＿

见票＿＿＿＿＿日后　　(本汇票之副本未付) 付交

At 30 <u>DAY AFTER</u> sight of this FIRST of Exchange (Second of Exchange being unpaid) pay to the order of <u>FU RONG GUANGDONG FOODSTUFFS I/E (GROUP) CORPORATION</u>

金额

the sum of <u>SAY U.S. DOLLARS SEVENTY THOUSAND ONLY</u>.

此致

To <u>SEMARANG BANK 1286　VTRA　SEMARANG</u>

FU RONG GUANGDONG FOODSTUFFS I/E (GROUP) CORPORATION

李红

图 10.11　已填制的汇票

参考答案

技能强化训练

技 能 提 高

项目小结

（一）填单题

2015 年 4 月广东肇庆 ABC 进出口公司与日本公司签订了一份买卖桂皮的合同，按 CIF OSAKA 成交，即期信用证付款，合同金额为 365 000 美元。

试根据下面信用证的资料，缮制一份信用证项下的汇票。

卖方：ZHAO QING ABC IMPORT & EXPORT TRADE CORPORATION 12 NORTH KANG LE ROAD,ZHAO QING ,GUANG DONG,CHINA

买方：TAKADA CORPORATION 6-8, KAWARAMACHI, OSAKA, JAPAN

在线测试及
参考答案

货物、单价及数量：CINNAMON ART.NO.1 USD110.00/KG CIF OSAKA，1000KG；ART.NO.2 USD100.00/KG CIF OSAKA,1200KG；ART.NO.3 USD90.00/KG CIF OSAKA, 1500KG.

开证行：FUJI BANK 1022 SAKURA OTOLIKINGZA MACHI, OSAKA, JAPAN

信用证号：JA162

信用证类型：L/C AT SIGHT

开证日期：MAY 12,2015

有效期：JUNE 30.2015

桂皮

议付行：BANK OF CHINA,ZHAO QING BRANCH

发票号：ZH322

参考答案

（二）审单改错题

根据下列信用证资料审核已填制好的汇票（见图 10.12），指出其错误并改正。

信用证号码：FPA-HZJ56

开证行：WEST LB (EUROPA) A.G. P.O.BOX 1252 3021 CE COPEN-HAGEN, THE DANMARK

开证日期：JAN.09　2015

开证人：F.L.SMIDTH &CO. A/S 86，VIGERSLEV ALLE, DK-2120

VALBY COPENHAGEN DANMARK

受益人：ZHAO QING XI JIANG ROAD NO. 8, GUANG DONG，CHINA

参考答案

货物：1 600SETS OF PHOENIX BRAND BICYCLE

金额：USD96 200.00

付款期：D /P AT 60 DAYS AFTER DATE OF B/L

议付行：BANK OF CHINA，ZHAO QING BRANCH

BILL OF EXCHANGE

ZHAO QING CHINA Date APR. 22，2015

凭

Drawn   under   WEST LB   (EUROPA) A.G , FPA-HZJ56, JAN.09, 2015

支取   按_____息_____付款_____

Payable With Interest @ _____%_____

号码   汇票金额

No. TH-ZH165 Exchange for:__UAD96 200__

见票_____日 后 （本 汇 票 之 副 本 未 付）付 交

At 60 DAYS AFTER DATE OF B/L sight of this FIRST of Exchange (Second of Exchange being unpaid) pay to the order of BANK

OF CHINA，ZHAO QING BRANCH

金额

the sum of U.S DOLLARS NINETY-SIX THOUSAND AND TWO HUNDRED.

此致

To WEST LB (EUROPA) A.G. P.O.BOX 1252 3021 CE COPENHAGEN, THE DANMARK

ZHAO QING XI JIANG ROAD NO. 8, GUANG DONG，CHINA

图 10.12　汇票

项目十一

综合实训

知识目标

1. 了解电汇项下的全套结汇单据；
2. 了解托收项下的全套结汇单据；
3. 了解信用证项下的全套结汇单据。

能力目标

1. 能正确缮制电汇项下全套结汇单据；
2. 能正确缮制托收项下全套结汇单据；
3. 能正确缮制信用证项下全套结汇单据。

任务一　　缮制电汇项下全套结汇单据

任务导航

　　肇庆市富庆五金塑料有限公司出口了价值 240 107 美元的货物，电约以电汇方式付款。

　　要求：

　　联系本公司开户银行中国农业银行肇庆高新支行，申请结汇、缮制结汇单据。

知识准备

一、电汇的定义基本概念

　　电汇（telegraphic transfer，T/T），是汇出行应汇款人的申请，拍发加押电报或电传（tested cable/telex）或者通过 SWIFT 给国外汇入行，指示其解付一定金额给收款人的一种汇款结算方式。

二、电汇的业务流程

　　电汇是目前使用较多的一种汇款方式，其业务流程：汇款人电汇申请书并交款付费给汇出行→汇出行拍加押电报或电传给汇入行→汇入行给收款人电汇通知书→收款人接到通知后去汇入行兑付→汇入行解付→汇入行发出借记通知书给汇出行，同时汇出行给汇款人电汇回执。

　　电汇时，由汇款人（进口方）填写汇款申请书，并在申请书中注明采用电汇方式。同时，将所汇款项及所需费用交汇出行，取得电汇回执。汇出行接到汇款申请书后，为防止因申请书中出现的差错而耽误或引起汇出资金的意外损失，汇出行应仔细审核申请书，不清楚的地方与汇款人及时联系。

　　汇出行办理电汇时，根据汇款申请书内容，以电报或电传向汇入行发出解付指示。电文内容主要有汇款金额及币种、收款人名称、地址或账号、汇款人名称、地址、附言、头寸拨付办法、汇出行名称或 SWIFT 地址等。为了使汇入行证实电文内容确实是由汇出行发出的，汇出行在正文前要加列双方银行所约定使用的密押（test key）。

　　汇入行收到电报或电传后，即核对密押是不是相符，若不符，应立即拟电文向汇出行查询。若相符，即缮制电汇通知书，通知收款人取款。

收款人持通知书一式两联向汇入行取款，并在收款人收据上签章后，汇入行即凭以解付汇款。

实际业务中，如果收款人（出口方）在汇入行开有账户，汇入行往往不缮制汇款通知书，仅凭电文将款项收入收款人收户，然后给收款人一份收账通知单，也不需要收款人签具收据。最后，汇入行将付讫借记通知书（debit advice）寄给汇出行。

■ 课堂思考

参考答案

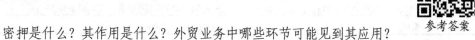

密押是什么？其作用是什么？外贸业务中哪些环节可能见到其应用？

小 贴 士

结汇申请书（模板）

××银行××支行：

本单位 于 年 月 日收到一笔境外汇入款，币种及金额为（外币，小写）_____，该笔款项的性质为_____。我单位现申请办理结汇，结汇金额_____，外币资金在账号_____中扣划，人民币资金划入账号_____中，结汇资金用于_____。

特此申请

申请单位公章：
年 月 日

职业判断

案例资料：

在T/T结汇方式中，A类企业不需向结算银行交付任何书面资料。

思考：

我国对外贸企业是如何分类的？

参考答案

任务实施

肇庆市富庆五金塑料有限公司出具的结汇业务申请书、结算说明和结汇后银行结算水单（结汇通知书），如图11.1～图11.3所示。

中国农业银行广东省分行"跨境结汇通"业务申请书

致：中国农业银行肇庆高新支行

业务申请人（名称）	肇庆市富庆五金塑料有限公司		
在途收汇资金信息			
付汇币种及金额	USD240101.00	付款人国家/地区	台湾
付汇人名称	余瀚五金××有限公司	业务编号	449998HR15387475
收汇人名称	肇庆市富庆五金××有限公司	收汇人账号	4465010404×××905
开户行名称	中国农业银行肇庆高新支行	资金用途	货款
业务申请人不可撤销地授权贵行将上述外币款项在入账前办理跨境结汇通业务，结汇要素如下：			
跨境结汇通币种、金额	USD 240 107.00		
结汇方式	☑ 即期　□ 择期	择期交割期间　年　月　日至　年　月　日	
申请结汇汇率	6.4808		
业务申请人不可撤销地授权贵行将兑换后的人民币款项汇入境内如下账户			
收款银行	中国农业银行肇庆高新支行		
收款账号	4465010404×××905		
收款人全称	肇庆市富庆五金塑料有限公司		

业务须知

1. 在填写申请结汇汇率前，业务申请人应先向受理银行询价，以提高成交的可能性。2. 申请择期结汇方式的，在受理银行已收到外汇资金的前提下，业务申请人可以在择期交割期间内的任何一日向受理银行提出按申请结汇汇率进行交割，申请结汇汇率在择期交割期间内不变。3. 受理银行办理结汇的时间可能会受到资金交易系统、外汇管制等因素影响。4. 办理该业务涉及的境外合作银行由受理银行选择并自行确立权利义务关系，受理银行不对业务申请人承担披露义务，业务申请人对境外合作银行不享有任何权利。5. 受理银行按约定将结汇资金汇入收款人账户即视为已完成本笔"跨境结汇通"交易。

业务申请人声明与保证

1. 本公司签署本申请书前已充分了解贵行"跨境结汇通"产品的原理、流程和相关权利义务，并知悉签署本申请书的法律后果。本公司承诺委托贵行结汇的外币汇入款具有真实和正常贸易收汇背景，所提供给贵行的资料均真实有效，不违反国家反洗钱和外汇管理的法律法规。本公司不可撤销地授权贵行对上述外币汇入款项在入账前协助安排由境外合作银行提供结汇服务，并将兑换后的人民币资金划至本公司上述人民币收款账户。

2. 本公司确认贵行为本公司办理"跨境结汇通"业务以贵行收到上述外汇资金作为前提，无论贵行在办理"跨境结汇通"业务过程中与境外合作银行协商的具体汇率形式及大小，贵行仅需按本公司申请结汇汇率为本公司办理结汇并支付兑换后的人民币款项。如因本公司或付汇人的原因导致无法履行上述交易，给贵行或境外合作银行带来损失，本公司愿意承担相关资金损失并授权贵行在本公司的账户中扣收损失金额。

3. 本公司清楚，贵行在操作过程中如因市场汇率价格剧烈波动超出本公司可接受的申请结汇汇率范围，贵行及境外合作银行保留取消本次交易的权利，由此引起的损失由本公司承担。

4. 如果结汇后人民币汇入款项因非贵行失误的原因造成退款，所产生的损失及合理费用由本公司承担。

经办：　　　企业客户（盖章）：　　　日期：2015 年 12 月 29 日

银行成交确认信息

已按客户申请结汇汇率成交，结汇后入账人民币金额：1 550 085.45

经办：　　　复核：　　　银行盖章

日期：2015 年 12 月 29 日

图 11.1　结汇业务申请书

跨境业务人民币结算收款说明

填表日期：　　　年　月　日

收款企业名称：肇庆市富庆五金塑料有限公司			组织机构代码：		
组织机构代码（身份证件号）：			收款日期：　　　年　月　日		
收款金额合计：			元		
货物贸易金额：			元		
预收货款项下：	元	占合同金额比例：	%	预计	天后报关（结账期）

已报关	报关经营单位名称：肇庆市富庆五金塑料有限公司				
	组织机构代码：				
	人民币报关 □	一般贸易：	元	进料加工：	元
	外币报关 □	其他贸易：	元	边境贸易：	元
无货物报关	海关特殊监管区域及保税监管场所进出境物流货物：				元
	离岸转手买卖：	元	其他：		元
服务贸易：	元	国际收支编码：			
投资收益：	元	国际收支编码：			
		批准证书号（仅汇入直投收益时填报）：			
经常转移：	元	国际收支编码：			
资本账户：	元	国际收支编码：			
直接投资：	元	国际收支编码：		批准证书号：	
证券投资：	元	国际收支编码：			
其他投资：	元	国际收支编码：			
备注：					

本企业申明：本表所填内容真实无误。如有虚假，视为违反跨境人民币结算管理规定，将承担相应后果。

单位公章或财务专用章　　　　　　填报人：　　　　　　　联系电话：

填表说明：

一般贸易：指海关监管贸易方式为"0110"的贸易类型。

进料加工贸易：指海关监管贸易方式为"0615进料对口"、"0654进料深加工"、"0664进料料件复出"、"0700进料料件退换"、"0715进料非对口"、"0864进料边角料复出"。

边境贸易：指根据国家相关规定在指定口岸与毗邻国家之间开展的货物贸易。

其他贸易：不在上列范围内的海关监管贸易方式。

无货物报关：包括海关特殊监管区域及保税监管场所进出境物流货物、离岸转手买卖，以及其他未达到海关规定申报金额的邮寄进口或从境外付款但境内交货等方式。

图 11.2　结算说明

中国农业银行即期实时结汇通知书

合约编号：44JJ850115000649-001　　　　　　　　交易日期：2015-12-29

客户名称：肇庆市 ABC 塑料有限公司

客户卖出：USD240107.00　　　　　　　账号：4465×××××0905

客户买入：CNY1566085.45　　　　　　　账号：4465×××××3062

汇率：　6.4808

交割日期：2015-12-29

附言：

经办：袁欣　　　　　复核：卢海彬　　　　　盖章：中国农业银行肇庆高新支行

　　　　　　　　　　　　　　　　　　　　　　　　2015-12-29

　　　　　　　　　　　　　　　　　　　　　　　　袁欣

中国农业银行肇庆市高新支行　　客户回单

2015 年 12 月 29 日

币种：USD　　　编号：449999HR15387475　　业务办讫章：中国农业银行肇庆高新支行

　　　　　　　　　　　　　　　　　　　　　　　　　　　　　2015-12-29

　　　　　　　　　　　　　　　　　　　　　　　　　　　　　袁欣

账号	客户	金额
44650114040000905	肇庆市 ABC 塑料有限公司	USD240107.00

汇入汇款　　收汇日期：20151229　　收汇金额：USD240107.00

汇款人：YUHANXX METAL LIMITED

　　　　2/2F,KEJING ROAD,TAIPEI, TAIWAN

受益人：44650114040000640 ZHAOQING FUQING METAL

　　　　LIMITED

申报号：4412000000×××1229N001

图 11.3　银行结算水单

任务再现

肇庆市 WARM SING 进出口贸易有限公司出口了价值 20 520 美元的铝箔箱到智利，双方约定的付款方式是电汇方式。请向该司的开户银行中国银行肇庆市支行申请结汇。

参考答案

任务二 缮制托收项下全套结汇单据

项目小结

任务导航

顺德纺织品进出口公司向突尼斯某公司出口了一批货物后，向中国农业银行容桂支行申请托收结汇。图 11.4 是结汇的托收申请书。

中国农业银行
AGRICULTURAL BANK OF CHINA

ABCS(2007)3021

跟 单 托 收 申 请 书
APPLICATION FOR DOCUMENTARY COLLECTION

Date 日期_2013-06-14

To: Agricultural Bank of China　　　　　　Branch 致：中国农业银行股份有限公司　　容桂支　　　　行 We enclose the following draft(s)/documents as specified hereunder which please collect in accordance with the instructions indicated herein. 兹附上汇票和单据如下，谨请贵行依照本申请书的要求为我公司办理托收。 This collection is subject to URC 522. 此托收遵循国际商会第 522 号出版物《托收统一规则》。	Collecting Bank (Full name & address 代收行（全称和地址） BANQUE NATIONALE AGRICOLE BNA DIRECTION REGIONAL SFAX 43 RUE HABIB MAAZOUN 3000 SFAX TUNISIA A/C 03-026156011500403301

Drawer (Full name & address) 收款人（全称和地址） SHUNDE TEXTILES IMP/EXP CO. LTD OF GUANGDONG	Tenor（期限） At Sight	
	Draft/Inv. No. 汇票/发票号码	Currency and Amount 币种及金额
Drawee(Full name & address) 付款人（全称和地址） Tunisia Trading Co.ltd. 342,NIX Road,MAAZOUN,Tunisia	AF362267771088	USD44750.00

DOCUMENTS 单据

DP AFT	COM. INV.	PACKING LIST	B/L	N/N B/L	AWB.	ORIGIN CERI	INS. POL.	INSP. CERT.	CERT	CABLE COPY		
	3	3	3	1								

图 11.4 银行托收申请书

Special Instructions （See box marked "×" 特殊条款（用"×"在方框中表明）:

☐ please deliver documents against ☐payment at sight /☐payment ____ after sight /☐acceptance.

　　请办理☐即期付款交单/☐远期付款交单/☐承兑交单。

☐ All your charges are to be borne by ☐the drawee /☐us.

　　你行所有费用由☐付款人/☐我司承担。

☐ In case of a time bill, please advise us of acceptance giving maturity date.

　　如果托收包含远期汇票，请通知我公司承兑到期日。

☐ In case of dishonour, please do not protest but advise us of non-payment ☐non-acceptance giving reasons.

　　如果发生拒付，无须拒绝证书但应该通知我公司拒绝付款或拒绝承兑的原因。

☐ Please instruct the Collecting Bank to deliver documents only upon receipt of all their banking charges.

　　请指示代收行收妥全部银行费用后再提示单据。

☐ We will take on all the results caused by choosing the above bank as the collecting bank.

　　请选择我司选定的代收行，由此引起的问题和其他后果由我司负责。

Disposal of proceeds upon collection　（款项收妥后，请按照以下要求办理）

联系人：　　　　　　　　　　　　　　　电话：

　　　　　　　　　　　　　　　　　　　　　　　　　　　　申请人（盖章）

图 11.4　银行托收申请书（续）

要求：

根据跟单托收申请书中的单据要求及附页内容，缮制全套结汇单据。

一、托收的概念

　　托收是建立在商业信誉的基础上的、由出口方委托银行根据其要求通过进口地银行向进口方提示单据，收取货款的一种结算方式，即卖方在交货后，通过托收行向买方当地银行（代收行）托收单据，并指示代收行做付款交单（D/P）或承兑交单（D/A）。

　　D/P 和 D/A 都属于跟单托收。其中，D/P 有即期和远期之分，就是说买方必须在向卖方付款之后才能够获得提取货物的单据，这种交易方式使卖方能够及时地收到货款；D/A 是说只要买方在收到付款通知时向卖方作出一定付款的承诺就可以得到提取货物的有关单据，因此 D/A 取决于买方信用，存在很大的风险。况且，若买家不付款银行不承担任何责任，在实际贸易中较少采用。

　　其优点是：费用低廉，操作简单。

　　其缺点是：D/P 托收情况下，如果市场发生变化，或买方经营不善倒闭，那么进口商就有可能不要货了，出口商就有收不到货款的风险；D/A 托收情况下，除了 D/P 可能遇到的风险外，如果进口商在提货后于汇票到期时不付款，那么出口商就有款货两空的风险。因此，D/A 比 D/P 的风险要大得多。所以，托收适合于买卖双方有深厚的合作基础，不会出现不付款情形的情况。

二、托收的流程

1. D/P AT SIGHT

（1）买卖双方约定以 D/P AT SIGHT 结算。

（2）出口人发运货物取得货运单据。

（3）出口人向寄单银行（国内银行）提交托收申请、即期汇票及单据。

（4）寄单银行邮寄托收委托书及即期跟单汇票给代收银行（进口方银行）。

（5）代收银行提示即期跟单汇票要求进口人付款。

（6）进口人付清票款给代收银行。

（7）收银行提交货运单据给进口人。

（8）代收银行向寄单银行汇交收到的货款。

（9）寄单银行将所收货款划入出口方账户。

2. D/P AFTER SIGHT

（1）买卖双方约定以 D/P AFTER SIGHT 结算。

（2）出口人发运货物取得货运单据。

（3）出口人向寄单银行（国内银行）提交托收申请、远期汇票及单据。

（4）寄单银行邮寄托收委托书及远期跟单汇票给代收银行（进口方银行）。

（5）代收银行提示远期跟单汇票要求进口人承兑。

（6）进口人在远期汇票上做承兑。

（7）汇票到期代收银行向进口人做付款指示。

（8）进口人向代收银行付清货款。

（9）代收银行向进口人提交货运单据。

（10）代收银行向寄单银行汇交收到的货款。

（11）寄单银行将所收货款划入出口方账户。

3. D/A AFTER SIGHT

（1）买卖双方约定以 D/A AFTER SIGHT 结算。

（2）出口人发运货物取得货运单据。

（3）出口人向寄单银行（国内银行）提交托收申请、远期汇票及单据。

（4）寄单银行邮寄托收委托书及远期跟单汇票给代收银行（进口方银行）。

（5）代收银行提示远期跟单汇票要求进口人承兑。

（6）进口人在远期汇票上做承兑。

（7）代收银行向进口人提交货运单据，留存承兑汇票。

（8）汇票到期代收银行向进口人做付款指示。

（9）进口人向代收银行付清货款。

（10）代收银行向寄单银行汇交收到的货款。

（11）寄单银行将所收货款划入出口方账户。

参考答案

■ 课堂思考

（1）阅读"任务导航"项目，本次托收的全套结汇单据包括哪些？

（2）本次托收的全套结汇单据中为什么没有汇票？

参考答案

小 贴 士

跟单托收申请书样本如图 11.5 所示。

中国农业银行
AGRICULTURAL BANK OF CHINA

ABCS(2007)3021

跟 单 托 收 申 请 书
APPLICATION FOR DOCUMENTARY COLLECTION

Date 日期＿＿＿＿＿＿＿

To：Agricultural Bank of China Branch 致：中国农业银行股份有限公司行 We enclose the following draft(s)/documents as specified hereunder which please collect in accordance with the instructions indicated herein. 兹附上汇票和单据如下，谨请贵行依照本申请书的要求为我公司办理托收。 This collection is subject to URC 522. 此托收遵循国际商会第 522 号出版物《托收统一规则》。	Collecting Bank（Full name & address） 代收行（全称和地址）	
Drawee（Full name & address） 收款人（全称和地址）	Tenor（期限）	
	Draft/Inv.No. 汇票/发票号码	Currency and Amount 币种及金额

图 11.5　跟单托收申请书样本

Drawee（Full name & address） 付款人（全称和地址）											
DOCUMENTS 单据											
DR AFT	COM. INV.	PACKING LIST	B/L	N/N B/L	AWB.	ORIGIN CERT.	INS. POL.	INSP. CERT.	CERT	CABLE COPY		

Special Instructions（See box marked "×"）特殊条款（用 "×" 在方框中表明）：

☐ please deliver documents against ☐payment at sight /☐payment ＿＿after sight /☐acceptance.

　请办理☐即期付款交单/☐远期付款交单/☐承兑交单。

☐ All your charges are to be borne by ☐the drawee /☐us.

　你行所有费用由☐付款人/☐我司承担。

☐ In case of a time bill, please advise us of acceptance giving maturity date.

　如果托收包含远期汇票，请通知我公司承兑到期日。

☐ In case of dishonour, please do not protest but advise us of non-payment/non-acceptance giving reasons.

　如果发生拒付，无须拒绝证书但应该通知我公司拒绝付款或拒绝承兑的原因。

☐ Please instruct the Collecting Bank to deliver documents only upon receipt of all their banking charges.

　请指示代收行收妥全部银行费用后再提示单据。

☐ We will take on all the results caused by choosing the above bank as the collecting bank.

　请选择我司选定的代收行，由此引起的问题和其他后果由我司负责。

Disposal of proceeds upon collection（款项收妥后，请按照以下要求办理）

联系人：　　　　　　　　　　　电话：

申请人（盖章）

图 11.5　跟单托收申请书样本（续）

任务实施

　　　　顺德纺织品进出口公司出具的全套结汇单据（Commercial Invoice, Packing list & B/L），如图 11.6 所示。

SHUNDE TEXTILES IMP/EXT CORPORATION LTD OF GUANGDONG

ADD: 2,CHUANGYE ROAD, RONGGUI, SHUNDE, FOSHAN, GUANGDONG, CHINA

COMMERCIAL   INVOICE

To: Tunisia Trading Co.ltd   Date: May.20,2013

ADD: 342,NIX ROAD,MAAZOUN,TUNISIA

Invoice No. AF36226777108

Description of Goods:

MJ300 Sliding Table saw according to Proforma Invoice No. 87943210(K)

Shipping Marks	Description of Goods	Quantity(sets)	Unit price	Amount
TT1-20	MJ300 Sliding Table saw	20	USD2237.5	44750.00
Total		20		44750.00

SAY US DOLLARS FORTY FOUR THOUSAND SEVEN HUNDRED FIFTY ONLY.

(a)

SHUNDE TEXTILES IMP/EXT CORPORATION LTD OF GUANGDONG

ADD: 2,CHUANGYE ROAD, RONGGUI, SHUNDE, FOSHAN, GUANGDONG, CHINA

PACKING   LIST

TO: MS ×××

Add.:   Date: May 20,2013

Description of Goods: Invoice No. ×××

MJ300 Sliding Table Saw according to Proforma Invoice No. ×××:

Shipping Marks	Description of Goods	PKGS (Wooden Cases)	QTY (sets)	N.W (KGS)	G.W (KGS)	MEAS (CBM)
×××	MJ300 Sliding Table saw	40	20	15000.00	16000.00	63.20
Total		40	20	15000.00	16000.00	63.20

(b)

1. Shipper	SCAC MAEU	B/L No.866918959
SHUNDE TEXTILES IMP/EXP CORPORATION OF GUANGDONG 2,CHUANGYE ROAD, RONGGUI, SHUNDE, FOSHAN, GUANGDONG, CHINA		Booking No.866918959
2. Consignee **Tunisia Trading Co.ltd** **342,Nix Road, Maazoun, Tunisia**		**MAERSK LINE ORIGINAL**

图 11.6　结汇单据

3. Notify Party			Port-to-Port or Combined Transport

BILL OF LADING

RECEIVED in external apparent good order and condition except as other-Wise noted. The total number of packages or unites stuffed in the container, The description of the goods and the weights shown in this Bill of Lading are Furnished by the Merchants, and which the carrier has no reasonable means Of checking and is not a part of this Bill of Lading contract. The carrier has Issued the number of Bills of Lading stated below, all of this tenor and date, One of the original Bills of Lading must be surrendered and endorsed or sig-Ned against the delivery of the shipment and whereupon any other original Bills of Lading shall be void. The Merchants agree to be bound by the terms And conditions of this Bill of Lading as if each had personally signed this Bill of Lading.

SEE clause 4 on the back of this Bill of Lading (Terms continued on the back Hereof, please read carefully).

*Applicable Only When Document Used as a Combined Transport Bill of Lading.

4. Combined Transport * Pre - carriage by	5. Combined Transport* Place of Receipt
6. Ocean Vessel Voy. No. MAERSK EVORA 1304	7. Port of Loading NANSHA PORT, CHINA
8. Port of Discharge FSAX PORT,TUNISIA	9. Combined Transport * Place of Delivery

Marks & Nos. Container / Seal No.	No. of Containers or Packages	Description of Goods (If Dangerous Goods, See Clause 20)	Gross Weight Kgs	Measurement
TT1-40	40 Wooden cases	MJ300 Sliding Table saw	16000.00(KGS)	63.20CBM
		Description of Contents for Shipper's Use Only (Not part of This B/L Contract)		

10. Total Number of containers and/or packages (in words) FORTY   wooden cases only

Subject to Clause 7 Limitation

11. Freight & Charges	Revenue Tons	Rate	Per	Prepaid	Collect
				prepaid	
Declared Value Charge					

Ex. Rate:	Prepaid at NANSHA PORT, CHINA	Payable at	Place and date of issue May, 20,2013
	Total Prepaid USD 380.40	No. of Original B(s)/L THREE	Signed for the Carrier,

LADEN ON BOARD THE VESSEL

Date	May,20,2013	BY	MAERSK LINE

(c)

图 11.6 结汇单据（续）

任务再现

广东德庆某公司向印度出口了一批产品后，向中国农业银行德庆支行申请托收结汇。图 11.7 是跟单托收申请书。

试根据跟单托收申请书缮制全套结汇单据。

中国农业银行
AGRICULTURAL BANK OF CHINA

ABCS(2007)3021

跟 单 托 收 申 请 书
APPLICATION FOR DOCUMENTARY COLLECTION

Date 日期 2015-12-30

To: Agricultural Bank of China DEQING Branch 致：中国农业银行股份有限公司　德庆支行 We enclose the following draft(s)□documents as specified hereunder which please collect in accordance with the instructions indicated herein. 兹附上汇票和单据如下，谨请贵行依照本申请书的要求为我公司办理托收。 This collection is subject to URC 522. 此托收遵循国际商会第 522 号出版物《托收统一规则》。	Collecting Bank (Full name ＆ address) 代收行（全称和地址） India National bank, Dehli Branch 2, Saint Road, Dehli, India

Drawer (Full name ＆ address) 收款人（全称和地址） DEQING FOREST PRODUCTS IMP/EXP CO. LTD OF GUANGDONG 7,CHANGGAN ROAD, DECHENG TOWN,ZHAOQING,GUANGDONG, CHINA	Tenor（期限） 90 Days D/A From B/L Date	
Drawee(Full name ＆ address) 付款人（全称和地址） Dehli Forest Products, Ltd 57, Gandhi Road, Dehli, India	Draft/Inv. No. 汇票/发票号码 US15126	Currency and Amount 币种及金额 USD26647.50

DOCUMENTS 单据

DP AFT	COM. INV.	PACKING LIST	B/L	N/N B/L	AWB.	ORIGIN CERI	INS. POL.	INSP. CERT.	CERT	CABLE COPY		
	3/3	3/3	3/3	3			3/3+2	3/3				

图 11.7　跟单托收申请书

Special Instructions （See box marked "×"） 特殊条款（用"×"在方框中表明）：

×□ please deliver documents against □payment at sight /□payment ____ after sight /□acceptance.

  请办理□即期付款交单/□远期付款交单/□承兑交单。

□ All your charges are to be borne by □the drawee /□us.

  你行所有费用由□付款人/□我司承担。

□ In case of a time bill, please advise us of acceptance giving maturity date.

如果托收包含远期汇票，请通知我公司承兑到期日。

×□ In case of dishonour, please do not protest but advise us of non-payment □non-acceptance giving reasons.

如果发生拒付，无须拒绝证书但应该通知我公司拒绝付款或拒绝承兑的原因。

□ Please instruct the Collecting Bank to deliver documents only upon receipt of all their banking charges.

请指示代收行收妥全部银行费用后再提示单据。

□ We will take on all the results caused by choosing the above bank as the collecting bank.

  请选择我司选定的代收行，由此引起的问题和其他后果由我司负责。

参考答案

项目小结

Disposal of proceeds upon collection （款项收妥后，请按照以下要求办理）

联系人：   电话：

申请人（盖章）

图 11.7　跟单托收申请书（续）

任务三　缮制信用证项下全套议付单据

任务导航

　　顺德纺织品进出口有限公司向孟加拉国出口了一批货物后，向中国农业银行容桂支行提交了客户交单联系单。

　　要求：根据客户交单联系单（见图 11.8）和 107614010048 号信用证（见图 11.9）缮制全套结汇单据。

致：中国农业银行股份有限公司　容桂支　行

　　兹随附下列信用证项下出口单据一套，请按《跟单信用镇统一惯例》（2007 年修订版）国际商会第 600 号出版物和下属标识"×"的事项办理寄单索汇。

开证行： AL-ARAFAH ISLAMI BANK LTD CHITTAGONG BD					信用证号码： 107614010048				附信用证及其他修改共　页 信用证修改共　次					
通知行：渣打（上海）					汇票号码：				发票号码：						
通知行编号：333113911891-1					汇票金额：USD17579.00				发票金额：USD17579.00						
单据名称	汇票	商业发票	海运提单正本	海运提单副本	空运单	铁路运单	公路运单	保险单	装箱/重量单	数量/质量/重量证	检验/分析证	产地证	GSP FORM A	装船通知	受益人证明	电抄	船证
份数	代打	8	3	3					6			1/2		1	2		1×2

经我司审核，单据有下列不符点

□如单据有不符点。
□请联系我司改单。
□请向开证行直接寄单，我司承担一切责任。
□请向开证行寄单同时表提不符点，我司承担一切责任。
□请向开证行电提不符点，待开证行同意接受电提之不符点后，贵行再寄单。
①请代打汇票 ②在面函上打资信证明。

寄单方式	索汇方式
公司联系人　　　　　联系电话　　　　　公司盖章：广东省顺德纺织品进出口有限公司	

银行审单记录：	接单日期
	汇票/发票金额
	交单参考号
	寄单日期
	银行费用由承担
	经办：

单据处理记录：　　　　　　　　　复核：

如为可转让信用证，请贵司修改可转让信用证换单后产生的不符点，并于　年　月　日之前向我行重新交单（请贵司仔细阅读《信用证换单通知》的提示事项）

图 11.8　客户交单联系单

282

FORM OF DOCUMENTARY CREDIT

IRREVOCABLE

DOCUMENTARY CREDIT NUMBER

107614010048

DATE OF ISSUE

140116

APPLICABLE RULES

UCP LATEST VERSION

DATE AND PLACE OF EXPIRY

140410 CHINA

APPLICANT

M/S *** ENTERPRISE, *** KADER PLAZA,ANEX *** JUBILEE ROAD

NANDONKANON,CHITTAGONG, BANGLADESH

BENEFICIARY

SHUNDE TEXTILES IMPORT AND EXPORT COMPANY OF GUANGDONG

ADD; NO.2 CHUANGYE ROAD, RONGGUI, SHUNDE, FOSHAN, GUANGDONG, CHINA

CURRENCY CODE, AMOUNT: USD34854.00

AVAILABE WITH ANY BANK OF CHINA

BY NEGOTIATION OF DRAFT(S) AT SIGHT

DRAWEE

ALARBDDH076

AL-ARAFAH ISLAMI BANK LTD.CHITTAG0NG

PARTIAL SHIPMENTS ALLOWED

TRANSHIPMENT ALLOWED

PORT OF LOADING/AIRPORT OF DEPARTURE

ANY SEA PORT OF CHINA

PORT OF DISCHARGE/AIRPORT OF DESTINATION

CHITTAGONG SEA PORT,BANGLADESH

LATEST DATE OF SHIPMENT

140326

DESCRIPTION OF GOODS AND/OR SERVICES

***BRAND DISTRIBUTION BOX (EMBEDDED)

CFR CHITTAGONG SEA PORT, BANGLADESH. THE UNIT PRICE, QUANTITY, QUALITY, PACKING AND ALL OTHER SPECIFICATIONS OF THE GOODS MUST BE AS PER PROFORMA INVOIVE NO.******** DATED 25,12,2013 ISSUED BY THE BENEFICIARY MUST APPEAR   IN COMMERCIAL INVOICE.

DOCUMENTS REQUIRED

01.   DRAFT IN DUPLICATE DRAWN AT SIGHT ON OURSELVES.

02.   BENEFICIARY'S SIGNED INVOICE IN OCTUPLICATE IN ENGLISH CERTIFYING MERCHABDISE TO BE CHINA ORIGIN MENTIONING H.S. CODE NO.8538.90.00 IRC NO.BA-0166510 LCAF NO.37197 TIN NO.313-106-3421. VAT REGISTRATION NO.*********** AND BANK BIN NO.19011031524

03.   DETAILS PACKING LISTSIX FOLD

04.   FULL SET OF ORIGINAL PLUS 3 N/N COPIES OF CLEAN SHIPPED OB BOARD OCEAN BILL OF LADING DRAWN OR ENDORSED TO THE ORDER OF AL-ARAFAH ISLAMI BANK LIMITED,JUBILEE ROAD BRANCH, CGITTAGONG,

图 11.9 信用证

BANGLADESH SHOWING FREIGT PREPAID MARKED NOTIFY APPLICANT AND US.

CERTIFICATE OF ORIGIN ISSUED BY THE CHAMBER OF COMMERCE OF THE BENEFICIARY'S COUNTRY MUST ACCOMPANY THE SHIPPING DOCUMENTS.

05. INSURANCE COVERED BY THE OPENERS.BENEFICIARY MUST ADVISEDETAILS OF SHIPMENT(LC NUMBER,DATE OF SHIPMENT,QUANLITY,NAME AND VALUE THEREOF AND APPROXIMATE DATWE OF ARRIVAL AT CHITTAGONG PORT AND INVOICE VALUE PLUS 10 PCT TO REPUBLIC INSURANCE CO. LMITED FAX NO.880-031-2865624-5, APPLICANT AND US WITHIN THREE DAYS AFTER SHIPMENT REFERRING COVER NOTE NO.RICL/LDG/MC-0026/01-2014 DATED 16-01-2014. A COPY OF THIS ADVICE MUST ACCOMPANY THE ORIGINAL SHIPPING DOCUMENTS.

06. COUNTRY OF ORIGIN INCLUDING DETAILS OF MERCHANDISE MUST BE PRINTED IN ENGLISH ON EACH AND EVERY PACKAGE/BUNDLE/CARTON. A CERTIFICATE TO THIS EFFECT MUST ACCOMPANY THE ORIGINAL SHIPPING DOCUMENTS.

07. APPLICANT NAME AND ADDRESS, BIN NUMBER MUST EITHER BE PRINTED OR WRITTEN IN UNREMOVEABLE INK MINIMUN 2 PERCENT SPACE OF THE CARTON OR OTHER BIGGEST CARTON OF THE SHIPMENT. A CERTIFICATE IN THIS REGARD MUST ACCOMPANY THE ORIGINAL SHIPPING DOCUMENTS.

08. A SATISFACTORY CREDIT REPORT OF THE BENEFICIARY FROM HIS BANK ON THE BANK PAD DULY SIGNED BY BANK'S OFFICIALS MUST ACCOMPANY THE ORIGINAL SHIPPING DOCUMENTS.

09. SHIPMENT/TRANSHIPMENT OF GOODS BY ISRAELI, SERBIAN AND MONTENEGRO FPAGE VESSEL/CARIER PROHIBITED. A CERTIFICATE IN THIS REGARD ISSUED BY CARRIER/ITS AGENT MUST BE INCORPORATED IN THE ORIGINAL SHIPPING DOCUMENTS.

ADDITIONAL CONDITIONS:

1. BANK BIN NO.,VAT REGISTRATION NO.,LC NO. AND DATE MUST BE QUOTED ON AL SHIPPING DOCUMENTS.

2. NO DOCUMENTS SHOULD BE EARLIER DATED THAN THE DATE OF THIS LC.

3. CHARTER PARTY/STALE/SHORT FORM/BLANK BACKED/CLAUSED/THOROUGH BILL OF LADING NOT ACCEPTABLE.

4. BROSS AND NET WEIGHT OF GOODS MUST BE MENTIONED IN INVOICES,PACKING LIST AND BILL OF LADING

5. NAME OF LOCAL SHIPPING AGENT WITH DETAIL ADDRESS, TELEPHONE/FAX NUMBER AND NAME OF CONTACTING PERSON MUST BE MENTIONED IN BILL OF LADING.

6. GOODS MUST BE PACKED IN XPORT STANDARD SEA-WORTHY PACKING TO AVOID DAMAGE/PILFERAGE DURING THE TRANSIT, WHICH MUST BE CERTIFIED BY THE BENEFICIARY IN THE INVOICE AND THE PACKING LIST.

7. AN AMOUNT OF USD 75.00 WILL BE DEDUCTED FROM BILL AMOUNT FOR EACH SET OF DISCREPANT DOCUMENT.

8. CABLE/HANDLING CHARGES OF USD 60.00 WILL BE DEDUCTED FROM BILL AMOUNT AT THE TIME OF PAYMENT.

9. SHIPMENT MUST BE EFFECTED BY 2X40 FEET HQ CONTAINER.

10. SHIPPING MARK:******

11. ALL DOCUMENTS MUST BE PRESENTED IN ENGLISH LANGUAGE CHARGES

ALL CHARGES OUTSIDE BANGLADESH INCLUDING RE-IMBURSEMENT CHARGE ARE ON BENEFICIARY ACCOUNT.

PERIOD FOR PRESENTATION

15 DAYS FROM THE DATE OF SHIPMENT BUT NOT LATER THAN THE CREDIT VALIDITY.

CONFIRMATION INSTRUCTIONS

WITHOUT

INSTRUCTIONS TO THE PAYING/ACCEPTING/NEGOTIATING BANK

图 11.9　信用证（续）

01. UPON RECEIPT OF THE COMPLYING PRESENTATION OF ORIGINAL SHIPPING DOCUMENTS, WE SHALL REMIT THE PROCEEDS AS PER INSTRUCTION.

02. DOCUMENTS WITH DISCREPANCY MUST NOT BE NEGOTIATED EVEN AGAINST GUARANTEE OR UNDER RESERVE WITHOUT PRIOR APPROVAL.

03. ORIGINAL SHIPPING DOCUMENTS TO BE SENT UNDER THE FOLLOWING ADDRESS:AL-ARAFAH ISLAMI

BANK LIMITED,JUBILEE ROAD BRANCH, CHITTAGONG,

BANGLADESH,PHONE:880-31-637681,FAX:637680

04. ON THE DATE OF NEGOTIATION,THE NEGOTIATING BANK SHALL SEND A FAX (NUMBER: 880-031-2868497/SWIFT(ALARBDDH076) TO THE LC OPENING BANK ADVISING THE VALUE OF DOCUMENT NEGOTIATED.

ADVISED THROUGH

BANK OF CHINA (FOSHAN BRANCH), FOSHAN

SENDER TO RECEIVER INFORMATION

THIS IS SUBJECT TO UCPDC-600(REV.-2007)

图 11.9 信用证（续）

知识准备

在信用证模式下的出口结汇业务中，银行是中间人，它的义务是保证理论上/形式上实现"一手交钱，一手交货"。一方面，信用证开证行要拿到出口方提交的交货凭证（全套单据，等于货物），另一方面，信用证开证行还要拿到货物进口方的货款。银行赚取的主要是手续费等费用。

参考答案

信用证业务中的各方关系人、各自的责任以及业务操作流程，在本书的项目二中有详述，在此不再重复。

课堂思考

出口用的集装箱的种类有哪些？

小 贴 士

（1）常见的标准集装箱：①20 英尺集装箱，简称 20 尺集装箱（20GP）；②40 英尺集装箱，简称40 尺集装箱（40GP）；③40 英尺加高集装箱（40HQ）；④40 尺可折叠平台用集装箱；⑤45 尺加高集装箱。

（2）特种集装箱。如果货物要求装特种集装箱，一般在订舱时要向船公司预订，因为船公司不可能在每一港口都配有这种特种箱。特种集装箱有以下几种：开顶集装箱（open top container）、通风集装箱（ventilated container）、台式集装箱（platform-based container）、平台式集装箱（plat-form container）、冷藏集装箱（reefer container）、罐式集装箱（tank container）、汽车集装箱（car container）、动物集装箱（pen container or live stock container）、服装集装箱（garment container）、散货集装箱（solid bulk container）、20英尺加重集装箱（heavy container）。

小 贴 士

客户交单联系单样本如图 11.10 所示。

客 户 交 单 联 系 单

致：中国农业银行股份有限公司

　　兹随附下列信用证项下出口单据一套，请按《跟单信用证统一惯例》（2007年修订版）国际商会第 600 号出版物和下属标识"×"的事项办理寄单索汇。

开证行：						信用证号码：					附信用证及其他修改共　　页 信用证修改共　　次			
通知行：						汇票号码：					发票号码：			
通知行编号：						汇票金额：					发票金额：			
单据名称	汇票	商业发票	海运提单正本	空运单	铁路运单	公路运单	保险单	装箱/重量单	数量/质量/重量证	检验/分析证	产地证	GSP FORMA	装船通知	受益人证明	电抄
分数														

经我司审核，单据有下列不符点：	我司审核，单据有下列不符点： □ 如单据有符点 □ 请联系我司改单 □ 请向开证直接寄单，我司承担一切责任 □ 请向开证行寄单同时表提不符点，我司承担一切责任 □ 请向开证行电提不符点，持开证行同意接受电提之不　　符点后，贵行再寄单
寄单方式：□特快专递　　□航空挂号	索汇方式：□电索　　□信索（□特快专递/□航空挂号）
公司联系人：　　　　联系电话：	公司盖章：

银行审单记录：	接单日期：
	汇票/发票金额：
	交单参考号：
银行审单记录：	寄单日期：
	银行费用： 由　　　　　　　　承担
	经办：
单据处理记录：	复核：

如为可转让信用证，请贵司修改转让信用证换单后产生的不符点，并于　　年　　月　　日之前向我行重新交单。（请贵司仔细阅读《信用证换单通知书》的提示事项）。

图 11.10　信用证项下的出口单据

参考答案

■ 课堂思考

审读 107614010048 号信用证（图 11.9），其中要求受益人提供哪几种证明？

任务实施

顺德纺织品进出口公司缮制的 107614010048 号信用证项下的全套结汇单据有发票、提单、装箱单、原产地证书、装船通知书副本、受益人证明三种），如图 11.11～图 11.18 所示。

SHUNDE TEXTILES IMP/EXT CORPORATION LTD OF GUANGDONG

ADD: 2,CHUANGYE ROAD, RONGGUI, SHUNDE, FOSHAN, GUANGDONG, CHINA

COMMERCIAL   INVOICE

TO: MS ABC ENTERPRISE

43,KADER PLAZA ,ANEX EAST F-14

JUBILER ROAD, NANDONKANON

CHITTAGONG, BANGLADESH

Date: Mar.25,2014

Invoice No. ××××

Shipping Marks: ××××

Description of Goods:

MJ300 Brand Distribution Box (Embedded)

CFR Chittagong Sea Port, Bangladesh. All other specifications of   the goods are as per Proforma Invoice No. ××× issued by the beneficiary.

Description of Goods	Quantity	G.W. of Goods（KGS）	N.W.of Goods(KGS)	Unit Price	Amount
Distribution Box (embedded)					
JB-4-6A 4-6 Units	3000pcs	2952.00	USD 2595.00	1.35/pc	USD4050.00
JB-7-9A 7-9 Units	4300pcs	5117.00	USD 4687.00	1.53/pc	USD6579.00
JB-10-13A 10-13 Units	2500pcs	3917.00	USD 3425.00	1.90/pc	USD4750.00
JB-14-16 14-16 Units	1000pcs	1784.00	USD 1580.00	2.20/pc	USD2200.00
H.s. Code No.8538.90.00					
TOTAL	10800PCS	13770.00	12287.00		17579.00

SAY US DOLLARS SEVENTEEN THOUSAND FIVE HUNDRED SEVENTY NINE ONLY.

We are certifying that merchandise to be China origin:

H.S Code No.8538.90.00   IRC No.BA-0166510   LCFA No. 37195

TIN No. ××× VAT Registration No. ×××   Bank BIN No.19011631524.

L/C No.107614010048 dated 140116

We as beneficiary hereby certifying that goods are packed in export standard sea-worthy packing to avoid damage/pilferage during the transit.

图 11.11   发票

1. Shipper (Name, Address and Phone)			B/L No. SZUE1403416			
SHUNDE TEXTILES IMP/EXT CORPORATION LTD OF GUANGDONG 　ADD: 2,CHUANGYE ROAD, RONGGUI, SHUNDE, FOSHAN, GUANGDONG, CHINA			**COSCO** **ORIGINAL**			
2. Consignee(Name, Address and Phone)						
To the order of AL-ARAFAH ISLAMI BANK LTD JUBILER ROAD BRANCH, CHITTAGONG, BANGLADESH BIN NO.19011031524			**BILL OF LADING** RECEIVED in external apparent good order and condition except as other-Wise noted. The total number of packages or unites stuffed in the container, The description of the goods and the weights shown in this Bill of Lading are. Furnished by the Merchants, and which the carrier has no reasonable means Of checking and is not a part of this Bill of Lading contract. The carrier has Issued the number of Bills of Lading stated below, all of this tenor and date, One of the original Bills of Lading must be surrendered and endorsed or signed against the delivery of the shipment and whereupon any other original Bills of Lading shall be void. The Merchants agree to be bound by the terms and conditions of this Bill of Lading as if each had personally signed this Bill of Lading. SEE clause 4 on the back of this Bill of Lading (Terms continued on the back Hereof, please read carefully).* Applicable Only When Document Used as a Combined Transport Bill of Lading.			
3. Notify Party (Name, Address and Phone)						
ABC ENTERPRISE　　　43,KADER PLAZA ,ANEX EAST F-14 JUBILER ROAD, NANDONKANON CHITTAGONG, BANGLADESH VAT Register No.24040-118-2380 AND AL-ARAFAH ISLAMI BANK LTD JUBILER ROAD BRANCH, CHITTAGONG, BANGLADESH						
4. Combined Transport *		5. Combined Transport*				
Pre - carriage by		Place of Receipt	LELIU SEA PORT OF CHINA			
6. Ocean Vessel Voy. No.		7. Port of Loading				
COSCO VIETNAM 010W		NANSHA SEA PORT OF CHINA				
8. Port of Discharge		9. Combined Transport *				
CHITTAGONG SEA PORT,BANGLADESH		Place of Delivery	CHITTAGONG SEA PORT,BANGLADESH			
Marks & Nos. Container / Seal No.	No. of Containers or Packages	Description of Goods (If Dangerous Goods, See Clause 20)		Gross Weight Kgs	Measurement	
CONTAINER/SEAL No:CBHU9037933/40HQ/ Q22052/1080 CARTONS/13770.500KGS 68.5110CBM	1X40HQ Container 1080 Cartons	MJ300 Brand Distribution Box(Embedded)		13770.50KGS	68.5110CBM	
		Description of Contents for Shipper's Use Only (Not part of This B/L Contract)				
10. Total Number of containers and/or packages (in words)　SAY ONE 1X40HQ CONTAINER ONLY						
Subject to Clause 7 Limitation						
11. Freight & Charges	Revenue Tons		Rate	Per	Prepaid	Collect
					prepaid	
Declared Value Charge						
Ex. Rate:	Prepaid at	Payable at		Place and date of issue		
	NANSHA			Mar. 26,2014		
	Total Prepaid	No. of Original B(s)/L		Signed for the Carrier, as agent		
	USD 530.40	THREE		TRANSNATIONAL FREIGHT SERVICES,INC		
LADEN ON BOARD THE VESSEL						
DATE　Mar. 26.2014		BY	COSCO CONTAINER LINES			

图 11.12　提单

SHUNDE TEXTILES IMP/EXT CORPORATION LTD OF GUANGDONG,

ADD: 2,CHUANGYE ROAD, RONGGUI, SHUNDE, FOSHAN, GUANGDONG, CHINA

DETAILS PACKING LIST

TO: MS ABC ENTERPRISE

43,KADER PLAZA ,ANEX EAST F-14

JUBILER ROAD, NANDONKANON

CHITTAGONG, BANGLADESH

Date: Mar.25,2014

Invoice No. ×××

Shipping Marks: ×××

Description of Goods:

MJ300 Brand Distribution Box (Embedded).

The Unit price, Quantity, Quality.Packing and All other specifications of the goods are as per Proforma Invoice No. ××× dated 25,12,2013 issued by the beneficiary.

Description of Goods	QNTY	PCS/ CTN	CTNS	N.W. /CTN (KGS)	N.W.of Goods (KGS)	G.W. /CTN (KGS)	G.W. of Goods （KGS）	VOL. (CBM /CTN)	TTL MEAS (CBM)	CONTAINER NO.
Distribution Box (embedded)										
JB-4-6A 4-6 Units	3000pcs	10	300	8.65	2595.00	9.84	2952.00	0.04898	14.6940	CBHU903793
JB-7-9A 7-9 Units	4300pcs	10	430	10.90	4687.00	11.90	5117.00	0.06041	25.9760	3/40HQ
JB-10-13A 10-13 Units										
JB-14-16 14-16 Units	2500pcs	10	250	13.70	3425.00	15.67	3917.00	0.07578	18.9450	
H.s. Code No.8538.90.00										
	1000pcs	10	100	15.80	1580.00	17.84	1784.00	0.08896	8.8960	
Total	10800 pcs		1080		12287		13770.5		68.511	

We as beneficiary hereby certify that goods are packed in export standard sea-worthy packing to avoid damage/pilferage during the transit.

Bank BIN No.19011631524   VAT Registration No. ×××   L/C No.107614010048 dated 140116

图 11.13　装箱单

ORIGINAL

1. Exporter: SHUNDE TEXTILES IMP/EXP CORPORATION LTD OF GUANGDONG ADD: 2, CHUANGYE ROAD, RONGGUI,SHUNDE,FOSHAN,GUANGDONG, CHINA	Certificate No. CCPIT1255109999
2. Consignee: TO THE ORDER OF AL-ARAFAH ISLAMI BANK LTD JUBILER ROAD BRANCH, CHITTAGONG, BANGLADESH	1404406A0004/00362# Certificate of Origin Of The People's Republic of China

图 11.14　原产地证书

3. Means of Transportation and Route: ON/AFTER MAR. 26,2014 FROM LELIU SEA PORT OF CHINA TO NANSHA SEA PORT OF CHINA BY SEA. THENCE, TRANSHIPPED TO CHITTAGONG,BANGLADESH BY SEA.		5.For Authority use Only **China Council for the Promotion of International Trade is China Chamber Of International Commerce.**		
4. Country/region of destination: BANGLADESH				
6.Marks and Numbers	7.Number & Kind of Packages; Description of Goods	8.H.S.Code	9.Quantity	10.Number and date of Invoice
No Marks	Total: One Thousand and Eighty (1080) Cartons Only Distribution Box(embedded) BANK BIN No.19011031524 VAT Registration No. ××× L/C No.107614010048 Dated 140116	8538.90.00	10800pcs	××× Mar.25,2014

11.Declaration By the Exporter:
   The undersigned hereby declare that the above details and statements are correct, that   all the goods were produced in China and that they comply with the Rules of Origin of the People's Republic of China.
 	
   Shunde   China   Mar.25,2014
		12.Certification:
		
		It is hereby certified that the declaration by the exporter is correct.
		
		   Shunde China Mar.25,2014		

图 11.14   原产地证书（续）

SHUNDE TEXTILES IMP/EXP CORPORATION LTD OF GUANGDONG
ADD: 2, CHUANGYE ROAD, RONGGUI, SHUNDE,   FOSHAN, GUANGDONG, CHINA

COPY OF ADVICE   DATE: Mar. 27, 2014
TO: REPUBLIC INSURANCE, LIMITED
FAX NO.: 880-031-2865624-5
And MS ABC Enterprise, 43, KADER PLAZA , ANEX EAST F-14
JUBILER ROAD, NANDONKANON   CHITTAGONG, BANGLADESH
And AL-ARAFAH ISLAMI BANK LTD JUBILER ROAD BRANCH, CHITTAGONG, BANGLADESH

COVER NOTE No.: RICI/LDG/MC-0026/01/2014 Dated 16,01,2014

We as beneficiary hereby advise details of shipment as follows:
Invoice No.: ×××
Bank BIN No.: 19011031524 VAT Registration No.×××
L/C No.:107614010048 dated 140116
Date of shipment: Mar.26, 2014
Quantity: 10800pcs
Name of the Vessel with Voyage No.: COSCO Vietnam V.010W
B/L No.: SZUE1403416
Quantity shipped:10800 pcs
Value thereof: USD17579.00
Approximate Date of Arrival at Chittagong port: Apr. 12, 2014
Invoice value plus 10 pct is USD19336.90

图 11.15   装船通知书副本

SHUNDE TEXTILES IMP/EXP CORPORATION LTD OF GUANGDONG,

ADD: 2, CHUANGYE ROAD, RONGGUI, SHUNDE, FOSHAN, GUANGDONG, CHINA

CERTIFICATE

TO WHOM IT MAY CONCERN   Date: Mar. 26,2014

BANK BIN NO.: 19011031524 VAT Registration No.: ×××
L/C No.: 107614010048 dated 140116

We hereby certify to this effect that country of origin including details of merchandise have been printed in English on each and every package/bundle/carton.

图 11.16 受益人证明（一）

SHUNDE TEXTILES IMP/EXP CORPORATION LTD OF GUANGDONG

ADD: 2, CHUANGYE ROAD, RONGGUI, SHUNDE, FOSHAN, GUANGDONG, CHINA

CERTIFICATE

TO WHOM IT MAY CONCERN   Date: Mar. 26,2014

We hereby certify in this regard that Applicant name & address, TIN number have either been printed or written in unmovable ink minimum 2 pct space of the carton or other biggest carton of the shipment.

图 11.17 受益人证明（二）

TRANSNATIONAL FREIGHT SERVICES, INC

CERTIFICATE

Date: Mar. 26, 2014
BILL OF LADING NUMBER: SZUE1403416

We hereby certify in this regard that shipment/transshipment of goods by Israeli, Serbian, and Montenegro flags vessel/carrier prohibited.

BANK BIN No.: 19011031524
VAT Registration No. ×××
L/C No.: 107614010048 dated 140116

For and on behalf of
TRANSNATIONAL FREIGHT SERVICES, INC

As agent for the carrier:
COSCO CONTAINER LINES, CO. LTD

图 11.18 受益人证明（三）

任务再现

顺德纺织品进出口公司向西班牙某公司（L/C 里的 APPLICANT、单据中被涂掉的某些地方）出口了一批打蛋器（light beater）。根据信用证通知书、相关信用证和信用证修改书（见图 11.19～图 11.21），缮制全套结汇单据。

中国银行
BANK OF CHINA SHUNDE BRANCH

信用证通知书

致：SHUNDE TEXTILES IMP/EXP CORPORATION LTD OF GUANGDONG

通知编号：AD××××××

日期：2013-04-26

迳启者：

我行收到如下信用证一份：

开证行：BANCO SANTANDER S.A. MADRID

开证日： 2013-04-26

信用证号： 107614010048

金额：USD17052.00

现随附通知。贵司交单时，请将本通知及正本信用证一并提示。其他注意事项如下：

本信用证之通知 系遵循国际商会《跟单信用证统一惯例》第 600 号出版物。

如有任何问题及疑虑，请与中国银行股份有限公司联络。

电话：   传真：

附言：   签章：中国银行股份有限公司

顺德容桂支行

图 11.19 信用证通知书

SEND BANK: BSCHHKHHXXX

BANCO SANTANDER, S.A. HONGKONG BRANCH

RECEIVE BANK BKCHCNBJ44A

BANK OF CHINA FOSHAN BRANCH

FORM OF DOCUMENTARY CREDIT IRREVOCABLE

WITHOUT OUR CONFIRMATION

DOCUMENTARY CREDIT NUMBER 5494BTY201677

DATE OF ISSUE 130426

APPLICABLE RULES UCP LATEST VERSION

DATE AND PLACE OF EXPIRY 130515 SPAIN

ISSUING BANK BSCHESMM×××

APPLICANT ×××

BENEFICIARY SHUNDE TEXTILES IMP&EXP COMPANY OF GUANGDONG

　　　　　　NO 2 CHUANGYE ROAD RONGGUI SHUNDE GUANGDONG CHINA

CURRENCY CODE AMOUNT USD17052,00

MAXIMUM CREDIT AMOUNT NOT EXCEEDING

AVAILABLE WITH BY

　　　　　　BSCHESMM×××

　　　　　　BY DEF PAYMENT

DEFERRED PAYMENT DETAILS 90 DAYS AFTER DOCUMENTS APPROVAL PAYMENT WILL BE EFFECTED THE FOLLOWING 10 OR 20 PARTIAL SHIPMENTS ARE PROHIBITED TRANSHIPMENTS ARE ALLOWED.

PORT OF LOADING: SHUNDE PORT, CHINA

PORT OF DISCHARGE: ANY PORT IN BRAZIL

LATEST DATE OF SHIPMENT: 130430

DESCRIPTION OF GOODS OR SERVICES: LIGHT BEATER, 70 000 PCS UNIT PRICE 0.2436

TOTAL AMOUNT: USD17 052.00

AS PER ORDER No.×××

DELIVERY TERMS FOB SHUNDE PORT CHINA

DOCUMENTS REQUIRED

1. ORIGINAL SEALED AND STAMPED COMMERCIAL INVOICE ISSUED TO NAME OF APLICANT IN 2 ORIGINALS AND 3 COPIES. INVOICE MUST STATE THE ORIGIN COUNTRY OF THE GOODS.

2. ORIGINAL PACKING LIST IN 2 ORIGINALS AND 3 COPIES（THE PACKING LIST MUST DESCRIBE ALL THE PRODUCTS WHICH WILL BE LOADED—IT MUST BE DETAILED）.

3. FULL SET OF CLEAN ON BOARD BILL OF LADING SHOWING SHIPPER ×××（BENEFICIARY NAME IS ALSO

图 11.20　信用证

ACCEPTABLE AS SHIPPER）.CONSIGNEE TO: XXX AND NOTIFY TO: ×××.

A) UNIT PRICE, TOTAL AMOUNT, OR ANY VALUE OF THE GOODS CAN'T BE SHOWN ON BL. ON DESCRIPTION OF GOODS, BENEFICIARY IS NOT ALLOWED TO STATE "FREE OF CHARGE", OR FOC. IF IT IS STATED, A PENALTY OF USD100.00 WILL BE DEDUCTED FROM LC PAYMENT.

B) BL MUST STATE THE MONEY CODE.

C) IF SHIPMENT DOESN'T INCLUDE ANY SPARE PARTS, IT'S NOT ALLOWED THE BL STATES THE WORD "SPARE PARTS" MARKED FREIGHT COLLECT.

4. ONE ORIGINAL QUALITY CONTROL REPORT WITH THE HEADLINE "MALLORY, MARKED ACCEPTED FOR EACH TYPE OF GOODS DESCRIBED IN THIS DOCUMENTARY CREDIT. THIS QUALITY CONTROL IS NOT NECESSARY FOR THE FOC SPARE PARTS, FOC GIFT BOXES AND FOC MASTER CARTONS. THIS DOCUMENT MUST BE SIGNED AND STAMPED BY MALLORY AND MANUFACTURER. IF PENALTY SECTION IS MARKED: 200.00 USD MUST BE DEDUCTED FROM LC PAYMENY, AND A PENALTY OF 1 000.00 USD MUST BE DEDUCTED FROM LC PAYMENT WITHOUT THE PRESENTATION OF THIS DOCUMENT.

5. COPY OF SHIPMENT ADVICE FAXED OR E-MAILED, SPECIFYING:ORDER NUMBER, SHIPMENT DATE, ARRIVAL DATE, QUALTITY, DESCRIPTION OF GOODS,AND VESSEL NAME. THIS DOCUMENT MUST BE SIGNED AND STAMPED BY ×××× VIA FAX OR E-MAIL AS SUPPORTING DOCUMENT.

ADDITIONAL CONDITIONS:

+ A DISCREPANCY FEE OF USD140.00 WILL BE DEDUCTED FROM THE PROCEEDS ON EACH SET OF DOCUMENTS PRESENTED WITH DISCREPANCIES.

+ ORDER NUMBER MUST BE WRITTEN IN ALL DOCUMENTS REQUIRED.

+ THIRD PARTY DOCUMENTS ACCEPTABLE.

+ IF SPARE PARTS ARE INCLUDED IN THE SHIPMENTS,FULL DESCRIPTION AND QUANTITIES MUST BE DETAILED IN COMMERCIAL INVOICE AND PACKING LIST.

+ PAYMENT DOCUMENTS RECEIVED IN GOOD ORDER. PAYMENT DATE WILL BE CALCULATED AFTER THE DATE APPLICANT'S BANK RECEIVED THE DOCUMENTS AND THE FOLLOWING 10TH OR 20TH OF THE MONTH.

+ PAYMENT DOCUMENTS WITH SOME DISCREPANCIES: THE MATURITY FOR PAYMENT WILL BE CALCULATED AFTER THE DATE WHEN THE DISCREPANCIES HAVE BEEN LIFTED BY APPLICANT AND THE FOLLOWING 10TH OR 2OTH OF THE MONTH.

+ SHOULD THE BENEFICIARY FAIL TO DELIVER THE DOCUMENTS IN THE ABOVE SPECIFIED DELAY, A PENALTY FEE OF USD200.00 WILL BE DEDUCTED WITHOUT PRIOR APPROVAL OF NEGOTIATING BANK.

+ SANTANDER S.A. HONGKONG BRANCH IS PLEASED TO OFFER THE DISCOUNT OF EXPORT BILLS UNDER THIS LC UPON ACCEPTANCE BY THE ISSUING BANK. PLEASE REQUEST YOUR BANK TO INDICATE. CLEARLY THE DISCOUNTING INSTRUCTIONS IN THE COLLECTION ORDER SENT TOGETHER WITH THE EXPORT BILLS. IN CASE YOU NEED FURTHER CLARIFICATION YOU CAN CONTACT MS SYLINA WONG AT:+852 2101 2184

图 11.20　信用证（续）

+ ALL BANK COMMISSIONS AND CHARGES OUTSIDE SPAIN ARE FOR THE BENEFICIARY ACCOUNT.

+ PERIOD FOR PRESENTATION: DOCUMENTS MUST BE PRESENTED WITHIN 15 DAYS AFTER SHIPMENT DATE AND WITHIN VALIDITY TERMS OF THIS DOCUMENTARY CREDIT.

+ CONFIRMATION INSTRUCTIONS: WITHOUT.

+ INSTRUCTIONS TO THE PAYING/ACCEPTING /NEGOTIATING BANK: BANCO SANTANER S.A. HONGKONG HOLDS SPECIAL REIMBURSEMENT INSTRUCTIONS.

PRESENTING BANK WILL BE FULLY RESPONSIBLE FOR THE CONSEQUENCES OF SENDING DOCUMENTS TO THE WRONG ADDRESS.

OUR ADVISING COMMISSION USD50.00 WILL BE DEDUCTED FROM THE PROCEEDS OF THE DRAWING OF THE LC.ALL DOCS DRAWN UNDER THIS LC MUST BE PRESENTED TO US THROUGH THEM AT: BANCO SANTANER S.A. HONGKONG,ROOM 1501,ONE EXCHANGE SQUARE, 8 CONNAUGHT PLACE, CENTRAL, HK BY COURTIER SERVICES.

图 11.20　信用证（续）

SEND BANK: BSCHHKHH×××

BANCO SANTANDER, S.A. HONGKONG　BRANCH

RECEIVE BANK：BKCHCNBJ44A

BANK OF CHINA FOSHAN BRANCH

SENDER'S REFERENCE: ×××

RECEIVER'S REFERENCE: NONREF

ISSUING BANK'S REFERENCE: ×××

ISSUING BANK: HSCHESMM×××

DATE OF ISSUE: 130426

DATE OF AMENDMENT: 130430

NUMBER OF AMENDMENT:

01

BENEFICIARY (BEFORE THIS AMENDMENT)

SHUNDE TEXTILES IMP. AND EXP. COMPANY OF GUANGDONG

NO.2 CHUANGYE ROAD, RONGGUI, SHUNDE

FOSHAN, GUANGDONG ,CHINA

02

NEW DATE OF EXPIRY: 130525

LATEST DATE OF SHIPMENT: 130510

ALL OTHER TERMS AND CONDITIONS REMAIN UNCHANGED.

参考答案

图 11.21　信用证修改书

项目小结

在线测试及
参考答案

参考答案

技能强化训练

技 能 提 高

1. 在实际业务的操作中，在跟单托收和信用证结汇两种方式下，结汇单据中都出现了没有汇票的情况，为什么？

2. 肇庆土产进出口公司向以色列的 TOSAF COMPOUNDS LTD 出口了一批黑色色母（BLACK MASTERBATCH CARBON）后，根据对方开来的信用证制单结汇。图 11.22 和图 11.23 是有关的信用证通知书和电开的信用证。试按信用证中有关单据的条款，缮制全套结汇单据。

信用证通知书 ORIGINAL

致： ZHAOQING NATIVE PRODUCE IMPORT AND EXPORT COMPANY LTD. OF GUANGDONG

通知编号： AD33805150000189

日期： 2015-09-08

送启者：

我行收到如下信用证一份：

开证行： BANK HAPOALIM B.M. TEL-AVIV

开证日： 2015-09-08

信用证号： 167-01-001508-3

金额： USD 105,000.00

现随通知。贵司交单时，请将本通知书及正本信用证一并提示。其他注意事项如下：

本信用证之通知系遵循国际商会《跟单信用证统一惯例》第600号出版物。

如有任何问题及疑虑，请与中国银行股份有限公司联络。

电话： 传真 .

附言：

图 11.22 信用证通知书

```
Eximbills Enterpriste Incoming Swift
===================================================================
Message Type:MT700
Send Bank:POALILITXXX
BANK HAPOALIM B.M. TEL-AVIV

Recv Bank:BKCHCNBJ43A
BANK OF CHINA ZHAOQING (ZHAOQING BRANCH)

User Name:gd156019
Print Times:2
Print Date:2015-09-09 MIR:150908POALILITAXXX2953083522
===================================================================

:27:[Sequence of Total]
1/1
:40A:[Form of Documentary Credit]
IRREVOCABLE
:20:[Documentary Credit Number]
167-01-001508-3
:31C:[Date of Issue]
150908
:40E:[Applicable Rules]
UCPURR LATEST VERSION
:31D:[Date and Place of Expiry]
151031 CHINA
:50:[Applicant]
TOSAF COMPOUNDS LTD.
INDUSTRIAL ZONE ALON TAVOR
AFULA 18126
ISRAEL
:59:[Beneficiary]
/643157736640
ZHAOQING NATIVE PRODUCE IMPORT AND
EXPORT COMPANY LIMITED OF GUANGDONG
18 JIANG BIN RD WEST GUANGDONG
ZHAOQING CHINA
:32B:[Currency Code, Amount]
USD105000,
:39A:[Percentage Credit Amount Tolerance]
5/5
:41A:[Available With...By...]
BKCHCNBJ43A
BY PAYMENT
:43P:[Partial Shipments]
PROHIBITED
:43T:[Transshipment]
ALLOWED
:44E:[Port of Loading/Airport of Departure]
ANY PORT IN CHINA
:44F:[Port of Discharge/Airport of Destination]
HAIFA PORT
:44C:[Latest Date of Shipment]
151010
:45A:[Description of Goods and/or Services]
+/- 5 PCT. 100,000 KGS OF BLACK MASTERBATCH CARBON
AS PER PO 15MO2716 AND PROFORMA INVOICE NO.
20150902
TERMS:CIF HAIFA PORT ,INCOTERMS 2010
:46A:[Documents Required]
+ ORIGINAL COMMERCIAL INVOICE HAND SIGNED BY THE BENEFICIARY IN 4
COPY(IES) CERTIFYING THAT GOODS ARE OF CHINA ORIGIN
+ 3 / 3 ORIGINAL PLUS 3 NON NEGOTIABLE COPIES OF CLEAN 'SHIPPED
```

图 11.23　信用证

ON BOARD' MARINE BILLS OF LADING MADE OUT TO THE ORDER OF BANK
HAPOALIM B.M. NOTIFY: APPLICANT, MARKED: FREIGHT PREPAID,
SPECIFYING THE FOLLOWING ARABIAN UNLOADING CLAUSE: IN VIEW OF THE
DANGER OF CONFISCATION, WARRANTED VESSEL NOT TO CALL AT PORTS AND
NOT TO ENTER THE TERRITORIAL WATERS OF ANY ARAB COUNTRIES
BELLIGERENT TO THE STATE OF ISRAEL AND/OR ACTIVELY SUPPORTING THE
ARAB BOYCOTT, PRIOR TO UNLOADING AT PORT OF DESTINATION UNLESS IN
DISTRESS OR SUBJECT TO FORCE MAJEURE
+ ORIGINAL INSURANCE CERTIFICATE/POLICY IN 2 COPY(IES) DATED NOT
LATER THAN TRANSPORT DOCUMENT DATE, MADE OUT TO THE ORDER OF BANK
HAPOALIM B.M., FOR AT LEAST 110 PERCENT OF CIF VALUE, IN L/C
CURRENCY ONLY, IRRESPECTIVE OF PERCENTAGE AS PER INSTITUTE CARGO
CLAUSES(A), INSTITUTE WAR CLAUSES AND STRIKES CLAUSES, ALSO
CLAUSED CLAIMS PAYABLE IN ISRAEL AND INDICATING THE NAME AND
PHONE/FAX NO. OF A CLAIMS-SETTLING- AGENT IN ISRAEL.
+ PACKING LIST IN 3 FOLD(S).
:47A:[Additional Conditions]
+ OUR DISCREPANT DOCUMENTS FEES, IF ANY, FOR USD 60 (FOR EACH
PRESENTATION) PLUS SWIFT CHARGES FOR USD 15 FOR EACH SWIFT (OR
EQUIVALENT AMOUNT IN L/C CURRENCY) ARE FOR BENEFICIARY'S ACCOUNT,
REGARDLESS OF WHETHER ADVICE OF REFUSAL HAD BEEN SENT.
+ ALL DOCUMENTS MUST BE ISSUED IN ENGLISH LANGUAGE.
:71B:[Charges]
ALL BANKING CHARGES OUTSIDE ISRAEL
INCL YOUR SWIFT/TELEX/MAIL/COURIER
ARE FOR BENEFICIARY'S ACCOUNT.
:49:[Confirmation Instructions]
WITHOUT
:53A:[Reimbursing Bank]
IRVTUS3N
:78:[Instructions to the Paying/Accepting/Negotiating Bank]
UPON PRESENTATION OF DOCS YOU ARE REQUESTED TO ADVISE US BY SWIFT
MT750/MT754 AMOUNT AND VALUE DATE OF YOUR CLAIM, NAME OF VESSEL
AND B/L NO. AND DATE. PAYMENT TO BE EFFECTED 7 BUSINESS DAYS
AFTER YR SFT ADVICE.
DOCS MUST BE SENT BY COURIER TO BANK HAPOALIM INTERNATIONAL TRADE
CENTER 40, HAMASGER STREET TEL AVIV 67211 ISRAEL. EACH REMITTANCE
LETTER MUST INDICATE OUR L/C NO. AND THE ADVISING BANK REF. NO. +
IF DISCREPANCIES FOUND PLS INFORM US BY SFT, AND DO NOT REIMBURSE
YOURSELVES UNTIL RECEIPT OF OUR APPROVAL. +++PLS ADVISE THIS L/C
THROUGH YOUR ZHAOQING BRANCH AT: 2ND FL., SHENG DI MING XUNAN,
XIN'AN ROAD, DUANZHOU DISTRICT, ZHAOQING, GUANGDONG++++
:72:[Sender to Receiver Information]
PLEASE ACKNOWLEDGE RECEIPT OF THIS
L/C BY MT730
/PHONBEN/
-}{5:{MAC:A38EA68B}{CHK:8F0D968ABF1F}}

图 11.23　信用证（续）

参考答案

298

参 考 文 献

崔瑾，陆梦青. 2011. 外贸单证实务. 3 版. 北京：高等教育出版社.

杜清萍，杨荔. 2012. 国际商务单证实务. 广州：广东省语言音像电子出版社.

樊红霞，潘茹. 2014. 外贸单证缮制. 北京：外语教学与研究出版社.

何剑，郑淑媛. 2012. 国际商务单证. 北京：北京理工大学出版社.

娄珺. 2011. 进出口贸易实务. 北京：中国三峡出版社.

陆梦青，崔瑾. 2007. 外贸单证实务学习指导与训练. 2 版. 北京：高等教育出版社.

马朝阳，丛凤英. 2007. 外贸单证实务. 北京：科学出版社.

宁波对外经济贸易培训中心. 2007. 外贸单证实务. 2 版. 上海：上海交通大学出版社.

全国国际商务单证专业培训考试办公室. 2014. 国际商务单证专业培训考试大纲及复习指南. 北京：中国商务出版社.

上海市对外经济贸易交易培训中心. 2008. 国际商务单证应试指导. 2 版. 上海：同济大学出版社.

施旭华. 2012. 国际商务单证. 大连：东北财经大学出版社.

孙明贺. 2011. 国际贸易操作实务. 北京：科学出版社.

童宏祥. 2005. 外贸单证实务操作练习与解答. 上海：华东理工大学出版社.

童宏祥. 2008. 常用国际商务单证制作. 上海：华东师范大学出版社.

童宏祥，童莉莉. 2012. 常用国际商务单证制作. 上海：华东师范大学出版社.

王炯. 2011. 电子单证师制单实务. 北京：高等教育出版社.

王胜华. 2008. 国际商务单证操作实训教程. 重庆：重庆大学出版社.

魏翠芬. 2012. 国际贸易实务教程. 北京：清华大学出版社，北京交通大学出版社.

吴穗珊. 2011. 外贸单证实务. 北京：电子工业出版社.

吴穗珊. 2012. 外贸单证实务学习指导与练习. 北京：电子工业出版社.

许宝良. 2013. 外贸制单. 北京：高等教育出版社.

余世明. 2006. 国际商务单证实务练习题及分析解答. 3 版. 广州：暨南大学出版社.

余世明. 2013. 国际商务单证实务练习册. 2 版. 广州：暨南大学出版社.

余世明. 2014. 国际商务单证实务. 7 版. 广州：暨南大学出版社.

余世明，丛凤英. 2001. 国际贸易单证. 广州：暨南大学出版社.

俞涔，朱春兰. 2004. 外贸单证. 杭州：浙江大学出版社.

周树玲，郝冠军. 2011. 外贸单证实务. 北京：对外经济贸易大学出版社.